Programmer's Guide to Fortran 90

Walter S. Brainerd
Charles H. Goldberg
Jeanne C. Adams

Intertext Publications
McGraw-Hill Book Company

New York St. Louis San Francisco Auckland Bogotá
Hamburg London Madrid Mexico Milan Montreal
New Delhi Panama Paris São Paolo
Singapore Sydney Tokyo Toronto

Library of Congress Catalog Card Number 90-81424

10 9 8 7 6 5 4 3 2 1

ISBN 0-07-000248-7

Intertext Publications/Multiscience Press, Inc.
One Lincoln Plaza
New York, NY 10023

McGraw-Hill Book Company
1221 Avenue of the Americas
New York, NY 10020

Composition by UNICOMP

Preface

The new standard version of Fortran, informally known as Fortran 90, has many excellent new features that will assist the programmer in writing efficient, portable, and maintainable programs. However, because Fortran 77 is contained completely within Fortran 90, new features may be learned at whatever pace seems appropriate. For example, it is possible to concentrate on the array processing features, saving for later methods to encapsulate data types using the new global data feature, modules.

Programmer's Guide to Fortran 90 is organized so that it may be read from beginning to end, but also is organized so that particular topics may be emphasized by reading some chapters before previous ones are mastered. To the extent that is reasonable, all of the material about one topic is presented together, making the book suitable as a reference work, once much of the material has been assimilated.

All of the important features of the Fortran programming language are covered, beginning with the simplest constructs with examples. The book concentrates to some extent on the new features of the Fortran 90 programming language. This is natural because the new features often provide the best facilities to accomplish a particular programming task. Both the style of the many example programs and the selection of topics discussed in detail guide the reader toward acquiring programming skills to produce Fortran programs that are readable, maintainable, and efficient.

Case studies are used to illustrate the practical use of features of Fortran 90 and to show how complete programs are put together. There are simple problems to enable the reader to exercise knowledge of the topics learned.

An unusual feature of the book is that the first chapter contains a complete discussion of all the basic features needed to write complete Fortran programs: the form of Fortran programs, data types, simple expressions and assignment, and simple input and output. Subsequent chapters contain detailed discussions of control constructs, procedures, arrays, character strings, data structures, derived types, modules, recursion, and pointer variables.

From the beginning, Fortran has had extensive facilities for input and output; however, this is a topic that is not explored fully in many books because it is a little more difficult than other features and maybe just not as interesting as some features. The use of these facilities is very important in production programs, so this book contains, in Chapter 9, an extensive discussion of the input/output facilities in Fortran.

Features that are obsolete because better equivalent features are available are covered only briefly in Chapter 10. These features should never be used when writing a new program or modifying an old one; they are presented so that someone who must maintain an old program will understand enough about how they work to read and modify these statements.

No knowledge of Fortran 77 is assumed. However, footnotes indicate some important differences between Fortran 77 and Fortran 90; these will be of special interest to the Fortran 77 programmer. Readers familiar with Fortran 77 may skip immediately to Chapter 2 after looking over some of the examples in Chapter 1 to learn about kind parameters and to see what the new source form and declarations look like.

Appendices A and B give the complete syntax specifications for the language and descriptions of the many intrinsic functions, but there still will be occasions when an obscure property of the language must be learned, and in these cases it will be necessary to consult the official standard, published by the International Standards Organization and the American National Standards Institute, or the reference work *The Fortran 90 Handbook*, by Adams, Brainerd, Martin, Smith, and Wagener, McGraw-Hill, 1990.

Walter S. Brainerd, Charles H. Goldberg, and Jeanne C. Adams
April 1990

Contents

1

Introduction to Programming in Fortran 90

The best way to learn a programming language is to start reading and writing programs immediately. If a computer is available, write and *run* programs modeled on the simple sample programs in this chapter. You will need a short set of directions to show you how to enter and run a program at your local installation.

1.1 Programs That Calculate and Print

Since computers are very good at arithmetic and Fortran is designed to be very good at expressing numerical computations, one reasonable thing to learn first about Fortran 90 is how to tell a computer to do the sort of arithmetic that otherwise might be done by hand or with the aid of a hand calculator. This section describes how to write programs to calculate and to print the answer.

1.1.1 Simple Calculations

The first example is a program that prints the result of an addition

```
PROGRAM CALCULATION_1
    PRINT *, 84 + 13
END PROGRAM CALCULATION_1
```

The program CALCULATION_1 tells the computer to add the numbers 84 and 13 and then to print the sum, 97.[1] When the computer is told to run CALCULATION_1, it does precisely that: it adds the two numbers and prints their sum. The execution printout will look something like this.

```
RUN CALCULATION_1

    97
```

1.1.2 Default Print Format

The asterisk following the keyword PRINT tells the computer that the programmer will not be specifying the exact **format** or layout for the printed answer. Therefore, the Fortran system will use a **default format**, also called a list-directed format (9.8.21), designed to be satisfactory in most cases. The Fortran standard allows some freedom in the design of default formats, so your output may differ slightly from the sample execution shown above.

1.1.3 Printing Messages

If you want the computer to print the exact typographic characters that you specify, you enclose them in quotation marks (double quotes) or apostrophes (single quotes), as illustrated by the program QUOTES.[2] The quotes are not printed in the output.

```
PROGRAM QUOTES
    PRINT *, "84 + 13"
END PROGRAM QUOTES
```

---

1. Fortran 77 programmers will notice that, at long last, the 6-character limit on identifiers has been changed to a 31-character limit.
2. Previous versions of Fortran accepted only single quotes as character string delimiters.

```
RUN  QUOTES

   84 + 13
```

In a Fortran program, a sequence of typographic characters enclosed in quotes or apostrophes is a **character string**. A character string may contain alphabetic characters as well as numeric characters and may contain other special characters such as punctuation marks and arithmetic symbols.

Printing both exact literal characters and a computed numeric value produces the following easy-to-read output.

```
PROGRAM CALCULATION_1_V2
   PRINT *, "84 + 13 =", 84 + 13
END PROGRAM CALCULATION_1_V2

RUN CALCULATION_1_V2

   84 + 13 =  97
```

In the program CALCULATION_1_V2 (calculation 1 version 2), there are two items in the list in the PRINT statement, a **character constant** "84 + 13 =" to be printed exactly as written (but without the delimiting quotation marks) and an arithmetic expression whose value is first calculated and then printed. Although the two items may look similar, they are treated quite differently. Enclosing the character string in quotes means that it is to be transcribed *character for character*, including the three blank characters (spaces, in ordinary typing), while the same expression written without quotes or apostrophes is to be evaluated so that the sum can be printed. Commas are used to separate the items in the list of a PRINT statement.

1.1.4 The PROGRAM Statement

Each Fortran program may begin with a **PROGRAM statement**. It consists of the keyword PROGRAM followed by a **program name** of the programmer's choosing. The name must start with a letter and consist of at most 31 letters, digits, and underscores. The program name CALCULATION_1 has no significance except to the human reader.

1.1.5 The END Statement

The **END statement** begins with the keyword END. It may be followed by the keyword PROGRAM, which may in turn be followed by the name of the program. Every Fortran program must have an END statement as its last statement.

> *Style Note:* Include the keyword PROGRAM and the name of the program on every END statement.

1.1.6 Exercises

1. Write and run a program that prints your name.

2. Write and run a program that computes the sum of the integers 1 through 9, preceded by a short message, explaining what the output is.

3. What computer output might be expected when the following program is run?

```
PROGRAM SIMPLE
    PRINT *, 1, "AND", 1, "EQUALS", 1 + 1
END PROGRAM SIMPLE
```

1.2 The Intrinsic Data Types

The five intrinsic (i.e., built-in) **data types** in Fortran are integer, real, complex, logical, and character. Each data type has a set of values that may be represented in that type and operations that can be performed on those values. We already have seen examples of the use of two of these data types. "84 + 13" (including the quotation marks) is a character string constant, and 84 + 13 is an expression whose value is type integer.

The following subsections discuss each of the five intrinsic types and the way that constants of those types are written in Fortran.

1.2.1 Integer Type

The **integer type** is used to represent values that are whole numbers. In Fortran, integer constants are written much like they are written in ordinary usage. An **integer constant** is a string containing only the digits 0 to 9, possibly followed by an underscore (_) and an unsigned integer kind parameter as described in 1.2.9. The following are examples of integer constants.

23   0   1234567   42_1   42_SHORT

A **signed integer constant** is an integer constant optionally preceded by a + or – sign. A signed integer constant may be considered a restricted kind of expression, but often may be used wherever an integer constant may be used.

Every Fortran system must have at least one integer kind, although the integer kind number used for this kind may vary from one computer to another. Many Fortran systems have several integer kinds, with different kind numbers corresponding to different ranges of representable values.

1.2.2 Real Type

There are two forms of a **real constant** in Fortran. The first is called **positional form** because the place value of each digit is determined by its position relative to the decimal point. The positional form of a real constant consists of an integer followed by a decimal point followed by a string of digits representing the fractional part of the value, possibly followed by an underscore and a kind parameter. Assuming that DOUBLE and QUAD are names of integer constants that are permissible real kinds on the Fortran system being used (see Section 1.2.9), all the following are real constants written in positional form.

13.5   0.1234567   123.45678   00.30_DOUBLE   3.0
3.   12345.   .0   .1234567_QUAD

A real constant written in the positional form may have no digits to the left of the decimal point or it may have no digits to the right of the decimal point, but a decimal point by itself is not a legal real constant.

The **exponential form** of a real number consists of either an integer or a real number written in positional form followed by the letter E and a signed integer (without a kind parameter) and optionally followed by an underscore and kind parameter. The letter E is read as "times 10 to the power" and the integer following the E is a power of 10 to be multiplied by the number preceding the E. Exponential notation is useful for writing very large or very small numbers. For example, 2.3E5 represents 2.3 times 10 to the power 5, 2.3×10^5, or $2.3 \times 100{,}000 = 230{,}000$. The integer power may contain a minus or plus sign preceding it, as in the real constant 2.3E–5, which is 2.3×10^{-5} or $2.3 \times 0.00001 = 0.000023$. Two more examples are 1E9_DOUBLE, which is one billion with kind parameter DOUBLE, and 1E–3, which is one one-thousandth.

Every Fortran system must have at least two real kinds,[3] although the kind numbers used for these kinds may vary from one computer to another. Many Fortran systems have several real kinds, with different kind numbers corresponding to different precisions or ranges of values.

1.2.3 Complex Type

The Fortran **complex type** is used to represent the mathematical complex numbers, which consist of two real numbers and often are written as $a + b\,i$. The first real number is called the **real part** and the second is called the **imaginary part** of the complex number. In Fortran, a **complex constant** is written as two integer or real numbers, separated by a comma and enclosed in parentheses. Examples of complex constants are:

```
(1, -1)
(3.14_DOUBLE, -7)
(-1.0, 3.1E-27_QUAD)
```

If the two parts are type integer, the kind parameter of the complex constant is the default complex kind. If one part is integer and the other is real, the kind parameter of the complex constant is the kind of the real. If both parts are real, the kind parameter of the complex constant is the same as the part with the greater precision.

1.2.4 Arithmetic Operators

The operators that may be used to combine two numeric values include +, -, *, /, and **. Except for **, these symbols have their usual meaning indicating addition, subtraction, multiplication, and division. The two asterisks indicate exponentiation; that is, the value of 2 ** 4 is 16. The symbols + and - may be used as unary operators to indicate the identity and negation operations, respectively.

Integer division always produces an integer result obtained by chopping off any fractional part of the mathematical result. For example, since the mathematical result of 23/2 is 11.5, the value of the Fortran arithmetic expression

```
23.0 / 2.0
```

is 11.5, but the value of the expression

---

3. The two required kinds of real representations correspond to the Fortran 77 REAL and DOUBLE PRECISION data types.

23 / 2

which is the quotient of two integer constants, has the value 11. Similarly, the value of both the expressions

−23 / 2   23 / −2

is –11.

1.2.5 Relational Operators

Numeric values may be compared with **relational operators**. The two forms for each relational operator are given in Table 1-1.[4]

Table 1-1 The relational operators.

<	.LT.	less than
<=	.LE.	less than or equal to
==	.EQ.	equals
/=	.NE.	is not equal to
>=	.GE.	greater than or equal to
>	.GT.	greater than

Complex values may be compared only with the relational operators == and /=. However, due to roundoff error, it is poor programming practice to compare either real or complex values using either the == or the /= operator.

The result of a relational operator is type logical.

1.2.6 Mixed Mode Expressions

Mathematically, the integers are a subset of the real numbers and the real numbers are a subset of the complex numbers. Thus, it makes sense to combine two numeric values, even if they are not the same Fortran type. The two operands of a numeric operator do not have to be the same data type; when they are different, one is converted to the type of the other prior to executing the operation. If one is type integer and the other is type real, the integer is converted to a real value; if one is type integer and the other is type complex, the integer is converted to a complex value; if one is type real and the other is type complex, the real is converted to a complex value. As an example, the value of the expression

---

4. Note that the Fortran 77 relational operators each have new equivalents in Fortran 90.

23.0 / 2

is 11.5, because the integer 2 is converted to a real value and then a division of two real values is performed.

The two operands of a numeric operand also may have different kind parameter values. In this case, if the two operands have the same type or one is real and one complex, the result has the kind parameter of the operand with the greater precision. For example, if kind 5 has greater precision than kind 2, the value of

1_2 + 3_5

is 4 with kind parameter 5. Assuming that kind 4 has greater precision than either kind 2 or kind 3, the value of

1.1_4 + (2.2_2, 3.3_3)

is $3.3 + 3.3i$ with kind parameter 4. If one operand is type integer and the other is real or complex, the kind parameter of the result is that of the real or complex operand.

1.2.7 Logical Type

The Fortran **logical type** is used to represent the two truth values "true" and "false". A **logical constant** is either .TRUE. or .FALSE.

The operators that may be used to combine logical values are .NOT., .AND., .OR., .EQV., and .NEQV. They are all binary operators except the unary operator .NOT. The value resulting from the application of each logical operator is given in Table 1-2.

Table 1-2 Values of the logical operators.

x_1 x_2	.NOT.x_2	x_1.AND.x_2	x_1.OR.x_2	x_1.EQV.x_2	x_1.NEQV.x_2
true true	false	true	true	true	false
true false	true	false	true	false	true
false true	false	false	true	false	true
false false	true	false	false	true	false

To give one simple example, the value of

.FALSE. .EQV. .FALSE.

is true.

1.2.8 Character Type

The **character type** is used to represent strings of characters. The form of a **character constant** is a sequence of any characters representable in the computer delimited by either quotation marks (double quotes) or apostrophes (single quotes). If the delimiting character is to occur in the character string, it is represented by two of the delimiters with no intervening blanks. A character constant may be preceded by a kind parameter and an underscore. Note that the kind parameter for a character constant goes in front of the constant, rather than after it, as is the case for kind parameters on all other types of constants. The following are examples of character constants.

```
"Joan"
ASCII_'John Q. Public'
"Don't tread on me."
'He said, "Don''t tread on me."'
```

There is only one character operator that produces a character result, **concatenation**. The symbol used is // and the result of the binary operator is a string of characters consisting of those in the first string followed by those in the second string. For example, the value of "John Q." // "Public" is the string "John Q.Public". Note that there is no blank after the period. The kind parameter of the two operands must be the same.

Relational operators (1.2.5) may be used to compare character values.

1.2.9 Kind Parameters

Kind parameters provide a way to parameterize the selection of different possible machine representations for each of the intrinsic data types. If the programmer is careful, this provides a mechanism for making selection of numeric precision and range portable. For the character data type, it permits the use of more than one character set, such as Japanese, Chinese, and chemistry symbols, within a program.

Each intrinsic data type (integer, real, complex, logical, and character) has a parameter, called its **kind parameter**, associated with it. A kind parameter is intended to designate a machine representation for a particular data type. As an example, an implementation might have three real kinds, informally known as single, double, and quadruple precision.

The kind parameter is an integer. These numbers are processor dependent, so that kind parameters 1, 2, and 4 might be single, double, and quadruple precision, or on a different system, kind parameters 4, 8, and 16 could be used for the same things. The only requirements are that there must be at least two real and complex kinds, representing default real and double precision, and at least one kind for the integer, logical, and character data types. Note that the value of the kind parameter has nothing to do with the number of decimal digits of precision or range.

You need to check your Fortran manual for the computer system being used to determine which kind parameters are available for each type and which kind parameters are the default for each type. Kind parameters are optional in all cases, so it is possible to always use the default kind if that is sufficient for your application.

The intrinsic functions SELECTED_INT_KIND and SELECTED_REAL_KIND may be used to select an appropriate kind for a variable or a named constant (1.3.9). These functions provide the means for making a program portable in cases where values need to be computed with a certain specified precision that may use single precision on one machine, but require double precision on another machine. They are described in Section 1.5.1.

For the logical data type, an implementation may have representations with the property that logical values are packed one per bit; or it may be that due to the type of addressing and instruction set, putting one logical value per byte turns out to be more efficient. These representations can be selected by the programmer by specifying a kind parameter value.

When a kind parameter is a part of another constant, it may be either an integer constant or a named integer constant (parameter). In integer, real, and logical constants, it follows the underscore character (_) at the end.

```
12345_4
1.345_2
```

In character constants, it occurs at the front and is followed by an underscore.

```
ASCII_"abcde"
GREEK_"αβγδε"
```

The kind of a complex constant is indicated by the kinds of the two real components.

1.2.10 Exercises

1. Convert the following type real numbers from positional notation to exponential notation.

    48.2613   .00241_4   38499.0

2. Convert the following type real numbers from exponential notation to positional notation.

    9.503E2   4.1679E+10_DOUBLE   2.881E-5
    -4.421E2   -5.81E-2_8   7.000001E0

3. Write a program that prints the sum $.1 + .2 + .3 + \cdots + .9$.

4. Determine the number of one real kind that has precision greater than that of the default real kind on your computer system.

5. Write a program that prints the sum of the complex numbers $(.1 + .1i) + (.2 + .2i) + (.3 + .3i) + \cdots + (.9 + .9i)$.

6. Write a program that prints the logical value of each of the following expressions:

        2 > 3
        2 < 3
        .1 + .1 == .2
        .5 + .5 /= 1.0

7. Write a program that computes and prints the concatenation of all of your names (e.g., first, middle, and last).

1.3 Variables and Input

One benefit of writing a computer program for doing a calculation rather than obtaining the answer using pencil and paper or a hand calculator is that when the same sort of problem arises again, the program already written can be reused. The use of **variables** gives the programs in this section the flexibility needed for such reuse. The programs in Section 1.1 direct the computer to perform the indicated arithmetic operations on numeric constants appearing in the PRINT statements. The first sample program in this section, ADD_2, finds the sum of any two integers supplied as input. The numbers to be added do not appear in the program itself. Instead, two integer variables, X and Y, are reserved to hold the two values supplied as input. Since Fortran statements can operate on variables as well as constants, their sum can be calculated and printed. The first sample run shows how this new program could be used to find the sum of the numbers 84 and 13, calculated by the program CALCU-LATION_1 in Section 1.1.

```
PROGRAM ADD_2
    INTEGER :: X, Y
    READ *, X
    PRINT *, "Input data  X:", X
    READ *, Y
    PRINT *, "Input data  Y:", Y
    PRINT *, "X + Y =", X + Y
END PROGRAM ADD_2

RUN ADD_2

    Input data  X:   84
    Input data  Y:   13
    X + Y =  97
```

After declaring that the variables X and Y will hold integer values, the program ADD_2 tells the computer to read a number from an input device and call it X, then to read another number and call it Y, and finally to print the value of X + Y, identified as such. Two additional PRINT statements that echo the values of the input data complete the program ADD_2. During the execution of this program, the two numbers which are the values for X and Y must be supplied to the computer, or the computer cannot complete the run.

1.3.1 Declaration of Variables

Type statements appear between the PROGRAM statement and the beginning of the executable part of the program. Each declaration consists of a keyword specifying a Fortran intrinsic type, followed by two colons and a list of variable names separated by commas. For example, the program ADD_2 uses the type declaration

```
INTEGER :: X, Y
```

Corresponding to the integer, real, complex, logical, and character constants introduced in Section 1.2, there are integer, real, complex, logical, and character variables. For example, if the variables Q, T, and K are to be real variables in a program and the variables N and B are to be integer variables, then the following lines contain the necessary declarations.[5]

```
REAL :: Q, T, K
INTEGER :: N, B
```

Variables may be declared to have a particular kind parameter by putting KIND = followed by the kind parameter value in parentheses after the keyword representing the data type. For example, if more significant digits are needed than your system keeps in the default real type and the kind parameter for extra precision is 2, the variables DPQ, X, and LONG may be declared to be extra precision reals by the following declaration.

```
REAL (KIND = 2) :: DPQ, X, LONG
```

In the case of character variables, the keyword CHARACTER should be followed by LEN = and an integer indicating the number of characters in the character string in parentheses after the keyword CHARACTER. If the character variable is to have a kind parameter other than the default, that too can be specified inside the same parentheses. If the variable NAME is to be a string of 20 characters, it may be declared as follows.

```
CHARACTER (LEN = 20) :: NAME
```

If, in addition, the variable name is to be of kind KANJI, assumed to be the name of an integer constant, the declaration might be

```
CHARACTER (LEN = 20, KIND = KANJI) :: NAME
```

Style Note: As a matter of good programming practice, every variable that is used in a Fortran program should be listed in a type declaration.

It is possible to give a variable an **initial value** when it is declared. For example the variable COUNT may be declared to by type integer and set to 0 by the statement

---

5. Fortran 77 programmers will note the new syntax for type declarations. Older forms of type declarations (see Chapter 10) are still accepted by Fortran compilers, but it is good programming practice to use the new forms in all new programs.

```
INTEGER :: COUNT = 0
```

and the variables A, B, and C may be declared type real and set initially to the values 1.1, 2.2, and 3.3, respectively, by the statement

```
REAL :: A = 1.1, B = 2.2, C = 3.3
```

The value of a variable initialized in this way may be changed during execution of the program.

1.3.2 Implicit Typing

In its earliest days, the Fortran language did not have type declarations. Instead, variables were assigned a type by **implicit typing** based on the first letter of their names. Only real and integer variables were permitted. Variables whose names started with the letters I–N were type integer. All other variables were type real. Although it is now common practice to declare all variables, those that accidentally or intentionally remain undeclared are still assigned the default types based on the first letter of the variable name. Implicit typing can be turned off with the statement:

```
IMPLICIT NONE
```

Style Note: Every program and procedure should contain the

```
IMPLICIT NONE
```

statement to turn off implicit typing. *Note:* this style rule may be broken for very short programs.

1.3.3 Supplying Input Data

The two input values 84 and 13 for the variables X and Y, shown in the sample execution of the program ADD_2, did not appear in the computer by magic. They were typed in by the user. To run the program, it is assumed that there is a command "RUN" that compiles and runs a Fortran program, reading input from a file whose name is the same as the program, but with the characters "_IN" appended. Thus, the command

```
RUN ADD_2
```

compiles and runs the program ADD_2 and reads the input data from the file ADD_2_IN. For the Fortran system used to run this execution of ADD_2, an input file named ADD_2_IN must be prepared using the same editor used to type in the program. The file contains the two lines

84
13

On some Fortran systems, the input data is typed at the end of the file containing the program. On other systems, the data is typed at the keyboard during execution. You will have to find out what method your Fortran system uses.

1.3.4 Echo of Input Data

In Fortran, as well as most other programming languages, it is good programming practice for the user to provide an **echo of the input data** using PRINT statements, so that the output contains a record of the values used in the computation. Each READ statement in the program ADD_2 is followed by an echo of the input data just read.

> *Style Note:* It is good programming practice to echo all input data. However, it will be impractical to follow this rule in some cases, such as when there is a large amount of input data.

1.3.5 Rerunning a Program with Different Data

The program ADD_2 contains echoes, whose importance is demonstrated when the program is rerun using different input data. The echoes of input data help identify which answer goes with which problem. Other important uses of input echoes will appear later. In showing another sample run of the program ADD_2, this time adding two different numbers, it is not necessary to repeat the program listing. The program does not change; only the input data change. This time, the data file ADD_2_IN had the following two lines.

4
7

```
RUN ADD_2

    Input data  X:  4
    Input data  Y:  7
    X + Y =  11
```

The final PRINT statement of ADD_2 refers to the variables X and Y. As the execution printout for the two sample runs shows, what actually is printed is the value of the character string constant "X + Y = " followed by the value of the expression X + Y at the moment the PRINT statement is executed.

The program ADD_2_REALS is obtained from the program ADD_2 simply by changing the keyword INTEGER in the variable declaration to the keyword REAL, which causes the type of the variables X and Y to be real. The program ADD_2_REALS can be used to add two quantities that are not necessarily whole numbers. This execution of the program also illustrates that the input data values may be negative. The input file for this sample execution contains two lines

```
97.6
-12.9
```

```
PROGRAM ADD_2_REALS
    IMPLICIT NONE
    REAL :: X, Y
    READ *, X
    PRINT *, "Input data  X:", X
    READ *, Y
    PRINT *, "Input data  Y:", Y
    PRINT *, "X + Y =", X + Y
END PROGRAM ADD_2_REALS
```

```
RUN ADD_2_REALS

    Input data  X:    97.6000
    Input data  Y:   -12.9000
    X + Y =    84.7000
```

Some Fortran systems habitually print real quantities in exponential format. On such a system, the sample execution will more closely resemble the following:

```
RUN ADD_2_REALS

    Input data  X:    0.976000E+02
    Input data  Y:   -0.129000E+02
    X + Y =    0.847000E+02
```

1.3.6 Reading Several Values

The READ statement may be used to obtain values for several variables at a time, as shown in the program AVERAGE, that calculates the average of any four numbers. The four numbers to be averaged are supplied as data, rather than appearing as constants in the program. This permits the same program to be used to average different sets of four numbers.

```
PROGRAM AVERAGE
    IMPLICIT NONE
    REAL :: A, B, C, D
    READ *, A, B, C, D
    PRINT *, "Input data  A:", A
    PRINT *, "            B:", B
    PRINT *, "            C:", C
    PRINT *, "            D:", D
    PRINT *, "Average =", (A + B + C + D) / 4
END PROGRAM AVERAGE
```

The input data file in the sample execution has one line

```
58.5 60 61.3 57
```

When we run the program AVERAGE using this data file, the following output is produced.

```
RUN AVERAGE

    Input data  A:    58.5000
                B:    60.0000
                C:    61.3000
                D:    57.0000
    Average =   59.2000
```

This program does a computation more complicated than any discussed so far, but the meaning of the program should be obvious.

As shown in the sample execution, the data are supplied to the variables in the order they are listed in the READ statement. Note that the four variables in the READ statement are separated by commas and that there is a comma between the asterisk and the first variable in the input list. Although it is not required in Fortran, it is often desirable to put all input data for a READ statement on one line in the input file, creating a correspondence between READ statements and data lines. However, the input data file

    58.5
    60
    61.3
    57

also would have produced the same execution output.

Execution of each READ statement normally reads data from a new line in the input file. Thus, if four separate READ statements were to be used to read the variables A, B, C, and D, the four input values must be on four separate data lines in the input file.

1.3.7 Default Input Format

The asterisk in the READ statement indicates that the format of the input data is left to the preparer of the input file, except that the individual values must be separated by at least one blank character or a comma.

1.3.8 Rules for Names

X and Y are **names** of variables used in the program with the name ADD_2; the variable names A, B, C, and D are used in the program with name AVERAGE. The following are the rules for names of variables as well as most other kinds of things with names in a Fortran program:

1.   The first character of the name must be a letter.

2.   The remaining characters may be any mixture of letters, digits, or underscore characters (_).

3.   There must be at most 31 characters in a name.

These rules allow ordinary names like LISA, PAMELA, and JULIE to be used as names. They also allow ordinary English words like SUM and AREA and more technical-looking names like X3J3 and WG5 to be used as names. The underscore allows longer names to be more readable, as in DISTANCE_TO_THE_MOON and NUMBER_OF_VOWELS_IN_THE_TEXT.

The name of a program follows the rules given above.

1.3.9 Parameters/Named Constants

The program METERS_TO_INCHES that converts a length in meters to the equivalent length in inches illustrates the use of a **parameter**, which is a **named constant**. Parameters are declared much like variables, except that the keyword PARAMETER is added after the type and the value of the parameter follows the name of the parameter and an equals sign (=). Parameter names are subject to the same rules as variable names. For example,

```
REAL, PARAMETER :: PI = 3.14159
```

declares PI to be a real parameter with the value 3.14159.

The value of a parameter is fixed by its declaration and cannot change during execution. On the other hand, if the keyword PARAMETER is omitted, the objects being declared become variables and their values can be changed at any time, even if they are given an initial value.

A parameter name may be used any place in a Fortran program the corresponding constant may be used; this is why it is also called a named constant.

> *Style Note:* It is good programming practice to declare quantities to be parameters whenever possible. Assigning a value to a parameter rather than a variable tells the reader of the program that the value corresponding to that name will never change when the program is running. It also allows the computer to provide a diagnostic message if the programmer inadvertently tries to change its value.
>
> Since parameters are named constants, use of a parameter name instead of the corresponding constant makes a program more readable. It is easy to forget what role an unnamed constant plays in a program.
>
> Perhaps the most important reason for using a parameter declaration is that the program can be modified very easily if the particular value represented by the parameter name needs to be changed. The programmer can then be sure that the constant will be correct whenever it is used throughout the program.

```
PROGRAM METERS_TO_INCHES
! Converts length in meters to length in inches

   REAL :: METERS
   REAL, PARAMETER :: INCHES_PER_METER = 39.37

   READ *, METERS
   PRINT *, METERS, "meters =", METERS * INCHES_PER_METER, "inches."
END PROGRAM METERS_TO_INCHES

RUN METERS_TO_INCHES

   2.00000  meters =    78.7400  inches.
```

1.3.10 Reading and Writing Character Strings

Since computers can process character data as well as numeric information, computer languages provide for the reading and printing of character strings. The somewhat facetious program WHO shows how this is
done in Fortran.

```
   PROGRAM WHO
      CHARACTER (LEN = 20) :: WHATS_HIS_NAME

      PRINT *, "Do I remember whatshisname?"
      READ *, WHATS_HIS_NAME
      PRINT *, "Of course, I remember", WHATS_HIS_NAME
   END PROGRAM WHO

   RUN WHO

   Do I remember whatshisname?
   Of course, I remember  Roger Kaputnik
```

When the default input format, indicated by the asterisk, is used to read
a character string, the string must be enclosed in quotes or apostrophes,
the same as a character constant used within a program. Neither quotes
nor apostrophes appear in the printed output when using the default output format. The input file for the execution of the program WHO
shown above consists of one line.

```
   "Roger Kaputnik"
```

1.3.11 Input Data from a Terminal

We close this section with a version of the program METERS_TO_INCHES designed to be run on a Fortran system in which input data is supplied for the READ statements by typing the data at a computer terminal *during* the execution of the program. This is called **interactive input**. The only change is to add a PRINT statement prompting the user about what data to type. This **input prompt** immediately precedes the READ statement.

```
PROGRAM METERS_TO_INCHES
! Converts length in meters to length in inches.
! The length in meters is typed
! when prompted during execution.

  REAL :: METERS
  REAL, PARAMETER :: INCHES_PER_METER = 39.37

  PRINT *, "Enter a length in meters"
  READ *, METERS
  PRINT *, METERS, "METERS =", meters * INCHES_PER_METER, "inches."
END PROGRAM METERS_TO_INCHES

RUN METERS_TO_INCHES

  Enter a length in meters
2
  2.00000  meters =   78.7400  inches.
```

1.3.12 Exercises

1. Which of the following are valid names for variables?

NAME	ADDRESS	PHONE_#	PHONEY	REAL
IOU	IOU_2	4GOTTEN	PACKET	_LAURIE

2. The program INCHES_TO_FEET is similar to the program METERS_TO_INCHES described in this section. What output is produced when INCHES_TO_FEET is run using 110 inches as the input value?

```
PROGRAM INCHES_TO_FEET
   REAL :: INCHES
!  There are 12 inches per foot
   REAL, PARAMETER :: INCHES_PER_FOOT = 12.0

   READ *, INCHES
   PRINT *, INCHES, "inches =",  &
            INCHES / INCHES_PER_FOOT, "feet."
END PROGRAM INCHES_TO_FEET
```

3.   In the program RHYME, both JACK and JILL are parameters. What does a computer print when this program is run?

```
PROGRAM RHYME
   INTEGER, PARAMETER :: JACK = 1, JILL = 2
   PRINT *, JACK + JILL, "went up the hill."
END PROGRAM RHYME
```

4.   Write a program that reads in a first name, a middle initial, and a last name as the values of three different character variables and prints out the full name.

1.4 The Form of a Fortran Program

A Fortran program consists of a sequence of statements; these statements are written on lines that may contain from 0 to 132 characters. Often there is one Fortran statement on one line, but a statement can be continued onto more lines if the last character of the line to be continued is an ampersand (&).

```
PRINT *, &
   "I hope this is the right answer."
```

Conversely, more than one statement can occur on a line, provided the statements are separated by a semicolon (;).

```
A = 0; B = 0
```

The important fact is that, in the absence of a continuation symbol, the end of a line marks the end of a statement.

A statement must not contain more than 2640 characters, including blanks.

Each Fortran statement except the assignment statement begins with a **keyword**, such as PRINT, that identifies the kind of statement it is.

1.4.1 Significant Blank Characters

Blank characters are significant in a Fortran program.[6] In general, they must not occur within things that normally would not be typed with blanks in English text, such as names of things and numbers. On the other hand, they must be used between two things that look like "words". An example is that in the first line of a program the keyword PROGRAM and the name of the program must be separated by one or more blanks, as in the example

        PROGRAM ADD_2

Keywords and names such as PRINT and NUMBER must contain no blank characters, except that keywords that consist of more than one English word may contain blanks between the words, as in the Fortran statement

        END DO

Two or more consecutive blanks are always equivalent to one blank unless it is in a character string. The end of a line is also equivalent to one blank unless it is in a character string.

On the other hand, there are places where blank characters are not significant, but can and should be used to improve the readability of the program. For example, all of the programs in this book have blanks surrounding operator symbols, such as + and –, and have a blank after each comma in an input/output list or procedure argument list.

Style Note: Blank characters and blank lines should be used freely in a Fortran program to make it easier to read.

---

6. Significant blank characters in Fortran 90 are a big change from previous versions of Fortran in which no blanks were significant within the statement part of a program line. The old source form with fixed columns and insignificant blanks is still legal; it is described in Chapter 10. Even when using old source form, it is a good idea to use blanks to improve the readability of a Fortran program.

1.4.2 Comments

Any occurrence of the exclamation symbol (!) other than within a character string marks the beginning of a **comment**. The comment is terminated by the end of the line. All comments are ignored by the Fortran system.

1.4.3 Construct Names

Statements that begin an IF, CASE, or DO construct (2.3, 2.4, 2.5) may be preceded by a **construct name** and a colon. The rules for forming construct names are the same as for all other names (see Section 1.3.8).

1.4.4 The Fortran Character Set

A Fortran statement is a sequence of characters. The characters consist of the uppercase letters A to Z, the lowercase letters a to z, the digits 0 to 9, the underscore _, and the special characters in Table 1-3.

Table 1-3 The Fortran special characters.

Character	Name of Character	Character	Name of Character
	Blank	:	Colon
=	Equals	!	Exclamation Point
+	Plus	"	Quotation Mark or Quote
−	Minus	%	Percent
*	Asterisk	&	Ampersand
/	Slash	;	Semicolon
(	Left Parenthesis	<	Less Than
)	Right Parenthesis	>	Greater Than
,	Comma	?	Question Mark
.	Decimal Point or Period	$	Currency Symbol
'	Apostrophe or Single Quote		

Corresponding uppercase and lowercase letters are considered equivalent in a Fortran program except within a character constant. This means, for example, that a PRINT statement could be written

```
PRINT *, 84 + 13   ! Uppercase letters
```

or

```
Print *, 84 + 13   ! Mixed uppercase and lowercase letters
```

and the effect would be the same.

Two of the characters, $ and ?, have no special use.

1.4.5 Fixed Source Form

Until the advent of Fortran 90, parts of the Fortran statement had to be placed in certain columns on the line. This traditional fixed source form is described in Section 10.4.1.

1.4.6 Exercise

1. What does the following program print? Its style is *not* recommended.

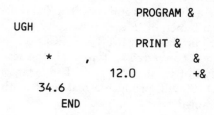

```
          PROGRAM &
     UGH
          PRINT &
      *      ,        &
            12.0      +&
       34.6
       END
```

1.5 Some Intrinsic Functions

There are many **built-in** or **intrinsic functions** in Fortran. To use these functions, simply type the name of the function followed by the arguments to the function enclosed in parentheses. For example, ABS (X) produces the absolute value of X and MAX (A, B, C) yields the maximum of the values of A, B, and C.

1.5.1 KIND Intrinsic Functions

The KIND function returns the kind parameter value of its argument. For example, KIND (X) is the kind parameter of the variable X. KIND (0) is the default integer kind; KIND (0.0) is the default real kind; KIND (.FALSE.) is the default logical kind; and KIND ("A") is the default character kind.

There is an intrinsic function SELECTED_REAL_KIND that produces a kind value whose representation has at least a certain precision and range. For example SELECTED_REAL_KIND (8, 70) will produce a kind (if there is one) that has at least 8 decimal digits of precision and allows values between -10^{70} and $+10^{70}$. This permits the programmer to select representations having required precision or range.

For the integer data type, there is an intrinsic function SELECTED_INT_KIND with only one argument. For example, SELECTED_INT_KIND (5) produces an integer type allowing representation of all integers between (but not including) -10^5 and $+10^5$.

1.5.2 Numeric Type Conversion Functions

There are built-in functions that convert any numeric values to each of the numeric types. These functions are named INT, REAL, and CMPLX. For example the value of INT (4.7) is the integer 4, the value of REAL ((2.7, –4.9)) is 2.7, the real part of the complex number $2.7 - 4.9i$. and the value of CMPLX (2) is $2 + 0i$. These functions are essential in some situations, such as when it is necessary to convert an integer to a real to avoid an integer division or when the type of a procedure actual argument must match the type of a dummy argument. For example, if a variable SUM holds the sum of a bunch of integer test scores and it is necessary to divide by the integer variable NUMBER_OF_SCORES to find the average, unless one or both are converted to type real, the result will be an integer, which is probably not what is desired. The expression REAL (SUM) / NUMBER_OF_SCORES will produce a real result with the fractional part of the average retained.

In other cases, explicit conversion is not required, but can improve the clarity of the program. For example, if I is an integer variable and R is a real variable, the assignment of the value of R to the variable I can be done with the statement

```
I = R
```

When this is done, any fractional part of the value of R is dropped, so that if R were 2.7, the value of I would be 2 after execution of the assignment. That this is happening can be made clearer to the reader of the program if the statement

```
I = INT (R)
```

is used instead.

> *Style Note:* In a context that requires conversion from complex to integer or real or requires conversion from real to integer, use the intrinsic type conversion functions, even if they are not required.

The numeric type conversion functions also may be used to convert from one kind to another within the same data type or to specify the kind parameter of the result of conversion between data types. For example, INT (X, KIND = SHORT) converts the real value X to an integer with kind parameter SHORT and, if Z is complex, the value of REAL (Z, KIND (Z)) has the same kind parameter as Z and has a value equal to the real part of Z.

1.5.3 The LOGICAL Function

The function named LOGICAL converts from one logical kind to another. For example, if L is type logical and PACKED is an integer named constant, LOGICAL (L, PACKED) is the truth value of L represented as a logical with kind parameter PACKED and LOGICAL (L) is the value of L represented as a logical with default kind parameter.

1.5.4 Mathematical Functions

There are several functions that perform common mathematical computations. The following is a list of some of the most useful ones. Appendix B should be consulted for a complete list with descriptions of each of the functions. Most of them do what would be expected, but the functions MAX and MIN are a little unusual in that they may be used with an arbitrary number of arguments. The mathematical functions are

ABS
ACOS
AIMAG
ASIN
ATAN
CEILING
CONJG
COS
COSH
EXP
FLOOR
LOG
LOG10
MAX
MIN
MODULO
SIN
SINH
SQRT

TAN
TANH

Some of these functions will be used in the case studies at the end of this chapter. Other intrinsic functions, such as those on array processing and character processing, will be discussed in relevant chapters.

1.5.5 Exercises

1.   Write a program that prints the kind of each of the constants

```
0
0.0
(0.0, 0.0)
.FALSE.
"A"
```

These are the default kinds.

2.   Print the value of SELECTED_INT_KIND and SELECTED_REAL_ KIND for about a dozen different argument values to see which kind values are available on the computer you are using. Check your results with the Fortran manual for your system.

1.6 Expressions and Assignment

A Fortran **expression** can be used to indicate many sorts of computations and manipulations of data values. So far we have seen simple examples of expressions as values to be printed using the PRINT statement. We now discuss in more detail just what can appear in this list of things to be printed.

1.6.1 Primaries

The basic component of an expression is a **primary**. Primaries are combined with operations and grouped with parentheses to indicate how values are to be computed. A primary is a constant, variable, function reference (3.2.2), array element (4.1.2), array section (4.1.6), structure component (6.1.1), substring (5.1.12), array constructor (4.1.4), structure constructor (6.2.3), or an expression enclosed in parentheses. Note that this is a recursive definition because the definition of an expression involves primaries. Examples of primaries are

```
2.7E43_4            ! constant
NUMBER_OF_BANANAS   ! variable
F (X, Y)            ! function value
(A + 3)             ! expression enclosed in parentheses
```

Primaries can be combined using the operators discussed in Section 1.2 as well as with user-defined operators discussed in Section 3.8 to form more complicated expressions. Any expression can be enclosed in parentheses to form another primary. Examples of more complicated expressions are

```
-A + D * E + B ** C
X // Y // "abcde"
(A + B ) /= C
A .AND. B .EQV. .NOT. C
A + B == C * D
```

1.6.2 The Interpretation of Expressions

When more than one operation occurs in an expression, parentheses and the **precedence** of the operations determines the operands to which the operations are applied. Operations with the highest precedence are applied first to the operand or operands immediately adjacent to the operand. For example, since * has higher precedence than +, in the expression A + B * C, the multiplication is first applied to its operands B and C; then the result of this computation is used as an operand by adding it to the value of A. If the programmer intends to add A and B and multiply the result by C, parentheses must be used as in the expression (A + B) * C.

When two operators have the same precedence, they are applied left-to-right, except for exponentiation, which is applied right-to-left. Thus, the value of 9 – 4 – 3 is 5 – 3 = 2, but the value of 2 ** 3 ** 2 is $2^9 = 512$.

Table 1-4 shows the operations with the highest precedence at the top of the list and the ones with the lowest precedence at the bottom.

1.6.3 The Evaluation of Expressions

Once it is determined by use of parentheses and precedence of operations which operations are to be performed on which operands, the computer may actually evaluate the expression by doing the computations in any order that is mathematically equivalent to the one indicated by the correct interpretation, *except that it must evaluate each subexpression within parentheses before combining it with any other values.* For example, the

Table 1-4 Operator precedence.

Operator	Precedence
User-defined unary operation	Highest
**	.
* or /	.
unary + or −	.
binary + or −	.
//	.
.EQ., .NE., .LT., .LE., .GT., .GE.	.
==, /=, <, <=, >, >=	.
.NOT.	.
.AND.	.
.OR.	.
.EQV. or .NEQV.	.
User-defined binary operation	Lowest

interpretation of the expression A + B + C indicates that A and B are to be added and the result added to C. Once this interpretation is made, it can be determined that a mathematically equivalent result will be obtained by first adding B and C and then adding this sum to A. Thus, the computer may do the computation either way. However, if the programmer writes the expression (A + B) + C, the computer must first do the computation as required by the parentheses. Note that the expression (A + B) + (C + D) can be done by first adding C and D, but then the computer must add A and B and add that result to the first sum obtained. To evaluate this expression, the computer must not first add B and C or any other pair in which one operand is taken from (A + B) and the other is taken from (C + D), because doing this would violate the integrity of parentheses.

Note that integer division is an oddity in that it does not satisfy the rules of arithmetic for ordinary division. For example (I / 2) * 2 is not equal to I if I is an odd integer. Thus, a computer may not make this substitution to optimize the evaluation of the expression.

Table 1-5 contains examples of expressions with allowable alternative forms that may be used by the computer in the evaluation of those expressions. A, B, and C represent arbitrary real or complex operands; I and J represent arbitrary integer operands; X, Y, and Z represent arbitrary operands of any numeric type; and L1, L2, and L3 represent arbitrary logical operands.

Table 1-5 Allowable alternative expressions.

Expression	Allowable Alternative Form
X + Y	Y + X
X * Y	Y * X
−X + Y	Y − X
X + Y + Z	X + (Y + Z)
X − Y + Z	X − (Y − Z)
X * A / Z	X * (A / Z)
X * Y − X * Z	X * (Y − Z)
A / B / C	A / (B * C)
A / 5.0	0.2 * A
I > J	J − I < 0
L1 .AND. L2 .AND. L3	L1 .AND. (L2 .AND. L3)
ABS (I) > −1 .OR. LOGICAL (L1)	.TRUE.

Table 1-6 contains examples of expressions with forbidden alternative forms that must not be used by a computer in the evaluation of those expressions.

Table 1-6 Forbidden alternative expressions.

Expression	Nonallowable Alternative Form
I / 2	0.5 * I
X * I / J	X * (I / J)
(X + Y) + Z	(X + Y + Z)
I / J / A	I / (J * A)
(X + Y) + Z	X + (Y + Z)
(X * Y) − (X * Z)	X * (Y − Z)
X * (Y − Z)	X * Y − X * Z

A computer needs to evaluate only as much of a character expression as is needed in the context in which it occurs. For example, the statements

```
CHARACTER (LEN = 2) C1, C2, C3, CF
C1 = C2 // CF (C3)
```

do not require the function CF to be evaluated, because only the two characters making up the value of C2 are needed to determine the value of C1, because C1 contains only two characters.

1.6.4 Assignment

The **assignment statement** is the most common way of giving a variable a value. An assignment statement consists of a variable, an equals sign (=), and an expression. The expression is evaluated and assigned to the variable. An example of an assignment statement is

```
X = A + 2 * SIN (B)
```

Note for later that the variable on the left-hand side may be an array, an array element, an array section, a substring, or a structure component.

Complete agreement of the variable and expression type and kind is not always required. In some cases the data type or kind parameter of the expression may be converted in order to assign it to the variable. If the variable on the left is any numeric type, the expression may be any numeric type and any kind. If the variable is type character, the expression must be type character and have the same kind parameter. If the variable is type logical, the expression must be type logical but may be any kind. If the variable is a derived type (6.2), that is, a user-defined type, the expression must be the same derived type.

1.6.5 Exercises

1. What computer output might be expected when the following program is run?

    ```
    PROGRAM CALCULATION_2
        PRINT *, (201 + 55) * 4 - 2 * 10
    END PROGRAM CALCULATION_2
    ```

2. The program CALCULATION_3 uses a confusing sequence of arithmetic operations whose meaning would be clearer if written with parentheses. What computer output might be expected when it is run? Insert parentheses in the PRINT statement in a way that does not change the value printed, but makes it easier to understand.

    ```
    PROGRAM CALCULATION_3
        PRINT *, 343 / 7 / 7 * 2
    END PROGRAM CALCULATION_3
    ```

3. What computer output might be expected when CALCULATION_4 is run?

```
PROGRAM CALCULATION_4
    PRINT *, 2 * (3 * (5 - 3))
END PROGRAM CALCULATION_4
```

4. What computer output might be expected when the program POWER_OF_2 is run?

```
PROGRAM POWER_OF_2
    PRINT *, 2 * 2 * 2 * 2 * 2 * 2 * 2 * 2 * 2 * 2
END PROGRAM POWER_OF_2
```

5. Write an expression that rounds the value of the variable X to the nearest tenth.

6. When is INT (X / Y) equal to X / Y for real values X and Y?

7. If X and Y are type integer, the value of the intrinsic function MODULO (X, Y) is the remainder when X is divided by Y. For example, MODULO (18, 5) = 3. Rewrite the following expression using the built-in function MODULO. Assume N is type integer with a positive value.

```
N - (N / 100) * 100
```

8. Write an expression using the built-in function MODULO that has the value 1 when N is odd and 0 when N is even.

9. Write an expression using the built-in function MODULO that is true if the value of the variable N is even and is false if N is odd.

10. Write a program to compute the quantity $e^{i\pi}$. The constant π can be computed by the formula $\pi = 4 * \text{ATAN}(1.0)$ since $\tan(\pi/4) = 1$. The complex constant i can be written (0, 1). The built-in function EXP (Z) is used for raising the mathematical constant e to a power. The sample output should look like:

```
RUN EIPI

The value of e to the power i*pi is ___
```

1.7 Introduction to Formatting

Fortran has extremely powerful, flexible, and easy-to-use capabilities for output formatting. This may seem surprising since Fortran is often considered a scientific programming language, but Fortran has always had better formatting facilities than many commercial languages. This section describes the basic formatting features that enable you to produce really good looking output, if you like. If the default formatting on your Fortran system is good enough, there is no necessity to learn formatting right away. This section appears early because some Fortran systems do not have satisfactory default formats, especially for reals. On such systems, the techniques of this section are essential.

1.7.1 Roundoff

Just as $1/3$ cannot be represented exactly as a decimal, though .333333 comes very close, $1/10$ and $1/100$ cannot be represented exactly when the representation uses a number base two instead of ten. The base two or **binary system** of notation is used internally in most computers for storage and calculation of numeric values. As a result, when reals are converted from input represented in decimal notation to the computer's internal representation and back again during execution of a program, the original numbers may not be recovered precisely.

Perhaps you have already seen this in your own output, in the form of a tell-tale sequence of 9s in the last decimal digits printed. For example, using the program ADD_2_REALS in Section 1.3.5, the same input data, 97.6 and –12.9, and a different computer, the following output resulted.

```
RUN ADD_2_REALS

    Input data  X:    0.9759999E+02
    Input data  Y:   -0.1289999E+02
    X + Y =      0.8469999E+02
```

The value of the variable X prints as $9.759999E+01 = 97.59999$ although the value supplied in the input file is 97.6. The difference between the intended and calculated values, –0.00001 in this case, is **roundoff** or **roundoff error**. It is normally of no consequence in practical calculations because it is virtually impossible to distinguish between such nearly equal values as 97.59999 and 97.6.

Similarly, the printed value of the variable Y is 0.00001 too large at -12.89999 instead of -12.9. The printed value of X + Y is 84.69999, differing by 0.00001 from both the sum of the intended values and the sum of the printed values of X and Y, a hint to the expert that the computer being used probably does not use decimal arithmetic for its internal calculations.

Minor cases of roundoff are hidden easily by rounding values before printing. For example, if the unexpected echoes of input data above are rounded to 4 decimal places before printing, the results will appear precisely as expected: 97.6000 + (−12.9000) = 84.7000.

Depending in large measure on whether the default format for reals rounds answers to fewer decimal places than are actually calculated, you rarely see any trace of roundoff on many computer systems. These extra guard digits may actually contain roundoff, but rounding answers before printing guarantees that the user will not see small roundoff errors. We mention roundoff at this point to forewarn the beginner whose Fortran system shows it in output that roundoff is not a malfunction of the computer's hardware, but a fact of life of type real arithmetic on computers.

In the remainder of this section we introduce the simplest forms of user-specified PRINT formatting, including the facility for rounding real values to a specified number of decimal places before printing.

1.7.2 Format Specifications

Extremely flexible and versatile control over the appearance of printed output is available in Fortran if you are willing to forego the convenience of the default format. In place of the asterisk denoting the default format, you write a format specification or some alternative means of locating a format specification in the program. A **format specification** is basically a list of **edit descriptors**, separated by commas and enclosed in parentheses. An example is

        (F5.1, A, I4)

For each expression to be printed, one of the edit descriptors in the format specification is used to determine the form of the output. For example if $X = 6.3$ is type real and $N = -26$ is type integer, then

        PRINT "(F5.1, A, I4)", X, " and ", N

would produce the output line

            6.3 and   −26

This example shows the three most frequently used edit descriptors, F (floating point) for positional notation printing of reals, A (alphanumeric) for character strings, and I (integer) for integers. The edit descriptor F5.1 means that a total of 5 columns are reserved for printing a real value rounded to one place after the decimal point. The decimal point occupies a column and a minus sign, if needed, occupies another column, so the largest number printable in F5.1 format is 999.9 and −99.9 is the smallest. I4 editing reserves 4 columns for printing an integer. The minus sign takes up one of the 4 columns. The A edit descriptor reserves space for character output. The actual length of the character constant to be printed or the declared length of the character variable determine how many columns are used. It is also possible to reserve a specific number of columns for a character string. The edit descriptor A10, for example, reserves 10 columns, regardless of the data to be printed. See Section 9.8.14 for details.

1.7.3 Placement of Format Specifications

In the preceding example, the format specification is in the form of a character constant. Now the necessity of the comma after the asterisk or other format specifier in the PRINT statement becomes apparent. It is the means of separating the format specifier from the first item in the list of expressions to be printed.

Since the format is a character expression, in the simplest case it is simply a character constant that appears in the input/output statement. For example, the following two sets of statements would produce the same output. It is assumed that X is real, N is integer, and FMT is character.

```
PRINT "(F5.1, A, I4)", X, " and ", N

FMT = "(F5.1, A, I4)"
PRINT FMT, X, " and ", N
```

It is also possible to give a format in the FORMAT statement, but this method is somewhat old fashioned and so is described in Chapter 10 with the obsolete features.

1.7.4 Tab and Line Feed Edit Descriptors

The slash (/) edit descriptor starts a new line in the printed output. Thus, a single PRINT statement can produce several lines of output. For example

```
PRINT "(A, /, A, /, A)", "These character strings", &
      "all appear", "on separate lines"
```

produces the three lines of output

```
These character strings
all appear
on separate lines
```

Commas may be omitted around slash edit descriptors.

The T (tab) edit descriptor is used to skip to a specified column of the output line for precise control over the appearance of the output. Tabs may be either forward or backward on the current line. For example,

```
PRINT "(T30, I5, T50, I5, T10, I5)", A, B, C
```

will print the integer values of C in columns 10-14, A in columns 30-34, and B in columns 50-54. Some printing devices do not print column 1 of any output line. Instead, the character appearing in column 1 is used to control single and double spacing, overprinting, and skips to the top of a new page. If you have such a printer on your system, a T2 edit descriptor will skip to column 2 to get single spacing, or a T1 edit descriptor will skip to column 1 to use one of the line feed codes described in Section 9.1.4.

1.7.5 Repeated Edit Descriptors

If one or more edit descriptors are to be repeated, they may be enclosed in parentheses and preceded by the positive integer representing the number of repetitions.

```
3(I4) is equivalent to 3I4 or I4,I4,I4
5(/) is equivalent to /,/,/,/,/ or /////
2(A4,/,T2) is equivalent to A4,/,T2,A4,/,T2
```

The parentheses may be omitted if there is only one E, F, I, or A edit descriptor inside the parentheses. The E edit descriptor is used for printing reals in exponential notation. For example, the E10.3 descriptor uses 10 columns and prints the mantissa rounded to three decimal places. For more details, see Section 9.8.8.

1.7.6 Examples of Formatted Output

The following examples illustrate how formatted output works. If these lines are printed on many printers, the first character may not appear, but may affect the vertical spacing.

```
PRINT "(3I2)", 2, 3, 4

 2 3 4

X = 7.346E-9
PRINT "(A, E10.3)", " The answer is ", X

 The answer is    .735E-08

Q1 = 5.6
Q2 = 5.73
Q3 = 5.79
F123 = "(A, 3(/, T2, A, I1, A, F3.1))"
PRINT F123, " Here come the answers--", &
      " Q", 1, "=", Q1, &
      " Q", 2, "=", Q2, &
      " Q", 3, "=", Q3
 Here come the answers--
 Q1=5.6
 Q2=5.7
 Q3=5.8
```

1.7.7 Formatted Input

A format specification can be used with the READ statement to indicate
how the columns of the input line are to be interpreted. Formatted input
is not as essential as formatted output because most natural arrangements
of input data are accepted by the default READ formats. However,
there are two major exceptions, which sometimes make the use of input
formatting desirable. First, default formats for character input usually
require quotes or apostrophes around the input strings; character input
read under an A edit descriptor does not. Second, it is a small convenience not to have to separate numbers with commas or blanks when
large amounts of data are read by a program. For example, it is much
harder to type 10 one-digit integers on a line of input with separating
commas than without them. Rather than discuss the rules in detail for
using formatted input, one example is given.

```
REAL :: X1, X2, X3
INTEGER :: J1, J2, J3
CHARACTER (LEN = 4) :: C
READ "(A, 3 (F2.1, I1))", C, X1, J1, X2, J2, X3, J3
```

If the input line is

1234567890123

then executing the READ statement is equivalent to executing the following assignment statements. Notice that quotes or apostrophes for A format input data must be omitted and that decimal points for F format input data are assumed when they are omitted.

```
C = "1234"
X1 = 5.6
J1 = 7
X2 = 8.9
J2 = 0
X3 = 1.2
J3 = 3
```

Style Note: It is good programming practice to use the default READ format whenever possible. Explicit input format specifications demand strict adherence to specified columns for each value in the input data. The slightest misalignment of the input data usually results in incorrect values assigned to the variables. By comparison, the default input format is usually relatively tolerant of variations in alignment and is user-friendly.

1.7.8 Exercises

1. If the variable X has value 2.5, what does the output for the following statement look like? Show blank columns with a "*b*".

    ```
    PRINT "(F6.3, E11.1)", X, X ** 2
    ```

2. What are the largest and smallest values that can be printed by the statement

    ```
    PRINT "(F8.3)", VALUE
    ```

3. What does the following statement print? Use "*b*" for blank columns.

    ```
    PRINT "(A, F9.5, A)", "|", 1.0/3.0, "|"
    ```

1.8 Case Studies: Quadratic Formula

A quadratic equation is an equation involving the square of the unknown x and no higher powers of x. Algorithms for solution of quadratic equations equivalent to the quadratic formula are found in Old Babylonian texts dating to 1700 B.C. It is now routinely taught in high school algebra. In this section, we show how to write a Fortran program to evaluate and print the roots of a quadratic equation. We also discuss improving the efficiency of the calculation by isolating common subexpressions.

1.8.1 The Problem

The most general quadratic equation has the form

$$ax^2 + bx + c = 0$$

where a, b, and c are constants and x is the unknown. The quadratic formula says that the roots of the quadratic equation, that is, the values of x for which the equation is true, are given by the formula

$$x = \frac{-b \pm \sqrt{b^2 - 4ac}}{2a}$$

This means that one root is obtained by adding the square root term and the other root is obtained by subtracting the square root term.

The problem is to write a program that reads as input the three coefficients, a, b, and c, and prints as output the values of the two roots. Since there is very little input, and we wish to discuss the answers as they are computed, we write the program for interactive execution with input from a terminal keyboard and output to the display screen or printing element.

1.8.2 The Solution

Experienced programmers may regard the following pseudocode solution as obvious, as indeed it is, but the three steps of the pseudocode solution must be thought, if not necessarily written down.

```
Read the coefficients a, b, and c
Calculate the two roots by the quadratic formula
Print the two roots
```

It is but a small step to the Fortran program that implements the pseudocode solution.

```
PROGRAM QUADRATIC_EQUATION_SOLVER
!  Calculates and prints the roots of a quadratic equation

!  Variables:
!     A, B, C: coefficients
!     X1, X2: roots

   IMPLICIT NONE
   REAL :: A, B, C, X1, X2

!  Read the coefficients
   PRINT *, "Enter A, the coefficient of X ** 2"
   READ *, A
   PRINT *, "Enter B, the coefficient of X"
   READ *, B
   PRINT *, "enter C, the constant term"
   READ *, C

!  Calculate the roots by the quadratic formula
   X1 = (-B + SQRT (B ** 2 - 4 * A * C)) / (2 * A)
   X2 = (-B - SQRT (B ** 2 - 4 * A * C)) / (2 * A)

!  Print the roots
   PRINT *, "The roots are"
   PRINT *, "X1 =", X1
   PRINT *, "X2 =", X2
END PROGRAM QUADRATIC_EQUATION_SOLVER
```

In the input section, each READ statement is preceded by an input prompt, that is, a PRINT statement telling the user at the computer terminal what input is expected. In the calculation section, the quadratic formula illustrates the use of the function SQRT.

1.8.3 Program Testing

To test the program QUADRATIC_EQUATION_SOLVER, we made up several quadratic equations with known roots. Since all variables are type real, our first test case has simple real roots. The solutions of the quadratic equation

$$x^2 - 5x + 6 = 0$$

are 2 and 3.

```
RUN QUADRATIC_EQUATION_SOLVER

   Enter A, the coefficient of X ** 2
1
   Enter B, the coefficient of X
-5
   Enter C, the constant term
6
   The roots are
   X1 =   3.00000
   X2 =   2.00000
```

The next quadratic equation has negative and fractional roots to test whether the program will work in these cases. The solutions of the quadratic equation

$$4x^2 + 8x - 21 = 0$$

are –3.5 and 1.5, testing both possibilities.

```
RUN QUADRATIC_EQUATION_SOLVER

   Enter A, the coefficient of X ** 2
4
   Enter B, the coefficient of X
8
   Enter C, the constant term
-21
   The roots are
   X1 =   1.50000
   X2 =  -3.50000
```

Notice that X1 is always the greater of the two roots because its formula adds the square root term.

The next case tests irrational roots of the quadratic equation. The golden ratio is a ratio famous from Greek mathematics. Renaissance artists thought that the golden ratio was the most pleasing ratio for the sides of a rectangular painting or the facade of a building. The spiral shells of snails and the arrangement of seeds in a sunflower are related to it. The golden ratio also is the limit of the ratio of successive terms of the Fibonacci sequence. The two roots of the following equation are the golden ratio and the negative of its reciprocal.

$$x^2 - x - 1 = 0$$

```
RUN QUADRATIC_EQUATION_SOLVER

    Enter A, the coefficient of X ** 2
1
    Enter B, the coefficient of X
-1
    Enter C, the constant term
-1
    The roots are
    X1 =    1.61803
    X2 = -0.618034
```

The exact solutions are $(1 + \sqrt{5}) / 2$ and $(1 - \sqrt{5} / 2$, which check with the output of the program using a hand calculator. The golden ratio has many interesting properties, including the fact that $1 / 1.6180339 = .6180339$.

The quadratic equation

$$x^2 - 6x + 9 = 0$$

has only one solution, $x = 3$. You might wonder what a program designed to find two roots will do with this equation.

```
RUN QUADRATIC_EQUATION_SOLVER

    Enter A, the coefficient of X ** 2
1
    Enter B, the coefficient of X
-6
    Enter C, the constant term
9
    The roots are
    X1 =    3.00000
    X2 =    3.00000
```

Mathematicians call the solution of this quadratic equation a *double root*. For this equation, the quantity $b^2 - 4ac$ is zero, so it doesn't matter whether its square root is added or subtracted in the calculation of a root. The answer is the same for both roots.

Finally, we try a test case which we know the program QUADRATIC_EQUATION_SOLVER will not handle. The quadratic equation

$$x^2 + 1 = 0$$

has no real roots. Instead, the roots are $x = \pm\sqrt{-1} = \pm i$, complex numbers with no real part. We still try it anyway, just to see what happens.

```
RUN QUADRATIC_EQUATION_SOLVER

   Enter A, the coefficient of X ** 2
1
   Enter B, the coefficient of X
0
   Enter C, the constant term
1
*** Error: attempt to take square root of negative quantity ***
*** Execution terminated ***
```

Since $b^2 - 4ac$ is -4, the error message is right on the money. Two ways to cope with this situation are discussed in Sections 1.8.5 and 2.3.

1.8.4 Common Subexpressions

The arithmetic expressions for calculating the roots X1 and X2 both involve the same subexpression, SQRT (B ** 2 - 4 * A * C). As written, the program QUADRATIC_EQUATION_SOLVER asks the computer to recalculate this subexpression as part of the calculation of X2. We can force the computer to calculate this subexpression only once by assigning it to a new intermediate variable SUB_EXPRESSION, and then calculating both roots in terms of the variable SUB_EXPRESSION.

```
PROGRAM QUADRATIC_EQUATION_SOLVER_2
! Calculates and prints the roots of a quadratic equation
```

```
!  Variables:
!     A, B, C: coefficients
!     SUB_EXPRESSION: value common to both roots
!     X1, X2: roots

      IMPLICIT NONE
      REAL :: A, B, C, X1, X2, SUB_EXPRESSION

!  READ THE COEFFICIENTS
      PRINT *, "Enter A, the coefficient of X ** 2"
      READ *, A
      PRINT *, "Enter B, the coefficient of X"
      READ *, B
      PRINT *, "Enter C, the constant term"
      READ *, C

!  Calculate the roots by the quadratic formula
      SUB_EXPRESSION = SQRT (B ** 2 - 4 * A * C)
      X1 = (-B + SUB_EXPRESSION) / (2 * A)
      X2 = (-B - SUB_EXPRESSION) / (2 * A)

!  Print the roots
      PRINT *, "The roots are"
      PRINT *, "X1 =", X1
      PRINT *, "X2 =", X2
END PROGRAM EQUATION_SOLVER_2
```

Some optimizing Fortran compilers will recognize that the program QUADRATIC_EQUATION_SOLVER, in its original form, calls for the calculation of the same subexpression twice without change of any of the variables in the subexpression. Such a compiler would produce the more efficient machine language code corresponding to the second version, QUADRATIC_EQUATION_SOLVER_2, even when the programmer writes the less efficient first version.

1.8.5 Complex Roots of a Quadratic Equation

The quadratic formula was used in the program QUADRATIC_EQUATION_SOLVER to calculate the roots of a quadratic equation. The program worked well when the two roots were real, but it failed in the test case of a quadratic whose roots were imaginary. In that case, the quadratic formula calls for taking the square root of a negative number, a function evaluation with no real answer. In the next program, QUADRATIC_EQUATION_SOLVER_3, we use complex values to compute the correct answer whether the roots of the quadratic are real or complex.

The subexpression

$$d = b^2 - 4ac$$

is called the **discriminant** because it discriminates between the cases of two real roots, a double real root, and two complex roots. If d is positive, then there is a real square root of d and the quadratic formula gives two real roots, one calculated by adding the square root of d and the other by subtracting it. If d is zero, then so is its square root. Consequently, when d is zero the quadratic formula gives only one real root, $-b/2a$.

When d is negative, on the other hand, its square root is imaginary. The complex square root of a negative number is obtained by taking the square root of its absolute value and multiplying the result by i, the basis of the complex number system. For example, if $d = -4$, then $\sqrt{d} = 2i$. Thus when d is negative, the two roots of the quadratic equation are given by the formulas

$$x_1 = \frac{-b}{2a} + \frac{\sqrt{|d|}}{2a}\, i$$

and

$$x_2 = \frac{-b}{2a} - \frac{\sqrt{|d|}}{2a}\, i$$

However, with the use of the complex data type, the formula for calculating the roots looks just like it does when the roots are real. The only thing that makes QUADRATIC_EQUATION_SOLVER_3 look different from the real version is that the coefficients are read in as real values and then converted to complex values. The two sample executions show one case where the roots are complex and one case where they are both real.

```
PROGRAM QUADRATIC_EQUATION_SOLVER_3

    !  Calculates and prints the roots of a quadratic formula
    !  even if they are complex
```

```
!  Variables:  A, B, C = coefficients
!              CA, CB, CC = complex coefficients
!              Z1, Z2 = roots

   IMPLICIT NONE
   REAL :: A, B, C
   COMPLEX :: CA, CB, CC, Z1, Z2

!  Read the coefficients
   READ *, A, B, C
   PRINT *, "Input data  A:", A
   PRINT *, "            B:", B
   PRINT *, "            C:", C

!  Convert coefficients to type complex
   CA = CMPLX (A)
   CB = CMPLX (B)
   CC = CMPLX (C)

!  Calculate the roots
   Z1 = (-CB + SQRT (CB ** 2 - 4 * CA * CC)) / (2 * CA)
   Z2 = (-CB - SQRT (CB ** 2 - 4 * CA * CC)) / (2 * CA)

!  Print the roots
   PRINT *, "The roots are:"
   PRINT *, "Z1 =", Z1
   PRINT *, "Z2 =", Z2
END PROGRAM EQUATION_SOLVER_3

RUN QUADRATIC_EQUATION_SOLVER_3

   Input data  A:   1.00000
               B:   0.
               C:   1.00000
   The roots are:
   Z1 = (  0.,   1.00000)
   Z2 = (  0.,  -1.00000)


RUN QUADRATIC_EQUATION_SOLVER_3

   Input data  A:   4.00000
               B:   8.00000
               C:  -21.0000
```

```
The roots are:
Z1 = (    1.50000,   0.)
Z2 = (   -3.50000,   0.)
```

1.9 Case Study: Debugging Pendulum Calculations

The time it takes a pendulum to complete one swing is virtually independent of the amplitude or maximum displacement of the pendulum at the height of its swing, as long as the swing is relatively small compared with the length of the pendulum. For this reason, pendulums have long been used to keep accurate time. The problem in this section is to write a program to calculate the frequency f (the number of swings per second) of a pendulum, and its period T (the time it takes to complete one swing). The input data is the length of the pendulum in meters.

The formula for the frequency of a pendulum is

$$f = \frac{1}{2\pi} \sqrt{\frac{g}{L}}$$

where g is the gravitational acceleration constant 9.80665 meters/sec^2 for bodies falling under the influence of gravity near the surface of the earth, L is the length of the pendulum in meters, and π is the mathematical constant 3.14159. In addition, the formula for the period T is

$$T = \frac{1}{f}$$

The solution to this problem uses everything we learned in this chapter: it has variables, input data, computational formulas, and even the built-in square root function. Nevertheless, it seems to be a straightforward calculation for which a Fortran program can be written quite easily. Here is the first attempt.

```
PROGRAM PENDULUM
!  Calculates the frequency and period
!  of a pendulum of length L

   IMPLICIT NONE
   REAL :: L, F, T
   REAL, PARAMETER :: PI = 3.14159, &
                      G = 9.80665
```

```
      READ *, L
      PRINT *, "Input data L: ", L
      F = (1.0 / 2.0 * PI) SQRT (G / L)
      T = 1.0 / F
END PROGRAM PENDULUM
```

When this program is entered into the computer, it will not compile and run. The error messages we show below are illustrative approximations of the messages we get from actual Fortran compilers. The quality and amount of useful information contained in error messages varies widely. We suggest comparing the error messages shown here with the messages your system produces for the same errors.

```
RUN PENDULUM
   *** Error -- syntax error in REAL statement ***
   REAL, PARAMETER :: PI = 3.14159,
   *** Missing parameter assignment ***

   *** Error -- undeclared variable: G ***
   G = 9.80665

   *** Error -- syntax error in assignment statement ***
   F = (1.0 / 2.0 * PI) SQRT (G / L)
   *** Expecting operator when sqrt found ***

   *** Severe errors -- no execution ***
```

Only three syntax errors isn't really too bad for a first attempt. The first error message is puzzling. What missing parameter assignment? The assignment PI = 3.14159 is right there, echoed in the error message, and the parameter assignment G = 9.80665 clearly is there in the next line. Why can't the compiler find them? The second error message is even more puzzling. G was supposed to be a parameter, not a variable, and besides, it is declared right in the line flagged by the error message. The crucial clue is before us, but as in a good detective mystery, only the practiced eye can see it. When the compiler detects an error in a REAL statement, it prints the offending REAL statement, the whole REAL statement, and nothing but the REAL statement. Looking back at the first error message, we now see that the compiler does not consider the line G = 9.80665 to be a part of this REAL statement. Now the problem is clear. Both error messages are related, and both are caused by the same mistake. There is no continuation character at the end of the first line of the statement declaring the parameters. It should read

```
REAL, PARAMETER :: PI = 3.14159, &
                    G = 9.80665
```

The compiler sees the comma, and therefore expects another parameter assignment but, in the absence of the continuation character, it finds the end-of-statement instead; so it says that there is a missing parameter assignment. Sometimes, when a compiler gets confused, it gets very confused. It would take a very clever compiler to print the error message

```
*** Error -- missing continuation character ***
```

The third error message said that the compiler was expecting an operator such as +, -, or * when SQRT was found instead. The rule is that the asterisk for multiplication cannot be omitted in Fortran in places where a multiplication sign can be omitted in ordinary algebraic notation. We correct this assignment statement to the following.

```
F = (1.0 / 2.0 * PI) * SQRT (G / L)
```

1.9.1 The Second Compilation and Run

Since all known errors have been corrected, we rerun the program. This is what happens.

```
RUN PENDULUM
    *** Execution error -- file PENDULUM_IN not found
    *** Severe error -- no execution ***
```

What went wrong this time? First, note that the situation is actually much improved over the first attempt. There are no syntax errors. This means that the current version is a syntactically correct Fortran program that compiled successfully and died during execution. Recalling that on this system, the file PENDULUM_IN is the default input file associated with the program PENDULUM, the cause of the error message is clear. We never prepared the input file for this program.

1.9.2 Choice of Input Data for Testing

The data in the input file should consist of one number, the length of the pendulum in meters. Visualizing the size of a grandfather clock, and rounding the length of its pendulum to the nearest whole meter, we will use an input length of one meter. We now prepare an input data file with the single line

1

and run the program again.

1.9.3 The Third Compilation and Run

This time, there are no error messages.

```
RUN PENDULUM

    Input data  L:    1.00000
```

Unfortunately, there is only one line of output, and that line is the echo of the input data. At least we know that the input data was read correctly. But why didn't the computer print the answers? The reason is very simple and embarrassing. The computer didn't print the answers because we didn't provide PRINT statements for them. It is clear to most people reading the program that we calculated values for the variables F and T for a purpose, but nothing is clear to the computer. If we include statements to print the answers, we obtain the following version of the program PENDULUM.

```
PROGRAM PENDULUM
!  Calculates the frequency and period
!  of a pendulum of length L

   IMPLICIT NONE
   REAL :: L, F, T
   REAL, PARAMETER :: PI = 3.14159, &
                      G = 9.80665

   READ *, L
   PRINT *, "Input data  L:", L
   F = (1.0 / 2.0 * PI) * SQRT (G / L)
   T = 1.0 / F
   PRINT *, "The frequency of the pendulum is", &
                  F, "swings / sec."
   PRINT *, "Each swing takes", T, "sec."
END PROGRAM PENDULUM
```

1.9.4 The Fourth Compilation and Run

Assuming we have not introduced any syntax errors in the two new PRINT statements, we expect the program PENDULUM to run, and this time, to print the correct answers. Here is what the fourth run produces.

```
RUN PENDULUM

    Input data  L:    1.00000
    The frequency of the pendulum is    4.91903  swings / sec.
    Each swing takes  0.203292  sec.
```

The program does run to completion; it prints the echo of the input data and it prints the answers, but they are wrong! The pendulum of a grandfather clock does not make almost five complete swings per second. One swing every two seconds is more like it, with each half of the swing producing a tick at one second intervals. Just because the computer prints an answer, it doesn't necessarily mean that the answer is right. The computer's arithmetic is almost certainly perfect, but the formula it was told to compute might be in error.

All the evidence seems to be pointing a finger at the assignment statement to calculate the frequency f:

```
F = (1.0 / 2.0 * PI) * SQRT (G / L)
```

or, if that statement is correct, at the statements that assign values to the variables and parameters that appear on the right in that statement. The assignment statement for F seems at first glance to be the Fortran equivalent of the algebraic formula for the frequency, so we shift our attention to the assignment of the parameters PI and G and the reading of the variable L. The echo of input data shows that L is correct. The PARAMETER statement assigning PI and G seems to be correct, so we shift our attention back to the assignment statement calculating F. The error must be in this statement. If we still don't believe that it is wrong, we could print the values of PI and G just before this statement to further narrow the focus.

Remember the rule that a sequence of multiplications and divisions is executed from left to right. Thus, the assignment statement executes as though it were written

```
F = (( 1.0 / 2.0) * PI) * SQRT (G / L)
```

The correct Fortran version of the statement is

```
F = (1.0 / (2.0 * PI)) * SQRT (G / L)
```

1.9.5 The Fifth Compilation and Run

This time, the answers look correct. We expected a pendulum one meter long to swing once every two seconds.

```
RUN PENDULUM

    Input data  L:    1.00000
    The frequency of the pendulum is  0.498403  swings / sec.
    Each swing takes   2.00641  sec.
```

To check it we calculate the algebraic formulas on a hand calculator and get the same answers, and we could also try other pendulum lengths in the computer.

1.9.6 Post Mortem Discussion

The authors are really not incompetent enough to make all of the errors shown in this 14-line program, at least not in one grand tour de force. However, even experienced programmers will make each of these errors, one at a time or in combination, over the course of writing several dozen longer programs. Thus, it is vital for programmers not only to know how to write programs, but also to have effective strategies for debugging programs when the inevitable bugs appear. The techniques illustrated above: compiler error messages, echoes of input data, well-chosen test cases worked by hand, and diagnostic printed output will serve the programmer in good stead throughout a career.

2

Control Constructs

The programs in Chapter 1 performed simple calculations and printed the answers, but each statement in these programs was executed exactly once. Almost any useful program has the properties that some collections of statements are executed many times and different sequences of statements are executed depending on the values of the input data.

The Fortran statements that control which statements are executed, together with the statements executed, are called **control constructs**. There are three kinds of control constructs, the **IF construct**, the **CASE construct**, and the **DO construct**. These constructs will be discussed in this chapter.

2.1 Statement Blocks

A collection of statements whose execution is controlled by one of the control constructs is called a **block**. For example, the statements between an IF statement and the next matching ELSE IF statement form a block. Transferring control into a block from outside is not permitted, but it is permitted to leave a block with a transfer of control, such as an EXIT or

CYCLE statement. Any block may contain a complete IF, CASE, or DO construct, so that these constructs may be nested to any level.

Indentation of the blocks of a construct improves the readability of a program. The subordinate placement of the controlled blocks visually reinforces the fact that their execution is conditional or controlled.

> *Style Note:* The statements of each block of a construct should be indented some consistent number of spaces more than the statements that delimit the block.

2.2 Construct Names

Any IF, CASE, or DO construct may have a **construct name** on its first statement. It consists of an ordinary Fortran name followed by a colon. The END statement that ends the construct may be followed by the same construct name. This permits more complete checking that constructs are nested properly and, in the case of the DO construct, provides a means of exiting or cycling more than one level of nested loop. Construct names are particularly useful when there are nested constructs.

2.3 The IF Construct and IF Statement

The IF construct is a simple and elegant decision construct that permits the selection of one of a number of blocks during execution of a program. The general form of an IF construct is

        IF (*logical expression*) THEN
          block of statements
        ELSE IF (*logical expression*) THEN
          block of statements
        ELSE IF (*logical expression*) THEN
          block of statements
        ELSE IF . . .
            .
            .
            .
        ELSE
          block of statements
        END IF

The ELSE IF clauses are optional and may be omitted, as may be the ELSE clause. The END IF statement must not be omitted. Some simple examples follow.

```
IF (A == B) THEN
   C = A
   PRINT *, C
END IF


IF (DICE < 3 .OR. DICE == 12) THEN
   PRINT *, "You lose!"
ELSE IF (DICE == 7 .OR. DICE == 11) THEN
   PRINT *, "You win!"
ELSE
   PRINT *, "You have to keep rolling until you get"
   PRINT *, "either a 7 or a ", DICE
END IF


!  30 days has September, April, June, and November
IF (MONTH == 9 .OR. MONTH == 4 .OR. &
   MONTH == 6 .OR. MONTH == 11) THEN
   NUMBER_OF_DAYS = 30
!  All the rest have 31, except February
ELSE IF (MONTH /= 2) THEN
   NUMBER_OF_DAYS = 31
ELSE IF (MONTH == 2) THEN
   IF (LEAP_YEAR) THEN
      NUMBER_OF_DAYS = 29
   ELSE
      NUMBER_OF_DAYS = 28
   END IF
ELSE
   PRINT *, MONTH, "is not the number of a month"
END IF
```

The IF-THEN statement is executed by evaluating the logical expression. If it is true, the block of statements following it is executed. Execution of this block completes the execution of the entire IF construct. If the logical expression is false, the next matching ELSE IF, ELSE, or END IF statement following the block is executed. The execution of an ELSE IF statement is exactly the same; the difference is that an IF statement must begin an IF construct and an ELSE IF statement must not. The ELSE and END IF statements merely serve to separate blocks in an IF construct; their execution has no effect.

The effect of these rules is that the logical expressions in the IF statement and the ELSE IF statements are tested until one is found to be true. Then the block following the statement containing that test is executed, which completes execution of the IF construct. If all of the logical conditions are false, the block following the ELSE statement is executed, if there is one.[1]

2.3.1 Case Study: Escape Velocity of a Rocket

If a rocket or other object is projected directly upward from the surface of the earth at a velocity v, it will reach a maximum height h above the center of the earth given by the formula

$$h = \frac{R_E}{1 - v^2 \,/\, 2gR_E}$$

where R_E is the radius of the earth (6.366×10^6 m) and g is the acceleration due to gravity at the surface of the earth (9.80 m/s^2). This formula is not an unreasonable approximation, since a rocket reaches its maximum velocity within a relatively short period of time after launching, and most of the air resistance is confined to a narrow layer near the surface of the earth.

A close examination of this formula reveals that it cannot possibly hold for all velocities. For example, if the initial velocity v is such that $v^2 = 2gR_E$, then $1 - v^2/2gR_E$ is zero and the maximum height h is infinite. This velocity $v = 1.117 \times 10^4$ m/s (approximately 7 mi/s) is called the **escape velocity** of the earth. Any object, either rocket or atmospheric gas molecule, attaining this vertical velocity near the surface of the earth will leave the earth's gravitational field and not return. A particle starting at the escape velocity will continue rising to arbitrarily great heights above the earth. As it does so, it will slow to practically, but not quite, zero velocity.

At initial velocities greater than the escape velocity, the particle or rocket's velocity will not drop to zero. Instead it will escape from the earth's gravitational field with a final velocity v_{final} given by the formula

$$v_{final} = \sqrt{v^2 - 2gR_E}$$

The original formula for the maximum height h gives negative answers in these cases and should not be used. The maximum height is infinite.

---

1. The usage of the term "block" has changed from Fortran 77. In Fortran 77 the term "IF block" referred to the entire Fortran IF construct from the IF-THEN statement to the END IF statement; a Fortran 90 block of statements was called a "clause" in Fortran 77.

2.3.2 The Problem

We wish to write a Fortran program that reads an initial velocity of a rocket or molecule (in meters per second) and prints an appropriate description of the fate of the rocket or molecule. That is, if the rocket reaches a maximum height before falling back to earth, the maximum height should be printed. On the other hand, if the rocket escapes the earth's gravitational field, the final velocity with which it escapes should be printed.

2.3.3 The Solution in Pseudocode

From the preceding discussion, we see that the fate of the rocket or molecule can be determined by comparing the initial velocity to the escape velocity of the earth, or equivalently, by comparing v^2 to $2gR_E$. If v^2 is smaller, then a maximum height h is reached before the rocket or molecule falls back to earth. If the initial velocity is greater, then the object in question escapes with a nonzero final velocity given by the second formula. In the pseudocode solution below, the control structure is modeled exactly on the Fortran IF construct.

```
Read the initial velocity v
Echo the input data
IF (v² < 2gRₑ) THEN
    Calculate maximum height h above center of earth
    Print that the object attains maximum height h - Rₑ
        above the surface of the earth before returning to earth
ELSE IF (v² = 2gRₑ) THEN
    Print that the initial velocity is the escape velocity
ELSE
    Calculate the final velocity
    Print that the object escapes earth
        with the calculated final velocity
END
```

The IF construct extends from the keyword IF that begins the IF construct to the keyword END IF that ends the construct. The two lines of pseudocode between the keyword THEN and the keyword ELSE IF constitute a block. They are executed if and only if $v^2 < 2gR_E$. The line of pseudocode between the second keyword THEN and the keyword ELSE is the first and only block controlled by an ELSE IF statement in this IF construct. It is executed whenever $v^2 = 2gR_E$. Finally, the two lines of pseudocode between the keyword ELSE and the keyword ELSE IF are the ELSE block. They are executed in case none of the preceding IF or ELSE IF conditions are true.

2.3.4 The Fortran Solution

Little remains to be done to refine the pseudocode solution to an executable Fortran program except to choose names for the Fortran variables and parameters that most nearly resemble the variable names in the formulas and to translate the pseudocode to Fortran nearly line by line.

```fortran
PROGRAM ESCAPE
!  Accepts as input an initial velocity V
!  Prints maximum height attained,
!     if object does not escape earth
!  Prints final escape velocity, VFINAL,
!     if object escapes

!  Parameters
!     G  = acceleration of gravity near earth's surface
!              in meters / sec ** 2  (m/s**2)
!     RE = radius of the earth (in meters)

   IMPLICIT NONE
   REAL :: V, H, VFINAL
   REAL, PARAMETER :: G = 9.80, RE = 6.366E6

   READ *, V
   PRINT *, "Initial velocity of object =", V, "m/s"
   IF (V ** 2 < 2 * G * RE) THEN
      H = RE / (1 - V ** 2 / (2 * G * RE))
      PRINT *, "The object attains a maximum height of", H - RE, "m"
      PRINT *, "above the earth's surface before returning to earth."
   ELSE IF (V ** 2 == 2 * G * RE) THEN
      PRINT *, "This velocity is the escape velocity of the earth."
      PRINT *, "The object just barely escapes from earth's gravity."
   ELSE
      VFINAL = SQRT (V ** 2 - 2 * G * RE)
      PRINT *, "The object escapes from earth with a velocity of", &
                VFINAL, "m/s."
   END IF
END PROGRAM ESCAPE
```

```
RUN ESCAPE

   Initial velocity of object =   1000.00  m/s
   The object attains a maximum height of   51432.5  m
   above the earth's surface before returning to earth.

RUN ESCAPE

   Initial velocity of object =   20000.0  m/s
   The object escapes from earth with a velocity of   16589.9  m/s.

RUN ESCAPE

   Initial velocity of object =   11170.0  m/s
   The object attains a maximum height of   1.69255E+11  m
   above the earth's surface before returning to earth.
```

2.3.5 Testing an IF Construct

The goal in testing an IF construct is to design test cases that exercise each alternative in the IF construct. The first sample execution shows an initial velocity of 1.0×10^3 m/s (1 km/s), which is well below the escape velocity of the earth. The sample execution shows that the rocket reaches a maximum height of 5.14×10^4 m (51.4 km) before falling back to earth. Calculating the appropriate formula using a hand calculator gives the same answer.

The second sample execution shows an initial velocity of 2.0×10^4 m/s (20 km/s), which is well above the escape velocity. As expected, the printed output shows that the rocket will escape from the earth's gravitational field, so the correct block in the IF construct is executed. It may seem surprising at first that the final velocity on escape is such a large fraction of the initial velocity. We rechecked it using a hand calculator and got the same answer. The explanation is that an initial velocity of nearly twice the escape velocity carries with it an initial kinetic energy (energy of motion) of nearly four times the energy of the escape velocity. So it is not really surprising that nearly three-fourths of the initial kinetic energy is retained and carried away with the rocket in the form of a large final velocity.

The third sample execution is designed to test the program using the escape velocity 1.117×10^4 m/s (11.17 km/s) as the initial velocity. Unfortunately, there is a little bit of roundoff in the calculations, and the middle block in the IF construct is not executed. The printed answer is not bad. It says that the rocket will rise to a height of 1.69×10^{11} m above the surface of the earth before returning. Since this height is farther than the distance to either Mars or Venus at their nearest approach to earth, for all practical purposes the program has reported that the rocket will escape.

You must expect some roundoff in any calculation using reals. The largest source of roundoff in this problem is the fact that the physical constants, the radius of the earth and the gravitational acceleration, are given to only 3 or 4 significant digits, as is the escape velocity. Even if the physical constants were given and used to more digits, each arithmetic calculation in the computer is calculated to a fixed number of digits. If you run this program on your computer, you will probably notice that the last one or more digits of your computer's printed answers differ from the ones shown. This is to be expected. We suggest that you try initial velocities slightly larger than 1.117×10^4 m/s in an attempt to hit the escape velocity exactly on the nose. Quite likely there is no computer-representable number on your machine to use as input to cause execution of the middle alternative in the IF block. *Equality tests for reals are rarely satisfied.* The best you can reasonably expect is even larger maximum heights or extremely low final escaping velocities. To avoid this test for equality, test for *approximate equality* instead. In our case, the two values v^2 and $2gR_E$ probably should be considered equal if they agree to within three significant digits. This test for approximate equality can be used to replace the ELSE IF statement in the program ESCAPE.

```
ELSE IF (ABS (V**2 - 2*G*RE) / (2*G*RE)) < 1.0E-3) THEN
```

2.3.6 Flowchart for an IF Construct

In standard flowcharting conventions, a diamond-shaped box is used to indicate a decision or fork in the flow of the program execution. A rectangular box represents processing of some sort. Using these standard conventions, the flowchart in Figure 2-1 indicates how an IF construct is executed.

2.3.7 Case Study: Graduated Income Tax

The U.S. federal income tax is a graduated or progressive tax, which means that each income level is taxed at a different rate. After all deductions, progressively higher incomes are taxed at increasing rates. A program to calculate federal income tax uses a multi-alternative IF block to select the correct tax computation formula for each income level.

The resulting program illustrates the use of some of the logical operators .AND., .OR., and .NOT.

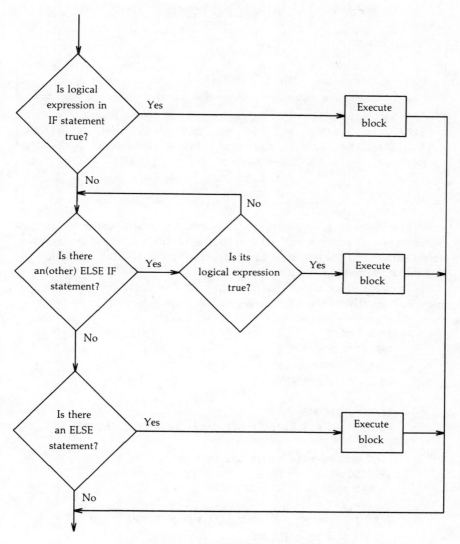

Figure 2-1 Flowchart for the IF construct.

To calculate a person's income tax liability, income for the year is modified by various exclusions, deductions, and adjustments to arrive at a taxable income. The problem treated in this section is that of writing a program to compute the federal income tax liability for an unmarried taxpayer based on taxable income. Schedule X in Table 2-1 indicates how the tax is computed.

Table 2-1 Schedule X tax table.

If taxable income is				
more than	but not more than	then income tax is		
$0	$17,850		15% of taxable income	
$17,850	$43,150	$2,677.50 plus	28% of excess over	$17,850
$43,150	$81,560	$9,761.50 plus	33% of excess over	$43,150
$81,560	. . .	Use worksheet to figure your tax.		

The input to the program is the person's taxable income, after all deductions and adjustments. The output is both the tax due on that taxable income and the person's tax bracket, that is, the rate at which the last dollar earned is taxed.

The central section of the program TAX to solve this problem corresponds directly to the alternatives in Tax Rate Schedule X.

```
PROGRAM TAX
    IMPLICIT NONE
    REAL :: INCOME, TAX
    INTEGER :: BRACKET

    READ *, INCOME
    PRINT "(A, F15.2)", "Input data  INCOME:", INCOME

!   Find appropriate range and compute tax
    IF (INCOME == 0) THEN
        TAX = 0
        BRACKET = 0
    ELSE IF (INCOME > 0 .AND. INCOME <= 17850) THEN
        TAX = 0.15 * INCOME
        BRACKET = 15
    ELSE IF (INCOME > 17850 .AND. INCOME <= 43150) THEN
        TAX = 2677.50 + 0.28 * (INCOME - 17850)
        BRACKET = 28
    ELSE IF (INCOME > 43150 .AND. INCOME <= 81560) THEN
        TAX = 9761.50 + 0.33 * (INCOME - 43150)
        BRACKET = 33
    END IF
!   End of tax computation section
```

```
IF (INCOME <= 81560) THEN
    PRINT "(A, F8.2, A, F7.2)", &
           "The tax on $", INCOME, " is $", TAX
    PRINT "(A, I2, A)", &
           "This income is in the ", BRACKET, "% tax bracket."
ELSE
    PRINT *, "Tax must be figured using worksheet."
END IF
END PROGRAM TAX
```

Each line in Tax Rate Schedule X corresponds to an IF or ELSE IF test and a corresponding block in the tax computation IF construct. If INCOME lies in the indicated range for that IF test, then the variables TAX and BRACKET are calculated by the formula in the following IF block. The conditions describing the ranges for INCOME follow the form of Schedule X exactly. They guarantee that only one range and one tax computation formula applies for each possible value of INCOME less than or equal to $81,560.

To be more specific, let us look at a few sample executions of TAX, in which the computer is supplied with different values as input for the variable income.

```
RUN TAX

Input data  INCOME:      1000.00
The tax on $ 1000.00 is $  150.00
This income is in the 15% tax bracket.

RUN TAX

Input data  INCOME:      20850.00
The tax on $20850.00 is $ 3517.50
This income is in the 28% tax bracket.

RUN TAX

Input data  INCOME:      63150.00
The tax on $63150.00 is $16361.50
This income is in the 33% tax bracket.
```

```
RUN TAX
```

```
Input data  INCOME:      95000.00
   Tax must be figured using worksheet.
```

Consider the second run with a taxable income of $20,850. The only condition in the tax computation section which this taxable income satisfies is

```
INCOME > 17850 .AND. INCOME <= 43150
```

The tax is computed by the formula in the block following:

```
TAX = 2677.50 + 0.28 * (INCOME - 17850)
```

so that the tax computed is $2677.50 + .28 \times (20850 - 17850) = 2677.50 + .28 \times 3000 = 2677.50 + 840 = 3517.50$. The second assignment statement of this block assigns a tax bracket of 28 (percent) to the variable BRACKET. The remaining ELSE IF test in the tax computation section is skipped, but even if it were made, its condition would not be satisfied and so no other action would be taken for a taxable income of $20,850.

The final IF test of the program controls the printout. Since the value of INCOME is $20,850, which is less than $81,560, the two sentences giving the tax and the tax bracket are printed.

In the last of the sample executions, using a taxable income of $95,000, none of the conditions in the tax computation section is satisfied. Since this IF construct contains no ELSE statement, the variables TAX and BRACKET are not assigned values at all. In this execution, the final IF test causes the computer to print a statement that the tax cannot be computed using Schedule X.

Style Note: It is good programming practice to warn the user when a situation occurs that the program is not designed to handle.

2.3.8 Non-Exclusive IF Conditions

Because the tax computation IF construct in the program TAX is based so closely on Tax Rate Schedule X, the alternative IF and ELSE IF conditions are mutually exclusive. Just as one and only one line of Tax Rate Schedule X applies to each taxable income, one and only one condition in the tax computation IF construct in the program TAX is true (up to $81,560).

The test conditions in an IF construct need not be mutually exclusive. Fortran permits more than one condition to be true. However, even if several conditions are true, only the first such condition selects its block for execution. The remaining conditions are not even tested. Executing the selected block completes execution of the entire IF construct.

Using this rule for breaking ties when several conditions are satisfied, we may rewrite the main IF block of the program TAX with shorter test conditions.

```
!  Find appropriate range and compute tax
   IF (INCOME == 0) THEN
      TAX = 0
      BRACKET = 0
   ELSE IF (INCOME <= 17850) THEN
      TAX = 0.15 * INCOME
      BRACKET = 15
   ELSE IF (INCOME <= 43150) THEN
      TAX = 2677.50 + 0.28 * (INCOME - 17850)
      BRACKET = 15
   ELSE IF (INCOME <= 81560) THEN
      TAX = 9761.50 + 0.33 * (INCOME - 43150)
      BRACKET = 33
   END IF
!  End of tax computation section
```

What is to be gained by shortening the IF tests? Certainly, there is less typing to enter the program. In addition, since the IF tests are simpler, they will execute more rapidly. Just how much more rapidly is not clear. Not only is the correspondence between the length of the Fortran source program and the speed of execution of the compiled machine language program rather loose, but input and output operations tend to be very time consuming when compared to computational statements. Thus, it is possible that most of the execution time is spent in the READ and PRINT statements, and even a significant improvement in the speed of the IF tests produces very little change in the total execution time.

What is lost? The most important thing that is lost is the closeness of the correspondence between the program and Tax Rate Schedule X. The original program TAX obviously implements Tax Rate Schedule X. If the IF construct were replaced by the one above, the new program also would implement Tax Rate Schedule X, but this fact would not be so obvious.

Another difference is that the second IF construct is slightly more fragile or less robust. This means that although it works perfectly in its present form, it is slightly more likely to fail if it is modified at a later date. For example, if the order of the alternatives in the program TAX is scrambled, perhaps listed in decreasing rather than in increasing order of taxable income, the tax computation IF construct in TAX still works properly. The alternatives in the replacement IF construct must remain in increasing order or the IF construct will fail to compute taxes properly. On balance, the slight gain in efficiency and the slightly fewer keystrokes needed do not justify the less robust program.

> *Style Note:* Don't sacrifice clarity of the program to shorten the execution time by a few nanoseconds. Not only is the program harder to get right and maintain, but with a good optimizing compiler the improvement in execution time may be smaller than anticipated or even nonexistent.

2.3.9 The IF Statement

There is a special form of test that is useful when there are no ELSE IF or ELSE conditions and the action to be taken when the condition is true consists of just one statement. It is the **IF statement**. The general form of an IF statement is

> IF *(logical expression) statement*

The statement to be executed when the logical expression is true must not be anything that does not make sense alone, such as an END IF statement. Also, it must not be another IF statement, but it may be the first statement of an IF construct.

When the IF statement is executed, the logical expression is evaluated. If the result is true, the statement following the logical expression is executed; otherwise, it is not executed. If the conditionally executed statement begins a construct, either the whole construct is executed or none of it is executed, depending on the value of the logical expression in the IF statement.

Using this form of testing has the drawback that if the program is modified in such a way that the single statement IF is no longer adequate, the IF statement must be changed to an IF construct. If an IF construct were used in the first place, the modification would consist of simply adding more statements between the IF-THEN statement that begins the IF construct and the END IF statement. However, in the cases where the computation to be done when a certain condition is true consists of just one short statement, using the IF statement probably makes it a little easier to read. Compare, for example

```
IF (VALUE < 0) VALUE = 0
```

with

```
IF (VALUE < 0) THEN
   VALUE = 0
END IF
```

2.3.10 Exercises

1. Write an IF construct that prints the word "vowel" if the value of the variable LETTER is a vowel (i.e., A, E, I, O, or U) and the word "consonant" if the value of LETTER is any other letter of the alphabet. Only uppercase letters can appear as values of LETTER.

2. Hand simulate the programs EXAMPLE_1 to EXAMPLE_4 using the values 45, 75, and 95 as input data (12 simulations in all). Check your answers with a computer, if possible. *Caution:* These simulations are tricky, but each program is syntactically correct. No indentation has been used in order not to give any hints about the structure of the IF constructs. We suggest correctly indenting each program before hand simulating it.

```
PROGRAM EXAMPLE_1
   INTEGER :: X
   READ *, X
   IF (X > 50) THEN
   IF (X > 90) THEN
   PRINT *, X, " is very high."
   ELSE
   PRINT *, X, " is high."
   END IF
   END IF
END PROGRAM EXAMPLE_1

PROGRAM EXAMPLE_2
   INTEGER :: X
   READ *, X
```

```
            IF (X > 50) THEN
            IF (X > 90) THEN
            PRINT *, X, " is very high."
            ELSE
            END IF
            PRINT *, X, " is high."
            END IF
        END PROGRAM EXAMPLE_2

    PROGRAM EXAMPLE_3
        INTEGER :: X
        READ *, X
        IF (X > 50) THEN
        IF (X > 90) THEN
        PRINT *, X, " is very high."
        END IF
        ELSE
        PRINT *, X, " is high."
        END IF
    END PROGRAM EXAMPLE_3

    PROGRAM EXAMPLE_4
        INTEGER X
        READ *, X
        IF (X > 50) THEN
        END IF
        IF (X > 90) THEN
        PRINT *, X, " is very high."
        ELSE
        PRINT *, X, " is high."
        END IF
    END PROGRAM EXAMPLE_4
```

3. A toll bridge charges $3.00 for passenger cars, $4.00 for buses, $6.00 for trucks under 10,000 pounds, and $10.00 for trucks over 10,000 pounds. The problem is to write a program to compute the toll. Use interactive input if it is available. The input data consists of first the letter C, B, or T for car, bus, or truck, respectively. If the class is T (truck), then prompt the user for another character which is either "<" (meaning less than 10,000 pounds) or ">" (meaning greater than 10,000 pounds). The following are sample executions:

```
                    Enter vehicle class (C, B, or T)
              T
                    Enter < or > to indicate weight class
              <
                    The toll is $6.00

                    Enter vehicle class (C, B, or T)
              C
                    The toll is $3.00
```

4. The Enlightened Corporation is pleased when its employees enroll
    in college classes. It offers them an 80 percent rebate on the first
    $500 of tuition, a 60 percent rebate on the second $400, and a 40
    percent rebate on the next $300. The problem is to compute the
    amount of the rebate. The input data consists of one number, the
    amount of tuition paid by the employee. A sample execution might
    produce the following:

```
        RUN TUITION_REBATE

        Input data  TUITION:  600
        The employee's rebate is $   460
```

2.4 The CASE Construct

The CASE construct is somewhat similar to the IF construct in that it
permits selection of one of a number of different alternative blocks of
instructions, providing a streamlined syntax for an important special case
of a multiway selection. The general form of a CASE construct is

> SELECT CASE (*expression*)
>   CASE (*case selector*)
>   *block of statements*
>   CASE (*case selector*)
>   *block of statements*
>
>   .
>   .
>   .
>
>   CASE DEFAULT
>   *block of statements*
> END SELECT

The value of the expression in the SELECT CASE statement must be a
single integer, character (of any length), or logical value. The case

selector in each CASE statement is a list of items that are either single values or ranges of values of the same type as the expression in the SELECT CASE statement. A range of values is two values separated by a colon and stands for all the values between and including the two values. The CASE DEFAULT statement and its block is optional.

The CASE block is executed by evaluating the expression in the SELECT CASE statement. Then the expressions in the CASE statements are examined until one is found with a value or range that includes the value of the expression. The block of statements following this CASE statement is executed, completing execution of the entire CASE construct. No more than one CASE statement may match the value of the expression. If no CASE statement matches the value of the expression and there is a CASE DEFAULT statement, the block following the CASE DEFAULT statement is executed. The CASE DEFAULT statement is optional in a CASE construct.

Any of the items in the list of values in the CASE statement may be a range of values, indicated by the lower bound and upper bound separated by a colon (:). The case expression matches this item if the value of the expression is greater than or equal to the lower bound and less than or equal to the upper bound.

A flowchart indicating how a CASE construct is executed appears in Figure 2-2.

Some simple examples follow.

```
SELECT CASE (DICE)
   CASE (2:3, 12)
      PRINT *, "You lose!"
   CASE (7, 11)
      PRINT *, "You win!"
   CASE DEFAULT
      PRINT *, "You have to keep rolling until you get"
      PRINT *, "either a 7 or a ", DICE
END SELECT

SELECT CASE (TRAFFIC_LIGHT)
   CASE ("red")
      PRINT *, "Go"
   CASE ("yellow")
      PRINT *, "Caution"
   CASE ("green")
      PRINT *, "Stop"
```

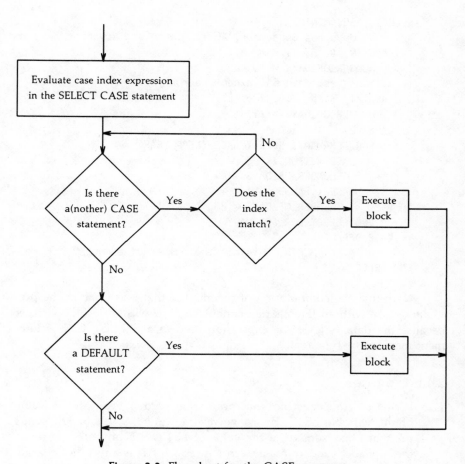

Figure 2-2 Flowchart for the CASE construct.

```
    CASE DEFAULT
        PRINT *, "Illegal value:", TRAFFIC_LIGHT
END SELECT

SELECT CASE (B > 0)
    CASE (.TRUE.)
        A = B
    CASE (.FALSE.)
        A = -B
END SELECT
```

```
SELECT CASE (MONTH)
   ! 30 days has September, April, June, and November
   CASE (9, 4, 6, 11)
      NUMBER_OF_DAYS = 30
! All the rest have 31, except February
   CASE (1, 3, 5, 7:8, 10, 12)
      NUMBER_OF_DAYS = 31
   CASE (2)
      FOR_FEBRUARY: SELECT CASE (LEAP_YEAR)
         CASE (.TRUE.)
            NUMBER_OF_DAYS = 29
         CASE (.FALSE.)
            NUMBER_OF_DAYS = 28
      END SELECT FOR_FEBRUARY
   CASE DEFAULT
      PRINT *, MONTH, " is not the number of a month"
END SELECT
```

Note that the computation of income tax that was done in the previous section with an IF construct cannot be done with a CASE construct because the data type of the expression used in a SELECT CASE statement may not be type real.

2.4.1 Exercises

1. Write a CASE construct that prints the word "vowel" if the value of the variable LETTER is a vowel (i.e., A, E, I, O, or U), prints the word "consonant" if the value of LETTER is any other letter of the alphabet, and prints an error message if it is any other character.

2. A toll bridge charges $3.00 for passenger cars, $2.00 for buses, $6.00 for trucks under 10,000 pounds, and $10.00 for trucks over 10,000 pounds. The problem is to write a program to compute the toll. Use interactive input if it is available. The input data consists of first the letter C, B, or T for car, bus, or truck, respectively. If the class is T (truck), then prompt the user for another character which is either "<" (meaning less than 10,000 pounds) or ">" (meaning greater than 10,000 pounds). The following are sample executions:

```
    Enter vehicle class (C, B, or T)
T
```

```
Enter < or > to indicate weight class
<
The toll is $6.00

Enter vehicle class (C, B, or T)
C
The toll is $3.00
```

2.5 The DO Construct

All of the programs so far suffer from the defect that each instruction is executed at most once. At the enormous speed at which computers execute instructions, it would be difficult to keep a computer busy for very long using this type of program. By the simple expedient of having the computer execute some instructions more than once, perhaps a large number of times, it is possible to produce a computer program that takes longer to execute than to write. More important is the fact that a loop increases the difficulty of writing a program very little, while it greatly increases the amount of useful data processing and calculation done by the program.

The only looping construct in Fortran is the **DO construct**. The general form of the DO construct is

DO *loop control*
    block of statements
END DO

The block of statements is executed repeatedly as indicated by the loop control. Figure 2-3 shows a flowchart showing the execution of a DO construct.

There are three types of loop control. In one case the loop control is missing, in which case the loop is executed until some instruction inside the block of statements, such as an EXIT statement, causes the loop to stop. In the second type of loop control, a variable takes on a progression of values and, in the third type, the loop is executed as long as a logical expression is true. After a very brief discussion of the EXIT statement and CYCLE statement, we will look at examples of the different types of loop control.

2.5.1 The EXIT Statement

The **EXIT statement** causes termination of execution of a loop. If the keyword EXIT is followed by the name of a DO construct, that named loop (and all loops nested within it) is exited.

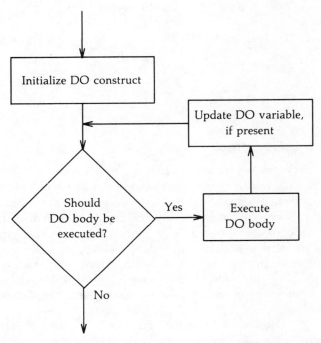

Figure 2-3 Flowchart for the DO construct.

2.5.2 The CYCLE Statement

The **CYCLE statement** causes termination of the execution of *one iteration* of a loop. In other words, control is transferred back to the beginning of the block of statements that comprise the DO construct. If the keyword CYCLE is followed by the name of a DO construct, all loops nested within that named loop are exited and control is transferred back to the beginning of the block of statements that comprise the named DO construct.

2.5.3 Loops with No Loop Control

For a DO construct with no loop control, the block of statements between the DO statement and the matching END DO statement are executed repeatedly until an EXIT statement causes it to terminate. Suppose we wish to print out all powers of two that are less than 1000. This is done with a simple DO construct with no loop control and an EXIT statement.

```
PROGRAM SOME_POWERS_OF_2

    IMPLICIT NONE
    INTEGER :: POWER_OF_2

    POWER_OF_2 = 1   ! THE ZERO POWER OF 2
    DO
        PRINT *, POWER_OF_2
        POWER_OF_2 = 2 * POWER_OF_2
        IF (POWER_OF_2 >= 1000) EXIT
    END DO
END PROGRAM SOME_POWERS_OF_2
```

As another example, suppose a file contains integers, one per line. All of the integers are nonnegative, except the last integer in the file, which is negative. The following program reads the file and computes the average of the integers, treating the first negative integer it finds as a signal that the file has all been read.

```
PROGRAM AVERAGE
! This program finds the average of a file of nonnegative integers,
! which occur one per line in the input file.
! The first negative number is treated as an end-of-file signal.

    IMPLICIT NONE
    INTEGER :: NUMBER, NUMBER_OF_NUMBERS, SUM

    SUM = 0
    NUMBER_OF_NUMBERS = 0
    DO
        READ *, NUMBER
        IF (NUMBER < 0) EXIT
        PRINT *, "Input data: ", NUMBER
        SUM = SUM + NUMBER
        NUMBER_OF_NUMBERS = NUMBER_OF_NUMBERS + 1
    END DO

    PRINT *, "The average of the numbers is", &
            REAL (SUM)  / NUMBER_OF_NUMBERS
END PROGRAM AVERAGE
```

To illustrate a simple use of the CYCLE statement, suppose a file of integers similar to the one used above is presented and the task is to count the number of odd numbers in the file prior to the first negative number in the file. The following program accomplishes this.

```
PROGRAM ODD_NUMBERS
!  This program counts the number of odd numbers
!  in a file of nonnegative integers,
!  which occur one per line in the input file.
!  The first negative number is treated as an end-of-file signal.

   IMPLICIT NONE
   INTEGER :: NUMBER, NUMBER_OF_ODD_NUMBERS

   NUMBER_OF_ODD_NUMBERS = 0
   DO
      READ *, NUMBER
      PRINT *, "Input data: ", NUMBER
      IF (NUMBER < 0) THEN
         EXIT
      ELSE IF (MODULO (NUMBER, 2) == 0) THEN
         CYCLE
      ELSE
         NUMBER_OF_ODD_NUMBERS = NUMBER_OF_ODD_NUMBERS + 1
      END IF
   END DO

   PRINT *, "The number of odd numbers is",  &
            NUMBER_OF_ODD_NUMBERS
END PROGRAM ODD_NUMBERS
```

These last two programs have a structure similar to that of the heart of many programs, both simple and complex. That structure is

```
DO
   Attempt to read some data
   If all data have been processed, then exit
   Process the data
END DO
```

For this kind of loop, a DO construct with no loop control and an EXIT statement are just right.

2.5.4 Loop Control with a DO Variable

Quite frequently, the successive values taken by a variable follow a simple pattern, like 1, 2, 3, 4, 5, 6, 7, 8, 9, 10, or 9, 7, 5, 3. Because these
sequences occur so often in programming, there is a simple means of
assigning successive values to a variable in Fortran using the DO construct and variable loop control. A simple example that prints the
squares and cubes of the integers 1–20 follows:

```
DO NUMBER = 1, 20
   PRINT *, NUMBER, NUMBER ** 2, NUMBER ** 3
END DO
```

The block of this DO construct consists of a single PRINT statement.
The first time the PRINT statement is executed, the **DO variable** NUM-
BER has the value of 1, and this number is printed as the first output
line, followed by its square and its cube. Then the DO variable NUM-
BER takes on the value 2, which is printed on the next line, followed by
its square and its cube. Then the DO variable takes on the values 3, 4,
5, up to 20 for successive repetitions of the PRINT statement. At this
point, the possible values for the DO variable NUMBER specified in the
DO statement are exhausted and execution of the DO construct terminates.

The general forms of loop control using a DO variable are

variable = *expression, expression*

and

variable = *expression, expression, expression*

The three expressions specify the starting value, the stopping value, and
the step size between successive values of the DO variable. The DO
statement in the DO construct above used constants 1 and 20 for the
starting and stopping values. When the step size expression is omitted,
as it is in the DO construct above, a step size of one is used.

The data type of a DO variable must be either integer or real.

Style Note: Do not use a real DO variable because of roundoff error. Problems include systematic drift of successive values and the fact that one cannot always guarantee that the
DO block will be executed with the real DO variable equal to
the stopping value.

The number of times the loop is executed (unless terminated by an
EXIT statement, for example) is given by the formula

$$\max\left(\left\lfloor\frac{m_2 - m_1 + m_3}{m_3}\right\rfloor, 0\right)$$

where m_1 is the starting value, m_2 is the stopping value, and m_3 is the step size. $\lfloor x \rfloor$ denotes the floor function, the greatest integer less than or equal to x..

For example, the following DO loop is executed $\left\lfloor\dfrac{10 - 2 + 2}{2}\right\rfloor =$ 5 times with the DO variable assigned the values 2, 4, 6, 8, and 10.

```
DO NUMBER = 2, 10, 2
   PRINT *, NUMBER
END DO
```

If the DO statement were changed to

```
DO NUMBER = 2, 11, 2
```

The DO loop would be executed $\left\lfloor\dfrac{11 - 2 + 2}{2}\right\rfloor = 5$ times, as before, and the values of the DO variable NUMBER would be the same: 2, 4, 6, 8, 10. The DO statement

```
DO NUMBER = 1, UPPER_LIMIT
```

causes its DO block to be executed no times if the value of the variable UPPER_LIMIT is less than or equal to zero.

2.5.5 Counting Backward

If the step size is negative, the DO variable counts backwards. Thus, it is possible to print the complete words to the popular camp song "Ninety-Nine Bottles of Beer on the Wall" using a DO statement with a negative step size. The program BEER, which tells the computer to print the verses, is given below. In the program, a PRINT statement with no print list is used to print a blank line between verses.

```
PROGRAM BEER
!  Prints the words of a camp song
```

```
      IMPLICIT NONE
      INTEGER :: N

      DO N = 99, 1, -1
         PRINT *
         PRINT *, N, "bottles of beer on the wall."
         PRINT *, N, "bottles of beer."
         PRINT *, "If one of those bottles should happen to fall,"
         PRINT *, "there'd be", N - 1, "bottles of beer on the wall."
      END DO
END PROGRAM BEER

RUN BEER


    99  bottles of beer on the wall.
    99  bottles of beer.
    If one of those bottles should happen to fall,
    there'd be  98  bottles of beer on the wall.

    98  bottles of beer on the wall.
    98  bottles of beer.
    If one of those bottles should happen to fall,
    there'd be  97  bottles of beer on the wall.

    97  bottles of beer on the wall.
    97  bottles of beer.
    If one of those bottles should happen to fall,
    there'd be  96  bottles of beer on the wall.
             .
             .
             .
    1  bottles of beer on the wall.
    1  bottles of beer.
    If one of those bottles should happen to fall,
    there'd be  0  bottles of beer on the wall.
```

A short name N is chosen for the DO variable to make it easier to sing the program listing. The execution printout shown is abbreviated after three full verses, with the last verse also given to show how the loop ends.

2.5.6 Case Study: Approximating a Definite Integral

The value of a definite integral is the area of an "almost rectangular" region of the plane bounded by the three straight lines. $x = a$, $y = 0$, $x = b$, and the curve $y = f(x)$ as shown in Figure 2-4. The better part of a semester in any calculus sequence is spent seeking analytic solutions to the area problem, that is, expressing the area by an algebraic or trigonometric expression. At the conclusion, the calculus student acquires a modest repertoire of useful functions that can be integrated in "closed form".

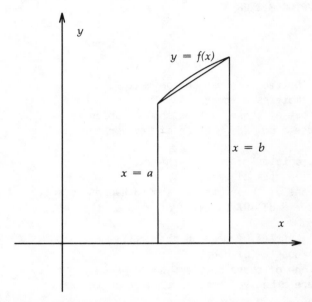

Figure 2-4 Trapezoidal approximation to the area under a curve.

It turns out to be easier to approximate the area of such "almost rectangular" regions numerically, if you have a computer available. Moreover, the numerical approximation method works even for functions that cannot be integrated algebraically. If we replace the curve $y = f(x)$ by a straight line with the same endpoints, the region in question is converted to a trapezoid, a simple four-sided figure whose area is given by the formula

$$A = (b - a) \times \frac{f(a) + f(b)}{2}$$

Of course, the area of this trapezoid is not exactly equal to the area of the original region with curved boundary, but the smaller the width of the trapezoid, the better the approximation.

Specifically, the problem we wish to solve is to find the area of one arch of the curve $y = sin(x)$, that is, the area under this curve for x from 0 to π radians (180°) as shown in Figure 2-5. We will do it by writing a program to calculate trapezoidal approximations to the area, choosing a number of trapezoids sufficient to give the answer to three decimal places.

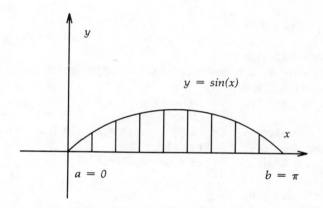

Figure 2-5 Approximating the area under the curve $y = sin(x)$.

If we call the width of each trapezoid h, we have the relationship

$$h = \frac{b - a}{n}$$

After a little algebra, the sum of the areas of the n trapezoids may be expressed by the formula

$$T_n = h \left[\frac{f(a)}{2} + f(a + h) + f(a + 2h) + \cdots + f(b - h) + \frac{f(b)}{2} \right]$$

In the following program INTEGRAL, the sum is formed by first computing

$$\left[\frac{f(a)}{2} + \frac{f(b)}{2} \right] = 0.5 \times [f(a) + f(b)]$$

To compute the remaining terms, it would be possible to use a real DO variable X to take on the values

$$a + h, \ a + 2h, \ ..., \ b - h$$

but we shall follow our style suggestion and use an integer variable I that counts $1, 2, ..., n - 1$ and compute the expression $A + I * H$ to obtain the sequence of values

$$a + h, \ a + 2h, \ ..., \ b - h = a + (n - 1)h$$

The program follows.

```
PROGRAM INTEGRAL
!  Calculates a trapezoidal approximation to an area
!  using N trapezoids.
!  N is read from the input file.

!  The region is bounded by lines X = A, Y = 0, X = B,
!  and the curve Y = SIN (X).
!  A and B also are read from the input file.

   IMPLICIT NONE
   REAL :: A, B, H, SUM
   INTEGER :: N, I

   READ *, N
   PRINT *, "Input data  N:", N
   READ *, A, B
   PRINT *, "Input data  A:", A
   PRINT *, "            B:", B

   H = (B - A) / N
!  Calculate the sum 1/2 F(A) + F(A+H) +...+ F(B-H) + 1/2 F(B)
!  Do the first and last terms first
   SUM = 0.5 * (SIN (A) + SIN (B))
   DO I = 1, N - 1
      SUM = SUM + SIN (A + I * H)
   END DO

   PRINT *, "Trapezoidal approximation to the area =", H * SUM
END PROGRAM INTEGRAL
```

```
RUN INTEGRAL

    Input data  N:  100
    Input data  A:  0.
                B:  3.14159
    Trapezoidal approximation to the area =   1.99885

RUN INTEGRAL

    Input data  N:  1000
    Input data  A:  0.
                B:  3.14159
    Trapezoidal approximation to the area =   1.99997
```

Since these two answers differ by only one in the third decimal place, we may conclude that the approximation using 100 trapezoids is almost sufficiently accurate for our purposes, and that the approximation using 1000 trapezoids is accurate to more than three decimal places. There is no need to rerun the program using more trapezoids to meet the limits of accuracy specified in the problem statement. The answer is 1.99997 rounded to three decimal places to get 2.000.

2.5.7 Exercises

1.   Hand simulate the execution of the following statements, keeping track of the value of N and PROD after the execution of each statement.

```
PROD = 1
DO N = 2, 4
    PROD = PROD * N
END DO
```

2.   What output is produced by the following program?

```
PROGRAM EXERCISE
   IMPLICIT NONE
   INTEGER :: M
   DO M = 1, 20
      IF (MODULO (M, 2) /= 0) THEN
         PRINT *, M
      END IF
   END DO
END PROGRAM EXERCISE
```

3.   What is the value of the variable SUM at the conclusion of the following loops?

```
SUM = 0
DO N = 1, 10
   SUM = SUM + 1
END DO

SUM = 0
DO N = 1, 5
   SUM = SUM + N * N
END DO

SUM = 0
DO N = 1, 14, 2
   SUM = SUM + N * N
END DO

SUM = 0
DO N = 5, 1, -1
   SUM = SUM + N
END DO
```

4.   An integer is a perfect square if it is the square of another integer. For example, 25 is a perfect square because it is 5 × 5. Write a program to selectively print those numbers less than 100 that are not perfect squares. Hint: One way to see if a number is a perfect square is to see if its square root is an integer. Using Fortran built-in functions, you can test whether INT (SQRT (REAL (X))) has the same value as SQRT (REAL (X)). Sample output for this program should look like the following.

```
RUN NOT_SQUARES

    2
    3
    5
    6
    7
    8
   10
    .
    .
    .
   99
```

5. Read integers from input until the value zero is read. Then print the number in the file just before the zero value. Sample input data might be

```
    3
    7
    2
   10
    0
    9
    4
    0
    5
```

Sample output for this input data is

```
RUN LAST_NUMBER_BEFORE_FIRST_ZERO

    Input data:   BUFFER   3
    Input data:   BUFFER   7
    Input data:   BUFFER   1
    Input data:   BUFFER   10
    Input data:   BUFFER   0
    The last number before the first zero is 10
```

6. Write a program that prints the smallest power of 3 that exceeds 5000.

7. In 1970, the population of New Jersey was 7,168,192 and it was increasing at the rate of 18% per decade. The area of New Jersey is

7521 square miles. On the basis of the 18% growth rate continuing indefinitely into the future, predict the population of New Jersey every decade from 1980 on. Stop the predictions when the average number of square feet per person is less than 100. Print out all estimates. Execution of the program should produce something like the following.

```
RUN POPULATION_OF_NJ

    Year     Population    Sq Ft / Person
    1980      8458466.         24789.6
    1990      9980990.         21007.3
      .           .               .
      .           .               .
      .           .               .
```

For partial confirmation of the validity of the prediction model, look up the 1980 and 1990 census data for New Jersey and compare the actual data with your program's predictions.

3

Procedures

The original release of Fortran did not have independent procedures, but within a year, six new statements were added to the language, all having to do with subroutines and functions. Thus, as early as 1958, it was realized that large programs were extremely difficult to debug and maintain unless they could be split into independent modules. Modern programming practice has gone even further. Even relatively short programs are greatly improved when their component parts are refined as procedures.

There are two kinds of **procedures**: **functions** and **subroutines**. A function looks much like a Fortran program, except that it begins with the keyword FUNCTION instead of the keyword PROGRAM. Once written, a function is used just like the built-in functions discussed in Section 1.5 to compute a value that may be used in any expression. A subroutine also looks like a Fortran program or a function, except that the first line begins with the keyword SUBROUTINE. A subroutine may be used to perform any computation and is used by executing a CALL statement.

Both subroutines and functions are classified as either **internal procedures** or **external procedures**. Very simply, an internal procedure is contained within another program, procedure, or module and an external procedure is not. An important distinction between these two kinds of procedures is that an internal procedure may use names of objects declared by the program or procedure that contains it, whereas an external procedure is not contained within another program or procedure. Subroutines and functions are treated in this chapter; modules are discussed in Section 6.3.

Functions and subroutines whose first statements begin with the keyword RECURSIVE are permitted to call themselves; this technique is used to write clear and simple programs for what might otherwise be difficult programming tasks.

Style Note: Self-contained subtasks should be written as procedures.

3.1 Subroutines

Suppose the task at hand is to read in three real numbers and print them in ascending order. We will revisit this problem several times, improving the program in the process. The main steps needed to accomplish this task are: (1) read in the numbers, (2) sort them, and (3) print them. The program SORT_3 does this.

```
PROGRAM SORT_3

    IMPLICIT NONE
    REAL :: N1, N2, N3, TEMP

    ! Read the numbers
    READ *, N1, N2, N3
    PRINT *, "Input data N1:", N1
    PRINT *, "          N2:", N2
    PRINT *, "          N3:", N3

    ! Sort the numbers
    IF (N1 > N2) THEN
        TEMP = N1; N1 = N2; N2 = TEMP
    END IF
    IF (N1 > N3) THEN
        TEMP = N1; N1 = N3; N3 = TEMP
    END IF
```

```
IF (N2 > N3) THEN
   TEMP = N2; N2 = N3; N3 = TEMP
END IF

! Print the numbers
PRINT *, "The numbers, in ascending order, are:"
PRINT *, N1, N2, N3

END PROGRAM SORT_3
```

Something that is noticeable is that there are three lines in the program, all doing the same kind of operation, namely, swapping the values of two variables if they are in the wrong order. This illustrates the first good reason to use a procedure: to write some statements once and use them many times, either within the same program or in different programs. In this case, the computation that is performed three times is represented the first time by the line containing three Fortran statements:

```
TEMP = N1; N1 = N2; N2 = TEMP
```

However, each time this swapping operation occurs in the program, different named variables are involved. This is no obstacle if a subroutine with arguments is used.

3.1.1 Writing a Subroutine

A subroutine is almost exactly like a program except that it begins with the keyword SUBROUTINE and may have arguments that are written in the **SUBROUTINE statement**.

The following subroutine uses arguments A and B to represent any two variables that need to be swapped.

```
SUBROUTINE SWAP (A, B)
   IMPLICIT NONE
   REAL :: A, B, TEMP
   TEMP = A
   A = B
   B = TEMP
END SUBROUTINE SWAP
```

3.1.2 The CALL Statement

The **CALL statement** is used to indicate that the computation represented by a subroutine is to be performed. The keyword CALL is followed by the name of the subroutine and, often, by a list of arguments (3.4) in parentheses.

With the subroutine SWAP available, the program SORT_3 can be rewritten as follows:

```
PROGRAM SORT_3

    IMPLICIT NONE
    REAL :: N1, N2, N3

    ! Read the numbers
    READ *, N1, N2, N3
    PRINT *, "Input data  N1:", N1
    PRINT *, "            N2:", N2
    PRINT *, "            N3:", N3

    ! Sort the numbers
    IF (N1 > N2) THEN
        CALL SWAP (N1, N2)
    END IF
    IF (N1 > N3) THEN
        CALL SWAP (N1, N3)
    END IF
    IF (N2 > N3) THEN
        CALL SWAP (N2, N3)
    END IF

    ! Print the numbers
    PRINT *, "The numbers, in ascending order, are:"
    PRINT *, N1, N2, N3

END PROGRAM SORT_3
```

In this case, the resulting program is not much shorter because the subroutine call replaces only three statements on one line, but even in this simple case, the purpose of the program is quite a bit easier to understand, in part because of the self-documenting subroutine name SWAP and the hiding from the calling program SORT_3 of inessential details of how the swapping actually is done. We will use this example to illustrate other possibilities when external and internal procedures are discussed.

3.1.3 Exercises

1. Write a subroutine SORT_4 (A, B, C, D) that arranges its four arguments into ascending order.

2. Write a subroutine that reads in values for a loan principal amount (P), an annual interest rate (R), and the number of months (M) in which the loan is to be paid off. The monthly payment is given by the formula:

$$PAY = \frac{R \times P\,(1 + r)^N}{(1 + r)^N - 1}$$

The subroutine should print out a monthly schedule of the interest, principal paid, and remaining balance. Note that if the annual interest rate is R, the monthly interest rate r is $R/12$.

3.2 Functions

If the purpose of a procedure is to compute one value (which may be a compound value consisting of a whole array or structure), a function is the kind of procedure to use.[1]

To illustrate a simple use of a function, suppose the task is to print out a table of values of the function

$$f(x) = \left[1 + \frac{1}{x}\right]^x$$

for values of x equal to 1, 10, 100, ..., 10^{10}. A program to do this is

```
PROGRAM FUNCTION_VALUES

    IMPLICIT NONE
    REAL :: X
    INTEGER :: I
```

---

1. Fortran 90 greatly extends the power of function procedures by allowing the result to be an array or structure and by allowing recursive functions. Older versions of Fortran permitted only simple scalar integer, real, character, and logical values.

```
DO I = 0, 10
  X = 10.0 ** I
  PRINT "(F15.1, F15.5)", X, (1 + 1/X) ** X
END DO

END PROGRAM FUNCTION_VALUES

RUN FUNCTION_VALUES
```

1.0	2.00000
10.0	2.59374
100.0	2.70481
1000.0	2.71692
10000.0	2.71815
100000.0	2.71827
1000000.0	2.71828
10000000.0	2.71828
100000000.0	2.71828
1000000000.0	2.71828
10000000000.0	2.71828

In this program the evaluation of the function occurs once for each execution of the DO construct, but the expression that evaluates the function occurs only once. In this case, a function is used to submerge the details of evaluating the function to another place, making the program a little easier to read. When this is done, there is also the advantage that if the same table is needed, but for a different function, the main program does not need to be changed; only the procedure that evaluates the function needs to be changed.

3.2.1 Writing a Function

A function is almost like a program or subroutine except that its first statement uses the keyword FUNCTION. It also may have arguments that are written in parentheses in the **FUNCTION statement**.

A difference between a subroutine and a function is that a function must provide a value that is returned as the value of the function. This is done by assigning a value to a **result variable** during execution of the function. This result variable is indicated by placing its name in parentheses at the end of the FUNCTION statement following the keyword RESULT. The result variable is declared within the function and is used just like any other local variable, but the value of this variable is the one that is returned as the value of the function to the program using the function.[2]

Style Note: Use a result variable in every function procedure.

The following function computes the values required in our example and uses the result variable F_RESULT to hold the result.

```
FUNCTION F (X)  RESULT (F_RESULT)

    IMPLICIT NONE
    REAL :: F_RESULT, X

    F_RESULT = (1 + 1/X) ** X

END FUNCTION F
```

3.2.2 Invoking a Function

A programmer-defined function is called by writing its name, followed by its arguments, in any expression in the same manner that a built-in function is invoked. With the function F available, the program FUNCTION_VALUES can be rewritten as follows:

```
PROGRAM FUNCTION_VALUES

    IMPLICIT NONE
    REAL :: F, X
    INTEGER :: I

    DO I = 0, 10
        X = 10.0 ** I
        PRINT "(F15.1, F15.5)", X, F (X)
    END DO

END PROGRAM FUNCTION_VALUES
```

Note that the type of F must be declared in the calling program, and must match the type of the result variable within the function itself.

---

2. When the RESULT keyword and variable is omitted, the function name is declared and used as the result variable, just as it was in Fortran 77.

3.2.3 Exercises

1. Write a function MEDIAN_OF_3 that selects the median of its three integer arguments. If all three numbers are different, the median is the number that is neither the smallest nor the largest. If two or more of the three numbers are equal, the median is one of the equal numbers.

2. Write a function AVERAGE_OF_4 that computes the average of four real numbers.

3. Write a function CONE_VOLUME (R, H) that returns the volume of a cone. The formula for the volume of a cone is $V = \pi r^2 h / 3$, where r is the radius of the base and h is its height.

4. Write a function ROUND (X, N) whose value is the real value X rounded to the nearest 10^N. For example, ROUND (463.2783, –2) should be 463.28, which has been rounded to the nearest hundredth.

3.3 External, Internal, and Module Procedures

We have discussed how to write and use functions and subroutines. We now discuss where to place these procedures in a Fortran program. A function or subroutine is an **external procedure** if it is not contained within any other procedure and it is not in a module (6.3). A function or subroutine is an **internal procedure** if it follows a CONTAINS statement in a main program, an external procedure, or a module procedure. A function or subroutine is a **module procedure** if it occurs in a module, but not inside another procedure in the module.

Both the function and the subroutine given as examples in this chapter could be used as internal, external, or module procedures. To illustrate the first two possibilities, let us return to the program SORT_3. If the subroutine SWAP is to be an external procedure, it remains outside the program SORT_3. On most systems, it could be in the same file or in a different file from the main program SORT_3.

```
PROGRAM SORT_3

    IMPLICIT NONE
    REAL :: N1, N2, N3
```

```
! Read the numbers
READ *, N1, N2, N3
PRINT *, "Input data  N1:", N1
PRINT *, "           N2:", N2
PRINT *, "           N3:", N3

! Sort the numbers
IF (N1 > N2) THEN
    CALL SWAP (N1, N2)
END IF
IF (N1 > N3) THEN
    CALL SWAP (N1, N3)
END IF
IF (N2 > N3) THEN
    CALL SWAP (N2, N3)
END IF

! Print the numbers
PRINT *, "The numbers, in ascending order, are:"
PRINT *, N1, N2, N3

END PROGRAM SORT_3

SUBROUTINE SWAP (A, B)
    IMPLICIT NONE
    REAL :: A, B, TEMP
    TEMP = A
    A = B
    B = TEMP
END SUBROUTINE SWAP
```

Rather than illustrate how SWAP could be used as an internal subroutine, let us modify the program SORT_3 to make its purpose and function even clearer, retaining SWAP as an external subroutine. We do this by creating subroutines to do the three main steps of the program: reading the input, sorting the numbers, and printing the results. This just amounts to taking the comments from the previous version and making them subroutine calls.

```
PROGRAM SORT_3

    IMPLICIT NONE
    REAL :: N1, N2, N3
```

```
CALL READ_THE_NUMBERS
CALL SORT_THE_NUMBERS
CALL PRINT_THE_NUMBERS

   . . .

END PROGRAM SORT_3
```

The three subroutines could be external provided N1, N2, and N3 were passed to them as arguments, but when they are internal, the objects declared in the program are also known within any contained internal procedures. The ellipses in the example above indicate that the three internal subroutines are missing. When they are supplied, they must be preceded by the CONTAINS statement.

3.3.1 The CONTAINS Statement

When procedures are internal to a program, another procedure, or within a module, they are preceded by a CONTAINS statement. The internal procedures must appear just before the last END statement of the program, procedure, or module containing them. Thus, to complete our example above, the CONTAINS statement is used and the subroutines follow. Note that the variables N1, N2, and N3 are *not* declared within these subroutines; they are the same variables that are declared in the main program.

```
PROGRAM SORT_3

   IMPLICIT NONE
   REAL :: N1, N2, N3

   CALL READ_THE_NUMBERS
   CALL SORT_THE_NUMBERS
   CALL PRINT_THE_NUMBERS

CONTAINS
```

```
SUBROUTINE READ_THE_NUMBERS
   READ *, N1, N2, N3
   PRINT *, "Input data  N1:", N1
   PRINT *, "            N2:", N2
   PRINT *, "            N3:", N3
END SUBROUTINE READ_THE_NUMBERS

SUBROUTINE SORT_THE_NUMBERS
   IF (N1 > N2) THEN
      CALL SWAP (N1, N2)
   END IF
   IF (N1 > N3) THEN
      CALL SWAP (N1, N3)
   END IF
   IF (N2 > N3) THEN
      CALL SWAP (N1, N3)
   END IF
END SUBROUTINE SORT_THE_NUMBERS

SUBROUTINE PRINT_THE_NUMBERS
   PRINT *, "The numbers, in ascending order, are:"
   PRINT *, N1, N2, N3
END SUBROUTINE PRINT_THE_NUMBERS

END PROGRAM SORT_3



SUBROUTINE SWAP (A, B)
   IMPLICIT NONE
   REAL :: A, B, TEMP
   TEMP = A
   A = B
   B = TEMP
END SUBROUTINE SWAP
```

This program assumes that SWAP is still available as an external subroutine. It is not made an internal program for two reasons. First, it naturally belongs within the subroutine SORT_THE_NUMBERS, but internal procedures may not be nested within other internal procedures. Second, it is a generally useful subroutine and so should be kept where it can be used by any program.

Note that none of the internal subroutines has any arguments; all values needed by the subroutines are declared within the main program that contains the subroutines. Internal procedures may have arguments, however, and it is possible to have external procedures with no arguments.

Module procedures will be discussed in Chapter 6.

3.3.2 Exercises

1.   Write a program that tests the function MEDIAN_OF_3 (Exercise 1 of Section 3.2) as an external function.

2.   Write a program that tests the function MEDIAN_OF_3 (Exercise 1 of Section 3.2) as an internal function.

3.4 Argument Passing

One of the important properties of both functions and subroutines is that information may be passed to the procedure when it is called and information may be returned from the procedure to the calling program when the procedure execution ends. This information passing is accomplished with procedure **arguments**. A one-to-one correspondence is set up between **actual arguments** in the calling program and **dummy arguments** in the procedure. The corresponding arguments need not have the same name, and the correspondence is temporary, lasting only for the duration of the procedure call.

3.4.1 Agreement of Arguments

Fortran 77 required complete agreement of actual and dummy argument types. With the introduction of the new language features of optional arguments, keyword-identified arguments, generic procedures, and assumed shape and size arrays, the rules for agreement of actual and dummy arguments are no longer simple.[3] In this subsection, we try to emphasize general principles, but for the sake of having all the important rules in one place, we list exceptions needed to implement these language features along with forward references to the sections where they are discussed.

---

3. The new procedure features of Fortran 90, optional arguments, keyword-identified arguments, generic procedures, and assumed size and shape arrays are so powerful and useful that the Fortran 77 programmer should make the effort to learn them and use them.

Except for dummy arguments declared as optional (3.4.7), the number of actual and dummy arguments must be the same. Each actual argument corresponds to a dummy argument. The default correspondence is the first actual argument with the first dummy argument, the second with the second, etc. However, keyword-identified arguments (3.4.6) can be used to override the default, and provide clear, order-independent specification of the correspondence between actual and dummy arguments.

The data type and kind parameter of each actual argument must match that of the corresponding dummy argument. If the arguments are type character, the length of the actual argument may be greater than that of the corresponding dummy. If this argument is passed by value (3.4.3), the character string is truncated to the length of the dummy argument. If this argument is passed by reference (3.4.2), only those characters up to the declared length of the dummy argument are accessible; the remaining characters in the actual argument are unchanged. If the length of the dummy argument is inquired about using the LEN intrinsic function in the procedure, it is reported as the length of the dummy argument.

Except for a few cases that should never be used in a Fortran program, the rank of an actual argument should match that of the corresponding dummy argument; that is, if one is a scalar, the other should be also, and if both are arrays (4), they should both have the same number of dimensions.

If the dummy argument is a pointer (8), the actual argument must be a pointer with the same type, kind parameter, and length (if character). An actual argument that is both pointer and character cannot have length greater than its corresponding dummy argument.

If the subroutine or function is generic (3.7), there must be exactly one specific procedure with that generic name for which all the above rules of agreement of actual and dummy arguments are satisfied. For given actual arguments, Fortran selects that specific procedure for which there is agreement of actual and dummy arguments.

3.4.2 Reference Arguments

A dummy argument whose actual argument is a variable (which includes an array name, an array element, an array substring, a structure component, or a substring) is **called by reference**. Any reference to the dummy argument in the subroutine causes the computer to behave as if the reference were to the corresponding argument supplied by the calling program. Statements in the subroutine causing changes to such a dummy argument cause the same changes to the corresponding actual argument.

It is bad programming practice to have such changes take place within a function procedure.

> *Style Note:* Do not change the values of any dummy arguments in a function procedure.

3.4.3 Value Arguments

A dummy argument whose actual argument is a constant (either literal or named) or an expression more complex than a variable can pass only a value to the corresponding dummy argument. This is known as **call by value**. The dummy argument then must not have its value changed during execution of the procedure. There is no way to pass a value back to the calling program using this argument.

3.4.4 An Example of Call by Reference

Let us look again at the subroutine SWAP discussed earlier and how it is used in the program SORT_3 in Sections 3.1.2 and 3.3. In the SUBROUTINE statement, the subroutine name SWAP is followed by a list (A, B) of variables enclosed in parentheses. The variables A and B in that list are the dummy arguments for the subroutine SWAP.

Suppose that in executing the first READ statement of the program SORT_3, the computer reads and assigns to the variable N1 the value 3, assigns to the variable N2 the value 2, and assigns to the variable N3 the value 1. Since 3, the value of N1, is greater than 2, the value of N2, the computer executes the CALL statement

```
CALL SWAP (N1, N2)
```

During this execution of the subroutine SWAP, it is as if every occurrence of the dummy argument A in SWAP were replaced by the variable N1, and every occurrence of the dummy argument B in SWAP were replaced by the variable N2, as shown below.

```
                     N1 N2
        SUBROUTINE SWAP (A, B)
                  N1 N2
          REAL :: A, B, TEMP
```

```
              N1
    TEMP = A̸
    N1   N2
    A̸ = B̸
    N2
    B̸ = TEMP
END SUBROUTINE SWAP
```

For example, in executing the statement

```
    TEMP = A
```

of the subroutine SWAP, the computer assigns to the variable TEMP the value 3 of the variable N1 in the program SORT_3, just as if the statement were written

```
    TEMP = N1
```

In executing the statement

```
    A = B
```

of the subroutine SWAP, the computer assigns to the variable N1 the value 2 of the variable N2, as though the statement were written

```
    N1 = N2
```

Finally, the value 3 that is saved as the value of the variable TEMP is assigned to the variable N2 by the statement

```
    B = TEMP
```

as though it were written

```
    N2 = TEMP
```

The variables N1 and N2 in the statement

```
    CALL SWAP (N1, N2)
```

are the actual arguments of the subroutine call. Whatever the names of the dummy arguments, during the execution of the subroutine, it is always as if the names of the actual arguments were copied in place of the dummy arguments.

At this point, execution of the CALL statement is complete and control returns to the main program SORT_3, which continues by testing whether the new value 2 of N1 is greater than the value 1 of N3. Since it is, the computer is directed to execute a second call to the subroutine SWAP

```
CALL SWAP (N1, N3)
```

with the actual arguments N1 and N3. This time the subroutine SWAP is executed as if every occurrence of the first dummy argument A were replaced by the first actual argument N1 and every occurrence of the second dummy argument B were replaced by the second actual argument N3.

3.4.5 An Example of Call by Value

Suppose a function is to be written that computes the following sum of certain terms of an arithmetic progression:

$$\sum_{i=m}^{n} (s + d\,i)$$

The arguments to this function are m, n, s (the starting value), and d, the difference between terms. A function to do this computation is

```
FUNCTION SERIES_SUM (M, N, S, D)   RESULT (SERIES_SUM_RESULT)

    IMPLICIT NONE
    INTEGER :: M, N, I
    REAL :: S, D, SERIES_SUM_RESULT

    SERIES_SUM_RESULT = 0
    DO I = M, N
       SERIES_SUM_RESULT = SERIES_SUM_RESULT + S + I * D
    END DO

END FUNCTION SERIES_SUM
```

This function may be used in a program, as in the following example:

```
PRINT *, SERIES_SUM (400, 700, 100.0, 0.1)
```

which produces the answer 1,950,650.

3.4.6 Keyword Arguments

With the use of **keyword arguments**, it is not necessary to put the arguments in the correct order, but it is necessary to know the names of the dummy arguments. The same computation may be made using the statement

```
PRINT *, SERIES_SUM (D = 0.1, M = 400, N = 700, S = 100.0)
```

It is even possible to call the function using keywords for some arguments and not for others. In this case, the rule is that all arguments prior to the first keyword argument must match the corresponding dummy argument correctly and once a keyword argument is used, the remaining arguments must use keywords. Thus, the following is legal:

```
PRINT *, SERIES_SUM (400, 700, D = 0.1, S = 100.0)
```

Under some circumstances using keyword arguments, an explicit procedure interface (3.6) is required. These circumstances do not include calls to contained procedures (3.3.1) or calls to procedures in a module named in a USE statement (6.3.1). An explicit interface also may be used to change the names of the keywords used in the calling program.

3.4.7 Optional Arguments

In our example computation of an arithmetic series, a common occurrence would be that the value of M is 0. It is possible to indicate that certain arguments to a procedure are **optional arguments** in the sense that they do not have to be present when the procedure is called. An optional argument must be declared to be such within the procedure; usually, there would be some instructions within the procedure to test the presence of the optional argument on a particular call and perhaps do something different if it is not there. In our example, suppose that if the function SERIES_SUM is called without the argument M, the value of M is to be set to zero. To do this, the intrinsic function PRESENT (3.4.7) is used to test whether an argument has been supplied for the dummy argument M, and if an actual argument is not present, the lower bound for the sum is set to zero. To handle both cases with the same DO loop, a different variable, TEMP_M, is used to hold the lower bound.

```
FUNCTION SERIES_SUM (M, N, S, D)  RESULT (SERIES_SUM_RESULT)

   IMPLICIT NONE
   INTEGER, OPTIONAL :: M
   INTEGER :: N, I, TEMP_M
   REAL :: S, D, SERIES_SUM_RESULT

   IF (PRESENT (M)) THEN
      TEMP_M = M
   ELSE
      TEMP_M = 0
   END IF

   SERIES_SUM_RESULT = 0
   DO I = TEMP_M, N
      SERIES_SUM_RESULT = SERIES_SUM_RESULT + S + I * D
   END DO

END FUNCTION SERIES_SUM
```

This new version of the function can now be called with any of the following statements:

```
PRINT *, SERIES_SUM (0, 700, 0.1, 100.0)
PRINT *, SERIES_SUM (0, 700, D = 0.1, S = 100.0)
PRINT *, SERIES_SUM (N = 700, D = 0.1, S = 100.0)
PRINT *, SERIES_SUM (D = 0.1, S = 100.0, N = 700)
PRINT *, SERIES_SUM (M = 0, N = 700, D = 0.1, S = 100.0)
```

Under some circumstances using optional arguments, an explicit procedure interface (3.6) is required.

3.4.8 Argument Intent

It is possible, and good programming practice, to indicate the **intent** of use of each dummy argument of a subroutine or function. The intent may be IN, which means that the dummy argument must not be changed within the procedure; it may be OUT, which means that the actual argument must be given a value by the procedure; or it may be INOUT, which means that the dummy argument both receives an initial value from, and is expected to return a value to the corresponding actual argument. Except in very rare cases, all arguments to a function should have intent IN to avoid problems with side effects.

The intent is an attribute given to an argument when it is declared within the procedure. In our series summation example, all arguments can be given intent IN by changing the function's declarations.

```
FUNCTION SERIES_SUM (M, N, S, D)  RESULT (SERIES_SUM_RESULT)

    INTEGER, INTENT (IN), OPTIONAL :: M
    INTEGER, INTENT (IN) :: N
    REAL, INTENT (IN) :: S, D
    REAL :: SERIES_SUM_RESULT
    INTEGER :: I, TEMP_M
    . . .

    END FUNCTION SERIES_SUM
```

The intent attribute is provided to make the program more easily understandable to a human reader and to allow the compiler to catch some possible errors when the programmer violates the stated intent.

3.4.9 Procedures as Arguments

An actual argument and the corresponding dummy argument may be a procedure. Any kind of procedure except an internal procedure may be passed as an actual argument. A function is used as an actual argument in the example numerical integration function in (3.10).

3.4.10 Exercises

1. Write a program that tests CONE_VOLUME (Exercise 3 of Section 3.2) as an internal function using keywords to call the function with arguments in the wrong order.

2. Rewrite the function CONE_VOLUME (Exercise 3 of Section 3.2) to make the radius an optional argument with a default value of 1 if it is not present. Test the revised function as an internal function by using it both with the argument present and with the argument missing.

3.5 Scope

Fortran has a long tradition of independence of main program and subroutines. Each procedure could be compiled separately, so that when changes were made to a large program, only the changed procedures would need to be recompiled. As a consequence of this feature, the names and types of variables declared in one procedure are not available when another external procedure is compiled. Names can be redeclared in external procedures, perhaps with different types, with no presumption of any relation between variables of the same name.

The **scope** of a name is the set of lines in a Fortran program where that name may be used and refer to the same variable, procedure, or type. The scope of a variable or type name declared in a program extends throughout that program from the PROGRAM statement to the END PROGRAM statement. The scope of such a name does not extend to external subroutines or functions. Similarly, a name declared in an external procedure has scope from the SUBROUTINE or FUNCTION statement to the corresponding END SUBROUTINE or END FUNCTION statement, but is unknown in the main program or in any other external procedure.

On the other hand, any name declared in a program or external procedure is known in all procedures internal to the one in which it is declared, that is, in all procedures following the CONTAINS statement in the program in which it is declared. This is consistent with the rule that the scope of a name extends from the opening PROGRAM, SUB-ROUTINE, or FUNCTION statement to its matching END statement. However, the scope of a name declared in a program or external procedure does not include any internal procedure in which the name is redeclared. A name declared in an internal procedure has scope extending only from the beginning to the end of that procedure, not to the program or procedure that contains it, nor to any other procedure internal to the same procedure. Recall that internal procedures cannot contain other procedures, so there is no further inheritance of a name declared in an internal procedure.

The name of an internal procedure, its number and type of arguments, as well as the type of its result variable if it is a function, are considered as declared in the containing program or procedure, and their scope therefore extends throughout the containing program and all other internal procedures of the containing program. The containing program or procedure therefore can call an internal procedure, as can any other internal procedure of the same containing procedure, but external procedures cannot call it.

Since a program must be able to call external procedures and external procedures must be able to call one another, an exception is made to the usual scoping rule to allow the name of an external procedure to be used in all other external procedures and in the main program. However, the independent compilation of external procedures is possible only if the calling program is restricted to call the external procedure in the ordinary way with the correct number, type, and kind of actual arguments, in exactly the same order that they are declared in the independent external procedure. If advanced calling features such as optional arguments or keyword arguments are desired in a call to an external procedure, an explicit interface block (3.6) must appear in the calling program to declare the name of the external procedure and the names and characteristics of all of its dummy arguments, thereby satisfying the scoping rule and permitting independent compilation of these advanced kinds of procedure calls.

Modules (6.3) follow a different paradigm. A module contains declarations of names of variables, parameters, types, kinds, etc., between the MODULE statement and the CONTAINS statement, followed by full source code of the procedures internal to the module between the CONTAINS statement and the END MODULE statement. When a module is included in a program or procedure, or another module with a USE statement, it is as if all declarations made in the module (except those declared PRIVATE in the module or not copied because of a USE ONLY option, 6.3.1) were made at the place where the USE statement appears. Thus, names declared in a module have as scope the full extent of any program that USEs the module. However, the scope of a name declared in a module does not include any internal procedure in which the name is redeclared. Similarly, procedures declared in a module may be called by any program that USEs the module. Several different external procedures may use the same module, in which case the names declared in the module have a scope that includes each of the procedures that USE it. A variable name declared in a module references the same variable in every program or external procedure that USEs the module.[4]

3.6 Interface Blocks

A **procedure interface** is the collection of information that is needed by a compiler to generate a correct call to the procedure. This information is always known to the compiler for intrinsic procedures, internal procedures, and module procedures. For external procedures that may be compiled separately, all of the necessary information may be not be available unless the programmer provides it in an **interface block** within

---

4. Modules provide a much better way to share values than COMMON, the error-prone mechanism used in Fortran 77.

the calling program.   An interface block is needed to call an external pro-cedure in the following cases:[5]

1.   If an external procedure is to be referenced with a keyword argu-ment, an interface block must indicate the name, type, kind, length (if character), number, and order of the arguments.

2.   If an external procedure is called with a missing optional argument, an interface block must provide enough information to determine the position, type, kind, and length (if character) of the omitted argument.

3.   If an external procedure is called using an operator symbol whose meaning has been extended (3.8), a procedure interface must associ-ate the operator symbol with the name of the function used to extend its meaning.

4.   If an external procedure is called using assignment extended to other data types (3.9), a procedure interface must associate the assignment operator with the name of the subroutine used to extend its meaning.

5.   If an external procedure is called that has an array-valued result (functions only); a dummy argument that is an assumed-shape array, a pointer, or a target; or a result that is neither a constant nor assumed length (character functions only); the calling program must contain an interface block declaring these objects.

6.   If a procedure is called using a generic name (3.7), an interface block must associate the generic name with the specific procedure name.

An interface block begins with a statement consisting of the key-word INTERFACE, optionally followed by a generic name or operator or assignment specification, and ends with a statement consisting of the key-words END INTERFACE. Between these statements are **procedure inter-faces**, that look like procedures but contain only declarations of dummy arguments and result variables and no executable statements.

An example of the necessity of an interface block is provided by our series summation function (3.4.6 to 3.4.8). If SERIES_SUM is an external function and it is to be called with either a keyword actual

---

5. In Fortran 77 and earlier versions, all procedure calls were to external procedures and used the default conventions for establishing correspondence and agreement between actual and dummy arguments. Explicit procedure interfaces were not required in Fortran 77, nor are they required in Fortran 77 programs run under Fortran 90.

argument or with a missing optional argument, the calling program must contain an interface block making the interface to the function explicit.

```
INTERFACE

    FUNCTION SERIES_SUM (M, N, S, D)  RESULT (SERIES_SUM_RESULT)

        REAL :: SERIES_SUM_RESULT
        INTEGER, INTENT (IN), OPTIONAL :: M
        INTEGER, INTENT (IN) :: N
        REAL, INTENT (IN) :: S, D

    END FUNCTION SERIES_SUM

END INTERFACE
```

When the interface is made explicit with an interface block, it is possible to change the names used to indicate the dummy arguments; however, it is important to keep the arguments in the correct order. Thus, the interface block could be changed to

```
INTERFACE

    FUNCTION SERIES_SUM (START, STOP, INITIAL_VALUE, DIFFERENCE) &
            RESULT (SERIES_SUM_RESULT)

        REAL :: SERIES_SUM
        INTEGER, INTENT (IN), OPTIONAL :: START
        INTEGER, INTENT (IN) :: STOP
        REAL, INTENT (IN) :: INITIAL_VALUE, DIFFERENCE

    END FUNCTION SERIES_SUM

END INTERFACE
```

and, with this different interface block, the function could be called with

```
PRINT *, SERIES_SUM (INITIAL_VALUE = 100.0,  &
                     DIFFERENCE = 0.1, STOP = 700)
```

3.6.1 Exercise

1. Write an interface block for the function CONE_VOLUME (Exercise 1 of Section 3.2 and Exercises 1 and 2 of Section 3.4) to test it as an

external function using both missing optional arguments and keyword arguments.

3.7 Generic Procedures

Our subroutine SWAP that swaps two real values works fine for that case; but suppose we also want subroutines available that swap two integers, two character strings, or even two reals with a kind different from the default. The requirement that the data types of actual and dummy arguments must match prevents the SWAP subroutine already exhibited from being used to swap two integer values. However, it is possible to create a **generic procedure** that selects one of several specific procedures based on the data types of the actual arguments.

First, let us rename the original SWAP subroutine that swaps two real values to SWAP_REALS.

```
SUBROUTINE SWAP_REALS (A, B)
   IMPLICIT NONE
   REAL, INTENT (INOUT) :: A, B
   REAL :: TEMP
   TEMP = A
   A = B
   B = TEMP
END SUBROUTINE SWAP_REALS
```

It is quite easy to modify SWAP_REALS to produce SWAP_INTEGERS that swaps two integer values.

```
SUBROUTINE SWAP_INTEGERS (A, B)
   IMPLICIT NONE
   INTEGER, INTENT (INOUT) :: A, B
   INTEGER :: TEMP
   TEMP = A
   A = B
   B = TEMP
END SUBROUTINE SWAP_INTEGERS
```

It is possible to make as many versions of SWAP as desired by creating a new subroutine name and changing the data type given in the declarations of the variables A, B, and TEMP. All of the various swapping subroutines may be called by the same name with the use of an interface block indicating a generic procedure name and its specific versions. This interface block must appear in or be included into the calling program to make the generic name accessible.

The name SWAP can be made a generic procedure by putting all of the versions of SWAP in one interface block. The name SWAP following the keyword INTERFACE indicates that the interface is specifying a generic procedure. With the following interface established, the subroutine SWAP may be called with two real arguments, two integer arguments, etc.

```
INTERFACE SWAP

    SUBROUTINE SWAP_REALS (A, B)
        REAL, INTENT (INOUT) :: A, B
        REAL :: TEMP
    END SUBROUTINE SWAP_REALS

    SUBROUTINE SWAP_INTEGERS (A, B)
        INTEGER, INTENT (INOUT) :: A, B
        REAL :: TEMP
    END SUBROUTINE SWAP_INTEGERS


    . . .


END INTERFACE
```

The name SWAP following the keyword INTERFACE indicates that the subroutines SWAP_REALS and SWAP_INTEGERS may be called by the generic name SWAP.

All of the specific procedures to be known by the same generic name may appear in one interface block or they may be scattered in several interface blocks, all specifying the same generic name. The compiler chooses that specific version of a generic procedure whose dummy arguments exactly match the number, type, and kind of the actual arguments in the generic procedure call. Of course, it is an error to use actual arguments for which no such match can be made.

3.7.1 Exercise

1. Extend the function AVERAGE_OF_4 (Exercise 2 of Section 3.2.3) to permit either all real arguments or all integer arguments. Write an interface block for the function and test it as an external function with each type of argument.

3.8 Defining and Overloading Operators

It is possible for one of the standard Fortran operators +, −, *, /, **, //, <, <=, ==, /=, >=, >, .LT., .LE., .EQ., .NE., .GE., .GT., .AND., .OR., or .NOT. to have a meaning when applied to operands other than those allowed by their intrinsic use. This commonly is called **operator overloading**. When this is done, the operator with its new meaning has the same precedence that is already established for the operator by the rules of Fortran. It is also possible to define new operators.

To illustrate, suppose that a character string operation is to be defined that concatenates two strings after stripping all trailing blanks from both arguments, and further suppose the symbol + is chosen for this operation. For example, the result of

```
"JOHN      " + "DOE        "
```

is to be

```
"JOHNDOE"
```

The first step is to write an ordinary function for this operation and give it a name, such as CONCAT.

```
FUNCTION CONCAT (S, T)  RESULT (CONCAT_RESULT)

    CHARACTER (LEN = *) :: CONCAT_RESULT
    CHARACTER (LEN = *), INTENT (IN) :: S, T

    CONCAT_RESULT (1 : LEN_TRIM (S)) = S
    CONCAT_RESULT (LEN_TRIM (S) + 1 :  &
                LEN_TRIM (S) + LEN_TRIM (T)) = T

END FUNCTION CONCAT
```

The intrinsic function LEN_TRIM returns the length of a string after all trailing blanks have been removed.

Then an interface block is created to indicate the operator that may be used in place of the function call.

```
INTERFACE OPERATOR (+)

    FUNCTION CONCAT (S, T)  RESULT (CONCAT_RESULT)
      CHARACTER (LEN = *) :: CONCAT_RESULT
      CHARACTER (LEN = *), INTENT (IN) :: S, T
    END FUNCTION CONCAT

END INTERFACE
```

After this interface is established the operator + may be used to concatenate two strings. It still may be used as an intrinsic operator to add two numerical values.

A function used to overload an intrinsic binary operator must have two dummy arguments and they may not both have the same type and kind as the operands in an intrinsic use of the same operator. Similarly, no two overloads of the same operator may have the same type and kind for both dummy arguments, because the compiler could not decide which meaning of the operator was intended.

A unary operator such as unary minus (-) or .NOT. similarly can be overloaded using a function with one dummy argument. Although minus (-) is also a binary operator, there is no confusion if both are overloaded, since the overloading functions have different numbers of arguments.

Instead of overloading an intrinsic operator, we can create a new unary operator .REVERSE. and overload it with the operation of reversing a character string, ignoring trailing blanks.

```
FUNCTION REVERSE_STRING (S)  RESULT (REVERSE_STRING_RESULT)

    CHARACTER (LEN = *) :: REVERSE_STRING_RESULT
    CHARACTER (LEN = *), INTENT (IN) :: S
    INTEGER :: I, L

    L = LEN_TRIM (S)
    DO I = 1, L
       REVERSE_STRING_RESULT (I : I) = S (L + 1 - I)
    END DO

    DO I = L + 1, LEN (S)
       REVERSE_STRING_RESULT (I : I) = S (I : I)
    END DO
END FUNCTION REVERSE_STRING
```

```
INTERFACE OPERATOR (.REVERSE.)
   FUNCTION REVERSE_STRING (S)   RESULT (REVERS_STRING_RESULT)
      CHARACTER (LEN = *) :: REVERSE_STRING_RESULT
      CHARACTER (LEN = *), INTENT (IN) :: S
   END FUNCTION REVERSE_STRING
END INTERFACE
```

If the character string C of length 8 has the value "abc   " and the length of .REVERSE. and CONCAT (+) are declared to be 8 in the calling program, the value of .REVERSE. C is "cba   " and the value of C + (.REVERSE. C) is "abccba ".

All programmer-defined unary operators have the same priority, which is lower than that of all intrinsic operators. All programmer-defined binary operators have the same priority, which is higher than that of all intrinsic binary operators. The name of a programmer-defined operator may be any sequence of up to 31 letters enclosed in periods, except that it may not be the same as an intrinsic operator (.EQ., .NE., .GT., .LT., .GE., .LE., .AND., .OR., or .NOT.) and it may not be the same as a logical constant (.TRUE. or .FALSE.).

3.8.1 Exercises

1.   Extend the operators .AND., .OR., and .NOT. so that the operands may be integers. The integer 0 is treated as false and all others are treated as true. The result should be either 0 or 1. For example, 0 .AND. −6 = 0, 1 .OR. 6 = 1, and .NOT. 6 = 0.

2.   Write interface blocks for the procedures in Exercise 1 and put them in a program to test the new versions of the operators .AND., .OR., and .NOT. as external functions.

3.9 Assignment Overloading

Just as it is possible to extend the meaning of any of the intrinsic operators to additional data types, it is also possible to extend the meaning of assignment to new data types. For example, suppose it is desired to extend assignment so that it is possible to assign a logical value to an integer such that a true value becomes 1 and a false value becomes 0. As before, the first step is to create an ordinary subroutine with two dummy arguments that does the assignment, then write an interface block to indicate that this subroutine is to be used when the overloaded assignment is specified as a Fortran statement.

Style Note: In subroutines that overload the assignment operator, it is good programming practice to declare the intents of the arguments; the second argument should be INTENT (IN) and the first INTENT (OUT).

```
SUBROUTINE LOGICAL_TO_INT (I, L)

    INTEGER, INTENT (OUT) :: I
    LOGICAL, INTENT (IN) :: L

    IF (L) THEN
        I = 1
    ELSE
        I = 0
    END IF

END SUBROUTINE LOGICAL_TO_INT
```

The interface block that indicates that this function may be used to perform assignment is

```
INTERFACE ASSIGNMENT (=)

    SUBROUTINE LOGICAL_TO_INT (I, L)
        INTEGER, INTENT (OUT) :: I
        LOGICAL, INTENT (IN) :: L
    END SUBROUTINE LOGICAL_TO_INT

END INTERFACE
```

The compiler decides which meaning to use for the assignment operator on the basis of the types and kinds of the expression on the right of the assignment operator and the variable on the left. It is an error to overload the assignment operator with a subroutine using the same types and kinds as an intrinsic assignment or to have accessible two different subroutines overloading the assignment operator that cannot be distinguished by the type and kind of their arguments. The subroutine LOGICAL_TO_INT causes no such problems because, although there is a logical-to-logical intrinsic assignment and an integer-to-integer intrinsic assignment, there is no intrinsic logical-to-integer assignment.

3.9.1 Exercises

1. Extend assignment so that an integer expression may be assigned to a logical variable. Zero should be assigned as the value false and all other integer values should be assigned as the value true.

2. Write an interface block for the overloaded assignment of Exercise 2 and test it as an external subroutine.

3.10 Case Study: Numerical Integration

In section 2.5.6, we wrote a program to approximate the definite integral

$$\int_a^b f(x)\,dx$$

by dividing the interval from a to b into n equal pieces, approximating the curve with straight lines, and computing the sum of the areas of the n trapezoids with the formula

$$T_n = h \left[\frac{f(a)}{2} + f(a+h) + f(a+2h) + \cdots + f(b-h) + \frac{f(b)}{2} \right]$$

In the program INTEGRAL, the values for a, b, and n were read as input data. Now that we have procedures, a better approach is to write a function INTEGRAL with arguments A, B, and N. The other problem with the program INTEGRAL is that the name of the function to be integrated (SIN, in the example), could not be changed without rewriting and recompiling the program. Since it is possible to pass a procedure as an argument, we can make the name of the function an additional argument F to our function INTEGRAL. The interface block in the function INTEGRAL describes the interface for F so that calls to F can be compiled correctly. It indicates that the first argument is a function and gives its type as well as the type of its argument. Even in cases where an interface block is not required, it provides good documentation for the reader and the maximum amount of information to the compiler.

All of these changes so far affect only the declarative part of the program INTEGRAL. The executable statements of the program are modified to use the dummy function argument F in place of the particular function SIN, resulting in the following function subprogram INTEGRAL.

```
FUNCTION INTEGRAL (F, A, B, N)  RESULT (INTEGRAL_RESULT)
!  Calculates a trapezoidal approximation to an area
!  using N trapezoids.

!  The region is bounded by lines X = A, Y = 0, X = B,
!  and the curve Y = F (X).

   IMPLICIT NONE
   REAL :: INTEGRAL_RESULT

   INTERFACE
      FUNCTION F (X)
      REAL :: F, X  ! F is default result variable
   END INTERFACE

   REAL, INTENT (IN) :: A, B
   INTEGER, INTENT (IN) :: N
   REAL :: X, H, SUM
   INTEGER :: I

   H = (B - A) / N
!  Calculate the sum 1/2 F(A) + F(A+H) +...+ F(B-H) + 1/2 F(B)
!  Do the first and last terms first
   SUM = 0.5 * (F (A) + F (B))
   DO I = 1, N - 1
      SUM = SUM + F (A + I * H)
   END DO

INTEGRAL_RESULT = H * SUM

END FUNCTION INTEGRAL
```

The function INTEGRAL can be tested by executing the statement

```
PRINT *, INTEGRAL (SIN, A = 0.0, B = 3.14159, N = 100)
```

assuming that INTEGRAL itself is in a module, is internal to the program containing the PRINT statement, or has been declared in an interface block to permit use with keyword actual arguments.

Some specific intrinsic functions may not be passed as actual arguments; see Section B.12.

3.11 Case Study: Calculating Probabilities

Consider the problem of calculating the probability that a throw of two dice will yield a 7 or an 11. One way to solve this problem is to have a computer simulate many rolls of the dice and count how many times the result is 7 or 11. The probability of throwing 7 or 11 is then the number of successful throws divided by the total number of times the throw of the dice was simulated.

3.11.1 The Built-In Subroutine RANDOM

The heart of a probabilistic simulation program is a procedure that generates pseudorandom numbers. In Fortran 90, such a procedure is built in; it is a subroutine named RANDOM. The subroutine places uniformly distributed real numbers greater than or equal to 0 and less than 1 in the actual argument. The argument may be a single real value or an array of real values. In this section, we will use RANDOM to generate one value at a time; in 4.6.1, we will use the same subroutine with an array as the argument to generate a whole array of random numbers with one subroutine call.

To simulate the roll of one die, we need a function that returns an integer from 1 to 6. The following function RANDOM_INT has two arguments, LOW and HIGH, and returns an integer that is greater than or equal to LOW and that is less than or equal to HIGH. For example, the expression RANDOM_INT (0, 9) returns one of the 10 one-digit integers 0, 1, 2, ..., 9. The function RANDOM_INT calls the built-in subroutine RANDOM.

```
FUNCTION RANDOM_INT (LOW, HIGH)  RESULT (RANDOM_INT_RESULT)

    IMPLICIT NONE
    INTEGER :: RANDOM_INT_RESULT
    INTEGER, INTENT (IN) :: LOW, HIGH
    REAL :: UNIFORM_VALUE

    CALL RANDOM (UNIFORM_VALUE)
    RANDOM_INT_RESULT = &
          INT ((HIGH - LOW + 1) * UNIFORM_VALUE + LOW)

END FUNCTION RANDOM_INT
```

3.11.2 Computing the Probability of a 7 or 11

Using the function RANDOM_INT, the program to estimate the probability of rolling 7 or 11 with two dice is not difficult.

```
PROGRAM SEVEN_11

    IMPLICIT NONE
    INTEGER, PARAMETER :: NUMBER_OF_ROLLS = 1000
    INTEGER :: DICE, I, WINS, RANDOM_INT

    WINS = 0
    DO I = 1, NUMBER_OF_ROLLS
       DICE = RANDOM_INT (1, 6) + RANDOM_INT (1, 6)
       IF ((DICE == 7) .OR. (DICE == 11)) WINS = WINS + 1
    END DO

    PRINT "(A, F6.2)", &
          "THE PERCENTAGE OF ROLLS THAT ARE 7 OR 11 IS", &
          100.0 * REAL (WINS) / REAL (NUMBER_OF_ROLLS)

END PROGRAM SEVEN_11

RUN SEVEN_11

THE PERCENTAGE OF ROLLS THAT ARE 7 OR 11 IS 22.40
```

The program SEVEN_11 simulates the event of rolling the dice 1000 times and computes a pretty good approximation to the true answer, which is $6/36 + 2/36 = 22.22$ percent.

3.11.3 Exercises

1. Write a program that determines by simulation the percentage of times the sum of two rolled dice will be 2, 3, or 12.

2. Two dice are rolled until a 4 or 7 comes up. Write a simulation program to determine the percentage of times a 4 will be rolled before a 7 is rolled.

3. Write a simulation program to determine the percentage of times exactly 5 coins will be heads and 5 will be tails, if 10 fair coins are tossed simultaneously.

4. Use the function RANDOM_INT to create a program that deals a five-card poker hand. Remember that the same card cannot occur twice in a hand.

4

Arrays

In ordinary usage, a **list** is a sequence of values, usually all representing data of the same kind, or otherwise related to one another. A list of students registered for a particular course and a list of all students enrolled at a college are examples.

In Fortran, a collection of values of the same type is called an **array**. We will also refer to a one-dimensional array as a list or a **vector**.

Frequently, the same operation or sequence of operations is performed on every element in an array. On a computer that performs one statement at a time, it makes sense to write such programs by specifying what happens to a typical element of the array and enclosing these statements in a sufficient number of DO constructs (loops) to make them apply to every element. Fortran 90 also has powerful intrinsic functions and operations that operate on whole arrays or sections of an array. Programs written using these array operations are often clearer and are more easily optimized by Fortran compilers. Especially on computers with parallel or array processing capabilities, such programs are more likely to take advantage of the special hardware to increase execution speed.

4.1 Declaring and Using Arrays in Fortran

We introduce the use of arrays with an example involving credit card numbers.

4.1.1 A Credit Card Checking Application

As an example of a problem concerned with a list, suppose that a company maintains a computerized list of credit cards that have been reported lost or stolen or that are greatly in arrears in payments. The company needs a program to determine quickly whether a given credit card, presented by a customer wishing to charge a purchase, is on this list of credit cards that can no longer be honored.

Suppose that a company has a list of 8262 credit cards reported lost or stolen, as illustrated in Table 4-1.

Table 4-1 Lost credit cards.

Account number of 1st lost credit card	2718281
Account number of 2nd lost credit card	7389056
Account number of 3rd lost credit card	1098612
Account number of 4th lost credit card	5459815
Account number of 5th lost credit card	1484131
.	.
.	.
.	.
Account number of 8262nd lost credit card	1383596

Since all of the 8262 numbers in the list must be retained simultaneously in the computer's main memory for efficient searching, and since a simple (scalar) variable can hold only one value at a time, each number must be assigned as the value of a variable *with a different name* so that the computer can be instructed to compare each account number of a lost or stolen card against the account number of the card offered in payment for goods and services.

4.1.2 Subscripts

It is possible to use variables with the 8262 Fortran names

```
LOST_CARD_1
LOST_CARD_2
LOST_CARD_3
    .
    .
    .
LOST_CARD_8262
```

to hold the 8262 values. Unfortunately, the Fortran language does not recognize the intended relationship between these variable names, so the search program cannot be written simply. The Fortran solution is to declare a single object name LOST_CARD that consists of many individual integer values. The entire collection of values may be referenced by its name LOST_CARD and individual card numbers in the list may be referenced by the following names:

```
LOST_CARD (1)
LOST_CARD (2)
LOST_CARD (3)
    .
    .
    .
LOST_CARD (8262)
```

This seemingly minor modification of otherwise perfectly acceptable variable names opens up a new dimension of programming capabilities. All the programs in this chapter, and a large number of the programs in succeeding chapters, cannot be written without this form.

The numbers in parentheses that specify the location of an item within a list are **subscripts**, a name borrowed from mathematics. Although mathematical subscripts are usually written below the line (hence the name), such a form of typography is impossible on most computer input devices. A substitute notation, enclosing the subscript in parentheses or brackets, is adopted in most computer languages. It is customary to read the expression X (3) as "X sub 3", just as if it were written X_3.

The advantage of this method of naming the quantities over using the variable names LOST_CARD_1, LOST_CARD_2, ..., LOST_CARD_8262 springs from the following programming language capability: *The subscript of an array variable may itself be a variable*, or an even more complicated expression.

The consequences of this simple statement are much more profound than would appear at first sight. This entire chapter, and much of the rest of this book, is devoted to exploring some of the uses of this facility.

For a start in describing the uses of a subscript that is itself a variable, the two statements

```
I = 1
PRINT *, LOST_CARD (I)
```

produce exactly the same output as the single statement

```
PRINT *, LOST_CARD (1)
```

namely, 2718281, the account number of the first lost credit card on the list. The entire list of account numbers of lost credit cards can be written by the subroutine PRINT_LOST_CARD.

```
SUBROUTINE PRINT_LOST_CARDS (LOST_CARD)

    IMPLICIT NONE
    INTEGER, DIMENSION (1:8262), INTENT (IN) :: LOST_CARD
    INTEGER :: I

    DO I = 1, 8262
       PRINT *, LOST_CARD (I)
    END DO

END SUBROUTINE PRINT_LOST_CARDS
```

As an example of an array feature in Fortran, the collection of card numbers as a whole can be referenced by the one statement

```
PRINT *, LOST_CARD
```

The replacement just made actually creates a different output. The difference is that using the DO loop to execute a PRINT statement 8262 times causes each card number to be printed on a separate line. The new version indicates that all the card numbers should be printed on one line, which is probably not acceptable if there are 8262 numbers. Adding a simple format for the PRINT statement instead of using the default produces the desired result. The slash in the format produces a new line after every eight-character integer field.

```
PRINT "(I8, /)", LOST_CARD
```

This is a little better, but another problem is that the number of lost and stolen cards varies daily. The subroutine will not be very useful if it makes the assumption that there are exactly 8262 cards to be printed. This can be fixed easily by changing the declaration to

```
INTEGER, DIMENSION (:), INTENT (IN) :: LOST_CARD
```

The colon indicates that the size of the array LOST_CARD is to be assumed from the array that is the actual argument given when the subroutine is called. Thus, we have created a general subroutine for printing a list of integers. However, it is so simple that it can be done with a single statement, so it is not worth showing it.

4.1.3 Array Declarations

The name of an array must obey the same rules as an ordinary variable name. Each array must be declared in the declaration section of the program. A name is declared to be an array by putting the dimension attribute in a type statement followed by a range of subscripts, enclosed in parentheses. For example,

```
REAL, DIMENSION (1 : 9) :: X, Y
LOGICAL (-99 : 99) :: YESNO
```

declares that X and Y are lists of 9 real values and that YESNO is a list of 199 logical values. This declaration implies that a subscript for X or Y must be an integer expression with a value from 1 to 9 and that a subscript for YESNO must be an integer expression whose value is from -99 to +99.

A list of character strings may be declared in a form like the following.

```
CHARACTER (LEN = 8), DIMENSION (0 : 17) :: CHAR_LIST
```

In this example, the variable CHAR_LIST is a list of 18 character strings, each of length 8.

The declaration

```
REAL, DIMENSION (:, :), ALLOCATABLE :: A, B
```

indicates that the arrays A and B have two dimensions (rank 2). The colons mean that the extents along each dimension will be established later, when an ALLOCATE statement is executed.

A similar declaration using colons may occur for a dummy argument of a procedure, indicating that the shape of the dummy array is to be taken from the actual argument used when the procedure is called. This sort of dummy argument is called an **assumed-shape array**.

```
SUBROUTINE S (D)
    INTEGER, DIMENSION (:, :, :) :: D
```

The ALLOCATABLE attribute is not used for an assumed-shape dummy argument.

The declaration of arrays also may use values of other dummy arguments to establish extents. For example,

```
SUBROUTINE S2 (DUMMY_LIST, N, DUMMY_ARRAY)
    REAL, DIMENSION (:) :: DUMMY_LIST
    REAL, DIMENSION (SIZE (DUMMY_LIST)) :: LOCAL_LIST
    REAL, DIMENSION (N, N) :: DUMMY_ARRAY, LOCAL_ARRAY
    REAL, DIMENSION (2 * N + 1) :: LONGER_LOCAL_LIST
```

declares that the size of DUMMY_LIST is to be the same as the size of the corresponding actual argument, that the array LOCAL_LIST is to be the same size as DUMMY_LIST, and that DUMMY_ARRAY and LOCAL_ARRAY are both to be two-dimensional arrays with N × N elements. The last declaration shows that a certain amount of arithmetic on other dummy arguments is permitted in calculating array bounds.

In the main program, an array must either be declared with constant fixed bounds or be declared ALLOCATABLE and be given bounds by the execution of an ALLOCATE statement (4.1.5). In the first case, our lost and stolen card program might contain the declaration

```
INTEGER, DIMENSION (8262) :: LOST_CARD
```

This is not satisfactory if the number of lost cards changes frequently. In this situation, perhaps the best solution is to declare the array to have a sufficiently large upper bound so that there will always be sufficient space to hold the card numbers. Because the upper bound is fixed, there must be a variable whose value is the actual number of cards lost. Assuming that the list of lost credit cards is stored in a file connected to the standard input unit (*), the following program fragment reads, counts, and prints the complete list of lost card numbers. The READ statement has an IOSTAT keyword argument whose value is set to zero if no error occurs and is set to a negative number if there is an attempt to read beyond the last data item in the file.

```
INTEGER, DIMENSION (20000) :: LOST_CARD
DO I = 1, 20000
   READ (*, *, IOSTAT = IOSTAT_VAR), LOST_CARD (I)
   IF (IOSTAT_VAR < 0) THEN
      NUMBER_OF_LOST_CARDS = I - 1
      EXIT
   END IF
END DO
. . .
PRINT "(I8, /)", LOST_CARD (1:NUMBER_OF_LOST_CARDS)
```

Although the array LOST_CARD is declared to have room for 20,000 entries, the PRINT statement limits output to only those lost card numbers that actually were read from the file by specifying a range of subscripts 1 : NUMBER_OF_LOST_CARDS.

4.1.4 Array Constructors

It is convenient to give an array a set of values using an array constructor. An **array constructor** is a sequence of scalar values defined along one dimension only. An array constructor is a list of values, separated by commas and delimited by the pair of two-character symbols "(/" and "/)". There are three possible forms for the array constructor values:[1]

1.   A scalar expression as in

        X = (/ 1.2, 3.5, 1.1, 1.5 /)

2.   An array expression as in

        X = (/ A (I, 1:2), A (I+1, 2:3) /)

3.   An implied DO loop as in

        X = (/ (SQRT (REAL (I)), I = 1, 4) /)

If there are no values specified, the array is zero sized. If the values are of different types that are allowed in mixed mode expressions in assignment, the ordinary rules for mixed mode apply in placing the values in the array. Since the array constructor values are restricted to assignment into rank-one arrays only, the RESHAPE and MOLD

---

1. The array constructor uses a syntax for constructing lists similar to that of the DATA statement, but with more generality and expanded capability.

intrinsic functions can be used to define rank-two and greater arrays from the array constructor values.

4.1.5 Dynamic Arrays

In Fortran 77, all the storage that was required during execution of a program could be determined and allocated by the compiler. This is known as **static storage allocation**, as opposed to **dynamic storage allocation**, which means that storage may be allocated or deallocated during execution of the program.

With static allocation, the size of each array must be declared at compile time, usually as the largest size anticipated in any execution of the program. With dynamic storage allocation, the program can wait until it knows *during execution* exactly what size array is needed and then allocate only that much memory. Memory also can be deallocated dynamically, so that the storage used for a large array early in the program can be reused for other large arrays later in the program after the values in the first array are no longer needed.

For example, instead of relying on an end-of-file condition when reading in the list of lost cards, it is possible to keep the numbers stored in a file with the number of lost cards as the first value in the file, such as

```
8262
2718281
7389056
1098612
5459815
1484131
     .
     .
     .
1383596
```

The program can then read the first number, allocate the correct amount of space for the array, and read the lost card numbers.

```
INTEGER, DIMENSION (:), ALLOCATABLE :: LOST_CARD
INTEGER :: NUMBER_OF_LOST_CARDS
    . . .
```

```
! The first number in the file is
! the number of lost card numbers in the
! rest of the file.
READ *, NUMBER_OF_LOST_CARDS
ALLOCATE (LOST_CARD (NUMBER_OF_LOST_CARDS))

! Read the numbers of the lost cards
READ "(I7, /)", LOST_CARD
    . . .
```

In the declaration of the array LOST_CARD, the colon is used to indicate the rank (number of dimensions) of the array, but the bounds are not pinned down until the ALLOCATE statement is executed. Since the programmer doesn't know how many lost cards there will be, there is no way to tell the compiler that information. During execution, the system must be able to create an array of any reasonable size *after* reading from the input data file the value of the variable NUMBER_OF_LOST_CARDS. The **DEALLOCATE** statement may be used to free the allocated storage.

Pointers, discussed in Chapter 8, provide an additional and more general facility for constructing data structures with variable sizes.

4.1.6 Array Sections

In the following statement, used in the example that tests for an end-of-file condition, a section of the array LOST_CARD is printed.

```
PRINT "(I8, /)", LOST_CARD (1:NUMBER_OF_LOST_CARDS)
```

On many occasions such as the one above, only a portion of the elements of an array is needed for a computation. It is possible to refer to a selected portion of an array, called an **array section**. A **parent array** is an aggregate of array elements, from which a section may be selected.

In the following example

```
REAL A (10)
    . . .
A (2:5) = 1.0
```

the parent array A has 10 elements. The array section consists of elements A (2), A (3), A (4), and A (5). The section is an array itself and the value 1.0 is assigned to all four of the elements in A (2:5).

In addition to the ordinary subscript that can select a subobject of an array, there are two other mechanisms for selecting certain elements along a particular dimension of an array. One is a subscript triplet, an example of which was shown above, and the other is a vector subscript.

The syntactic form of a **subscript triplet** is

[*expression*] : [*expression*] [: *expression*]

where each set of brackets encloses an optional item and each expression must produce a scalar integer value. The first expression gives a lower bound, the second an upper bound, and the third a stride. If the lower bound is omitted, the lower bound that was declared is used. If the upper bound is omitted, the upper bound that was declared is used. The stride is the increment between the elements in the section referenced by the triplet notation. If omitted, it is assumed to be one. For example, if V is a one-dimensional array (vector) of numbers:

V (0:4)

represents elements V (0), V (1), V (2), V (3), and V (4) and

V (3:7:2)

represents elements V (3), V (5), and V (7).

Each expression in the subscript triplet must be scalar. The values of any of the expressions in triplet notation may be negative. The stride must not be zero. If the stride is positive, the section is from the first subscript to the upper bound in steps of the stride. If the stride is negative, the section is from the upper bound down to the first subscript decrementing by the stride.

Another way of selecting a section of an array is to use a vector subscript. A **vector subscript** is an integer array expression of rank one.

Ordinary subscripts, triplets, and vector subscripts may be mixed in selecting an array section from a parent array. An array section may be empty.

Consider a more complicated example. If B were declared in a type statement as

REAL B (10, 10, 5)

B (1:4:3, 6:8:2, 3) is a section of B, consisting of four elements, B (1, 6, 3), B (4, 6, 3), B (1, 8, 3) and B (4, 8, 3). The stride along the first dimension is 3; therefore, the notation references the first subscripts 1 and 4. The stride in the second dimension is 2, so the second subscript varies by 2 and takes on values 6 and 8. In the third dimension of B, there is no triplet notation, so the third subscript is 3 for all elements of the section. The section would be one that has a shape of (2, 2, 1), that is, it is three dimensional, with extents 2, 2, and 1.

To give an example using both triplet notation and a vector subscript, suppose again that B is declared as above:

```
REAL B (10, 10, 5)
```

then B (8:9, 5, (/ 4, 5, 4/)) is a 2 × 1 × 3 array consisting of the six values B (8, 5, 4), B (8, 5, 5), B (8, 5, 4), B (9, 5, 4), B (9, 5, 5), and B (9, 5, 4). If VS is a vector of three integers, and VS = (/ 4, 5, 4/), the expression B (8:9, 5, VS) would have the same value.

4.1.7 Array Assignment

Array assignment is permitted under two circumstances: when the array expression on the right has exactly the same shape as the array on the left, and when the expression on the right is a scalar. Note that, for example, if A is a 9 × 9 array, the section A (2:4, 5:8) is the same shape as A (3:5, 1:4), so the assignment

```
A (2:4, 5:8) = A (3:5, 1:4)
```

is valid, but the assignment

```
A (1:4, 1:3) = A (1:2, 1:6)
```

is not valid because even though there are 12 elements in the array on each side of the assignment, the left side has shape 4 × 3 and the right side has shape 2 × 6.

When a scalar is assigned to an array, the value of the scalar is assigned to every element of the array. Thus, for example, the statement

```
M (K+1:N, K) = 0
```

sets the elements M (K+1, K), M (K+2, K), ..., M (N, K) to zero.

4.1.8 The WHERE Statement and Construct

The **WHERE statement** may be used to assign values to only those elements of an array where a logical condition is true. For example, the following statement sets the elements of B to zero in those positions where the corresponding element of A is negative. The other elements of B are unchanged. A and B must be arrays of the same shape.

```
WHERE (A < 0) B = 0
```

The **WHERE construct** permits any number of array assignments to be done under control of the same logical "mask" and the **ELSEWHERE statement** within a WHERE construct permits array assignments to be done where the logical expression is false. The following statements assign to the array A the quotient of the corresponding elements of B and C in those cases where the element of C is not zero. In the positions where the element of C is zero, the corresponding element of A is set to zero and the zero element of C is set to 1.

```
WHERE (C /= 0)
   A = B / C
ELSEWHERE
   A = 0
   C = 1
END WHERE
```

Within a WHERE statement or WHERE construct, only array assignments are permitted. The shape of all arrays in the assignment statements must conform to the shape of the logical expression following the keyword WHERE. The assignments are executed in the order they are written, first those in the WHERE block, then those in the ELSE-WHERE block. WHERE constructs may not be nested.

4.1.9 Intrinsic Operators

All the intrinsic operators and functions may be applied to arrays, operating independently on each element of the array. A binary operation, such as *, may be applied only to two arrays of the same shape, in which case it multiplies corresponding elements of the two arrays. For example, the expression ABS (M (K:N, K)) results in a 1-dimensional array of (N−K+1) nonnegative real values. The assignment statement

```
M (K, K:N+1) = M (K, K:N+1) / PIVOT
```

divides each element of M (K, K:N+1) by the real value PIVOT. In essence, a scalar value may be considered an array of the appropriate size to make the operations on it legal, and with all its entries equal to the value of the scalar.

4.1.10 Element Renumbering in Expressions

An important point to remember about array expressions is that the elements in an expression no longer have the same subscripts as the elements in the arrays that make up the expression. They are renumbered with 1 as the lower bound in each dimension. Thus, it is legal to add Y (0:7) + Z (–7:0), which results in an array whose eight values are considered to have subscripts 1, 2, 3, .., 8.

The renumbering must be taken into account when referring back to the original array. Suppose V is a one-dimensional integer array that is given an initial value with the declaration:

```
INTEGER, DIMENSION (0:6), PARAMETER :: &
     V = (/ 3, 7, 0, -2, 2, 6, -1 /)
```

The intrinsic function MAXLOC returns a vector of subscripts giving the position of the largest element of an array. MAXLOC (V) is (/ 2 /) because position 2 of the vector V contains the largest number, 7, even though it is V (1) that has the value 7. Also, MAXLOC (V (2:6)) is the vector (/ 4 /) because the largest entry, 6, occurs in the fourth position in the section V (2:6).

4.1.11 Exercises

1. Write a statement that declares VALUES to be an array of 100 real values with subscripts ranging from –100 to –1. Use an array constructor to assign the squares of the first 100 positive integers to a vector of integers named SQUARES. For example, SQUARES (5) = 25.

2. If a chess or checkers board is declared by

   ```
   CHARACTER (LEN = 1), DIMENSION (8, 8) :: BOARD
   ```

   the statement

   ```
   BOARD = "W"
   ```

   assigns the color white to all 64 positions. Write a statement or statements that assigns "B" to the black positions. Assume that BOARD (1, 1) is to be white so that the board is as shown in Figure 4-1.

3. Suppose LIST is a one-dimensional array that contains N < MAX_SIZE real numbers in ascending order. Write a subroutine

W	B	W	B	W	B	W	B
B	W	B	W	B	W	B	W
W	B	W	B	W	B	W	B
B	W	B	W	B	W	B	W
W	B	W	B	W	B	W	B
B	W	B	W	B	W	B	W
W	B	W	B	W	B	W	B
B	W	B	W	B	W	B	W

Figure 4-1 A chess board.

INSERT (LIST, N, MAX_SIZE, NEW_ENTRY) that adds the number NEW_ENTRY to the list in the appropriate place to keep the entire list sorted.

4. Write a function that finds the angle between two three-dimensional real vectors. If $V = (v_1, v_2, v_3)$, the magnitude of V is $|V| = \sqrt{V \cdot V}$ where $\cdot$ is the vector dot product. The cosine of the angle between V_1 and V_2 is given by

$$\cos(\theta) = \frac{V_1 \cdot V_2}{|V_1|\ |V_2|}$$

The built-in function ACOS (arccosine) may be used to find an angle with a given cosine.

4.2 Searching a List

The previous section describes the appropriate terminology and some of the Fortran rules concerning arrays and subscripts. This section makes a start toward illustrating the power of arrays as they are used in meaningful programs. The application throughout this section is that of checking a given credit card account number against a list of account numbers of lost or stolen cards. Increasingly more efficient programs are presented here and compared.

4.2.1 The Problem: Credit Card Checking

When a customer presents a credit card in payment for goods or services, it is desirable to determine quickly whether it can be accepted or whether it previously has been reported lost or stolen or canceled for any other reason. The subroutines in this section perform this task.

4.2.2 Sequential Search through an Unordered List

The first and simplest strategy for checking a given credit card is simply to search from beginning to end through the list of canceled credit cards, card by card, either until the given account number is found in the list, or until the end of the list is reached without finding that account number. In the subroutine SEARCH_1, this strategy, called a **sequential search**, is accomplished by a DO construct with exit that scans the list until the given account number is found in the list or all of the numbers have been examined.

> *Style Note:* It is good programming practice to make the searching part of the program a separate subroutine. Other versions of the credit card program in this section will be obtained by modifying this subroutine.

The two ways of exiting from the search loop both pass control to the END statement that returns from the subroutine SEARCH_1. However, they have a different effect on the dummy argument FOUND. When the credit card being checked is not in the list, the search loop is executed until the list is exhausted. This normal completion of the DO construct allows control to fall through to the END statement with the value of FOUND still false. When the card being checked is found in the list, the logical variable FOUND is set to true before exiting the DO construct. The calling program can test the actual argument passed to the dummy variable FOUND to decide whether the card number was found in the list. The intrinsic function SIZE used in this subroutine returns an integer value that is the number of elements in the array LOST_CARD.

```
SUBROUTINE SEARCH_1 (LOST_CARD, CARD_NUMBER, FOUND)

    IMPLICIT NONE
    INTEGER, DIMENSION (:), INTENT (IN) :: LOST_CARD
    INTEGER, INTENT (IN) :: CARD_NUMBER
    LOGICAL, INTENT (OUT) :: FOUND
    INTEGER :: I
```

```
       FOUND = .FALSE.
       DO I = 1, SIZE (LOST_CARD)
          IF (CARD_NUMBER == LOST_CARD (I)) THEN
             FOUND = .TRUE.
             EXIT
          END IF
       END DO

    END SUBROUTINE SEARCH_1
```

This subroutine makes a nice example for illustrating how individual elements of an array can be manipulated; but in Fortran 90, it is often better to think of operations for processing the array as a whole. In fact, using the built-in array functions, it is possible to do the search in one line.

```
    FOUND = ANY (LOST_CARD (1 : SIZE (LOST_CARD)) == CARD_NUMBER)
```

The comparison

```
    LOST_CARD (1 : SIZE (LOST_CARD)) == CARD_NUMBER
```

creates a list of logical values with true in any position where the value of CARD_NUMBER matches a number in the list LOST_CARD. The function ANY is true if any of the elements in the resulting list of logical values is true, and is false otherwise.

The basic strategy of the program SEARCH_1 is to check a credit card account number, supplied as input, against each account number, in turn, in the list of canceled or lost cards, either until a match is found or until the list is exhausted. These alternatives are not equally likely. Most credit cards offered in payment for purchases or services represent the authorized use of active, valid accounts. Thus, by far the most usual execution of the subroutine SEARCH_1 is that the entire list is searched without finding the card number provided.

The number of comparisons a program must make before accepting a credit card is some measure of the efficiency of that program. For example, when searching for an acceptable credit card in a list of 10,000 canceled credit cards, the subroutine SEARCH_1 usually makes 10,000 comparisons. On a traditional computer, the elapsed computer time for the search depends on the time it takes to make one comparison and to prepare to make the next comparison. However, on a computer with vector or parallel hardware, many comparisons may be done simultaneously and the intrinsic functions, probably written by the implementor to take advantage of this special hardware, might provide very efficient searching.

If the search must be performed on a traditional computer by making one comparison at a time, the search can be made more efficient by maintaining the list in order of increasing card number. As soon as one canceled card number examined in the search is too large, all subsequent ones will also be too large, so the search can be abandoned early. The subroutine SEARCH_2 presumes that the list is in increasing order.

```
SUBROUTINE SEARCH_2 (LOST_CARD, CARD_NUMBER, FOUND)

    IMPLICIT NONE
    INTEGER, DIMENSION (:), INTENT (IN) :: LOST_CARD
    INTEGER, INTENT (IN) :: CARD_NUMBER
    LOGICAL, INTENT (OUT) :: FOUND
    INTEGER :: I

    FOUND = .FALSE.
    DO I = 1, SIZE (LOST_CARD)
       IF (CARD_NUMBER <= LOST_CARD (I)) THEN
          FOUND = (CARD_NUMBER == LOST_CARD (I))
          EXIT
       END IF
    END DO

END SUBROUTINE SEARCH_2
```

Before accepting a presented account number, SEARCH_1 always must search the entire list, but SEARCH_2 stops as soon as it reaches a number in the list of canceled account numbers that is larger than or equal to the presented number.

Roughly speaking, the average number of comparisons needed for an acceptance by SEARCH_2 is about half the list size, plus one additional comparison to determine whether the last entry examined was exactly the account number of the credit card being checked. For a list of 10,000 canceled cards, it would take an average of 5001 comparisons, significantly better than the 10,000 for SEARCH_1.

To a limited extent, this increased efficiency in the checking program is counterbalanced by some additional computer time needed to maintain the list of canceled credit cards in increasing order. However, the list is likely to be searched much more often than it is modified, so almost any increase in the efficiency of the checking program results, in practice, in an increase in the efficiency of the entire operation.

4.2.3 Program Notes

The sequential search loop in the subroutine SEARCH_2 is not quite as straightforward as it seems at first glance. When the presented card CARD_NUMBER is compared against an entry LOST_CARD (I), three things can happen:

1.   LOST_CARD (I) is too low, in which case the search continues.

2.   They match, in which case the presented card CARD_NUMBER has been found.

3.   LOST_CARD (I) is too high, in which case further search is futile.

The three possibilities are not equally likely. Case 1 can occur as many as 10,000 times in one search. Cases 2 and 3 can only happen once per search. It is important to test first for the most frequently occurring case. Otherwise, there will be two tests per iteration, slowing the search loop appreciably. This subroutine tests for the first case, and then, if it is false, determines whether case 2 or case 3 applies. The following IF construct also does the tests in this same optimal order; but if the order of testing alternatives is changed, twice as many tests are done.

```
DO I = 1, SIZE (LOST_CARD)
   IF (CARD_NUMBER < LOST_CARD (I)) THEN
      CYCLE
   ELSE IF (CARD_NUMBER == LOST_CARD (I)) THEN
      FOUND = .TRUE.
      EXIT
   ELSE
      EXIT
   END IF
END DO
```

4.2.4 Binary Search

Sequential search is a brute force technique. It works well for short lists but is very inefficient for large ones. A somewhat different strategy, **divide and conquer**, is employed in a **binary search**. Half of the list can be eliminated in one comparison by testing the middle element. Then half the remaining elements are eliminated by another test. This continues until there is only one element left; then this element is examined to see if it is the one being sought. The list must be ordered for binary search.

Table 4-2 shows how a binary search is used to try to find the number 2415495 in a list of 16 numbers. The numbers are given in increasing order in the first column. The presented number 2415495 is not in the list, but this fact plays no role in the search procedure until the very last step.

Table 4-2 A binary search that fails.

Before any comparisons	After one comparison	After two comparisons	After three comparisons	After four comparisons	Given number
1096633	1096633				
1202604	1202604				
1484131	1484131				
1627547	1627547*				
2008553	2008553	2008553			
2202646	2202646	2202646*			
2718281	2718281	2718281	2718281*	2718281 ≠	2415495
2980957*	2980957	2980957	2980957		
3269017					
4034287					
4424133					
5459815					
5987414					
7389056					
8103083					
8886110					

* An asterisk denotes the last entry of the first half of the segment still under active consideration.

As a first step in binary searching, the list is divided in half. An asterisk follows the eighth number in column 1 because it is the last entry in the first half of the list. Since the given number 2415495 is less than (or equal to) the eighth entry 2980957, the second half of the list can be eliminated from further consideration. Column 2 shows only the first half of the original list, entries 1 through 8, retained as the segment still actively being searched.

The procedure is repeated. An asterisk follows the fourth entry in column 2 because it is the last entry in the first half of the segment of the list still actively being searched. Since the given number 2415495 is greater than the fourth number 1627547, this time it is the first half of the active segment that is eliminated and the second half (entries 5 through 8 of the original list) that is retained. This is shown in column 3 of Table 4-2.

In the next stage, the second remaining number 2202646, which was the sixth entry in the original list, is marked with an asterisk because it is the last entry of the first half of the segment still being searched. Since this number is exceeded by the given number 2415945, the second half of the segment in column 3 (entries 7 and 8) is retained as the active segment in column 4. The seventh entry of the original list, the number 2718281, is the last entry of the first half of the remaining list of two entries and thus is marked with an asterisk in column 4 to indicate its role as a comparison entry. Since the given number 2415495 is less than this, the other entry (the eighth original entry) is discarded, and column 5 shows that after four comparisons, only the seventh entry 2718281 remains as a candidate.

Since only one entry remains, a test for equality is made between the given number 2415495 and the one remaining entry 2718281. They are not equal. Thus, the given number is not in the list. Note that the previous comparisons of these two numbers were merely to determine whether the given number was less than or equal to the seventh entry.

Table 4-3 shows how the binary search works for the number 7389056, which is found in the list of 16 numbers. As before, the first column lists the original numbers with an asterisk following the last number of the first half of the list, the eighth entry. The number 7389056 is greater than the eighth entry, so the second half of the list (entries 9 to 16) is retained in column 2. A comparison of the given number 7389056 with the last entry of the first half of the segment remaining in column 2, the twelfth original entry 5459815, eliminates entries 9 through 12.

A comparison with the fourteenth entry, marked with an asterisk in column 3, eliminates the fifteenth and sixteenth entries. One more comparison of the given number 7389056 against the thirteenth entry, marked with an asterisk in column 4, eliminates that entry and leaves only the fourteenth entry 7389056. The final test for equality of the given number and the only remaining candidate in the list yields success, and it can be reported that the given number is the fourteenth entry in the list.

For the purpose of explanation, it is most convenient to use a list size that is an exact power of 2, that is, 2, 4, 8, 16, 32, ... This avoids fractions when the size of the list segment still under consideration is halved repeatedly. However, this is not essential; the use of integer division by 2 in the subroutine BINARY_SEARCH permits it to search a list of any length.

Table 4-3 A binary search that is successful.

Before any comparisons	After one comparison	After two comparisons	After three comparisons	After four comparisons	Given number
1096633					
1202604					
1484131					
1627547					
2008553					
2202646					
2718281					
2980957*					
3269017	3269017				
4034287	4034287				
4424133	4424133				
5459815	5459815*				
5987414	5987414	5987414	5987414*		
7389056	7389056	7389056*	7389056	7389056 =	7389056
8103083	8103083	8103083			
8886110	8886110	8886110			

* An asterisk denotes the last entry of the first half of the segment still under active consideration.

```
SUBROUTINE BINARY_SEARCH (LOST_CARD, CARD_NUMBER, FOUND)

    IMPLICIT NONE
    INTEGER, DIMENSION (:), INTENT (IN) :: LOST_CARD
    INTEGER, INTENT (IN) :: CARD_NUMBER
    LOGICAL, INTENT (OUT) :: FOUND
    INTEGER :: I, FIRST, HALF, LAST, ONLY

    FIRST = 1
    LAST = SIZE (LOST_CARD)
    DO
        IF (FIRST == LAST) EXIT
        HALF = (FIRST + LAST) / 2
        IF (CARD_NUMBER <= LOST_CARD (HALF)) THEN
            ! Discard second half
            LAST = HALF
```

```
      ELSE
         ! Discard first half
         FIRST = HALF + 1
      END IF
   END DO

   ! The only remaining subscript to check is FIRST (= LAST)
   ONLY = FIRST
   FOUND = (CARD_NUMBER == LAST_CARD (ONLY))
END SUBROUTINE BINARY_SEARCH
```

When the part of the list still under consideration has been reduced to a single element by repeated bisection, the first element left is the last and only element left and the DO construct is exited to test it.

4.2.5 Efficiency of a Binary Search

As before, we can get a reasonable indication of the efficiency of a search method by seeing how many times the given account number is compared against account numbers in the list of lost or stolen cards in the most usual event that the card number is not in the list.

The number of comparisons required in the binary search can be counted easily. With one comparison, a list of items to be searched can be cut in half. When the list is reduced to one element, a final comparison determines whether that candidate is the credit card being searched for or not. Thus, with $n + 1$ comparisons, it is possible to search 2^n items. Turning it around the other way, n items may be searched using $\log_2 n + 1$ comparisons. Thus, for example, 15 comparisons suffice for binary searching all lists of length up to 16,384 ($= 2^{14}$). This is considerably better than the 8192 comparisons needed for a sequential search! However, keep in mind that on a computer with intrinsic parallelism, it may be better to use the intrinsic functions and hope that the implementation takes advantage of the parallelism to do many comparisons simultaneously. Even if it does, whether or not it is faster than the binary search depends on the size of the list and the amount of parallelism in the system.

4.2.6 Exercise

1. What changes need to be made to the subroutine BINARY_SEARCH to search a list of integers with kind 2?

4.3 Sorting

Frequently it is necessary to sort a list of numbers or character strings. One of the simplest ways to do this is to compare every number in the list with every other number in the list and swap them if they are out of order. As with the previous examples in this chapter, the sorting is done with a subroutine so that it may be put in a library and used by many programs.

```
SUBROUTINE SORT_1 (LIST)

    IMPLICIT NONE
    REAL, DIMENSION (:), INTENT (INOUT) :: LIST
    INTEGER :: I, J

    DO I = 1, SIZE (LIST) - 1
        DO J = I + 1, SIZE (LIST)
            IF (LIST (I) > LIST (J)) CALL SWAP (LIST (I), LIST (J))
        END DO
    END DO

END SUBROUTINE SORT_1
```

The subroutine SWAP of Section 3.7 that exchanges the values of two variables is assumed to be available. This is a very simple algorithm for sorting, but it is very inefficient and should not be used to sort more than a few hundred items.

A second approach to sorting a list is to find the smallest number in the list and put it in the first position, then find the smallest number in the remainder of the list and put it in the second position, etc. The built-in function MINLOC can be used effectively for this sort. For an array A of rank n, that is, with n subscripts, the value of MINLOC (A) is a one-dimensional array whose entries are the n subscripts of a smallest element of A. Since LIST is one-dimensional, the value of MINLOC (LIST) is a vector of one element; however, a vector with one element must be referenced differently from a scalar. Also note that because of renumbering, the subscripts in the array section LIST (I + 1 :) range from 1 to SIZE (LIST) – I and not from I + 1 to SIZE (LIST), so that a smallest element in LIST (I + 1 :) is LIST (I + MIN_LOC (1)).

```
SUBROUTINE SORT_2 (LIST)

   IMPLICIT NONE
   REAL, DIMENSION (:), INTENT (INOUT) :: LIST
   INTEGER :: I
   INTEGER, DIMENSION (1) :: MIN_LOC

   DO I = 1, SIZE (LIST) - 1
      MIN_LOC = MINLOC (LIST (I+1:))
      CALL SWAP (LIST (I), LIST (I + MIN_LOC (1)))
   END DO

END SUBROUTINE SORT_1
```

This subroutine appears to be just about as inefficient as SORT_1, because execution of the MINLOC function involves searching through the elements of LIST (I+1:) to find the smallest one. Indeed, it may be just as inefficient; however, if it is executed on a system with parallelism, the MINLOC function may be faster than a sequential search.

There is also an intrinsic function, MAXLOC, whose value is the vector of subscripts of a largest element of an array. For example, if

$$A = \begin{bmatrix} 1 & 8 & 0 \\ 5 & -1 & 7 \\ 3 & 9 & -2 \end{bmatrix}, \text{ the value of MAXLOC } (A) = (/3, 2/).$$

4.3.1 Quick Sort

One of the best sorting algorithms is called "quick sort" or "partition sort". Whereas SORT_1 needs to make approximately $n^2/2$ comparisons to sort n numbers, the quick sort needs approximately $n \log_2 n$ comparisons. To get an idea of the amount of improvement, for $n = 1000$ items, SORT_1 would require approximately 500,000 comparisons and the quick sort would require approximately 10,000 comparisons, a ratio of 50 to 1; for $n = 1,000,000$ items, SORT_1 would require approximately 500,000,000,000 comparisons and the quick sort would require approximately 100,000,000 comparisons, a ratio of 5000 to 1.

As might be expected, the quick sort is a bit more complicated. It is a divide-and-conquer algorithm like binary search. To sort a list of numbers, an arbitrary number (such as the first, last, or middle one) is chosen from the list. All the remaining numbers in turn are compared with the chosen number; the ones smaller are collected in a "smaller" set and the ones larger are collected in a "larger" set. The whole list is sorted by sorting the "smaller" set, following them with all numbers equal to the chosen number, and following them with the sorted list of "larger" numbers. Note that this last step involves using the quick sort routine recursively (7.1).

```
RECURSIVE SUBROUTINE QUICK_SORT (LIST)

    IMPLICIT NONE
    REAL, DIMENSION (:), INTENT (INOUT) :: LIST
    REAL, DIMENSION (SIZE (LIST)) :: SMALLER, LARGER
    INTEGER :: I, NUMBER_SMALLER, NUMBER_EQUAL, NUMBER_LARGER
    REAL :: CHOSEN

    IF (SIZE (LIST) > 1)
        CHOSEN = LIST (1)
        NUMBER_SMALLER = 0
        NUMBER_EQUAL = 1
        NUMBER_LARGER = 0

        DO I = 2, SIZE (LIST)
            IF (LIST (I) < CHOSEN) THEN
                NUMBER_SMALLER = NUMBER_SMALLER + 1
                SMALLER (NUMBER_SMALLER) = LIST (I)
            ELSE IF (LIST (I) = CHOSEN) THEN
                NUMBER_EQUAL = NUMBER_EQUAL + 1
            ELSE
                NUMBER_LARGER = NUMBER_LARGER + 1
                LARGER (NUMBER_LARGER) = LIST (I)
            END IF
        END DO

        CALL QUICK_SORT (SMALLER (1 : NUMBER_SMALLER))
        LIST (1:NUMBER_SMALLER) = SMALLER (1:NUMBER_SMALLER)
        LIST (NUMBER_SMALLER+1 : &
              NUMBER_SMALLER+NUMBER_EQUAL) = CHOSEN
        CALL QUICK_SORT (LARGER (1 : NUMBER_LARGER))
        LIST (NUMBER_SMALLER+NUMBER_EQUAL+1 :) = &
              LARGER (1 : NUMBER_LARGER)
    END IF

END SUBROUTINE QUICK_SORT
```

Although the subroutine QUICK_SORT follows the description fairly closely and sorts with order $n \log_2 n$ comparisons, it wastes a lot of space in each subroutine call creating new SMALLER and LARGER lists. However, by clever management of the available space, the entire list can be sorted without using any arrays except the original argument LIST itself. In the following version of the quick sort, the "smaller" numbers are collected together by placing them at the beginning of the list and the "larger" numbers are collected together by placing them at the end of the list. Also, every effort is made to eliminate unnecessary moving or swapping of elements in the list. To do serious sorting, this version should be used.[2]

The details of the quick-sorting algorithm are still quite tricky and must be clarified further before an efficient and bug-free subroutine can be written. First, while it is possible to maintain two lists in a single one-dimensional array, the list SMALLER that grows from the bottom of the array LIST, and the list LARGER that grows from the top of the array LIST, it is not possible to manage three lists in one array. Thus, the conditions for the sublists SMALLER and LARGER are relaxed to allow entries equal to the test element CHOSEN to qualify for either of these sublists. Since these elements are the largest elements in the sublist SMALLER, and the smallest elements in the sublist LARGER, they are reunited in the middle of the array LIST when both sublists are sorted in place.

Second, since there are (essentially) no extra storage spaces for list elements, the only way to remove an unsuitably large element from the left (i.e., SMALLER) part of the list is to swap it with an unsuitably small element from the right (i.e., LARGER) part of the list. Each pass through the main loop of the subroutine QUICK_SORT_1 consists of a search for an unsuitably large element on the left, a search for an unsuitably small element on the right, and a swap.

If the input list is in completely random order, it doesn't matter which element of the list is chosen as the test element. We use the middle element of the input list for two reasons: (1) one of the more likely nonrandom orders of a list is that the list is already sorted; choosing the middle element as test element provides much better splits than the first or last in this case; (2) if the test element is the middle element, both the search from the left for a "large" element and the search from the right for a "small" element are guaranteed not to run off the ends of the list,

---

2. The internal subprogram feature of Fortran 90 allows us to structure this second version of quick sort in a way impossible in earlier Fortrans. The outer level, the external subroutine QUICK_SORT, is nonrecursive and is used primarily to declare one copy of the dummy argument LIST that will be used by all the recursive calls of the internal subroutine QUICK_SORT_1. Each time QUICK_SORT_1 is called, it receives a left subscript and right subscript of the section of the list it is to sort, and it inherits the array variable LIST from the containing subroutine QUICK_SORT.

because the middle element will stop both searches. A test for invalid subscripts can be eliminated from these two inner loops if the test element is the middle element.

```
SUBROUTINE QUICK_SORT (LIST)

    IMPLICIT NONE
    REAL, DIMENSION (:), INTENT (INOUT) :: LIST
    CALL QUICK_SORT_1 (1, SIZE (LIST))

    CONTAINS

    RECURSIVE SUBROUTINE QUICK_SORT_1 (LEFT_END, RIGHT_END)

        INTEGER, INTENT (IN) :: LEFT_END, RIGHT_END
        INTEGER :: I, J
        REAL :: CHOSEN
        INTEGER, PARAMETER :: MAX_SIMPLE_SORT_SIZE = 6

        IF (RIGHT_END < LEFT_END + MAX_SIMPLE_SORT_SIZE) THEN
            ! Use interchange sort for small lists
            CALL INTERCHANGE_SORT (LEFT_END, RIGHT_END)
        ELSE
            ! Use partition ("quick") sort
            CHOSEN = LIST ((LEFT_END + RIGHT_END) / 2)
            I = LEFT_END - 1; J = RIGHT_END + 1

            DO
                ! Scan list from left end
                ! until element >= chosen is found
                DO
                    I = I + 1; IF (LIST (I) >= CHOSEN) EXIT
                END DO
                ! Scan list from right end
                ! until element <= chosen is found
                DO
                    J = J - 1; IF (LIST (J) <= CHOSEN) EXIT
                END DO
                IF (I < J) THEN
                    ! Swap two out of place elements
                    TEMP = LIST (I); LIST (I) = LIST (J); LIST (J) = TEMP
                ELSE IF (I = J) THEN
                    I = I + 1; EXIT
```

```
                ELSE
                    EXIT
                END IF
            END DO

            IF (LEFT_END < J) CALL QUICK_SORT_1 (LEFT_END, J)
            IF (I < RIGHT_END) CALL QUICK_SORT_1 (I, RIGHT_END)
        END IF

    END SUBROUTINE QUICK_SORT_1

    SUBROUTINE INTERCHANGE_SORT (LEFT_END, RIGHT_END)

        INTEGER, INTENT (IN) :: LEFT_END, RIGHT_END
        INTEGER :: I, J
        REAL :: TEMP

        DO I = LEFT_END, RIGHT_END - 1
            DO J = I + 1, RIGHT_END
                IF (LIST (I) >  LIST (J)) THEN
                    TEMP = LIST (I)
                    LIST (I) = LIST (J)
                    LIST (J) = TEMP
                END IF
            END DO
        END DO

    END SUBROUTINE INTERCHANGE_SORT

    END SUBROUTINE QUICK_SORT
```

4.3.2 Sorting Small Lists

The subroutine QUICK_SORT has been made more efficient by the addition of the following statements that test if the quantity of numbers to be sorted is small and calls an interchange sort if it is.

```
    IF (RIGHT_END < LEFT_END + MAX_SIMPLE_SORT_SIZE) THEN
        ! Use interchange sort for small lists
        CALL INTERCHANGE_SORT (LEFT_END, RIGHT_END)
```

Why be concerned about this? Quick sort rarely is used to sort such small lists, and even if is, it is only relative efficiency that suffers: the absolute time required to quick sort a small list is very small. The answer is that although the user might not call quick sort often to sort a very small list, because it is a divide-and-conquer technique, the quick-sort algorithm subdivides the list again and again until finally it calls itself recursively many times to sort very small lists. Thus, small inefficiencies in the quick sorting of small lists contribute many times over to form large inefficiencies in the quick sorting of large lists.

The solution is simple: for lists below a certain minimum size, INTERCHANGE_SORT is used. The subroutine QUICK_SORT_1 sorts all lists of size up to MAX_SIMPLE_SORT_SIZE using the compact and simple sorting algorithm of the subroutine SORT_1 for such lists. For larger lists, it uses the quick sort algorithm. Some experimenting with randomly generated large lists and different values of MAX_SIMPLE_SORT_SIZE indicates that for this simple sorting algorithm and this implementation of the quick-sort algorithm, MAX_SIMPLE_SORT_SIZE = 6 is probably the right choice.

4.3.3 Exercises

1.   Modify the subroutine QUICK_SORT so that a variable records the number of times two values are swapped. This provides a crude measure of the complexity of the sorting algorithm. Experiment with the program by generating 1000 numbers using the built-in subroutine RANDOM discussed in Section 3.11.1 and by varying the parameter MAX_SIMPLE_SORT_SIZE. If there is a way to do it on your system, collect data about actual running time also.

2.   Execute QUICK_SORT with randomly generated lists of numbers of various sizes n to see if the number of values swapped is proportional to $n \log_2 n$.

4.4 Selecting

A common problem is to find the median of a list of numbers, that is, the one that would be in the middle of the list if the list were in order. One way to do this is to sort the list and look at the element in the middle, but this is quite inefficient. The best sorting algorithms require $n \log_2 n$ steps to sort n numbers, whereas the median of n numbers can be found in n steps.

The trick is one that is often applicable to recursive procedures: solve a slightly more general problem instead. In this case the more general problem to solve is to find the number that would be in position k, $1 \leq k \leq n$, if a list of n numbers were in order. Then to find the median, simply find the number in position $n/2$.

A good algorithm to select the k th element is similar to the quick-sort algorithm. Arbitrarily pick one of the numbers in the list. As with the quick sort, separate the numbers into three collections: the numbers smaller than the chosen number, the numbers equal to the chosen number, and the numbers larger than the chosen number. Suppose the size of each of these collections is s, e, and l, respectively. If $k \leq s$, the number we are looking for is in the collection of smaller numbers, and, in fact, is the k th number in that collection in order; this number can be found by applying the same selection algorithm recursively to the list of smaller numbers. If $s < k \leq s + e$, then the number chosen is the one we are looking for and the search is complete. If $s + e < k$, the number we are looking for is in the collection of larger numbers; it is, in fact, the one in position $k - s - e$ in that list in order, so it can be found by recursively calling the selection procedure. Here is the Fortran program; the selected element is placed as the value of the variable ELEMENT and the logical value ERROR indicates if a value outside the bounds of the list is requested. The procedure QUICK_SELECT is written as a subroutine instead of a function because it returns two values.

```
RECURSIVE SUBROUTINE QUICK_SELECT (LIST, K, ELEMENT, ERROR)

    IMPLICIT NONE
    REAL, DIMENSION (:), INTENT (IN) :: LIST
    INTEGER, INTENT (IN) :: K
    REAL, INTENT (OUT) :: ELEMENT
    LOGICAL, INTENT (OUT) :: ERROR
    REAL, DIMENSION (SIZE (LIST)) :: SMALLER, LARGER
    INTEGER :: I, NUMBER_SMALLER, NUMBER_EQUAL, NUMBER_LARGER
    REAL :: CHOSEN

    IF (SIZE (LIST) <= 1) THEN
        ERROR = .NOT. (SIZE (LIST) == 1 .AND. K == 1)
        IF (ERROR) THEN
            ELEMENT = 0.0   ! A value must be assigned
                            ! because ELEMENT is INTENT (OUT)
        ELSE
            ELEMENT = LIST (1)
        END IF
```

```
    ELSE
        CHOSEN = LIST (1)
        NUMBER_SMALLER = 0
        NUMBER_EQUAL = 1
        NUMBER_LARGER = 0

        DO I = 2, SIZE (LIST)
            IF (LIST (I) < CHOSEN) THEN
                NUMBER_SMALLER = NUMBER_SMALLER + 1
                SMALLER (NUMBER_SMALLER) = LIST (I)
            ELSE IF (LIST (I) = CHOSEN) THEN
                NUMBER_EQUAL = NUMBER_EQUAL + 1
            ELSE
                NUMBER_LARGER = NUMBER_LARGER + 1
                LARGER (NUMBER_LARGER) = LIST (I)
            END IF
        END DO

        IF (K <= NUMBER_SMALLER) THEN
            CALL QUICK_SELECT (SMALLER (1 : NUMBER_SMALLER), &
                               K, ELEMENT, ERROR)
        ELSE IF (K <= NUMBER_SMALLER + NUMBER_EQUAL) THEN
            ELEMENT = CHOSEN
            ERROR = .FALSE.
        ELSE
            CALL QUICK_SELECT (LARGER (1 : NUMBER_LARGER), &
                K - NUMBER_SMALLER - NUMBER_EQUAL, ELEMENT, ERROR)
        END IF
    END IF

END SUBROUTINE QUICK_SELECT
```

4.4.1 Exercises

1. Modify the subroutine QUICK_SELECT so that a variable records the number of times two values are compared. This provides a crude measure of the complexity of the selection algorithm. Experiment with the program by generating 1000 numbers using the built-in subroutine RANDOM discussed in Section 3.11.1. If there is a way to do it on your system, collect data about actual running time also.

2. Execute QUICK_SELECT with randomly generated lists of numbers of various sizes n to see if the number of values compared is proportional to n.

4.5 Case Study: Solving Linear Equations

The operations of searching, sorting, and selecting discussed in previous sections involve, by their nature, mostly operations on a single element of a list, one at a time. In many situations, particularly in numerical computations, whole arrays or sections of arrays can be processed at once. To explore an example of this type, we look at the problem of solving n simultaneous equations of the form:

$$a_{11}x_1 + a_{12}x_2 + \cdots + a_{1n}x_n = b_1$$

$$a_{21}x_1 + a_{22}x_2 + \cdots + a_{2n}x_n = b_2$$

$$\cdot$$
$$\cdot$$
$$\cdot$$

$$a_{n1}x_1 + a_{n2}x_2 + \cdots + a_{nn}x_n = b_n$$

In matrix notation, this system of equations would be written as

$$
\begin{bmatrix}
a_{11} & a_{12} & \cdots & a_{1n} \\
a_{21} & a_{22} & \cdots & a_{2n} \\
 & & \cdot & \\
 & & \cdot & \\
 & & \cdot & \\
a_{n1} & a_{n2} & \cdots & a_{nn}
\end{bmatrix}
\begin{bmatrix}
x_1 \\
x_2 \\
\cdot \\
\cdot \\
\cdot \\
x_n
\end{bmatrix}
=
\begin{bmatrix}
b_1 \\
b_2 \\
\cdot \\
\cdot \\
\cdot \\
b_n
\end{bmatrix}
$$

Solving the equations is done by manipulating them, performing combinations of the following operations, none of which changes the values of the solutions. The three operations are interchanging equations (which amounts to interchanging rows in the matrix of coefficients), multiplying an equation (i.e., row) by a constant, and adding one equation (i.e., row) to another equation. The operations of interchanging columns in the matrix of coefficients (which amounts to renaming variables) and multiplying a column by a constant (which amounts to rescaling the values of the variable represented by that column) are sometimes used in solving simultaneous linear equations, but are not used in the solution presented below.

These equations will be solved by a process called **Gaussian elimination**. Combinations of these operations are performed until the equations are in a form where all coefficients below the diagonal of the coefficient matrix are zero and all coefficients on the main diagonal are one; this constitutes the first phase of Gaussian elimination. In broad outline, what happens in this phase is that the first equation is solved for the first variable x_1 (i.e., its coefficient is made 1), and then appropriate multiples of the first equation are subtracted from each of the remaining equations to eliminate the variable x_1 from equations 2 to n. Then the second equation is solved for x_2, and multiples of it are subtracted from the remaining equations to eliminate x_2 also from equations 3 to n. Eventually, all the variables x_1, x_2, ... x_{n-1} are eliminated from the nth equation, which can now be solved for x_n. At the end of the first phase, the set of equations takes the form

$$x_1 + c_{12}x_2 + c_{13}x_3 + \cdots + c_{1n-1}x_{n-1} + c_{1n}x_n = d_1$$
$$x_2 + c_{23}x_3 + \cdots + c_{2n-1}x_{n-1} + c_{2n}x_n = d_2$$
$$x_3 + \cdots + c_{2n-1}x_{n-1} + c_{2n}x_n = d_3$$
$$\vdots \qquad \vdots$$
$$x_{n-1} + c_{n-1}x_n = d_{n-1}$$
$$x_n = d_n$$

The second phase of Gaussian elimination is called **back substitution**. The last equation is already solved for $x_n = d_n$. The answer for x_n is substituted into the next to last equation, which contains only variables x_{n-1} and x_n after the first phase, so it can be solved for x_{n-1}. Then the answers for both x_n and x_{n-1} are substituted into the previous equation to solve for x_{n-2}, and so forth until all the variables x_n, x_{n-1}, ..., x_2 are substituted into the first equation to solve for x_1.

An equivalent form of the back-substitution phase, which is used sometimes, is to subtract appropriate multiples of the nth equation from all previous equations to eliminate x_n from equations 1 to $n-1$. Then multiples of equation $n-1$ are subtracted from equations 1 to $n-2$ to eliminate x_{n-1} from these equations. The process continues upward through the equations until each equation has only one variable, or equivalently, until every entry in the matrix of coefficients above the diagonal is zero. The equations now have the form

$$x_1 = e_1$$
$$x_2 = e_2$$

.   .

.   .

.   .

$$x_n = e_n$$

which is solved for all of its variables. In the program SOLVE_LINEAR_EQUATIONS, we use the first method, substituting directly without changing the triangular matrix of coefficients to this completely diagonalized form.

If all goes well, the process of solving the system of linear equations is no more complicated than what we just described; however, a general solution must foresee and provide for all possibilities, even the possibility that the set of equations is inconsistent and has no solution.

The first potential problem is that when we try to solve the first equation for the first variable x_1, we might find that the first equation does not involve x_1 (i.e., $a_{11} = 0$). If some other equation involves x_1, that is, if some $a_{k1} \neq 0$, then we can swap the first and k th equations (to make $a_{11} \neq 0$ after the swap) so that we can solve the new first equation for x_1 and proceed. On the other hand, if no equation involves x_1, then the system of equations does not uniquely determine x_1 and we must report this as an error.

A similar problem might occur when we try to solve the k th equation for x_k. If the coefficient a_{kk} is zero at this point in the computation, then we must seek a later equation, say the mth, for which $a_{mk} \neq 0$, and swap it with the k th equation before proceeding. If all remaining coefficients in the k th column are zero, then x_k is not uniquely determined.

Conventional wisdom, which we follow in this program, says that even if a_{kk} is nonzero, it is still better to swap the k th equation with that later equation for which the absolute value $|a_{mk}|$ is largest. Part of the reason is that roundoff error in calculations with the real coefficients often results in a coefficient that should be zero being calculated as a small nonzero value, but almost never results in it being calculated as a large nonzero value. Swapping a_{kk} with the largest coefficient a_{mk} greatly reduces the risk of dividing by a coefficient a_{kk} that should have been calculated as zero.

```
SUBROUTINE SOLVE_LINEAR_EQUATIONS (A, X, B, ERROR)

    IMPLICIT NONE
    REAL, DIMENSION (:, :), INTENT (IN) :: A
    REAL, DIMENSION (:), INTENT (OUT) :: X
    REAL, DIMENSION (:), INTENT (IN) :: B
    LOGICAL, INTENT (OUT) :: ERROR
    REAL, DIMENSION (SIZE (B), SIZE (B) + 1) :: M
    INTEGER, DIMENSION (1) :: MAX_LOC
    REAL, DIMENSION (SIZE (B) + 1) :: TEMP_ROW
    INTEGER :: N, K

    N = SIZE (B)
    M (1:N, 1:N) = A
    M (1:N, N+1) = B

    ! Triangularization phase
    ERROR = .FALSE.
    TRIANG_LOOP: DO K = 1, N - 1

        MAX_LOC = MAXLOC (ABS (M (K:N, K)))
        TEMP_ROW (K:N+1) = M (K, K:N+1)
        M (K, K:N+1) = M (K-1+MAX_LOC(1), K:N+1)
        M (K-1+MAX_LOC(1), K:N+1) = TEMP_ROW (K:N+1)

        IF (M (K, K) == 0) THEN
            ERROR = .TRUE.
            EXIT TRIANG_LOOP
        ELSE
            M (K, K+1:N+1) = M (K, K+1:N+1) / M (K, K)
            M (K, K) = 1
            M (K+1:N, K+1:N+1) = M (K+1:N, K+1:N+1) - &
                SPREAD (M (K, K+1:N+1), 1, N-K) * &
                SPREAD (M (K+1:N, K), 2, N-K+1)
            M (K+1:N, K) = 0   ! These values never will be used
        END IF

    END DO
```

```
    ! Back substitution phase
    IF (ERROR) THEN
       X = 0.0
    ELSE
       DO K = N, 1, -1
          X (K) = M (K, N+1) - SUM (M (K, K+1:N) * X (K+1:N))
       END DO
    END IF
```

END SUBROUTINE SOLVE_LINEAR_EQUATIONS

The array M is created in the subroutine SOLVE_ LINEAR_EQUATIONS because the constant terms are often subject to the same operations as the coefficients of the variables during the calculations of Gaussian elimination. It consists of the array A of coefficients enlarged by one column into which is placed the vector of constants B. This is accomplished using the statements:

```
REAL, DIMENSION (SIZE (B), SIZE (B) + 1) :: M
N = SIZE (B)
M (1:N, 1:N) = A
M (1:N, N+1) = B
```

Several array intrinsic functions are used in the subroutine SOLVE_LINEAR_EQUATIONS. The SIZE function is used to find the number of equations and variables, which is the size of the vector B. The function SPREAD takes an array and increases its dimension (i.e., number of subscripts) by one by duplicating entries along a chosen dimension. Suppose that M is the 3×4 array

```
11  12  13  14
21  22  23  24
31  32  33  34
```

then SPREAD (M (1, 2:4), 1, 2) is the array

```
12  13  14
12  13  14
```

which consists of two copies of M (1, 2:4) spread downward, duplicating entries that differ only in the first subscript. Similarly, SPREAD (M (2:3, 1), 2, 3) is the array

```
21  21  21
31  31  31
```

consisting of three copies of M (2:3, 1) spread to the right, duplicating entries that differ only in the second subscript. Since these two arrays are the same size and shape, they may be multiplied; the value of SPREAD (M (1, 2:4), 1, 2) * SPREAD (M (2:3, 1), 2, 3) is the array

$$12 \times 21 \quad 13 \times 21 \quad 14 \times 21$$
$$12 \times 31 \quad 13 \times 31 \quad 14 \times 31$$

Thus, the resulting value of M after executing the statement

```
M (2:3, 2:4) = M (2:3, 2:4) - &
        SPREAD (M (1, 2:4), 1, 2) * &
        SPREAD (M (2:3, 1), 2, 3)
```

is

11	12	13	14
21	22 − 12 × 21	23 − 13 × 21	24 − 14 × 21
31	32 − 12 × 31	33 − 13 × 31	34 − 14 × 31

The intrinsic function SUM finds the sum of all the elements of an array. If A is a one-dimensional array, then the statement

```
S = SUM (A)
```

gives the same result as the statements

```
S = 0
DO I = LBOUND (A), UBOUND (A)
   S = S + A (I)
END DO
```

For higher dimensional arrays, a nested DO loop is needed for each dimension of the array to achieve the effect of the built-in function SUM. Besides the added simplicity and clarity of using the expression SUM (A) in place of nested loops, it is much easier for compilers to recognize that SUM (A) applies the same operation to the entire array and therefore might be a suitable expression for parallel execution if the hardware permits. The DO loop versions explicitly ask for the calculations to be done in a specific order, and thus may not benefit from optimization.

Many other functions that operate on arrays are described briefly in Appendix B.

4.6 Case Study: Calculating Probabilities

In Section 3.11, we considered the problem of calculating the probability that a throw of two dice will yield a 7 or an 11. The resulting program used the built-in subroutine RANDOM to generate a real random number between 0 and 1. We now provide a slightly different solution using the same built-in procedure, but with an array as the argument.

4.6.1 Generating an Array of Random Numbers

When the argument to the built-in subroutine RANDOM is a real array, the array is filled with a collection of real numbers each greater than or equal to 0 and less than 1. In general, the numbers are not all the same, although, by chance, some pairs of them might be equal.

Also, in this section, we will rewrite the function RANDOM_INT to return an array of integers from LOW to HIGH. A third argument is added that indicates the number of pseudorandom integers to generate. The function RANDOM_INT calls the built-in subroutine RANDOM, but now with an array as the actual argument. Note that the computational part of the function is identical to the scalar version presented in Section 3.11.

```
FUNCTION RANDOM_INT (LOW, HIGH, N)  RESULT (RANDOM_INT_RESULT)

    IMPLICIT NONE
    INTEGER, DIMENSION (N) :: RANDOM_INT_RESULT
    INTEGER, INTENT (IN) :: LOW, HIGH, N
    REAL, DIMENSION (N) :: UNIFORM_VALUE

    CALL RANDOM (UNIFORM_VALUE)
    RANDOM_INT_RESULT = &
        INT ((HIGH - LOW + 1) * UNIFORM_VALUE + LOW)

END FUNCTION RANDOM_INT
```

Using the techniques discussed in Section 3.7, it is possible to make the function RANDOM_INT a generic function, so that when it is called with two arguments, it returns a single scalar value, and when it is called with three arguments, it returns an array of pseudorandom integer values.

4.6.2 Computing the Probability of a 7 or 11 Using Arrays

Using the array-valued function RANDOM_INT, the program to estimate the probability of rolling 7 or 11 with two dice is a bit shorter than the scalar version. We leave it to the reader to ponder whether it is easier or more difficult to understand than the scalar version.

```
PROGRAM SEVEN_11

    IMPLICIT NONE
    INTEGER, PARAMETER :: NUMBER_OF_ROLLS = 1000
    INTEGER, DIMENSION (NUMBER_OF_ROLLS) :: DICE
    INTEGER :: WINS
    INTEGER, DIMENSION (:) :: RANDOM_INT

    DICE = RANDOM_INT (1, 6, NUMBER_OF_ROLLS) +  &
           RANDOM_INT (1, 6, NUMBER_OF_ROLLS)
    WINS = COUNT ((DICE == 7) .OR. (DICE == 11))

    PRINT "(A, F6.2)",  &
          "THE PERCENTAGE OF ROLLS THAT ARE 7 OR 11 IS",  &
          100.0 * REAL (WINS) / REAL (NUMBER_OF_ROLLS)

END PROGRAM SEVEN_11
```

The built-in function COUNT returns the number of true values in any logical array; in this case the value in the array is true if the corresponding value in the array DICE is 7 or 11. This version of the program SEVEN_11 should produce an answer similar to the one produced by the scalar version.

4.6.3 Exercises

1. Use the array version of RANDOM_INT to write a program that determines by simulation the percentage of times the sum of two rolled dice will be 2, 3, or 12.

2. Two dice are rolled until a 4 or 7 comes up. Use the array version of RANDOM_INT to write a simulation program to determine the percentage of times a 4 will be rolled before a 7 is rolled.

3. Use the array version of RANDOM_INT to write a simulation program to determine the percentage of times exactly 5 coins will be heads and 5 will be tails, if 10 fair coins are tossed simultaneously.

4. Is it reasonable to use the array version of RANDOM_INT to create a program that deals a five-card poker hand? Remember that
the same card cannot occur twice in a hand.

5

Character Data

In a computer program, a piece of written text is called a **character string**. Character strings have been used throughout this book to retain messages and identify information printed out but not processed in any other way. This chapter reviews this simple use of character strings and presents computer programs in which the character strings themselves are the center of interest.

5.1 Use of Character Data in Fortran Programs

5.1.1 Character String Declarations

A character string variable in a Fortran program is declared to be type character. Each object of type character has a length, which is the maximum number of characters that the string may have. For example, the declaration

```
CHARACTER (LEN = 7) :: STRING_7
```

declares the variable STRING_7 to be a character string of length 7.

It is possible to have an array of character strings, all of the same length. The following declares STRING_ARRAY to be a 5 × 9 × 7 array of character strings of length 20.

```
CHARACTER (LEN = 20), DIMENSION (5, 9, 7) :: STRING_ARRAY
```

It is possible for a character string to have length zero. It is not particularly useful to declare a variable to have length zero because such a variable could only assume one value, called the **null string**. However, the null string can arise as a result of a computation, and a variable could be declared to be length zero in a program generated by another computer program.

5.1.2 Character Kinds

Although there is a requirement for a Fortran system to support only one kind of character set, it may allow others, such as Kanji, Greek, mathematical symbols, or chemical symbols. You must consult the Fortran manual for the system you are using to see what character kinds are available and determine the number indicating each of the character kinds. For example, if you find that your system supports Greek characters and the kind for Greek is 7, it would be possible to declare the variables GREEK_NAME and GREEK_CITY with the statements:

```
INTEGER, PARAMETER :: GREEK = 7
CHARACTER (LEN = 20, KIND = GREEK) :: GREEK_NAME, GREEK_CITY
```

Of course, it is not necessary to use the parameter GREEK, but it is a good idea, so that if Greek is supported on another machine but with a different kind number, only the PARAMETER attribute needs to be changed to run the program on the other machine.

If the kind parameter is missing from a declaration, a default character set is assumed. In many cases, this will be the international standard character set known as ASCII. A program that prints the default character set is given in Section 5.1.9.

5.1.3 Character Constants

Recall that a character constant is enclosed in quotation marks (double quotes) or in apostrophes (single quotes). This makes it possible for the computer to tell the difference between the character constant "YES" and the variable YES, or between the character constant "14" and the integer constant 14.

If a character constant is to be a kind other than the default kind, it must be preceded with a kind value. For example, if kind 9 indicates strings of mathematical symbols,

9_"∫∫"

or

MATH_"∫∫"

where MATH is an integer constant with the value 9, indicate a string of three integral signs. Note that the placement of the kind on constants is inconsistent. Integer, real, complex, and logical constants may have a kind suffix and character constants may have a kind prefix.

5.1.4 Character Parameters

A character constant may be given a name using the PARAMETER attribute. As a simple example, the program HELLO uses a character parameter or named character constant, instead of a literal character constant.

```
PROGRAM HELLO
   IMPLICIT NONE
   CHARACTER (LEN = *), PARAMETER :: &
        MESSAGE = "Hello, I am a computer."
   PRINT *, MESSAGE
END PROGRAM HELLO

RUN HELLO

   Hello, I am a computer.
```

Note that the name of the character parameter must be declared, just like a character variable, but the length may be declared as an asterisk indicating that the length is to be determined from the value of the string. Dummy arguments and function results also can have their length designated as an asterisk, indicating that their length will be determined by declarations in the calling program.

5.1.5 Assigning Values to Character Variables

A variable that has been declared to be a character string may be assigned a value that is a character string. A simple example is provided by the following program that assigns a string to a character variable used in a PRINT statement instead of executing alternative PRINT statements containing different messages.

```
PROGRAM TEST_SIGN
   IMPLICIT NONE
   REAL :: NUMBER
   CHARACTER (LEN = 8) :: SIGN

   READ *, NUMBER
   IF (NUMBER > 0) THEN
      SIGN = "positive"
   ELSE IF (NUMBER == 0) THEN
      SIGN = "zero"
   ELSE
      SIGN = "negative"
   END IF
   PRINT *, NUMBER, "is", SIGN
END PROGRAM TEST_SIGN

RUN TEST_SIGN

-2.30000  is  negative
```

5.1.6 Length of a Character String

The **length** of a character string is the number of characters in the string. The length of a Fortran character string is fixed and must not be negative. Each blank occurring in the string is counted in its length. The built-in function LEN gives the length of a character string. Thus,

LEN ("love") = 4
LEN ("Good morning.") = 13
LEN (" ") = 1
LEN ("   ") = 4
LEN ("BG7*5 AD") = 8

As with any other function, the argument of the function LEN may be a variable or more general expression, as well as a constant.

During execution of a program, a character string variable always has its declared length. However, the length of a character string assigned to a character variable may be different from the length declared for that variable. For example, if the input number is zero in the program TEST_SIGN, the 4-character constant "zero" is assigned to the 8-character variable SIGN. This assignment is legal. Four blanks are added to the end of the string "zero" to make its length 8, the declared length of the variable SIGN. Thus, the new value of the variable SIGN is "zero   ".

On the other hand, if the character string to be assigned to a variable is longer than the declared length of the variable, characters are truncated from the right end of the string prior to assignment. For example, if the string NAME has a declared length of 3, the assignment statement

```
NAME = "Jonathan"
```

results in the string "Jon" being assigned to NAME.

In a subprogram, the length of a character dummy argument may be given as an asterisk enclosed in parentheses (*), which means that the length of the corresponding actual argument is to be used. For example,

```
SUBROUTINE PROCESS (C)
CHARACTER (LEN = *) :: C
```

The length function provides information that is otherwise unobtainable only in this case where a character string, such as the variable C above, is a dummy argument with its length given by an asterisk. The programmer knows the length of all other character strings from their declarations.

5.1.7 Input of Character Strings

When character strings are supplied as input using a READ statement with the default format (*), the string must be enclosed in quotes or apostrophes, just like a character constant. When using an A format, however, surrounding quotes must be omitted; any quotes among the characters read are considered to be part of the character constant. Input and output of nondefault character kinds are implementation dependent, and details must be checked in the manuals for the computer system you are using.

5.1.8 Character Collating Sequences

Every Fortran 90 system is required to support a default character kind containing at least all of the standard characters permitted in a Fortran program and the ASCII character kind, if it is not the default character kind. Other character kinds are permitted, but not required. Many computers use either the 128-character ASCII character set or the 256-character EBCDIC character set as default. The acronym ASCII stands for "American Standard Code for Information Interchange" and the acronym EBCDIC stands for "Extended Binary Coded Decimal Inter-change Code".

Each character set has an intrinsic ordering of individual characters, derived originally from the most usual way characters were stored internally on computers that used these character sets. More recently the intrinsic ordering for characters of a specific kind, called the **collating sequence** for that character set, has been fixed by published standards, whether or not the computer uses the motivating internal representation. For example, the ASCII code is described in the ANSI standard X3.4-1986, which is the U. S. national version of the international standard ISO 646:1977. Tables 5-1 and Table 5-2 show a selection of printable characters in the ASCII and EBCDIC collating sequences.

Table 5-1 The collating sequence for printable ASCII characters.

```
blank ! " # $ % & ' ( ) * + , - . /
0 1 2 3 4 5 6 7 8 9 : ; < = > ? @
A B C D E F G H I J K L M N O P Q R S T U V W X Y Z [ ] ^ _ '
a b c d e f g h i j k l m n o p q r s t u v w x y z { | } ~
```

Table 5-2 The collating sequence for printable EBCDIC characters.

```
blank ] . < ( + ! & [ $ * ) ; ^ - / , % _ > ? : # @ ' = "
a b c d e f g h i j k l m n o p q r s t u v w x y z
A B C D E F G H I J K L M N O P Q R S T U V W X Y Z
0 1 2 3 4 5 6 7 8 9
```

One character is considered "less than" another character if it precedes the other character in the collating sequence for the kind of the characters. Comparison of characters of different kinds is not permitted. The result of a comparison of characters may depend on the kind. As Table 5-1 and Table 5-2 show, the collating sequences for the ASCII and EBCDIC character sets do not agree on important particulars, including the relative placement of uppercase letters, lowercase letters, and digits. However, they do agree that both uppercase letters and lowercase letters are in alphabetic order, and that digits are in numeric order.

5.1.9 The Built-In Functions ICHAR, CHAR, IACHAR, and ACHAR

The built-in function ICHAR gives an integer representing the internal code or position in the collating sequence of the character given as argument. The kind of the actual argument determines the collating sequence to be used.

The function CHAR returns the character with a given code. The kind of the character is the default unless an optional second argument is provided indicating the kind. For example, CHAR (20, KIND = 7) and CHAR (20, GREEK) would both give the character in position 20 for the character set of kind 7, assuming that GREEK is a named integer constant with value 7. The kind argument is identified by its keyword in the first case.

The built-in function IACHAR gives the integer code used to represent a given character in the ASCII collating sequence, and the built-in function ACHAR returns the character with a given ASCII code. The actual argument for IACHAR must be a character of default type.

5.1.10 A Testing Technique for Character Output

The program EXPLORE_CHARACTER_SET will allow you to explore the collating sequence of the default kind one character at a time. You type the ASCII or EBCDIC code and the computer prints the character with that code.

```
PROGRAM EXPLORE_CHARACTER_SET

! Prints the character with given character code
! in the default kind

    IMPLICIT NONE
    INTEGER :: CODE

    PRINT *, "Type a character code"
    READ *, CODE
    PRINT "(I5, 3A)", CODE, ">", CHAR (CODE), "<"

END PROGRAM EXPLORE_CHARACTER SET

RUN EXPLORE_CHARACTER_SET

Type a character code
65
    65>A<
```

The blank character is a perfectly valid character (ASCII code 32). To better see the value of CHAR, the value is printed surrounded by the printable characters " > " and " < ". A blank character will then conspicuously occupy the print or display position between its delimiters.

You must expect some surprises when you run the program EXPLORE_CHARACTER_SET. Most of the characters from 0 to 31 do not print. Some, like the line feed, CHAR (10) in ASCII, direct the printer to perform some action rather than print a character. The delimiters ">" and "<" will help you figure out what action was taken.

Table 5-3 summarizes all possible executions of the program EXPLORE_CHARACTER_SET. It is the output of a program similar to EXPLORE_CHARACTER_SET that uses loops to print all 128 ASCII codes and their corresponding characters, eight per line of output. Characters that are unprintable or are interpreted as control directives by the output device cause the misalignments in the output. This typical output was produced on a computer using the ASCII character code as default kind. The output device used for computer-controlled typesetting also modified the spacing.

Table 5-3 A computer printout of the ASCII character set.

0	1	...	2	3	4	5	6	7
8	9		10					
11	12	13	14	15				
16	17	18	19	20	21	22	23	
24	25	26	27	28	29	30	31	
32	33 !	34 "	35 #	36 $	37 %	38 &	39 '	
40 (	41)	42 *	43 +	44 ,	45 –	46 .	47 /	
48 0	49 1	50 2	51 3	52 4	53 5	54 6	55 7	
56 8	57 9	58 :	59 ;	60 <	61 =	62 >	63 ?	
64 @	65 A	66 B	67 C	68 D	69 E	70 F	71 G	
72 H	73 I	74 J	75 K	76 L	77 M	78 N	79 O	
80 P	81 Q	82 R	83 S	84 T	85 U	86 V	87 W	
88 X	89 Y	90 Z	91 [	92	93]	94 ^	95 _	
96 '	97 a	98 b	99 c	100 d	101 e	102 f	103 g	
104 h	105 i	106 j	107 k	108 l	109 m	110 n	111 o	
112 p	113 q	114 r	115 s	116 t	117 u	118 v	119 w	
120 x	121 y	122 z	123 {	124 |	125 }	126 ~	127	

5.1.11 Comparison of Character Strings

In Fortran the comparison operators[1]

$$<, \ <=, \ ==, \ /=, \ >, \ >=$$

---

1. Of course, the old versions of the relational operators, .LT., .LE., .EQ., .NE., .GT., and .GE., also still work.

may be used to compare character values according to the intrinsic ordering of the character kind being compared. It is not permitted to compare character expressions of different kinds. If strings are to be sorted on the ASCII collating sequence, the built-in functions LLT, LLE, LGT, and LGE may be used.

The ordering of strings is an extension of the ordinary lexicographic (i.e., dictionary) ordering of words, but uses the processor codes to order characters other than letters. If the first character of one character string precedes the first character of the second string in the collating sequence, then we say the first character string is less than the second. If the first characters are equal, the second characters are used to decide which character string is smaller. If the second characters match also, the third characters are used to decide, and so on. The character string with the the smaller character in the first position where the two strings disagree is considered the smaller character string. When character strings of different lengths are compared, the shorter one is treated as if it were padded with enough blanks at the end to make it the same length as the longer one. For example,

> "apple" < "bug" < "cacophony" < "doldrums"
> "earache" < "elephant" < "empathy" < "equine"
> "phlegmatic" < "phonograph" < "photosynthetic"
> "dipole" < "duplicate" == "duplicate " < "dynamic"

In the first line of expressions, decisions are made on the basis of the first letter of the strings. In the second line, since each string has first letter "e", decisions are made on the basis of the relative collating position of the second letters. In the third set of comparisons, third or fourth letters differ.

From these examples, it is clear that the natural order of character strings corresponds exactly to ordinary alphabetic order when the character strings are words written either entirely in lowercase or entirely in uppercase letters.

String ordering does not take meaning into account. For example, although

> "1" < "2" < "3" < "4"

as expected, it is also true that

> "four" < "one" < "three" < "two"

and, worse yet

> "12" < "2"

String ordering also is sensitive to upper and lower case. The two character strings

"word"   "WORD"

are not equal. Moreover, the ASCII and EBCDIC collating sequences do not agree on which comes first.

5.1.12 Substrings

Many character-processing applications require breaking down a string into individual characters or special sequences of characters. Examples are decomposing a word into letters or a sentence into words. The key idea in such a decomposition is a substring.

A **substring** of a character string is any consecutive sequence of characters in the string. For example, "J", "ne D", and "Doe" are substrings of the character string "Jane Doe", but "JDoe" is not a substring. Every character string is regarded as a substring of itself. The string of length zero (the null string) is a substring of every string; it occurs between every pair of characters and at both the beginning and end of the string. The following table indicates all the substrings of the character string "then".

Length 0:   " " (the null string)
Length 1:   "t" "h" "e" "n"
Length 2:   "th" "he" "en"
Length 3:   "the" "hen"
Length 4:   "then"

5.1.13 Referencing Substrings

There is a convenient way to refer to any contiguous subsequence of characters of a character string. This is done by writing after any character variable or array element two integer expressions that give the positions of the first and last characters in the substring. These two expressions are separated by a colon and enclosed in parentheses. An example is STRING $(K : L)$, where the values of K and L are positive integers less than or equal to the length of STRING if $K \leq L$. If $K > L$, the result is the null string. For example if C = "crunch",

C $(2 : 4)$ = "run"
C $(1 : 6)$ = "crunch"
C $(9 : 2)$ = " " (the null string)
C $(2 : 7)$ is illegal
C $(5 : 5)$ = "c"

The last example illustrates how to refer to a single character of a string. The program SINGLE_LETTERS tells the computer to print, one at a time, the characters of a string supplied as input.

```
PROGRAM SINGLE_LETTERS
!  Print individually the letters of an input string

    IMPLICIT NONE
    INTEGER :: K
    CHARACTER (LEN = 10) :: STRING

    READ "(A)", STRING
    PRINT *, "Input data  STRING:", STRING

    DO K = 1, LEN (STRING)
        PRINT *, STRING (K : K)
    END DO

    PRINT *, "====="
END PROGRAM SINGLE_LETTERS

RUN SINGLE_LETTERS

  Input data  STRING:  SHAZAM
  S
  H
  A
  Z
  A
  M




  =====
```

There are four blank lines in the output of the program SINGLE_LETTER because there are are four blank letters following the characters SHAZAM in the value of the variable STRING. This is because STRING is declared to have length 10, but SHAZAM contains only 6 characters.

5.1.14 Trimmed Length of a String

It is a nuisance that the length of a character variable is always the same regardless of its value. A definition of length that is suitable for many applications is the length of the substring that includes all characters up to and including the last nonblank character, but excluding terminal blanks. Using substrings, it is possible to write a function subprogram LEN_TRIM (trimmed length) that computes this value.

```
FUNCTION LEN_TRIM (STRING) RESULT (LEN_TRIM_RESULT)

    IMPLICIT NONE
    CHARACTER (LEN = *), INTENT (IN) :: STRING
    INTEGER :: LEN_TRIM_RESULT, K

    LEN_TRIM_RESULT = 0
    DO K = LEN (STRING), 1, -1
        !  or until nonblank found
        IF (STRING (K : K) /= ' ') THEN
            LEN_TRIM_RESULT = K
            EXIT
        END IF
    END DO

END FUNCTION LEN_TRIM
```

Style Note: It is almost always a good idea to use an asterisk as the length declaration for a dummy argument of type character and to use the built-in function LEN to find its true length when needed.

Actually, the function LEN_TRIM is a built-in function that computes exactly the same result as the one given above. In addition, there is a built-in function TRIM, whose value is the given character string with all trailing blanks removed. The value of TRIM (STRING) is the same as STRING (1 : LEN_TRIM (STRING)) and is used in the sample program PLURAL in Section 5.1.17.

The program SUBSTRINGS_LENGTH_2 (substrings of length two) prints all substrings of length two of any character string supplied as input. The upper bound LEN_TRIM (STRING) – 1 on the DO variable K is the starting point of the last substring of length two that doesn't contain a trailing blank.

```
PROGRAM SUBSTRINGS_LENGTH_2
    IMPLICIT NONE
    CHARACTER (LEN = 20) :: STRING
    INTEGER :: K

    READ "(A)", STRING
    PRINT *, "Input data  STRING:", STRING
    DO K = 1, LEN_TRIM (STRING) - 1
       PRINT *, STRING (K : K + 1)
    END DO

    PRINT *, "====="
END PROGRAM SUBSTRINGS_LENGTH_2

RUN SUBSTRINGS_LENGTH_2

  Input data  STRING:  High their!
  Hi
  ig
  gh
  h
   t
  th
  he
  ei
  ir
  r!
  =====
```

By adapting the method of the program SUBSTRINGS_LENGTH_2, we could write a program to print out all the substrings of any given length. By using a double loop, we could write a program that lists all substrings of all possible lengths. Tasks like these are provided as exercises at the end of this section.

5.1.15 Reassigning the Value of a Substring

It is possible to reassign the value of a substring without affecting the rest of the string. For instance, the three lines

```
NAME = "John X. Public"
INITIAL = "Q"
NAME (6 : 6) = INITIAL
```

tell the computer to change the value of the variable NAME from "John X. Public" to "John Q. Public". Similarly the three lines

```
NAME = "John Xavier Public"
NEW_MIDDLE_NAME = "Quincy"
NAME (6 : 11) = NEW_MIDDLE_NAME
```

direct the computer to change the value of the variable NAME from "John Xavier Public" to "John Quincy Public".

In reassigning the value of a substring as in the above two examples, it is necessary that the length of the new substring value exactly equal the length of the old substring value. The following example shows how to use a loop to make room for a longer replacement substring. It is assumed that the declared length of NAME is at least 17 characters.

```
NAME = "John Paul Public"
!  Move last name and blank one position to the right
DO LETTER = 16, 10, -1
    NAME (LETTER + 1 : LETTER + 1) = NAME (LETTER : LETTER)
END DO
!  Insert middle name
NAME (6 : 11) = "Peter"
```

Note that it would not be correct to have the DO variable count forward from 10 to 16. That loop would first move the blank in position 10 to position 11, which is what is desired. However, for the second iteration of the loop, the value of LTR would be 11 and the blank just placed in position 11 would be moved to position 12. Next, the blank in position 12 would be moved to position 13. The total effect of the loop would be to put blanks in positions 11 through 17.

It is possible to replace the DO block that moves the last name one position to the right with the single statement

```
NAME (11 : 17) = NAME (10 : 16)
```

This was illegal in Fortran 77, but not in Fortran 90.

5.1.16 Finding the Position of One String in Another

There are numerous reasons for wanting to know if one string is contained as a substring in another. We might want to know if a particular letter is in a word or if a certain word is in a sentence. The built-in function INDEX tells even more than that; it tells where to find the first instance of one character string as a substring of another. For example,

        INDEX ("monkey", "on") = 2

because the substring "on" begins at the second letter of the string "monkey" and

        INDEX ("monkey", "key") = 4

because the substring "key" begins at the fourth letter of "monkey".
    If the string supplied as the second argument occurs more than once as a substring of the string supplied as the first argument, the function value is the location of the beginning of the leftmost occurrence, so that

        INDEX ("banana", "ana") = 2

even though characters 4 to 6 of "banana" also are "ana". If the second argument is not a substring of the first argument, rather than calling it an error and halting, a signal function value of zero is used. For example,

        INDEX ("monkey", "off") = 0

A program that calls the function INDEX can test for the signal value zero if desired.
    The function INDEX is a built-in function in Fortran; but to provide a better understanding of how the function works, a programmer-defined version of the program follows.

```
FUNCTION INDEX (TEXT, STRING)  RESULT (INDEX_RESULT)
!  Searches for string as a substring of text.
!  If found, INDEX is the position of the first character
!  of the leftmost occurrence of string in text.
!  If not found, INDEX = 0

   IMPLICIT NONE
   INTEGER :: INDEX_RESULT
   CHARACTER (LEN = *), INTENT (IN) :: TEXT, STRING
   INTEGER LEFT_END, RIGHT_END
```

```
        INDEX_RESULT = 0
        DO LEFT_END = 1, LEN (TEXT) - LEN (STRING) + 1
           RIGHT_END = LEFT_END + LEN (STRING) - 1
           IF (TEXT (LEFT_END : RIGHT_END) == STRING) THEN
              INDEX_RESULT = LEFT_END
              EXIT
           END IF
        END DO

     END FUNCTION INDEX
```

5.1.17 Concatenation

The only built-in operation that can be performed on strings is concatenation. The concatenation of two strings is formed simply by placing one string after the other. The symbol for concatenation is two slashes (//). The concatenation operator in Fortran is less useful than it might be because strings are all fixed length. The program PLURAL attempts to form the plural of given words by the method of putting the letter "s" at the end. Obviously, this program is not very useful as it stands, but it does illustrate the use of the concatenation operator.

```
PROGRAM PLURAL
   IMPLICIT NONE
   CHARACTER (LEN = 18) :: WORD
   INTEGER :: IOS

   DO ! until out of words
      READ (*, "(A)", IOSTAT = IOS) WORD
      IF (IOS < 0) EXIT  ! End of file
      PRINT *, "Input data WORD:", WORD
      PRINT *, "Plural of word:", TRIM (WORD) // "s"
   END DO
END PROGRAM PLURAL

RUN PLURAL

   Input data WORD:  program
   Plural of word:  programs
   Input data WORD:  programmer
   Plural of word:  programmers
   Input data WORD:  matrix
   Plural of word:  matrixs
```

```
Input data WORD: computer
Plural of word: computers
Input data WORD: horses
Plural of word: horsess
```

The READ statement in the program PLURAL needs both a format specification and an option that sets the integer variable IOS to a negative value when attempting to read beyond the end of the file. Thus, the long form is required. However, we still want to use the default input unit, so we could write

```
READ (UNIT = *, FMT = "(A)", IOSTAT = IOS) WORD
```

If the first two options are respectively the unit number and format specifier, the introductory phrases for these two options may be omitted, resulting in the shorter form

```
READ (*, "(A)", IOSTAT = IOS) WORD
```

5.1.18 Exercises

1. What is the value of each of the following expressions?

   ```
   LEN ("5 FEET")
   LEN ("ALPHABET")
   LEN ("ABCDEFGHIJKLMNOPQRSTUVWXYZ")
   LEN ("42")
   ```

2. List all the substrings of length 3 of the string "ALPHABET".

3. Write a program that reads a character string of maximum length 50 and prints all substrings of length 3. If you can't think of anything better, use as input data:

   ```
   "These are the times that try men's souls."
   ```

   The output from this sample input should be

   ```
   RUN SUBSTRINGS_3

      The
      hes
      ese
   ```

.
.
.
```
uls
ls.
```

4. Write a program that reads a character string of maximum length 50 and prints all of its substrings.

5. Write a program that sorts a list of at most 200 character strings. Each character string is at most 50 characters long and occupies the leftmost positions of one line in the input file. Use the end-of-file test to terminate reading of input data. You may be surprised at what happens if you accidentally type a blank in the leftmost column of one of the lines in the input file. Then again, after you think about it, you might not be.

6. A computer system maintains a list of valid passwords. Write a program that accepts an 8-character password and checks it against its list of valid passwords. The program should print "OK" if the password is in the list and "Try again" if it is not. Give the user two additional tries, replying with successively nastier messages each time the user fails to give the correct password. **Hint:** Keep a list of responses as well as a list of passwords. A sample execution might produce the following output:

```
RUN CHECK_PASSWORD

    Welcome to the super special simulated system
    Enter your password:
BUG FREE
    Try again
    Enter your password:
SILICON
    Are you sure you have a password?
    Enter your password:
Fortran
    OK
```

7. Read a character string of maximum length 50 as input and print it in reverse order. Ignore trailing blanks. You must use a character-valued function REVERSE (STRING). If the input is

```
until
```

the output should be

```
RUN TEST_REVERSE

   Input data STRING: until
   litnu
```

8. Nicely displayed headings add impact to a document. Write a program to take a character string as input and print it surrounded by a border of asterisks. Again, ignore trailing blanks in the input. Leave one blank before the first character and after the last character in the display. If the input is

```
Payroll Report
```

the output should be

```
RUN BORDER

   Input data TITLE: Payroll Report

   ******************
   * Payroll Report *
   ******************
```

9. Write a logical-valued function FORTRAN_NAME that determines whether or not its character string argument is a legal Fortran name.

10. Write a function CHAR_TO_INT that accepts a character string and returns a vector of integers, one for each character in the substring. The integer value should be 1 through 26, reflecting the position in the alphabet if the character is either an uppercase or lowercase letter; the value should be zero, otherwise. For example, CHAR_TO_INT ("e") = 5 and CHAR_TO_INT ("%") = 0.

11. Write a function INT_TO_BINARY that converts an integer to a character string that is the binary representation of the integer. Adjust the 1s and 0s in the right-hand portion of the string and pad the remainder of the string with blanks. The string should contain no insignificant zeros, except that the integer 0 should produce the string consisting of all blanks and one character "0". If the integer is negative, the first nonblank character should be a minus sign; if it is positive, the first nonblank character should be "1". In the

function, the result should be declared to have length *. If the declared length of the function in the calling program is not long enough to contain the result, it should consist of all asterisks. For example, if the calling program declares INT_TO_BINARY to be length 5:

```
INT_TO_CHAR (3) = "bb101"
INT_TO_CHAR (0) = "bbbb0"
INT_TO_CHAR (-4) = "b-100"
INT_TO_CHAR (77) = "*****"
```

5.2 Text Analysis

There are numerous reasons for examining text in minute detail, word by word and letter by letter. One of the reasons is to determine the authorship of an historical or literary work. Such quantities as the average length of a word or the frequency of usage of certain letters can be important clues. Computers have been useful in studying text from this viewpoint.

5.2.1 Blanking Out Punctuation

We start with some routines that perform simple text manipulation processes. The subroutine BLANK_PUNCT (blank out punctuation) uses the substring value reassignment facility and the function INDEX. Keep in mind that a function value zero means the intrinsic function INDEX has determined that the second supplied argument is not a substring of the first supplied argument. The subroutine BLANK_PUNCT regards any character besides a letter or a blank as a "punctuation mark" to be blanked out.

```
SUBROUTINE BLANK_PUNCT (TEXT)
! Blank out punctuation
! Retain only letters and blanks

   IMPLICIT NONE
   CHARACTER (LEN = *), INTENT (INOUT) :: TEXT
   CHARACTER (LEN = *), PARAMETER :: LETTER_OR_B = &
      "ABCDEFGHIJKLMNOPQRSTUVWXYZabcdefghijklmnopqrstuvwxyz "
   INTEGER :: I

   ! Replace any character that is not a blank or letter
   ! with a blank
```

```
    DO I = 1, LEN_TRIM (TEXT)
      IF (INDEX (LETTER_OR_B, TEXT (I : I)) == 0) THEN
        TEXT (I : I) = " "
      END IF
    END DO
END SUBROUTINE BLANK_PUNCT
```

The program TEST_BP (test blank out punctuation) is intended to show how the subroutine BLANK_PUNCT works.

```
PROGRAM TEST_BP
  IMPLICIT NONE
  CHARACTER (LEN = *), PARAMETER ::  &
        TEXT = 'Suppress5$,superfluous*/3punctuation.'

  CALL BLANK_PUNCT (TEXT)
  PRINT *, TEXT
END PROGRAM TEST_BP

RUN TEST_BP

  Suppress    superfluous    punctuation
```

A slightly different version of the subroutine BLANK_PUNCT uses the VERIFY built-in function. The VERIFY function scans the first argument-checking that each character in the string is also in the string that is the second argument. If each character in the first argument is also in the second, the value of the function is 0. Otherwise, the value of the function is the character position of the leftmost character in the first argument that is not in the second argument. For example the value of VERIFY ("banana", "nab") is 0 and the value of VERIFY ("banana", "ab") is 3, the position in "banana" of the first "n".

```
SUBROUTINE BLANK_PUNCT (TEXT)
! Blank out punctuation
! Retain only letters and blanks

  IMPLICIT NONE
  CHARACTER (LEN = *), INTENT (INOUT) :: TEXT
  CHARACTER (LEN = *), PARAMETER :: LETTER_OR_B =  &
     "ABCDEFGHIJKLMNOPQRSTUVWXYZabcdefghijklmnopqrstuvwxyz "
  INTEGER :: I
```

```
          ! Replace any character that is not a blank or letter
          ! with a blank
          DO
             I = VERIFY (TEXT, LETTER_OR_B)
             IF (I == 0) EXIT
             TEXT (I : I) = " "
          END DO
       END SUBROUTINE BLANK_PUNCT
```

5.2.2 Excising a Character from a String

When a character of a string is blanked out, as by the subroutine
BLANK_PUNCT, that character is replaced by a blank and the length of
the character string remains unchanged. When a character is *excised*
from a string, not only is the character removed, but also all of the characters to the right of the excised characters are moved one position to the
left. Thus, when a character is excised from a string, the trimmed length
(that is, not including trailing blanks) of the string is decreased by one.
Of course, the declared total length of the string cannot change in Fortran. The character in position C of NAME can be excised by the statement:

```
       NAME (C :) = NAME (C + 1 :)
```

The subroutine COMPRES_BB (compress double blanks) removes
all double blanks from a string except those that occur at the right end.
It is called by a program WORDS that lists all the words in a string; the
program WORDS is discussed in the next subsection.

```
       SUBROUTINE COMPRESS_BB (TEXT)
       !  Removes double blanks, except at right end
          IMPLICIT NONE
          CHARACTER (LEN = *), INTENT (INOUT) :: TEXT
          INTEGER :: I

          DO
             I = INDEX (TRIM (TEXT), " ")
             IF (I == 0) EXIT
             TEXT (I :) = TEXT (I + 1 :)
          END DO
       END SUBROUTINE COMPRESS_BB
```

5.2.3 Listing All the Words

We now turn our attention to the problem of listing all the words in a text. For this purpose, the program WORDS regards a substring as a word if and only if it consists entirely of letters and both the character immediately before it (if any) and the character immediately after it (if any) are not letters. The computer does not consult a dictionary to see whether the word has been approved by a lexicographer.

```
PROGRAM WORDS
   IMPLICIT NONE
   CHARACTER (LEN = 200) :: TEXT
   INTEGER :: END_OF_WORD

   READ "(A)", TEXT
   PRINT *, "Input data  TEXT:", TEXT

   ! Blanking out the punctuation,
   ! compressing the multiple blanks,
   ! and ensuring that the first character is a letter
   ! are pre-editing tasks to simplify the job.
   CALL BLANK_PUNCT (TEXT)
   CALL COMPRESS_BB (TEXT)
   TEXT = ADJUSTL (TEXT)

   ! Print all the words.
   ! Each word is followed by exactly one blank.
   DO ! until all words are printed
      IF (LEN_TRIM (TEXT) == 0) EXIT
      END_OF_WORD = INDEX (TEXT, " ") - 1
      PRINT *, TEXT (1 : END_OF_WORD)

      ! Discard word just printed
      TEXT = TEXT (END_OF_WORD + 2 :)
   END DO
END PROGRAM WORDS

RUN WORDS

   Input data  TEXT:  Then, due to illness*, he resigned (for good).
   Then
   due
   to
   illness
```

```
he
resigned
for
good
```

If the string supplied as input to the program WORDS contains no letters, the pre-editing provides a string of all blanks to the DO block that prints all the words. The DO block exits correctly on the first iteration without printing any words because the trimmed length is zero. In the usual case, however, a word starts at position 1 of TEXT and stops immediately before the first blank. The computer prints the word and discards it and the blank immediately following it, so that the next word to be printed begins at location 1 of the resulting character string.

Even after the subroutines BLANK_PUNCT and COMPRESS_BB are called, it is possible that the first character of the string is a blank. Application of the built-in function ADJUSTL shifts the string to the left to eliminate any leading blanks, filling in the end of the string with a blank for each position shifted.

5.2.4 Average Word Length

To compute the average length of words in a given text, it is necessary to determine both the total number of letters in the text and the total number of words. The most direct way that comes to mind is used by the program AVG_WORD_LEN_1 (average word length, version 1).

```
PROGRAM AVG_WORD_LEN_1
    Initialize word count and letter count to zero
    Read text
    Start scan at leftmost character of the text
    Do until end of text is reached
        Locate the beginning and end of a word
        If no more words then exit the loop
        Increase the letter count by the number of letters
            in the word
        Increase the word count by 1
    Print "Average word length = ", letter count / word count
END PROGRAM AVG_WORD_LEN_1
```

After reading in the text, the computer starts to look for the first word at the extreme left. Blanks, commas, and other nonletters are passed over to find the beginning of a word. Then letters are counted until the first nonletter is reached, such as a blank or punctuation mark which signals the end of the word. These steps are repeated for each word in the text. Each time it locates a word, the computer increases the letter count by its length and the word count by one.

The refinement of AVG_WORD_LEN_1 is straightforward.

```
PROGRAM AVG_WORD_LEN_1
!  Calculate the average word length of input text

   IMPLICIT NONE
   CHARACTER (LEN = 200) :: TEXT
   INTEGER WORD_BEGIN, WORD_END
   INTEGER WORD_COUNT, LETTER_COUNT
   CHARACTER (LEN = *), PARAMETER :: ALPHABET =  &
      "ABCDEFGHIJKLMNOPQRSTUVWXYZabcdefghijklmnopqrstuvwxyz"

   LETTER_COUNT = 0
   WORD_COUNT = 0
   READ "(A)", TEXT
   PRINT *, "Input data  TEXT:", TEXT

   DO   ! until no more words
      WORD_BEGIN = SCAN (TEXT, ALPHABET)
      IF (WORD_BEGIN == 0) EXIT
      TEXT = TEXT (WORD_BEGIN :)
      WORD_END = VERIFY (TEXT, ALPHABET) - 1
      IF (WORD_END == -1) WORD_END = LEN (TEXT)
      LETTER_COUNT = LETTER_COUNT + WORD_END
      WORD_COUNT = WORD_COUNT + 1
      TEXT = TEXT (WORD_END + 2 :)
   END DO

   PRINT *, "Average word length =",  &
         REAL (LETTER_COUNT) / WORD_COUNT
END PROGRAM AVG_WORD_LEN_1

RUN AVG_WORD_LEN_1

   Input data  TEXT:  Never mind the whys and wherefores.
   Average word length =    4.83333

RUN AVG_WORD_LEN_1

   Input data  TEXT:  I computed the average word length.
   Average word length =    4.83333
```

The sample execution printouts of the program AVG_WORD_
LEN_1 might suggest that to use average word length as a test for
authorship, one should have a fairly large sample of text.

5.2.5 Modification for a Large Quantity of Text

If the amount of text is very large, then the computer might not have
enough memory to hold it all at one time. Also, in some Fortran systems, there is a maximum length for character strings. For these reasons,
it may be desirable to modify the program AVG_WORD_LEN_1 so that
it reads the text one line at a time, rather than all at once. The program
AVG_WORD_LEN_2 incorporates such a modification. Much of the
main program AVG_WORD_LEN_1 is put into the internal subroutine
ONE_LINE (process one line).

```
PROGRAM AVG_WORD_LEN_2
!   Calculate the average word length of input text.
!   Text may have many lines, terminated by end of file.

    IMPLICIT NONE
    CHARACTER (LEN = *), PARAMETER :: ALPHABET =  &
       "ABCDEFGHIJKLMNOPQRSTUVWXYZabcdefghijklmnopqrstuvwxyz"
    CHARACTER (LEN = 200) :: TEXT
    INTEGER :: WORD_COUNT, LETTER_COUNT

    LETTER_COUNT = 0
    WORD_COUNT = 0

    DO   ! until no more lines of text
       READ (*, "(A)", IOS = IOSTAT) TEXT
       IF (IOS < 0) EXIT
       PRINT *, "Input data  TEXT:", TEXT
       CALL ONE_LINE
    END DO

    PRINT *, "Average word length =",  &
          REAL (LETTER_COUNT) / WORD_COUNT

CONTAINS

SUBROUTINE ONE_LINE
!   Accumulate statistics on one line of input text.
```

```
      DO   ! until no more words
          WORD_BEGIN = SCAN (TEXT, ALPHABET)
          IF (WORD_BEGIN == 0) EXIT
          TEXT = TEXT (WORD_BEGIN :)
          WORD_END = VERIFY (TEXT, ALPHABET) - 1
          IF (WORD_END == -1) WORD_END = LEN (TEXT)
          LETTER_COUNT = LETTER_COUNT + WORD_END
          WORD_COUNT = WORD_COUNT + 1
          TEXT = TEXT (WORD_END + 2 :)
      END DO

  END SUBROUTINE ONE_LINE

  END PROGRAM AVG_WORD_LEN_2

  RUN AVG_WORD_LEN_2

     Input data  TEXT:  One of the more important uses
     Input data  TEXT:  of the character manipulation
     Input data  TEXT:  capability of computers is
     Input data  TEXT:  in the analysis of text.
     Average word length =   4.89474
```

5.2.6 Frequency of Occurrence of Letters

There are two basic ways to count the number of occurrences of each letter of the alphabet in a given text. Both ways use 27 counters, one for each letter of the alphabet and one to count all the other characters.

One way to tabulate letter frequencies in a line of text is first to scan it for all occurrences of the letter "A", then to scan it for all occurrences of the letter "B", and so on through the alphabet. This requires 26 scans of the whole line. This method is embodied in the program LETTER_COUNT_1.

```
  PROGRAM LETTER_COUNT_1
     Initialize
     DO
         Read line of text
         If no more text, exit loop
```

```
            DO LETTER = "A", "Z"
                Scan line of text, counting occurrences of that letter
                    (either uppercase or lowercase)
                Calculate the number of nonletters and
                    increment nonletter total
            END DO
        END DO
        Print the counts
    END PROGRAM LETTER_COUNT_1
```

The second way to count letter frequencies in a line of text is to begin with the first symbol of the text, to decide which of the 27 counters to increment, to continue with the second letter of the line of text, to see which counter to increment this time, and so on through the text. This second way is implemented by the program LETTER_COUNT_2

```
    PROGRAM LETTER_COUNT_2
        Initialize
        DO
            Read a line of text
            If no more text, exit loop
            DO for each character in the line of text
                If the character is a letter then
                    increment the count for that letter
                else
                    increment the nonletter count
                end if
            END DO
        END DO
        Print the counts
    END PROGRAM LETTER_COUNT_2
```

By the method of the program LETTER_COUNT_1, the text must be scanned completely for each letter of the alphabet. By the method of the program LETTER_COUNT_2, the text is scanned just once. Thus, the second program executes considerably faster than the first one and so only the program LETTER_COUNT_2 is refined.

Unfortunately, in Fortran, the subscripts of the array of counters cannot be "A", "B", etc. A subscript must be type integer. Therefore, subscripts 1 through 26 are used to count the number of occurrences of each letter of the alphabet and subscript 0 is used to count the characters that are not letters.

```
PROGRAM LETTER_COUNT_2
!  Count frequency of occurrence in a text
!  of each letter of the alphabet
!  Variables:
!      COUNT (0) = count of nonletters
!      COUNT (1) - COUNT (26) = counts of A/a - Z/z

   IMPLICIT NONE
   CHARACTER (LEN = *), PARAMETER :: ALPHABET =  &
         "ABCDEFGHIJKLMNOPQRSTUVWXYZabcdefghijklmnopqrstuvwxyz"
   CHARACTER (LEN = 200) :: TEXT
   INTEGER, DIMENSION (0 : 26) :: COUNT
   INTEGER :: IOS

   COUNT = 0   ! Set entire array to zero

   DO   ! until no more lines in file
      READ (*, "(A)", IOSTAT = IOS) TEXT
      IF (IOS < 0) EXIT
      PRINT *, "Input data  TEXT:", TEXT
      CALL COUNT_LETTERS
   END DO

   CALL PRINT_COUNTS

CONTAINS

SUBROUTINE COUNT_LETTERS
!  Count letters in one line of text
   INTEGER :: I, LETTER

   DO I = 1, LEN_TRIM (TEXT)
      LETTER = INDEX (ALPHABET, TEXT (I : I))
      IF (LETTER > 26) LETTER = LETTER - 26
      COUNT (LETTER) = COUNT (LETTER) + 1
   END DO
END SUBROUTINE COUNT_LETTERS

SUBROUTINE PRINT_COUNTS
!  PRINT THE FREQUENCY COUNTS

   PRINT *
   PRINT "(2A10)", "Letter", "Frequency"
```

```
    DO LETTER = 1, 26
        PRINT "(A10, I10)" &
                ALPHABET (LETTER : LETTER), COUNT (LETTER)
    END DO
    PRINT "(A10, I10)" "Other", COUNT (0)
END

END PROGRAM LETTER_COUNT_2

RUN LETTER_COUNT_2
```

    Input data TEXT: One of the important text analysis
    Input data TEXT: techniques (to determine authorship)
    Input data TEXT: is to make a frequency count of letters
    Input data TEXT: in the text.

Letter	Frequency
A	6
B	0
C	3
D	1
E	15
F	3
G	0
H	5
I	7
J	0
K	1
L	2
M	3
N	8
O	8
P	2
Q	2
R	5
S	6
T	16
U	4
V	0
W	0

```
        X        2
        Y        2
        Z        0
    Other       20
```

In the program LETTER_COUNT_2, the two internal subroutines are used to make the main part of the program easier to read.

5.2.7 Palindromes

Another aspect of text analysis is searching for patterns. Perhaps the text repeats itself every so often, or perhaps the lengths of the words form an interesting sequence of numbers. One pattern for which we search here is called a "palindrome", which means that the text reads the same from right to left as from left to right. The word "radar" is a palindrome, for example. Liberal palindromers customarily relax the rules so that punctuation, spacing, and capitalization are ignored. To liberal palindromers, the names "Eve", "Hannah", and "Otto" are all palindromes, as is the sentence

"Able was I ere I saw Elba."

something Napoleon might have said, except that he preferred speaking French.

The program PAL satisfies the most conservative palindromers. As the two sample runs show, it accepts the string

"NAT SAW I WAS TAN"

as a palindrome, but it rejects the string

"MADAM I'M ADAM"

It is easy to modify the program PAL to apply a more liberal test for palindromes; simply preprocess the text as in the program WORDS in Section 5.2.3. The subroutine BLANK_PUNCT converts all nonletters to blanks, the subroutine COMPRESS_BB can be modified to excise all blanks, and a subroutine FOLD_CASES can be written to change all lowercase letters to uppercase.

```
    PROGRAM PALINDROME
    ! Tests for a palindrome

    IMPLICIT NONE
    CHARACTER (LEN = 200) :: TEXT
    CHARACTER (LEN = *) :: C_OR_BLANK
    INTEGER :: I, J
```

```
LOGICAL MATCH

READ "(A)", TEXT
PRINT *, "Input data  TEXT:", TEXT

J = LEN_TRIM (TEXT)
MATCH = .TRUE.
DO I = 1, J / 2
    IF (TEXT (I : I) /= TEXT (J : J)) THEN
        MATCH = .FALSE.
        EXIT
    ELSE
        J = J - 1
    END IF
END DO

IF (MATCH) THEN
    PRINT *, "Palindrome"
ELSE
    PRINT *, "Not a palindrome"
    PRINT *, "Character", I, "from the left is", &
            C_OR_BLANK (TEXT (I : I))
    PRINT *, "Character", I, "from the right is", &
            C_OR_BLANK (TEXT (J : J))
END IF

CONTAINS

FUNCTION C_OR_BLANK (C)  RESULT (CB_RESULT)
! Tests if C is blank
! Returns "blank" if it is,
! Returns C otherwise
    CHARACTER (LEN = 5) :: CB_RESULT
    CHARACTER (LEN = *), INTENT (IN) :: C

    IF (C == " ") THEN
        CB_RESULT = "blank"
    ELSE
        CB_RESULT = C
    END IF
END

END PROGRAM PALINDROME
```

```
RUN PALINDROME

   Input data  TEXT:  NAT SAW I WAS TAN
   Palindrome

RUN PAL

   Input data  TEXT:  MADAM I'M ADAM
   Not a palindrome
   Character  5  from the left is  M
   Character  5  from the right is  blank
```

5.2.8 Exercises

1. Mark Twain wrote in "The Awful German Language" (in *A Tramp Abroad*) that he heard a California student in Heidelberg say, in one of his calmest moods, that he would rather decline two drinks than one German adjective. Write a program to help out this California student. The input data consists of a German adjective, for example,

    gut

    The output might be

    ```
    RUN DECLINE
    Input data  ADJ:  gut

       der gutes Mann      die gute Frau      das gute Kind
       des guten Mannes    der guten Frau     des guten Kindes
       dem guten Mann      der guten Frau     dem guten Kind
       den guten Mann      die gute Frau      das gute Kind
    ```

2. In a Fortran program using the old fixed-column source form, all blanks not within a character constant are ignored. Most Fortran compilers immediately remove these blanks to simplify the processing. (a) Write a program to move all blanks that occur in an input string to the end of the string. (b) Modify the program so that blanks within matched pairs of quotes or apostrophes are not removed. If the input data is

    DO 18 I = 1, 10

the output should be

```
RUN DEBLANK

    Input data  SOURCE:   DO 18 I = 1,  10
    DO18I=1,10
```

3.   Calculate the ratio of letters in the first half of the alphabet to letters in the second half of the alphabet in an input text.

4.   An alliteration is a sequence of words all starting with the same letter. Write a program ALLITERATION that counts how many consecutive words in an input text start with the letter P or p. For the sample input data:

```
In his popular paperback, "Party Pastimes People Prefer",
prominent polo player Paul Perkins presents pleasing
palindromes.
```

the output should be

```
RUN ALLITERATION

    14
```

6

Structures, Derived Types, and Modules

Fortran arrays allow data to be grouped, but only if all items have the same data type. It is often useful to use a structure, which is a compound object consisting of values that may be of different data types. Derived types are used to define the form of structures. It is possible to define new operations on defined types, creating abstract data types. Derived types and their operations may be defined in a module, making them globally available to all elements of a program, but a module also may be used to hold any global declarations.

6.1 Structures

A **structure** is a collection of values, not necessarily of the same type.

The objects that make up a structure are called its **components**. The components of a structure are identified by a Fortran name, whereas the elements of an array are identified by numerical subscripts.

A good example of the use of a structure might be provided by a simple text editor, such as the one supplied with many Basic programming language systems. Each line in a Basic program consists of a line number and one or more statements. When the editor is running, the program being edited could be represented in the editing program as two arrays, one to hold line numbers and one to hold the text of each line. Perhaps a better way to do this is to have a single object called LINE consisting of two components, an integer LINE_NUMBER and a character string STATEMENT. The entire program would then be an array of these structures, one for each line.

The components of a structure may be arrays or other structures. The elements of an array may be a structure. The elements of an array may not be arrays, but this functionality can be achieved with an array whose elements are structures whose only component is an array.

To give a slightly more complicated example, suppose we wish to store on our computer the contents of our little black book that contains names, addresses, phone numbers, and perhaps some remarks about each person in the book. In this case, each entry in the book can be treated as a structure containing four components: name, address, phone number, and remarks. The diagram in Figure 6-1 represents the organization of this information.

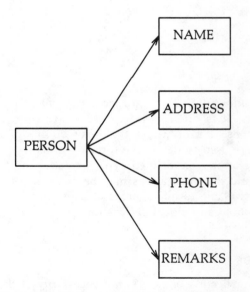

Figure 6-1 Diagram of the structure PERSON.

The name of the structure is PERSON, and it has four components: NAME, ADDRESS, PHONE, and REMARKS. Sometimes one or more components might be broken down into lower-level components. For instance, if the owner of the black book wanted to contact every acquaintance in a particular city, it would be helpful to have the component ADDRESS itself be a structure with components NUMBER, STREET, CITY, STATE, and postal ZIP_CODE. With this organization of the data, it would be possible to have a computer program scan the entries for city and state without having to look at the street address or zip code. For similar reasons, it might be convenient to subdivide each telephone number into a three-digit area code and a seven-digit local number, assuming all of the numbers are in North America. This more refined data organization is represented schematically by the structure in Figure 6-2.

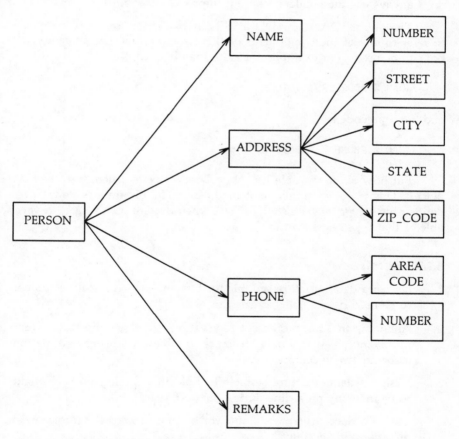

Figure 6-2 A more detailed diagram of the structure PERSON.

6.1.1 Referencing Structure Components

A component of a structure is referenced by writing the name of the structure followed by a percent sign (%) and then the name of the component. Suppose JOAN is a Fortran variable declared to be a structure with the components shown in the previous diagram. Then Joan's address is referenced by the expression:

    JOAN % ADDRESS

> *Style Note:* Blanks are permitted, but not required, around the percent sign in a structure component reference. We always use the blanks because it improves readability.

The object JOAN % ADDRESS is itself a structure. If it is desired to refer to one of the components of this structure, another percent symbol can be used. For example, the state Joan lives in is

    JOAN % ADDRESS % STATE

and her area code is

    JOAN % PHONE % AREA_CODE

But how is the variable JOAN declared to be a structure in the first place? This is not as simple as it might be. The programmer must first define a new type, say PERSON_TYPE, then declare JOAN to be a variable of that type, as shown in the next section.

6.1.2 Exercises

1. Design a data structure suitable for information on a college student to be used by the college registrar.

2. Assuming that airlines accept reservations for flights up to one year in advance, design a data structure suitable for storing information associated with each reservation.

3. Design a data structure suitable to hold information on each flight to be made by an airline during the next year.

4. Design a data structure suitable for a bank to keep the information on a checking account.

6.2 Derived Types

As was discussed in Section 1.2, there are five intrinsic Fortran data types: integer, real, complex, logical, and character. A programmer may **define** a new data type, called a **derived type**. In Fortran, a derived type always must be a structure. Conversely, a structure can only occur in a program as a value of some derived type.

6.2.1 Defining Types and Declaring Structures

A **type definition** begins with the keyword TYPE and is followed by the name of the type being defined. The components of the type are given in the form of ordinary type declarations. The type definition ends with the keywords END TYPE, optionally followed by the name of the type being defined.

Let's start first with the Basic editor example, for which each line of the program consists of a line number and some text. A definition of a type that would be useful in this example is

```
TYPE LINE
   INTEGER :: LINE_NUMBER
   CHARACTER (LEN = LINE_LENGTH) :: TEXT
END TYPE LINE
```

A variable NEW_LINE that could be used to hold the line number and text for one line of the program can then be declared by

```
TYPE (LINE) :: NEW_LINE
```

As shown in this example, a variable is declared to be a derived type with a declaration that is similar to the declaration of a variable of intrinsic type, except that the name of the intrinsic type is replaced by the keyword TYPE and the name of the type in parentheses. Note that in a type *definition*, the name of the type is not enclosed in parentheses, but in a type *declaration*, the name of the type is enclosed in parentheses.

The entire program to be edited could be represented by a single variable declared to be an array of values of type LINE:

```
TYPE (LINE), DIMENSION (MAX_LINES) :: BASIC_PROGRAM
```

With this declaration, some parts of the editor are a little easier to write and read because any operations that must be done to both a line number and the text can be expressed as a single operation on a line. For example, the PRINT statement of the subroutine LIST_PROGRAM that would have been written:

```
PRINT "(I5, X, A)", LINE_NUMBER (L), TEXT (L)
```

if two arrays were used is now written:

```
PRINT "(I5, X, A)", LINE (L)
```

Let us return to the example of the little black book. To define the type PHONE_TYPE in that example, AREA_CODE and NUMBER are each declared to be integer components:

```
TYPE PHONE_TYPE
    INTEGER :: AREA_CODE, NUMBER
END TYPE PHONE_TYPE
```

The definition of the type ADDRESS_TYPE is a little more complicated because some of the components are character strings and some are integers:

```
TYPE ADDRESS_TYPE
    INTEGER :: NUMBER
    CHARACTER (LEN = 30) :: STREET, CITY
    CHARACTER (LEN = 2) :: STATE
    INTEGER :: ZIP_CODE
END TYPE ADDRESS_TYPE
```

Now that the types ADDRESS_TYPE and PHONE_TYPE have been defined, it is possible to define a type suitable for one entry in the black book. Note that the names ADDRESS_TYPE and PHONE_TYPE were used for the names of the types, so that the names ADDRESS and PHONE could be used for the components of the type PERSON_TYPE.

```
TYPE PERSON_TYPE
    CHARACTER (LEN = 40) :: NAME
    TYPE (ADDRESS_TYPE) :: ADDRESS
    TYPE (PHONE_TYPE) :: PHONE
    CHARACTER (LEN = 100) :: REMARKS
END TYPE PERSON_TYPE
```

Finally, JOAN can be declared to be type PERSON_TYPE with the statement:

```
TYPE (PERSON_TYPE) :: JOAN
```

and the little black book can be declared to be an array of type PERSON_TYPE:

```
TYPE (PERSON_TYPE), DIMENSION (1000) :: BLACK_BOOK
```

6.2.2 Using Structures

To see how structures can be used in a program, suppose the contents of the little black book are stored as the value of the variable BLACK_BOOK declared above, and suppose we want an internal subroutine that will print out the names of all persons who live in a given postal zip code. The subroutine simply goes through the entire contents of the black book, one entry at a time, and prints out the name of any person with the appropriate zip code.

```
SUBROUTINE FIND_ZIP (ZIP)

    IMPLICIT NONE
    INTEGER, INTENT (IN) :: ZIP
    INTEGER :: ENTRY

    DO ENTRY = 1, NUMBER_OF_ENTRIES
       IF (BLACK_BOOK (ENTRY) % ADDRESS % ZIP_CODE == ZIP) THEN
          PRINT *, BLACK_BOOK (ENTRY) % NAME
       END IF
    END DO

END SUBROUTINE FIND_ZIP
```

This subroutine assumes, of course, that there is a variable named NUMBER_OF_ENTRIES with the appropriate value in the program that contains the subroutine FIND_ZIP.

> *Style Note:* If you use Fortran names followed by the suffix _TYPE to name derived types, the same name without the suffix is available for variables and structure components of that type. For example, the component NAME can be type NAME_TYPE and ADDRESS can be ADDRESS_TYPE. This convention is used frequently, but not always.

6.2.3 Structure Constructors

Each derived type declaration creates a function whose name is the same as that of the derived type. This function may be used to create a structure of the named type. The arguments for the function are values to be placed in the individual components of the structure. For example, using the type PHONE_TYPE in Section 6.2.1, an area code and telephone number may be assigned with the statement

```
JOAN % PHONE = PHONE_TYPE (505, 2750800)
```

It is not necessary that the function arguments be constants. If JOAN % ADDRESS has been given a value, the variable JOAN of type PERSON_TYPE can be assigned a value with the statement

```
JOAN = PERSON_TYPE ("JOAN DOE", JOHN % ADDRESS,  &
       PHONE_TYPE (505, FAX_NUMBER - 1),  &
       "Same address as husband John")
```

6.2.4 Exercises

1. Give a derived type declaration for a structure suitable for use by the U. S. Internal Revenue Service to hold information on each tax-payer.

2. Give a derived type declaration for the college student data structure designed in Exercise 1 of Section 6.1. Write statements to list all juniors with a gradepoint average of 2.8 or better in an array COLLEGE_STUDENTS of such structures.

3. Give a derived type declaration for the airline reservation data structure designed in Exercise 2 of Section 6.1. Write statements that tell the computer to list all the passengers on a given flight.

6.3 Modules

One way for procedures to share data is by passing values as arguments. This was discussed in Chapter 3. Passing arguments may not be the most effective way to share a large number of things among a large number of procedures, however. Just writing the lists of arguments and getting them all in the right order may be a significant chore. Also, on some systems, passing lots of arguments to procedures that are used frequently can reduce the efficiency of the program. Modules provide another way of sharing constants, variables, type definitions, and procedures; they also provide a useful way of packaging procedures in a "library" that may be accessible to many different programs.[1]

A **module** is a program unit that is not executed directly, but contains data specifications and procedures that may be utilized by other program units via the USE statement. To begin with a very simple example of a module, suppose we look again at the problem of storing and searching a list of lost credit cards discussed in Chapter 4. This application used an array LOST_CARD of integer card numbers and a single integer variable NUMBER_OF_LOST_CARDS. If several subroutines or functions need to use these variables, they can be placed in a module, here named LOST_CARD_MODULE.

```
MODULE LOST_CARD_MODULE

    INTEGER, DIMENSION (:), ALLOCATABLE :: LOST_CARD
    INTEGER :: NUMBER_OF_LOST_CARDS

END MODULE LOST_CARD_MODULE
```

Then a subroutine, such as one to search the list to see if a particular card is lost, can access this data with a USE statement.

```
SUBROUTINE SEARCH (CARD_NUMBER, FOUND)

    USE LOST_CARD_MODULE
    . . .
    DO I = 1, NUMBER_OF_LOST_CARDS
        IF (CARD_NUMBER == LOST_CARD (I)) THEN
        . . .
```

There is only one copy of each of the variables declared in the module. If two or more procedures USE the same module, all can reference the procedures and values of variables declared in their common module.

6.3.1 The USE Statement

The simple form of the USE statement is just the keyword USE followed by a list of the modules to be used.

A slightly different use of the MODULE might be to include the definition of constants that are different on various computer systems.

---

1. The sharing of values among procedures that was done quite awkwardly in Fortran 77 using the COMMON statement now may be done more cleanly using modules.

There could be a different version of this module for each Fortran compiler available at one site and the Fortran programmer could use the module appropriate for the computer being used. For example, there might be a module for the Ajax model 2002 computer that contains information such as the kind parameters that are available on the system. Part of it might look like the following:

```
MODULE AJAX_2002_PARAMETERS

    INTEGER, PARAMETER :: SINGLE = 4,   &
                          DOUBLE = 8,   &
                          QUAD = 12,    &
                          SHORT = 2,    &
                          ASCII = 1
        . . .
```

A program to be run on the Ajax 2002 could include this information and use the constants to declare variables. The program could then be transported to a different computer system by simply changing the USE statement to reference a different module.

```
PROGRAM EQUATION_SOLVER

    USE AJAX_2002_PARAMETERS
    REAL (KIND = QUAD) :: A, B, C
    INTEGER (KIND = SHORT) :: INDEX
    CHARACTER (LEN = 20, KIND = ASCII) :: NAME
        . . .
    NAME = ASCII_"John Doe"
    CALL CREATE_ARRAY (A, 100_SHORT)
        . . .
```

There are two ways to affect the way that variables and procedures in a module are accessed by another program unit. The first is that the names used in the module may be changed in the program unit using the module. This may be necessary because the program is using two or more modules that use the same name. Or it simply may be desirable to change the name to suit the taste or needs of the programmer of the program unit.

For example, in a subroutine using the lost card module, the programmer may have to write the variable name NUMBER_OF_LOST_CARDS many times and decide that the name is too long. This can be fixed by renaming the variable NOLC with the USE statement.

```
USE LOST_CARD_MODULE, NOLC => NUMBER_OF_LOST_CARDS
```

Any number of renames may appear in the USE statement.

The second way to affect the objects accessed in a module is to use the ONLY clause in the USE statement. Suppose, that from the AJAX_2002_PARAMETER module, only the values of DOUBLE and QUAD are needed. This can be accomplished with the USE statement:

```
USE AJAX_2002_PARAMETERS, ONLY :: DOUBLE, QUAD
```

If, in addition, it were desirable to rename the value of the parameter DOUBLE to DBL, this could be done with the statement:

```
USE AJAX_2002_PARAMETERS, ONLY :: DBL => DOUBLE, QUAD
```

There can be many names, with or without renaming, in a list after the double colon.

As we will see later in this chapter, it is possible for the programmer of the module to restrict the variables and procedures in the module that are accessible outside the module. This is done to "hide" implementation details in the module and is accomplished by declaring things PRIVATE.

6.3.2 Global Procedures

Modules may contain procedures that can be used by other program units. It would be reasonable, for example, to construct a module of special functions: Bessel, gamma, etc. This is done simply be placing subroutines or functions inside a module. Any program unit that uses that module will have access to all the procedures declared in that module, unless some have been designated as private.

However, the capability of having both data and procedures in a module can be used in a much more sophisticated way to create "abstract data types". An abstract data type is defined by indicating what values the data may assume and what operations may be performed on the data. Perhaps the best way to describe how all this works is to go through the steps of creating a new data type with some of its operations.

As described in Chapter 4, operations that are extended to arrays are performed on an element-by-element basis. This means, for example, that if A and B are arrays of real numbers, A * B means to multiple each element of A by the corresponding element of B. In many instances a Fortran array is used to represent a more structured mathematical object called a *matrix*. The addition of matrices is done by adding corresponding elements, but the multiplication of matrices is a more complicated operation than element-by-element multiplication. Suppose we want to provide to the Fortran programmer a new data type, MATRIX, together with a collection of operations suitable for the manipulation of matrices, such as addition, subtraction, multiplication, inversion, and eigenvalue calculation. This can be done by constructing a module called MATRIX_MODULE.

The first, and perhaps most important, decision is to figure out how to represent a matrix using the facilities built into Fortran. For an abstract data type used to model automobile traffic queues, this might be a more difficult task, but for matrices, it is pretty obvious that one of the possibilities is to use Fortran arrays. As we will see, this is not the only reasonable choice, and it is possible to change this decision if it becomes necessary to do so. The only way to create a new data type in Fortran 90 is by defining a new type that is a data structure. In our case, the structure could consist of one component that is an array, but it turns out to be convenient to store the dimensions of the matrix within the structure also. A definition that will do the trick is

```
TYPE MATRIX
    INTEGER :: M, N  ! Matrix is M x N
    REAL, DIMENSION (:, :), ALLOCATABLE :: A
END TYPE MATRIX
```

It might seem like the use of short names like M, N, and A is not good programming style, but it is common to use M and N as the number of rows and columns, referring to an $m \times n$ matrix. As we will see later, the name A will not ever be used except within the module, so it is not so important that the name be mnemonic. The component A is declared ALLOCATABLE so that we can represent matrices of any size.

The next thing to do is to define some operations for matrices. Addition is perhaps the easiest, but it is not completely trivial because a matrix, in our implementation, is not an array, but a structure with a component that is an array. One other complication is that the dimensions of the array must match if the addition is to make sense; we will produce a 0×0 array of results if this condition is not met. Thus, the function MATRIX_SUM might be written as

```
FUNCTION MATRIX_SUM (MATRIX_1, MATRIX_2)  &
      RESULT (MATRIX_SUM_RESULT)

   IMPLICIT NONE
   TYPE (MATRIX) :: MATRIX_SUM_RESULT
   TYPE (MATRIX), INTENT (IN) :: MATRIX_1, MATRIX_2

   IF (MATRIX_1 % M /= MATRIX_2 % M .OR.  &
      MATRIX_1 % N /= MATRIX_2 % N) THEN
      MATRIX_SUM_RESULT % M = 0
      MATRIX_SUM_RESULT % N = 0
      ALLOCATE (MATRIX_SUM_RESULT % A (0, 0))
   ELSE
      MATRIX_SUM_RESULT % M = MATRIX_1 % M
      MATRIX_SUM_RESULT % N = MATRIX_1 % N
      ALLOCATE (MATRIX_SUM_RESULT % A (MATRIX_1 % M,  &
                                       MATRIX_1 % N))
      MATRIX_SUM_RESULT % A = MATRIX_1 % A + MATRIX_2 % A
   END IF

END FUNCTION MATRIX_SUM
```

Subtraction and negation of matrices, as well as matrix multiplication, could be defined quite similarly. For matrix multiplication, there are two choices for the instructions that actually compute the values that go into the array. The first is to use the Fortran built-in function MATMUL; the other is to write instructions that do the computation using ordinary arithmetic operations. Which is used may depend on the quality of the MATMUL intrinsic available on your system.

It is nice to be able to add, subtract, negate, and multiply matrices, but how does one obtain the matrices to add, subtract, etc? One way to do this is to have another operation that creates a matrix and puts values in it. We will do this with a function whose argument is an ordinary Fortran array and whose result is type MATRIX.

```
FUNCTION ARRAY_TO_MATRIX (VALUES)  &
      RESULT (ARRAY_TO_MATRIX_RESULT)

   IMPLICIT NONE
   TYPE (MATRIX) :: ARRAY_TO_MATRIX_RESULT
   REAL, DIMENSION (:, :), INTENT (IN) :: VALUES
```

```
ARRAY_TO_MATRIX_RESULT % M = SIZE (VALUES, DIM = 1)
ARRAY_TO_MATRIX_RESULT % N = SIZE (VALUES, DIM = 2)
ALLOCATE (ARRAY_TO_MATRIX_RESULT % A &
      (ARRAY_TO_MATRIX_RESULT % M, ARRAY_TO_MATRIX_RESULT % N))
ARRAY_TO_MATRIX_RESULT % A = VALUES

END FUNCTION ARRAY_TO_MATRIX
```

The SIZE intrinsic function with the appropriate optional DIM arguments
give the dimensions of the array of values; this is the shape of the array
allocated to hold the result. Now we have ways of creating matrices and
computing with them, but no way to see the results of any of these computations. We need a subroutine PRINT_MATRIX to do this.

```
SUBROUTINE PRINT_MATRIX (MATRIX_1)

   IMPLICIT NONE
   TYPE (MATRIX), INTENT (IN) :: MATRIX_1
   INTEGER :: I, J

   DO I = 1, MATRIX_1 % M
      PRINT *, (MATRIX_1 % A (I, J), J = 1, MATRIX_1 % N)
   END DO

END SUBROUTINE PRINT_MATRIX
```

Of course, the subroutine to print the matrix must be a bit more
sophisticated if it is to be used to print a matrix with a large number of
columns.

6.3.3 Putting the Procedures in a Module

Now that we have enough operations defined on matrices to at least try
out something meaningful, we next need to package them all in a module. The structure of the module is as follows:

```
MODULE MATRIX_MODULE

   TYPE MATRIX
      INTEGER :: M, N   ! Matrix is M x N
      REAL, DIMENSION (:, :), ALLOCATABLE :: A
   END TYPE MATRIX

CONTAINS
```

```
FUNCTION MATRIX_SUM (MATRIX_1, MATRIX_2)  &
      RESULT (MATRIX_SUM_RESULT)
   . . .
END FUNCTION MATRIX_SUM

FUNCTION MATRIX_PROD (MATRIX_1, MATRIX_2)  &
      RESULT (MATRIX_PROD_RESULT)
   . . .
END FUNCTION MATRIX_PROD

FUNCTION ARRAY_TO_MATRIX (VALUES)  &
      RESULT (ARRAY_TO_MATRIX_RESULT)
   . . .
END FUNCTION ARRAY_TO_MATRIX

SUBROUTINE PRINT_MATRIX (MATRIX_1)
   . . .
END SUBROUTINE PRINT_MATRIX

END MODULE MATRIX
```

With the module available, we can write a simple program to test out the matrix manipulation facilities provided.

```
PROGRAM MATRIX_TEST

IMPLICIT NONE

USE MATRIX_MODULE

TYPE (MATRIX) :: M1, M2
REAL, DIMENSION (3, 3) :: A1, A2

! Set up two test arrays to be used
! to assign values to matrices M1 and M2
DO I = 1, 3
   A1 (I, :) = I
   A2 (:, I) = I
END DO

M1 = ARRAY_TO_MATRIX (A1)
M2 = ARRAY_TO_MATRIX (A2)
```

```
       CALL PRINT_MATRIX (MATRIX_SUM (M1, M2))
       CALL PRINT_MATRIX (MATRIX_PROD (M1, M2))

   END PROGRAM MATRIX_TEST
```

6.3.4 Generic Operators

The module works, but it is not very pretty. In mathematics, the symbols + and – are used to represent matrix operations. It would be nice to do the same in Fortran, and it is possible to do so by extending the generic properties of the operations already built into Fortran. Note that + already can be used to add two integers, two real values, or one of each. The intrinsic operator + also can be used to add two arrays of the same shape. In that sense, addition is already generic. We now extend the meaning of this operation to our own newly defined type, MATRIX. This is done with an interface block within the module as follows:

```
   INTERFACE OPERATOR ( + )

       FUNCTION MATRIX_SUM (MATRIX_1, MATRIX_2)  &
           RESULT (MATRIX_SUM_RESULT)

          IMPLICIT NONE
          TYPE (MATRIX), INTENT (IN) :: MATRIX_1, MATRIX_2
          TYPE (MATRIX) :: MATRIX_SUM_RESULT

       END FUNCTION MATRIX_SUM

   END INTERFACE
```

This says that the + operator is now to have meaning when both operands are matrices and that the operation to be performed is the one given by the function MATRIX_SUM. Similar interfaces can be written in the module to make the operations – and * be generic in the same sense.

This idea can be taken even further by making + a valid operation between a matrix and a scalar, or even also be a unary operation for matrices, just as + is a unary operation for integers and reals. To do this more lines are added to the same interface block and, of course, the functions must be written. With all this done, the interface block might look like:

```
INTERFACE OPERATOR ( + )

    FUNCTION MATRIX_SUM (MATRIX_1, MATRIX_2)  &
          RESULT (MATRIX_SUM_RESULT)
      TYPE (MATRIX), INTENT (IN) :: MATRIX_1, MATRIX_2
      TYPE (MATRIX) :: MATRIX_SUM_RESULT
    END FUNCTION MATRIX_SUM

    FUNCTION MATRIX_SCALAR_SUM (MATRIX_1, X_2)  &
          RESULT (MATRIX_SCALAR_SUM_RESULT)
      TYPE (MATRIX), INTENT (IN) :: MATRIX_1
      TYPE (MATRIX) :: MATRIX_SCALAR_SUM_RESULT
      REAL, INTENT (IN) :: X_2
    END FUNCTION MATRIX_SCALAR_SUM

    FUNCTION SCALAR_MATRIX_SUM (X_1, MATRIX_2)  &
          RESULT (SCALAR_MATRIX_SUM_RESULT)
      TYPE (MATRIX), INTENT (IN) :: MATRIX_2
      TYPE (MATRIX) :: SCALAR_MATRIX_SUM_RESULT
      REAL, INTENT (IN) :: X_1
    END FUNCTION SCALAR_MATRIX_SUM

    FUNCTION MATRIX_IDENT (MATRIX_SIZE)  &
          RESULT (MATRIX_IDENT_RESULT)
      INTEGER, INTENT (IN) :: MATRIX_SIZE
      TYPE (MATRIX) :: MATRIX_IDENT_RESULT
    END FUNCTION MATRIX_IDENT

END INTERFACE
```

Similar interface blocks and functions can be written to make the other operations utilize symbols, such as – and *. With all these in place, the test program can be revised:

```
PROGRAM MATRIX_TEST

    IMPLICIT NONE

    USE MATRIX_MODULE

    TYPE (MATRIX) :: M1, M2
    REAL, DIMENSION (3, 3) :: A1, A2
```

```
! Set up two test arrays to be used
! to assign values to matrices M1 and M2
DO I = 1, 3
    A1 (I, :) = I
    A2 (:, I) = I
END DO

M1 = ARRAY_TO_MATRIX (A1)
M2 = ARRAY_TO_MATRIX (A2)

CALL PRINT_MATRIX (M1 + M2)
CALL PRINT_MATRIX (M1 * M2)

END PROGRAM MATRIX_TEST
```

The only difference is that the infix operators + and * are used for matrix addition and multiplication; but this helps the reader, because these symbols correspond to those used for addition and multiplication of other data types in Fortran.

The precedence of the addition operator when used to add matrices is the same as when it is used to add integers. This holds true for all built-in operators that are extended.

6.3.5 User-Defined Operators

In addition to extending the meaning of the Fortran built-in operators, it is possible to make up new names for operators. If we were to add the operation of matrix inversion to the matrix module, there is probably not a good unary built-in operator that would be suitable to extend to this use. Any name consisting of from 1 to 31 letters preceded and followed by a period may be used, except for the names of logical constants and intrinsic operators. For example, we might pick .INVERSE. for the name of the matrix inversion function, place it in an interface, and write a function of one matrix argument to produce the matrix inverse.

```
INTERFACE OPERATOR (.INVERSE.)

    FUNCTION INVERSE (MATRIX_1)  RESULT (INVERSE_RESULT)

        TYPE (MATRIX), INTENT (IN) :: MATRIX_1
        TYPE (MATRIX) :: INVERSE_RESULT

    END FUNCTION INVERSE

END INTERFACE
```

After the function INVERSE is written, the inverse of a matrix can be calculated in an expression such as the following:

```
1.0 + .INVERSE. A
```

The generic binary operator + in this example is executed by a reference to the function SCALAR_MATRIX_SUM.

The precedence of a defined binary operator is always lower than all other operators, and the precedence of a defined unary operator is always higher than all other operators. This means, for example, that the previous example expression is treated as if it were written:

```
1.0 + (.INVERSE. A)
```

6.3.6 Generic Assignment

The name for the function ARRAY_TO_MATRIX was picked because it converts an array to a matrix. Another way to deal with the necessity of converting an array of real values into a structure of type matrix is to extend the assignment operator to work with matrix data types, just as some operators were extended. This also is done with an interface block, in which the keyword ASSIGNMENT is used. A property of assignment procedures is that they must be subroutines, not functions. Thus, the function ARRAY_TO_MATRIX is rewritten as a subroutine with two arguments, the first being the place the result is stored and the second being the array of values. An interface block is created indicating that this function extends the generic properties of assignment.

```
INTERFACE ASSIGNMENT ( = )

    SUBROUTINE ARRAY_TO_MATRIX (MATRIX_RESULT, VALUES)

        IMPLICIT NONE
        TYPE (MATRIX), INTENT (OUT) :: MATRIX_RESULT
        REAL, DIMENSION (:, :), INTENT (IN) :: VALUES

    END SUBROUTINE ARRAY_TO_MATRIX

END INTERFACE

SUBROUTINE ARRAY_TO_MATRIX (MATRIX_RESULT, VALUES)

    IMPLICIT NONE
    TYPE (MATRIX), INTENT (OUT) :: MATRIX_RESULT
    REAL, DIMENSION (:, :), INTENT (IN) :: VALUES

    MATRIX_RESULT % M = SIZE (VALUES, DIM = 1)
    MATRIX_RESULT % N = SIZE (VALUES, DIM = 2)
    ALLOCATE (MATRIX_RESULT % A (MATRIX_RESULT % M,  &
                                 MATRIX_RESULT % N))
    MATRIX_RESULT % A = VALUES

END SUBROUTINE ARRAY_TO_MATRIX
```

Now we can make the test program even a little more readable by using the newly created version of assignment.

```
PROGRAM MATRIX_TEST

    IMPLICIT NONE

    USE MATRIX_MODULE

    TYPE (MATRIX) :: M1, M2
    REAL, DIMENSION (3, 3) :: A1, A2
```

```
! Set up two test arrays to be used
! to assign values to matrices M1 and M2
DO I = 1, 3
   A1 (I, :) = I
   A2 (:, I) = I
END DO

M1 = A1
M2 = A2

CALL PRINT_MATRIX (M1 + M2)
CALL PRINT_MATRIX (M1 * M2)

END PROGRAM MATRIX_TEST
```

Assignment of one matrix to another is already allowed providing the dimensions of the array components match. Assignment could be extended further to allow assignment of a scalar real or integer value to a matrix, causing the scalar to be placed in each position of the array.

6.3.7 The PRIVATE Attribute

As was discussed above, the USE statement with the ONLY clause provides a way to exclude some of the objects in a module while including others. Conversely, the PRIVATE attribute allows the author of a module to prevent objects in the module from being used. To see why this is useful, suppose we decide that the implementation of the matrix module could be improved some way, or even that, for a particular application, the use of the module is primarily with sparse matrices and the values should be stored using linked lists rather than arrays. The way the module has been written, a program using the module can access any of the parts of the structure, such as

```
M1 % A (2, 3)
```

This may be quite useful, but if the underlying implementation is changed so that the elements are stored using a linked list, this notation will no longer make sense.

The module may specify that the internal structure of the type MATRIX is PRIVATE, which means that outside the module, none of its components may be accessed. This prevents programs using the module from accessing the structure directly and necessitates more functions to allow the user to get at individual elements of a matrix. The benefit is that if the form of the type MATRIX is changed for some reason, only programs within the module have to be changed; it is guaranteed that no programs using the module can access the components of the structure except through calls to functions within the module.

In the matrix module, it is possible to hide the internal structure of the data type MATRIX by changing its definition to

```
TYPE MATRIX
   PRIVATE
   INTEGER :: M, N   ! Matrix is M x N
   REAL, DIMENSION (:, :), ALLOCATABLE :: A
END TYPE MATRIX
```

It is also possible to list types, constants, variables, and procedures in a PRIVATE statement within a module. This prevents their use outside the module, which is desirable for objects that are only to be used in the module to build the functions that are intended to be exported. One simple example might be a subroutine that is called to do some of the computations necessary to invert a matrix. The matrix inversion routine would be available outside the module, but the lower-level routine would not be.

```
PRIVATE :: INV_SUB_1, INV_SUB_2
```

6.3.8 Exercises

1. Write a subroutine SCALAR_TO_MATRIX that assigns the scalar expression in the second argument to the first argument, a matrix. Assume that the size components M and N of the first argument are defined before the call or that the array component A is allocated. The value of the scalar expression should be placed in each position of the matrix. Extend the assignment interface to include this case.

2. Extend the operator * so that it applies to one scalar and one matrix. Note that two functions must be written, one for each position of the matrix. Add the appropriate information to the interface block for the operator *.

3. Write a function IDENT (N) that returns the N × N identity matrix. This would be a natural addition to the matrix module.

4. Assuming that the components of the type MATRIX have been given the PRIVATE attribute as shown above, how can the user of the module access one element of the matrix?

7

Recursion

Recursion may be thought of as a mechanism to handle flow of control in a program, but its implementation requires dynamic storage allocation; that is why it was not in Fortran 77. Each time a recursive function or subroutine is called, there must be space for the variables that are local to the procedure. There is no way to tell at compile time how many times the routine will call itself, hence there is no way to determine the amount of storage needed to store copies of the variables local to the procedure.

7.1 Recursive Procedures

The use of recursion is a very powerful tool for constructing programs that otherwise can be quite complex, particularly if the process being modeled is described recursively. However, depending on the implementation available, recursion can require a substantial amount of runtime overhead. Thus, the use of recursion illustrates the classic tradeoff between time spent in constructing and maintaining a program and execution time. In some cases, a process described recursively can be transformed into an iterative process in a very straightforward manner; in other cases, it is very difficult and the resulting procedure is very difficult to follow. It is in these cases that recursion is such a valuable tool. We will illustrate some examples that fall into each category.

7.1.1 The Factorial Function

First, let's look at the mathematical definition of the factorial function, $n!$, defined for nonnegative integers. It is a simple example that will illustrate many of the important ideas relating to recursion.

$$0! = 1$$

$$n! = n \times (n-1)! \quad \text{for } n > 0$$

To use this definition to calculate 4!, apply the second line of the definition with $n = 4$ to get $4! = 4 \times 3!$. To finish the calculation we need the value of 3!, which can be determined by using the second line of the definition again. $3! = 3 \times 2!$, so that $4! = 4 \times 3 \times 2!$. Using the second line of the definition two more times yields $2! = 2 \times 1!$ and $1! = 1 \times 0!$. Finally, the first line of the definition can be applied to compute $0! = 1$. Plugging all these values back in produces the computation

$$4! = 4 \times 3 \times 2 \times 1 \times 1 = 24$$

From this, it is pretty obvious that an equivalent definition for $n!$ is

$$n! = n \times (n-1) \times (n-2) \times \ \cdots \ \times 3 \times 2 \times 1$$

for integers greater than zero. So this is an example for which it should be quite easy to write an iterative program as well as a recursive one, but to illustrate the recursive technique, let's first look at the recursive version. It should be easy to understand because it follows the recursive definition very closely.

```
RECURSIVE FUNCTION FACTORIAL (N) RESULT (FACTORIAL_RESULT)

    INTEGER, INTENT (IN) :: N
    INTEGER :: FACTORIAL_RESULT
```

```
IF (N <= 0) THEN
    FACTORIAL_RESULT = 1
ELSE
    FACTORIAL_RESULT = N * FACTORIAL (N - 1)
END IF

END FUNCTION FACTORIAL
```

For a recursive function or subroutine, the keyword RECURSIVE must be placed on the procedure heading line. The RESULT clause is absolutely essential in this program; otherwise, there would be no way to distinguish the use of FACTORIAL as a result variable from the use of FACTORIAL as a function, as is done in the second assignment statement of the procedure. This version of the function returns a result of 1 for a negative value of N for which the mathematical factorial function $n!$ is undefined. Another alternative is to treat a negative argument as an error, but returning 1 keeps the example simple.

This program illustrates something often called **tail recursion**, which means that the only recursive call occurs as the very last step in the computation of the procedure. It is always easy to turn a process involving only tail recursion into an iterative process. Here is the iterative version of the factorial function. Although not strictly necessary, the result clause is still used in accordance with the style rules suggested in Chapter 3.

```
FUNCTION FACTORIAL (N)  RESULT (FACTORIAL_RESULT)

    INTEGER, INTENT (IN) :: N
    INTEGER :: FACTORIAL_RESULT
    INTEGER :: I

    FACTORIAL_RESULT = 1
    DO I = 2, N
        FACTORIAL_RESULT = I * FACTORIAL_RESULT
    END DO

END FUNCTION FACTORIAL
```

Note that the DO loop will be executed zero times for any value of N that is less than 2, so that the value of 1 will be returned in these cases.

7.1.2 Exponentiation

Exponentiation, like the factorial function, has both an iterative definition and a recursive definition. They are

$$x^0 = 1$$

$$x^n = x \times x^{n-1} \quad \text{for } n > 1$$

and

$$x^n = x \times x \times \ \cdots \ x \quad n \text{ times}$$

Since Fortran has an exponentiation operator (**) for real numbers, it is not necessary to write a procedure to do that. However, it may be necessary to write an exponentiation procedure for a new data type, such as matrices. So, let's suppose that you are writing a module to do matrix arithmetic and the representation of the matrix is the type MATRIX developed in the preceding sections. To make things look nicer, also suppose that the plus operator (+) and the multiply operator (*) have been overloaded to mean addition and multiplication for our matrix data type, and that there is a function IDENT (N) that returns the identity matrix. The task is to write a procedure for the module that will do matrix exponentiation. This time, the simple iterative procedure is presented first.

```
FUNCTION MATRIX_EXP (MATRIX_1, N)  RESULT (MATRIX_EXP_RESULT)

    TYPE (MATRIX), INTENT (IN) :: MATRIX_1
    INTEGER, INTENT (IN) :: N
    TYPE (MATRIX) :: MATRIX_EXP_RESULT
    INTEGER :: I

    MATRIX_EXP_RESULT = IDENT (MATRIX_1 % M)
    DO I = 2, N
       MATRIX_EXP_RESULT = MATRIX_EXP_RESULT * MATRIX_1
    END DO

END FUNCTION MATRIX_EXP
```

It would be straightforward to use the recursive factorial function as a model and construct a recursive version of the exponentiation function; but this is another example of tail recursion, and there is no real advantage to the recursive version. However, think about how you would calculate x^{18} on a calculator that does not have exponentiation as a built-in operator. The clever way is to compute x^2 by squaring x, x^4 by squaring x^2, x^8 by squaring x^4, x^{16} by squaring x^8, and finally x^{18} by multiplying the results obtained for x^{16} and x^2. This involves quite a lot fewer multiplications than doing the computation the hard way by multiplying x by itself 18 times. To utilize this scheme to construct a program is fairly tricky. It involves computing all of the appropriate powers x^2, x^4, x^8, ..., then multiplying together the powers that have a 1 in the appropriate position in the binary representation of n. For example, since $18 = 10010_2$, powers that need to be multiplied are 16 and 2. It happens that there is a recursive way of doing this that is quite easy to program. It relies on the fact that x^n can be defined with the following less obvious recursive definition below. The trick that leads to the more efficient recursive exponentiation function is to think of the problem "top-down" instead of "bottom-up". That is, solve the problem of computing x^{18} by computing x^9 and squaring the result. Computing x^9 is almost as simple: square x^4 and multiply the result by x. Eventually, this leads to the problem of computing x^0, which is 1. The recursive definition we are looking for is

$$x^0 = 1$$

$$x^n = \begin{cases} (x^{\lfloor n/2 \rfloor})^2 & \text{for } n \text{ even, } n > 0 \\ (x^{\lfloor n/2 \rfloor})^2 \times x & \text{for } n \text{ odd, } n > 0 \end{cases}$$

where $\lfloor\ \rfloor$ is the floor function, which for positive integers is the largest integer less than or equal to its argument. This definition can be used to construct a MATRIX_EXP function that is more efficient than the iterative version.

```
RECURSIVE FUNCTION MATRIX_EXP (MATRIX_1, N)  &
        RESULT (MATRIX_EXP_RESULT)

    TYPE (MATRIX), INTENT (IN) :: MATRIX_1
    INTEGER, INTENT (IN) :: N
    TYPE (MATRIX) :: MATRIX_EXP_RESULT
    TYPE (MATRIX) :: TEMP_M

    IF (N <= 0) THEN
        MATRIX_EXP_RESULT = IDENT (MATRIX_1 % M)
```

```
    ELSE
       TEMP_M = MATRIX_EXP (MATRIX_1, INT (N / 2))
       IF (MOD (N, 2) == 0) THEN
          MATRIX_EXP_RESULT = TEMP_M * TEMP_M
       ELSE
          MATRIX_EXP_RESULT = TEMP_M * TEMP_M * MATRIX_1
       END IF
    END IF

    END FUNCTION MATRIX_EXP
```

7.1.3 The Fibonacci Sequence

This next example illustrates not only the use of recursion when an iterative program would do as well, but a case in which a decision to implement a program based on a recursive definition yields an algorithm that has very poor running time even if recursive function calls had no overhead.

The **Fibonacci sequence** 1, 1, 2, 3, 5, 8, 13, 21, 34, ..., arises in such diverse applications as the number of petals in a daisy, the maximum steps it takes to recognize a sequence of characters, and the most pleasing proportions for a rectangle, the "golden section" of Renaissance artists and mathematicians. It is defined by the relations

$$f(1) = 1$$

$$f(2) = 1$$

$$f(n) = f(n-1) + f(n-2) \quad \text{for } n > 2$$

Starting with the third term, each Fibonacci number is the sum of the two previous Fibonacci numbers. Naive incorporation of the recurrence relation in a recursive function program produces an execution time disaster for all but the smallest values of n.

```
    RECURSIVE FUNCTION FIBONACCI (N) RESULT (FIBONACCI_RESULT)

       INTEGER, INTENT (IN) :: N
       INTEGER :: FIBONACCI_RESULT
```

```
      IF (N <= 2) THEN
          FIBONACCI_RESULT = 1
      ELSE
          FIBONACCI_RESULT = FIBONACCI (N - 1) + FIBONACCI (N - 2)
      END IF

  END FUNCTION FIBONACCI
```

If the function is used to calculate $f(7)$, for example, the recursive calls request computation of $f(6)$ and $f(5)$. Then the computation of $f(6)$ again calls for the computation of $f(5)$ as well as $f(4)$. Thus, values of f are computed over and over with the same argument. In fact, the number of recursive function calls resulting from a single call to FIBONACCI (N) exceeds the answer, which is approximately 0.447×1.618^N. The execution time of this function is called **exponential** because it depends on a number greater than 1 raised to the Nth power.

To make this computation much more efficient, values of f must be saved and reused when needed, rather than being recomputed. Perhaps the most straightforward way to do this is to first compute $f(1)$, then $f(2)$, then $f(3)$, etc. These values are stored in an array in the second attempt to implement the Fibonacci function.

```
  FUNCTION FIBONACCI (N)  RESULT (FIBONACCI_RESULT)

      INTEGER, INTENT (IN) :: N
      INTEGER :: FIBONACCI_RESULT
      INTEGER, DIMENSION (:), ALLOCATABLE :: F
      INTEGER :: I

      IF (N <= 2) THEN
          FIBONACCI_RESULT = 1
      ELSE
          ALLOCATE (F (N))
          F (1) = 1
          F (2) = 1
          DO I = 3, N
             F (I) = F (I - 1) + F (I - 2)
          END DO
          FIBONACCI_RESULT = F (N)
      END IF

  END FUNCTION FIBONACCI
```

This function is efficient in terms of the time it takes to do the computation, but it is inefficient in its use of storage because it reserves an array of size N when only the two most recently computed values are ever needed. The next function to compute the Fibonacci sequence simply uses the variables F_I and F_I_MINUS_1 to hold the two most recently computed values of f.

```
FUNCTION FIBONACCI (N) RESULT (FIBONACCI_RESULT)

    INTEGER, INTENT (IN) :: N
    INTEGER :: FIBONACCI_RESULT
    INTEGER :: F_I, F_I_MINUS_1, I

    IF (N <= 2) THEN
        FIBONACCI_RESULT = 1
    ELSE
        F_I_MINUS_1 = 1
        F_I = 1
        DO I = 3, N
            F_I = F_I + F_I_MINUS_1
            F_I_MINUS_1 = F_I - F_I_MINUS_1
        END DO
        FIBONACCI_RESULT = F_I
    END IF

    END FUNCTION FIBONACCI
```

This program, although containing two statements that take a little time to understand, is by far the most time and space efficient of those shown in this section. The increases are so dramatic in terms of both time and space that it is worth having a couple of lines of code that are not completely obvious.

7.1.4 The Towers of Hanoi

According to legend, there is a temple in Hanoi which contains a ritual apparatus consisting of 3 posts and 64 gold disks of graduated size that fit on the posts. When the temple was built, all 64 gold disks were placed on the first post with the largest on the bottom and the smallest on the top, as shown schematically in Figure 7-1. It is the sole occupation of the priests of the temple to move all the gold disks systematically until all 64 gold disks are on the third post, at which time the world will come to an end.

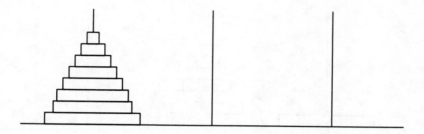

Figure 7-1 The towers of Hanoi.

There are only two rules that must be followed:

1. Disks must be moved from post to post one at a time.

2. A larger disk may never rest on top of a smaller disk on the same post.

A smaller version of this apparatus with only eight disks made of plastic is sold as a recreational puzzle. The sequence of moves necessary to solve the simpler puzzle is not obvious and often takes hours to figure out. We propose to write a simple recursive procedure HANOI that prints complete directions for moving any number of disks from one post to another. It is extremely difficult to write a nonrecursive procedure to print these directions.

The recursive procedure HANOI is based on the following top-down analysis of the problem. Suppose n disks are to be moved from a starting post to a final post. Because the largest of these n disks can never rest on a smaller disk, at the time the largest disk is moved, all $n - 1$ smaller disks must be stacked on the free middle post as shown in Figure 7-2.

For the number of disks $n > 1$, the algorithm has 3 steps.

1. Legally move the top $n - 1$ disks from the starting post to the free post.

2. Move the largest disk from the starting post to the final post.

3. Legally move the $n - 1$ disks from the free post to the final post.

The middle step involves printing a single move instruction. The first and third steps represent simpler instances of the same problem, simpler in this case because fewer disks must be moved. Therefore, the first and third steps may be handled by recursive procedure calls. In case $n = 1$, only the second step should be executed, and this provides a nonrecursive path through the procedure for the simplest case. The Fortran

Figure 7-2 Locations of the disks when the largest disk is to be moved.

subroutine HANOI, its test program TEST_HANOI, and a sample execution output for four disks is shown.

```
PROGRAM TEST_HANOI

    IMPLICIT NONE
    INTEGER :: NUMBER_OF_DISKS

    READ *, NUMBER_OF_DISKS
    PRINT *, "Input data  NUMBER_OF_DISKS: ", NUMBER_OF_DISKS
    PRINT *
    CALL HANOI (NUMBER_OF_DISKS, 1, 3);

CONTAINS

    SUBROUTINE HANOI (NUMBER_OF_DISKS, STARTING_POST, GOAL_POST)

        IMPLICIT NONE
        INTEGER :: NUMBER_OF_DISKS, STARTING_POST, GOAL_POST
        INTEGER :: FREE_POST
        INTEGER, PARAMETER :: ALL_POSTS = 6

        FREE_POST := ALL_POSTS - STARTING_POST - GOAL_POST
        IF (NUMBER_OF_DISKS > 1)  &
            CALL HANOI (NUMBER_OF_DISKS - 1,  &
                        STARTING_POST, FREE_POST)

        PRINT *, "Move disk ", NUMBER_OF_DISKS,  &
                " from post ", STARTING_POST,  &
                " to post ", GOAL_POST
```

```
      IF (NUMBER_OF_DISKS > 1)   &
          CALL HANOI (NUMBER_OF_DISKS - 1, FREE_POST, GOAL_POST)
      END SUBROUTINE HANOI

END PROGRAM TEST_HANOI

RUN TEST_HANOI

Input data  NUMBER_OF_DISKS: 4

Move disk 1 from post 1 to post 2
Move disk 2 from post 1 to post 3
Move disk 1 from post 2 to post 3
Move disk 3 from post 1 to post 2
Move disk 1 from post 3 to post 1
Move disk 2 from post 3 to post 2
Move disk 1 from post 1 to post 2
Move disk 4 from post 1 to post 3
Move disk 1 from post 2 to post 3
Move disk 2 from post 2 to post 1
Move disk 1 from post 3 to post 1
Move disk 3 from post 2 to post 3
Move disk 1 from post 1 to post 2
Move disk 2 from post 1 to post 3
Move disk 1 from post 2 to post 3
```

7.1.5 Indirect Recursion

It is possible for procedures A and B to be indirectly recursive in the sense that A calls B and B calls A. To illustrate this kind of recursion, suppose we need to write a procedure that will recognize certain character strings. An actual example might arise in biochemistry with the need to recognize certain chemical chains, or in cryptography to recognize repetitions of certain patterns that might help to crack the code, or in a compiler to recognize and parse syntactic constructs in a source program. To keep our example simple, suppose a type A string of characters is the letter "A" or a string of type B preceded by the letter "X" and followed by the letter "Z". A type B string of characters is a type A string preceded by two occurrences of the letter "B". Examples of type A strings are A and XBBXBBAZZ. Examples of type B strings are BBA and BBXBBAZ. To write logical functions that determine if a string is type A, just follow the definition. The function TYPE_A is recursive because it calls the function TYPE_B which, in turn, calls TYPE_A.

```
RECURSIVE FUNCTION TYPE_A (STRING) RESULT (TYPE_A_RESULT)

   LOGICAL :: TYPE_A_RESULT
   CHARACTER (LEN = *), INTENT (IN) :: STRING

   IF (STRING == "A") THEN
      TYPE_A_RESULT = .TRUE.
   ELSE IF (STRING (1:1) == "X") .AND.  &
        (STRING (LEN (STRING) : LEN (STRING)) == "Z") THEN
      TYPE_A_RESULT = TYPE_B (STRING (2 : LEN (STRING) - 1))
   ELSE
      TYPE_A_RESULT = .FALSE.
   END IF

END FUNCTION TYPE_A


RECURSIVE FUNCTION TYPE_B (STRING) RESULT (TYPE_B_RESULT)

   CHARACTER (LEN = *), INTENT (IN) :: STRING
   LOGICAL :: TYPE_B_RESULT

   IF (STRING (1:2) == "BB") THEN
      TYPE_B_RESULT = TYPE_A (STRING (3 : LEN (STRING)))
   ELSE
      TYPE_B_RESULT = .FALSE.
   END IF

END FUNCTION TYPE_A
```

7.1.6 Exercises

1.   Write a recursive function BC (N, K) to compute the binomial coefficient $\begin{pmatrix} n \\ k \end{pmatrix}$, $0 \le k \le n$, using the relations:

$$\begin{pmatrix} n \\ 0 \end{pmatrix} = 1 \qquad \begin{pmatrix} n \\ n \end{pmatrix} = 1$$

$$\binom{n}{0} = \binom{n-1}{k-1} + \binom{n-1}{k} = \text{for } 0 < k < n$$

2. Write an efficient program to compute the binomial coefficient $\binom{n}{k}$.

3. The following recurrence defines $f(n)$ for all nonnegative integer values of n.

$$f(0) = 0$$

$$f(1) = f(2) = 1$$

$$f(n) = 2f(n-1) + f(n-2) - f(n-3) \text{ for } n > 2$$

Write a function F to compute $f(n)$, $n > 0$. Also have your program verify that for $0 \le n \le 1000$, $f(n) = [(-1)^{n+1} + 2^n]/3$.

4. For positive integers a and b, the greatest common divisor of a and b satisfies the following recurrence relationship:

$$gcd(a, b) = b \ \text{ if } a \bmod b = 0$$

$$gcd(a, b) = gcd(b, a \bmod b) \ \text{ if } a \bmod b \ne 0$$

Write a recursive function GCD (A, B) using these recurrences. Test the program by finding $gcd(24, 36)$, $gcd(16, 13)$, $gcd(17, 119)$, and $gcd(177, 228)$.

7.2 Case Study: Numerical Integration

In Sections 2.5.6 and 3.10 we wrote function procedures to approximate the definite integral

$$\int_a^b f(x)\,dx$$

that represents the area bounded by the lines $x = a$, $x = b$, $y = 0$, and the curve $y = f(x)$, by a sum of the areas of n "inscribed" trapezoids, each of width h. If the answer so obtained is not sufficiently accurate, a better approximation is obtained by increasing the number of trapezoids, n, and proportionately decreasing the width of each trapezoid, h.

Decreasing the width of each trapezoid may not be the most efficient way to improve the accuracy of a trapezoidal approximation. In regions where the curve $y = f(x)$ is relatively straight, trapezoids approximate the area closely, and further reductions in the width of the trapezoids produces little further reduction in the error, which is already small. In regions where the curve $y = f(x)$ bends sharply, on the other hand, the area under the curve is approximated less well by trapezoids, and it would pay to concentrate the extra work of computing the areas of thinner trapezoids in such regions.

The recursive function INTEGRAL written in this section uses an **adaptive trapezoidal** method of approximating the area under a curve, requesting extra calculations through a recursive call only in those regions where the approximation by trapezoids is not yet sufficiently accurate.

Mathematicians tell us that the error $E(h)$ in approximating the area of the almost rectangular region with top boundary $y = f(x)$ by the area of one trapezoid is approximately $-1/12 f''(c) h^3$, where h is the width of the trapezoid, and c is any x value in the interval. The dependence of $E(h)$ on h^3 shows why the error drops rapidly as h decreases, and the dependence of $E(h)$ on $f''(c)$ shows why the error is smaller when $f''(x)$ is smaller, at places such as near inflection points (where the tangent line crosses the curve) where $f''(x) = 0$. If the same region is approximated by the sum of the areas of two trapezoids, each of width $h/2$, the error in each of them is approximately $-1/12 f''(c)(h/2)^3$, or $1/8 E(h)$, but since there are two trapezoids, the total error $E(h/2)$ is approximately $1/4 E(h)$. If $T(h)$ and $T(h/2)$ are the two trapezoidal approximations and I is the exact integral, we have

$$T(h/2) - T(h) = (I - E(h/2)) - (I - E(h))$$

$$= -E(h/2) + E(h)$$

$$= -E(h/2) + 4E(h/2)$$

$$= 3E(h/2)$$

approximately. This formula provides a way to check whether the trapezoidal approximations are better than a specified error tolerance ϵ. Since

$$|E(h/2)| = \frac{1}{3}|T(h/2) - T(h)|$$

approximately, the two-trapezoid approximation is sufficiently accurate if

$$\frac{1}{3} \mid T(h/2) - T(h) \mid < \epsilon$$

If not, then the error tolerance ϵ is split in two, and the adaptive trapezoidal function INTEGRAL is called again to approximate the area of each half of the region to within half of the original error tolerance. Thus, only regions where the approximation error is still large are further subdivided.

A side benefit of the adaptive trapezoidal strategy is that unlike the integration functions written earlier, the recursive function INTEGRAL in this section does not return an answer until the approximations are within the specified error tolerance.

```
RECURSIVE FUNCTION INTEGRAL (F, A, B, EPSILON) &
      RESULT (INTEGRAL_RESULT)

   INTERFACE
      FUNCTION F(X) RESULT (F_RESULT)
      REAL, INTENT (IN) :: X
      REAL :: F_RESULT
   END INTERFACE

   REAL, INTENT (IN) :: A, B, EPSILON
   REAL :: INTEGRAL_RESULT
   REAL :: H, MID
   REAL :: ONE_TRAPEZOID_AREA, TWO_TRAPEZOID_AREA
   REAL :: LEFT_AREA, RIGHT_AREA

   H = B - A
   MID = (A + B) /2
   ONE_TRAPEZOID_AREA = H * (F(A) + F(B)) / 2.0
   TWO_TRAPEZOID_AREA = H/2 * (F(A) + F(MID)) / 2.0 + &
                        H/2 * (F(MID) + F(B)) / 2.0
   IF (ABS(ONE_TRAPEZOID_AREA - TWO_TRAPEZOID_AREA) &
         < 3.0 * EPSILON) THEN
      INTEGRAL_RESULT = TWO_TRAPEZOID_AREA
```

```
    ELSE
        LEFT_AREA = INTEGRAL (F, A, MID, EPSILON / 2)
        RIGHT_AREA = INTEGRAL (F, MID, B, EPSILON / 2)
        INTEGRAL_RESULT = LEFT_AREA + RIGHT_AREA
    END IF

END FUNCTION INTEGRAL
```

The interface block for the function F (X) declares the types of the dummy argument and result variable of that function, so that even if the function subprogram INTEGRAL is compiled separately from the function subprogram F, the compiler will still be able to determine what type of actual argument to supply to F in each function call within INTEGRAL, and what type of returned value to expect.

To test the function INTEGRAL, we write a small test program and a function subprogram F. The test program will evaluate

$$\int_{-4}^{4} e^{-x^2} dx$$

to an accuracy of 0.01. The curve $y = e^{-x^2}$ is an unnormalized error distribution function, used extensively in probability and statistics. Its integral is approximately $\sqrt{\pi} = 1.7724531023$.

```
PROGRAM TEST_INTEGRAL

    REAL :: X_MIN, X_MAX
    REAL :: ANSWER, PI

    INTERFACE
        FUNCTION F (X)  RESULT (F_RESULT)
        REAL, INTENT (IN) :: X
        REAL :: F_RESULT
    END INTERFACE

    PI = 4 * ATAN (1.0)
    X_MIN = -4.0; X_MAX = 4.0
    ANSWER = INTEGRAL (F, X_MIN, X_MAX, 0.01)
```

```
    PRINT "(A, F15.10)", "The integral is approximately ",  &
                         ANSWER
    PRINT "(A, F15.10)", "The exact answer is              ",  &
                         SQRT (PI)

END PROGRAM TEST_INTEGRAL

FUNCTION F (X) RESULT (F_RESULT)

    REAL, INTENT (IN) :: X
    REAL :: F_RESULT

    F_RESULT = EXP (-X ** 2)

END FUNCTION F

RUN INTEGRAL_TEST
The integral is approximately 1.7770740699
The exact answer is           1.7724531023
```

Comparing the adaptive trapezoidal approximation to the exact answer, we see that the difference is approximately 0.0046, which is less than the specified error tolerance 0.01. Figure 7-3 shows the approximating trapezoids used between $x = -2$ and $x = +2$ to obtain the answer; trapezoids not shown have boundary points at $x = -4, -3, -2, 2, 3,$ and 4. Notice that more trapezoids are required to keep within the error tolerance in the highly curved regions near the maximum of the function and where it first approaches zero than are required in the relatively straight regions near the two inflection points where the curve switches from concave upward to concave downward.

7.2.1 Accelerated Convergence

Even better approximations to the integral can be squeezed out of the same calculations if the returned value INTEGRAL_RESULT is assigned an approximation to $I = T(h/2) - E(h/2)$ instead of settling for the approximation $I = T(h/2)$.

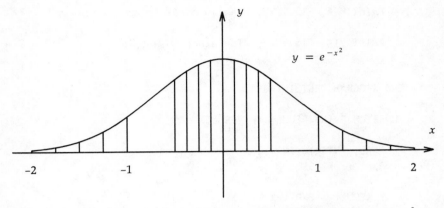

Figure 7-3 Approximating trapezoids used to calculate the integral of e^{-x^2}

$$I = T(h/2) + E(h/2)$$

$$= T(h/2) + \frac{T(h/2) - T(h)}{3}$$

$$= \frac{4T(h/2) - T(h)}{3}$$

Using this formula in the recursive function INTEGRAL in the form

```
INTEGRAL_RESULT = (4 * TWO_TRAPEZOID_AREA - ONE_TRAPEZOID_AREA) / 3
```

results in the same sequence of subdivisions and recursive calls, but an improved final answer of 1.7728076575, which differs from the exact answer, 1.7724531023, by approximately 0.00035.

It can be proved that this approximation formula is equivalent to approximating the area under $y = f(x)$ by the area under a parabola passing through the three points where the smaller trapezoids touch the curve. It is not surprising that parabolas can match the curve $y = f(x)$ more closely than the straight line boundaries of trapezoids, so that the resulting approximations, called **Simpson's approximations**, are more accurate for about the same number of calculated function values.

7.2.2 Exercises

1.   Determine the number of trapezoids needed to evaluate

$$\int_{-4}^{4} e^{-x^2} dx$$

to an accuracy of 0.01 using the nonadaptive integration function discussed in Section 3.10.

2.   Determine the approximate value of

$$\int_{0}^{2\pi} e^x \sin 2x \, dx$$

using both the adaptive integration method of this section and the nonadaptive integration method discussed in Section 3.10.

3.   The area under the curve $y = f(x)$ between $x = a - h$ and $x = a + h$ may be approximated by the area under a parabola passing through the three points $(a - h, f(a - h))$, $(a, f(a))$, and $(a + h, f(a + h))$. The approximation, called Simpson's approximation, is given by the formula

$$\int_{a-h}^{a+h} f(x) \, dx = \frac{h}{3} \left[f(a - h) + 4f(a) + f(a + h) \right]$$

with error $-1/90 f''''(c) h^5$ for some c in the interval of integration.

Use these facts to write a recursive adaptive Simpson's approximation subroutine patterned on the adaptive trapezoidal approximation subroutine INTEGRAL in this section. Compare the number of recursive function calls for your adaptive Simpson's approximation function with the number required to achieve the same accuracy with the adaptive trapezoidal rule.

4.   Use the accelerated convergence technique of Section 7.2.1 to improve the recursive adaptive Simpson's approximation subroutine written for Exercise 3 even more.

8

Pointer Variables

In Fortran, a **pointer variable** or simply a **pointer** is best thought of as a "free-floating" name that may be associated dynamically with or "aliased to" some data object. The data object already may have one or more other names or it may be an unnamed object.

Syntactically, a pointer is just any sort of variable that has been given the pointer attribute in a declaration. A variable with the pointer attribute may be used just like any ordinary variable, but it may be used in some additional ways as well. To understand how Fortran pointers work, it is almost always better to think of them simply as aliases. This will require a change of perspective for those programmers used to treating them as memory addresses, a scheme used in other programming languages and some previous extensions of Fortran. If you tend to fall back to this, at least think of the pointers as more general "descriptors", sufficient to describe a row of a matrix, for example.

8.1 The Use of Pointers in Fortran

Each pointer in a program is in one of the three following states:

1. It may be **undefined**, which is the condition of all pointers at the beginning of a program.

2. It may be **null**, which means that it is not the alias of any data object.

3. It may be **associated**, which means that it is the alias of some target data object.

8.1.1 The Pointer Assignment Statement

To start with a very simple example, suppose P is a real variable with the pointer attribute, perhaps given with the declaration

```
REAL, POINTER :: P
```

Suppose R is also a real variable. Then it is possible to make P an alias of R by the **pointer assignment statement**

```
P => R
```

For those that like to think of pointers, rather than aliases, this statement causes P to point to R.

Any variable aliased or "pointed to" by a pointer must be given the target attribute when declared and it must have the same type as the pointer. However, it is not necessary that the variable have a defined value. For our example above, these requirements are met by the presence of the following declaration:

```
REAL, TARGET :: R
```

A variable with the pointer attribute may be an object more complicated than a simple variable. It may be an array section or structure, for example. The following declares V to be a pointer to a one-dimensional array of reals:

```
REAL, DIMENSION (:), POINTER :: V
```

With V so declared, it may be used to alias any one-dimensional array of reals, including a row or column of some two-dimensional array of reals. For example,

```
V => REAL_ARRAY (4, :)
```

makes V an alias of the fourth row of the array REAL_ARRAY. Of course, REAL_ARRAY must have the target attribute for this to be legal.

```
REAL, DIMENSION (:, :), TARGET :: REAL_ARRAY
```

Once a variable with the pointer attribute is an alias for some data object, that is, it is pointing to something, it may be used in the same way that the other variable may be used. For the example above using V,

```
PRINT *, V
```

has exactly the same effect as

```
PRINT *, REAL_ARRAY (4, :)
```

and the assignment statement

```
V = 0
```

has the effect of setting all of the elements of the fourth row of REAL_ARRAY to 0.

A different version of the pointer assignment statement occurs when the right side also is a pointer. This is illustrated by the following example, in which P1 and P2 are both real variables with the pointer attribute and R is a real variable with the target attribute.

```
REAL, TARGET :: R
REAL, POINTER :: P1, P2
R = 4.7
P1 => R
P2 => P1
R = 7.4
PRINT *, P2
```

After execution of the first assignment statement, R is a name that refers to the value 4.7:

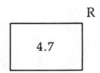

The first pointer assignment causes P1 to point to R, so that the value of the variable P1 is 4.7. The value 4.7 now has two names, R and P1, by which it may be referenced.

The next pointer assignment

```
P2 => P1
```

causes P2 to point to the same thing that P1 is pointing to, so the value of the variable P2 is also 4.7. The value 4.7 now has three names or aliases, R, P1, and P2.

Changing the value of R to 7.4 causes the value of both P1 and P2 also to change to 7.4 because they are both aliases of R. Thus, the next print statement

```
PRINT *, P2
```

prints the value 7.4.

The pointer assignment statement

```
P1 => P2
```

is legal whatever the status of P2. If P2 is undefined, P1 is undefined; if it is null, P1 is nullified; and if it is associated with a target, P1 becomes associated with the same target. Note that if P2 is associated with some target, say R, it is not necessary that R have a defined value.

8.1.2 The Difference between Pointer and Ordinary Assignment

We can now illustrate the difference between pointer assignment, which transfers the status of one pointer to another, and ordinary assignment involving pointers. In an ordinary assignment in which pointers occur, the pointers must be viewed simply as aliases for their targets. Consider the following statements:

```
REAL, POINTER :: P1, P2
REAL, TARGET  :: R1, R2
    . . .
R1 = 1.1;   R2 = 2.2
P1 => R1;   P2 => R2
```

This produces the following situation:

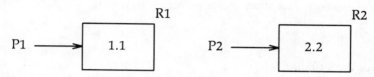

Now suppose the ordinary assignment statement

```
P2 = P1
```

is executed. This statement has exactly the same effect as the statement

```
R2 = R1
```

because P2 is an alias for R2 and P1 is an alias for R1. The situation is now:

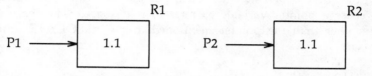

because the value 1.1 has been copied from R1 to R2. The values of P1, P2, R1, and R2 are all 1.1. Subsequent changes to R1 or P1 will have no effect on the value of R2.

If, on the other hand, the pointer assignment statement

P2 => P1

were executed instead, this statement would produce the situation

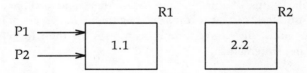

In this case, too, the values of P1, P2, and R1 are 1.1, but the value of R2 remains 2.2. Subsequent changes to P1 or R1 do change the value of P2. They do not change the value of R2.

Pointer assignment P1 => P2 assigns the current target of a pointer P2 to another pointer. Subsequent changes of target for the pointer P2 on the right do not affect the target of the pointer P1. In the above situation, execution of the pointer assignment

P1 => R2

creates the situation

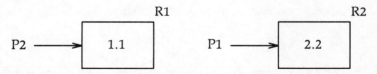

The pointer P2 remains an alias for R1; it does not remain associated with P1.

8.1.3 The ALLOCATE and DEALLOCATE Statements for Pointers

With the ALLOCATE statement, it is possible to create space for a value and cause a pointer variable to refer to that space. The space has no name other than the pointer mentioned in the ALLOCATE statement. For example,

ALLOCATE (P1)

creates space for one real number and makes P1 an alias for that space. No real value is stored in the space by the ALLOCATE statement, so it is necessary to assign a value to P1 before it can be used, just as with any other real variable.

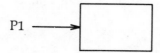

The statement

    P1 = 7.7

sets up the following situation.

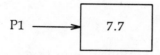

Before a value is assigned to P1, it must either be associated with an unnamed target by an ALLOCATE statement or be aliased with a target by a pointer assignment statement.

The DEALLOCATE statement throws away the space pointed to by its argument. For example,

    DEALLOCATE (P1)

returns P1 to the status it had at the beginning of the program, which is undefined.

P1 ⟶

After P1 is deallocated, it must not be referenced in any situation that requires a value; however it may be used, for example, on the right side of a pointer assignment statement. If other pointer variables were aliases for P1, they, too, no longer reference a value.

8.1.4 The NULLIFY Statement

At the beginning of a program, a pointer variable (just as all other variables) is not defined. A pointer variable must not be referenced to produce a value when it is not defined, but it is sometimes desirable to have a pointer variable be in the state of not pointing to anything. This occurs when it is nullified, which creates a condition that may be tested and assigned to other pointers by pointer assignment (= >). A pointer is nullified with the NULLIFY statement, which consists of the keyword

NULLIFY followed by the name of a pointer variable in parentheses, such as

```
NULLIFY (P1)
```

If the target of P1 and P2 are the same, nullifying P1 does not nullify P2. On the other hand, if P1 is null, then executing the pointer assignment

```
P2 => P1
```

causes P2 to be null also.

8.1.5 The ASSOCIATED Intrinsic Function

The **ASSOCIATED** intrinsic function may be used to determine if a pointer variable is pointing to, or is an alias for, another object. To use this function, the pointer variable must be defined; that is, it must either be the alias of some data object or be null. The ASSOCIATED function indicates which of these two cases is true.

The ASSOCIATED function may have a second argument. If the second argument is a target, the value of the function indicates whether the first argument is pointing to the second argument. If the second argument is a pointer, it must be defined; in this case, the value of the function is true if both pointers are null or if they are both aliases of the same target. For example, the expression

```
ASSOCIATED (P1, R)
```

indicates whether or not P1 is pointing to R, and the expression

```
ASSOCIATED (P1, P2)
```

indicates whether P1 is pointing to the same thing as P2 or they are both null.

8.1.6 Dangling Pointers and Unreferenced Storage

There are two situations that the Fortran programmer must try to avoid. The first is a **dangling pointer**. This situation arises when a pointer variable is an alias for some object that gets deallocated by an action that does not involve the pointer directly. For example, if P1 and P2 are both pointing to R, and the statement

```
DEALLOCATE (P2)
```

is executed, it is obvious that P2 is now disassociated, but the status of P1 appears to be unaffected, even though the object to which it was pointing has disappeared. A reference to P1 is now illegal and will produce unpredictable results. It is the responsibility of the programmer to keep track of the number of pointer variables referencing a particular object and to nullify each of the pointers whenever one of them is deallocated.

A related problem of **unreferenced storage** can occur when a pointer variable pointing to an object is nullified or set to point to something else without a deallocation. If there is no other alias for or pointer to this value, it is still stored in memory somewhere, but there is no way to refer to it. This is not important if it happens to a few simple values, but if it happens many times to large arrays, the efficient management of storage could be hampered severely. In this case, it is also the responsibility of the programmer to ensure that objects are deallocated before all pointers to the object are modified. Fortran systems are not required to have runtime "garbage collection" to recover the unreferenced storage.

8.2 Linked Lists

Linked lists have many uses in a wide variety of applications areas; one example in science and engineering is the use of a linked list to represent a queue in a simulation program. Lists of values can be implemented in Fortran 90 in more than one way. Perhaps the most obvious way is to use an array. Another is to use pointers and data structures to create a linked list. The choice should depend on which operations are going to be performed on the list and the relative frequency of those operations. If the only requirement is to add and delete numbers at one end of the list, as is done if the list is treated as a stack, then an array is an easy and efficient way to represent the list. If items must be inserted and deleted often at arbitrary points within the list, then a linked list is nice; with an array, many elements would have to be moved to insert or delete an element in the middle of the list. Another issue is whether storage is to be allocated all at once, using an array, or element by element in a linked list implementation. The implementation of linked lists using pointers also uses recursion effectively, but iteration also could be used.

A **linked list** of numbers (or any other objects) can be thought of schematically as a bunch of boxes, usually called *nodes*, each containing a number and a *pointer* to the box containing the next number in the list. Suppose, for example, the list contains the numbers 14, 62, and 83. In the lists discussed in this section, the numbers always will appear in numeric order, as they do in this example. Figure 8-1 contains a pictorial representation of the list.

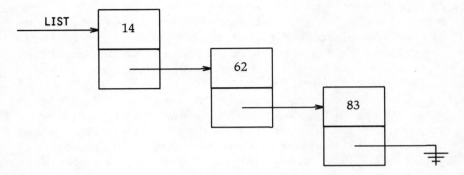

Figure 8-1 A linked list of integers.

We will illustrate the Fortran 90 techniques for manipulating linked lists by constructing a module to manipulate linked lists in which the nodes contain integers and the lists are sorted with the smallest number at the head of the list. The overall structure of the module is

```
MODULE SORTED_INTEGER_LISTS_1

    PRIVATE :: NODE

    TYPE NODE
        INTEGER :: VALUE
        TYPE (NODE), POINTER :: NEXT
    END TYPE NODE

    TYPE LIST
        PRIVATE
        TYPE (NODE), POINTER :: FIRST
    END TYPE LIST

CONTAINS

    . . .

END MODULE SORTED_INTEGER_LISTS_1
```

These declarations set up types for NODE, the "box" that contains a number and a pointer to the next node, and for LIST, which is a structure whose only component is a pointer to a node. The PRIVATE specifications indicate that although the procedures and some of the types in this module will be available to any external program or procedure that uses this module, the type NODE will not be accessible and the user also will not be able to access the internal structure of type LIST. The intent is to provide the user of the module with an **abstract data type**, that is, with the name of the list type and all necessary procedures to manipulate these lists. If it is desirable to change the implementation, we can be sure that no program has accessed the lists in any ways except those provided by the public procedures in this module.

The ability to declare which details of a module are private to the module and therefore hidden from all external users of the module, and which are public, that is, not private, and therefore available to users of the module, is important for two reasons, both of which we use in what follows.

1. In the course of implementing the module, we are free to change its private details, as long as we do not change the public interfaces with external procedures.

2. We will write two entirely different versions of this module that use different internal data structures for the lists, but which can be substituted for each other merely by changing the statement

    USE SORTED_INTEGER_LISTS_1

    to

    USE SORTED_INTEGER_LISTS_2

Now we must decide what operations are needed. We will supply a function NEW that returns an empty list; a function EMPTY (L) that returns the logical value indicating whether or not the list L is empty; a subroutine INSERT (L, NUMBER) that inserts NUMBER into list L; a subroutine DELETE (L, NUMBER) that deletes one occurrence of NUMBER from a list L, if it is there; and a subroutine PRINT_LIST (L) that prints the numbers in the list in order. Some of these are pretty simple and could be done easily without a procedure, but the purpose is to include all necessary operations in the module and be able to change the implementation, as we do later in this section.

The function that returns a new empty list is relatively easy. The only tricky point is that the type LIST is not a pointer, but a structure whose only component is a pointer. Thus, there is no need to allocate NEW_RESULT; all we need to do is nullify its pointer component FIRST.

```
FUNCTION NEW () RESULT (NEW_RESULT)

    IMPLICIT NONE
    TYPE (LIST) :: NEW_RESULT

    NULLIFY (NEW_RESULT % FIRST)

END FUNCTION NEW
```

With this function, the user of the module can create a new empty list and assign it to the variable X_LIST declared to be type LIST with the statement

```
X_LIST = NEW ()
```

Let's next do the subroutine that inserts a number into a list. This is a bit tricky. Suppose the list L has two numbers in it, 14 and 83, and we want to insert the number 62. The list is shown in Figure 8-2.

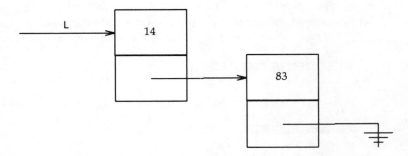

Figure 8-2 A list prior to insertion.

It is reasonable to move down through the list until a number in the list is found that is larger than the one to be inserted. In our example, this number is 83. Then the number 62 is inserted by creating a new node, linking the NEXT field of the new node to the node containing 83, and finally linking the NEXT field of the box containing 14 to the new box containing 62. The first two steps are easy, but to do the last step, it is necessary to have a variable that somehow references the box containing 14; but by the time we have found the number 83, unless we are careful, we no longer have anything pointing to the previous box and so cannot access it.

There are several solutions to this problem. One is to put two pointers in each box; one pointing forward in the list and one pointing backward. Another solution that we will pursue is to keep two temporary pointers as the list is traversed, one pointing at the current node and one pointing at the previous node. The latter pointer is often called a **trailing pointer**. In our example, when 83, the first number larger than 62, is found, the trailing pointer TRAIL_PTR will be pointing at the box containing 14 and the other pointer, TMP_PTR, will be pointing at the 83, as illustrated in Figure 8-3.

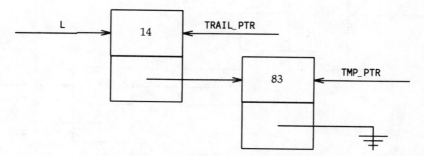

Figure 8-3 Locating the position of a new number in a linked list.

In this situation, the new number may be inserted with three statements. The first statement is

```
ALLOCATE (TRAIL_PTR % NEXT)
```

This statement creates a new unnamed node and sets the NEXT pointer in the box containing 14 to point to it, as shown in Figure 8-4.

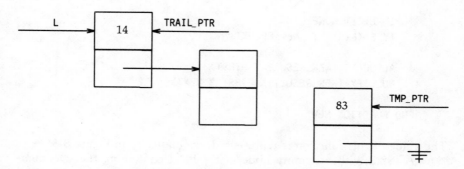

Figure 8-4 Allocating a new node for a linked list.

The other two statements put the number 62 into the VALUE field of the newly created node and make its NEXT field point to the node containing the number 83. The result is illustrated in Figure 8-5.

```
TRAIL_PTR % NEXT % VALUE = NUMBER
TRAIL_PTR % NEXT % NEXT => TEMP_PTR
```

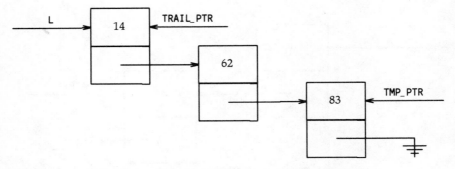

Figure 8-5 The linked list after the new number is inserted.

The introduction of a trailing pointer neatly solves the insertion problem most of the time, but it introduces another difficulty. When the list is empty, there can be no trailing pointer. This difficulty is solved by always having one extra unused node at the head of each list. Since an empty list now has one (unused) node, the function NEW must be rewritten.

```
FUNCTION NEW () RESULT (NEW_RESULT)

    IMPLICIT NONE
    TYPE (LIST) :: NEW_RESULT

    ALLOCATE (NEW_RESULT % FIRST)
    NULLIFY (NEW_RESULT % FIRST % NEXT)

END FUNCTION NEW
```

The value of this function is represented schematically in Figure 8-6.

A list L with a dummy node at the head containing the two numbers 14 and 83 is represented by the diagram in Figure 8-7.

As the list is traversed, the trailing pointer is initially set to point to the dummy node at the head and another pointer is set to start pointing

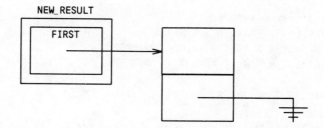

Figure 8-6 A newly created empty list.

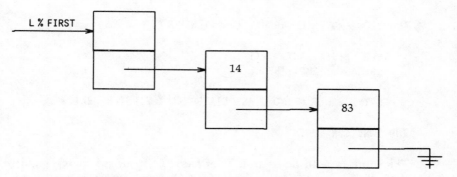

Figure 8-7 A linked list with a dummy node at the head.

at the rest of the list, which may be empty. We can now complete the
function INSERT.

```
SUBROUTINE INSERT (L, NUMBER)

    IMPLICIT NONE
    TYPE (LIST), INTENT (INOUT) :: L
    INTEGER, INTENT (IN) :: NUMBER
    TYPE (NODE), POINTER :: TRAIL_PTR, TMP_PTR

    ! Find location to put new number
    TRAIL_PTR => L % FIRST
    TEMP_PTR => TRAIL_PTR % NEXT
    DO
        IF (.NOT. ASSOCIATED (TMP_PTR)) EXIT
        IF (NUMBER < TMP_PTR % VALUE) EXIT
        TRAIL_PTR => TMP_PTR
        TMP_PTR => TMP_PTR % NEXT
    END DO
```

```
! Insert new node
ALLOCATE (TRAIL_PTR % NEXT)
TRAIL_PTR % NEXT % VALUE = NUMBER
TRAIL_PTR % NEXT % NEXT => TMP_PTR

END SUBROUTINE INSERT
```

The function that determines if a list is empty, that is, determines that only the dummy node is present, is straightforward. Recall that a pointer is not associated if it has been nullified.

```
FUNCTION EMPTY (L) RESULT (EMPTY_RESULT)

TYPE (LIST), INTENT (IN) :: L
LOGICAL :: EMPTY_RESULT

EMPTY_RESULT = .NOT. ASSOCIATED (L % FIRST % NEXT)

END FUNCTION EMPTY
```

The subroutine to delete a number from a list, if it is there, is quite similar to the subroutine to insert. First the number must be found. Then, to delete a node, it is only necessary to adjust the NEXT field of the node pointed to by the trailing pointer to "point around" the deleted node to the node following it. Also, it is a good idea to deallocate the space for the deleted node. If the number 62 is to be deleted, when its node is located by TEMP_PTR, the part of the list after the dummy node looks as shown in Figure 8-8.

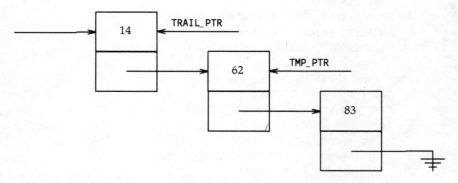

Figure 8-8 Locating an insertion position in a linked list with a dummy head.

The node containing 62 is removed from the list with the statement

```
TRAIL_PTR % NEXT => TMP_PTR % NEXT
```

and the node containing 62 is deallocated with the statement

```
DEALLOCATE (TMP_PTR)
```

The entire subroutine follows. The third argument, FOUND, indicates whether or not the number was found and deleted.

```
SUBROUTINE DELETE (L, NUMBER, FOUND)

    IMPLICIT NONE
    TYPE (LIST), INTENT (INOUT) :: L
    INTEGER, INTENT (IN) :: NUMBER
    LOGICAL, INTENT (OUT) :: FOUND
    TYPE (NODE), POINTER :: TRAIL_PTR, TMP_PTR

    ! Find location to put new number
    TRAIL_PTR => L % FIRST
    TEMP_PTR => TRAIL_PTR % NEXT
    DO
        IF (.NOT. ASSOCIATED (TMP_PTR)) THEN
            FOUND = .FALSE.
            EXIT
        ELSE IF (NUMBER = TMP_PTR % VALUE) THEN
            FOUND = .TRUE.
            EXIT
        ELSE
            TRAIL_PTR => TMP_PTR
            TMP_PTR => TMP_PTR % NEXT
        END IF
    END DO

    ! Delete node if found
    IF (FOUND) THEN
        TRAIL_PTR % NEXT => TMP_PTR % NEXT
        DEALLOCATE (TMP_PTR)
    END IF

END SUBROUTINE DELETE
```

The last subroutine needed to complete the module is one that prints the numbers in the list in order. This just involves traversing the list as in the subroutines INSERT and DELETE, except that no trailing pointer is required.

```
SUBROUTINE PRINT_LIST (L)

    IMPLICIT NONE
    TYPE (LIST), INTENT (IN) :: L
    TYPE (NODE), POINTER :: TMP_PTR

    TMP_PTR => L % FIRST % NEXT
    DO
        IF (.NOT. ASSOCIATED (TMP_PTR)) EXIT
        PRINT *, TMP_PTR % VALUE
        TMP_PTR => TMP_PTR % NEXT
    END DO

END SUBROUTINE PRINT_LIST
```

8.2.1 Sorting with a Linked List

With the integer list module just created, it is possible to write a simple but inefficient sorting program. The program works by reading in a file of numbers and inserting each number into a list as it is read. When all the numbers have been put into the list, it is printed, producing all the numbers in order.

```
PROGRAM LIST_SORT

    USE SORTED_INTEGER_LISTS_1

    IMPLICIT NONE
    TYPE (LIST) :: L
    INTEGER :: NUMBER, IOS
```

```
L = NEW ()
DO
    READ (*, *, IOSTAT = IOS) NUMBER
    ! A negative value for IOS indicates end of file
    IF (IOS < 0) EXIT
    CALL INSERT (L, NUMBER)
END DO

PRINT_LIST (L)

END PROGRAM LIST_SORT
```

8.2.2 Processing Lists Recursively

In this subsection we investigate how the procedures of the module SORTED_INTEGER_LISTS_1 would look if written using recursion. In these cases, the recursion is usually tail recursion, so, in one sense, not much is gained. However, it turns out that much of the detailed manipulation of pointers is eliminated and the recursive versions do not need a dummy node at the head of the list. This makes the routines a lot easier to write, understand, and maintain, but perhaps a little less less efficient to execute on systems that have a high overhead for procedure calls.

The approach to writing recursive routines to process the list is to view the list itself as a recursive data structure. That is, a list of integers is either empty or it is an integer followed by a list of integers. This suggests that to process a list of numbers, process the first number in the list and then process the rest of the list with the same routine, quitting when the list is empty.

To view the list as a recursive data structure as described above, the object of type NODE now should consist of a value and another object, REST_OF_LIST, of type LIST. In the module SORTED_INTEGER_LISTS_1, the second component of type NODE was a pointer to a node, but in SORTED_INTEGER_LISTS_2, it is an object of type LIST, which is slightly different; it is a structure consisting of one component that is the pointer to a node. With this change, the type definitions for the new module are

```
MODULE SORTED_INTEGER_LISTS_2

   PRIVATE :: NODE

   TYPE NODE
      INTEGER :: VALUE
      TYPE (LIST) :: REST_OF_LIST
   END TYPE NODE

   TYPE LIST
      PRIVATE
      TYPE (NODE), POINTER :: FIRST
   END TYPE LIST

CONTAINS

   . . .

END MODULE SORTED_INTEGER_LISTS_2
```

With the revised type definitions, the function NEW may be changed back to the original version, because there is no need for a dummy node at the head of the list.

```
FUNCTION NEW () RESULT (NEW_RESULT)

   TYPE (LIST) :: NEW_RESULT

   NULLIFY (NEW_RESULT % FIRST)

END FUNCTION NEW
```

Since the subroutines INSERT and DELETE were the most complicated, let's look at those next. The following is a recursive version of the subroutine INSERT.

```
RECURSIVE SUBROUTINE INSERT (L, NUMBER)

   IMPLICIT NONE
   TYPE (LIST), INTENT (INOUT) :: L
   INTEGER, INTENT (IN) :: NUMBER
   TYPE (NODE), POINTER :: TMP_PTR
```

```
    IF (.NOT. ASSOCIATED (L % FIRST)) THEN
        ALLOCATE (L % FIRST)
        L % FIRST % VALUE = NUMBER
        NULLIFY (L % FIRST % REST_OF_LIST % FIRST)
    ELSE IF (NUMBER < L % FIRST % VALUE) THEN
        ! Insert at the front of the list L
        ALLOCATE (TMP_PTR)
        TMP_PTR % VALUE = NUMBER
        TMP_PTR % REST_OF_LIST % FIRST => L % FIRST
        L % FIRST => TMP_PTR
    ELSE
        CALL INSERT (L % FIRST % REST_OF_LIST, NUMBER)
    END IF

END SUBROUTINE INSERT
```

To see just one more example of a recursive routine to process the list, let's look at the subroutine PRINT_LIST.

```
RECURSIVE SUBROUTINE PRINT_LIST (L)

    IMPLICIT NONE
    TYPE (LIST), INTENT (IN) :: L

    IF (ASSOCIATED (L % FIRST)) THEN
        PRINT *, L % FIRST % VALUE
        CALL PRINT_LIST (L % FIRST % REST_OF_LIST)
    END IF

END SUBROUTINE PRINT_LIST
```

Although this is just an instance of tail recursion, the procedure is quite a bit simpler than the iterative version.

Style Note: A very important point to note is that even when the procedures in the module SORTED_INTEGER_LISTS_1 are rewritten to be recursive, or even if arrays are used to represent the lists, creating yet another list module, a program such as LIST_SORT that uses one of these modules does not have to be changed at all. This illustrates one of the real benefits of using modules.

8.2.3 Exercise

1.   Use first the recursive version and then the nonrecursive version of
the programs to manipulate lists of integers to construct a program
that sorts integers. Experiment with each program, sorting different
quantities of randomly generated integers to determine an approximate formula for the complexity of the program. Is the execution
time (or some other measure of complexity, such as the number of
statements executed) proportional to $n \log_2 n$? Is it proportional to
n^2?

8.3 Trees

One of the big disadvantages of using a linked list to sort numbers is that
the resulting program has poor expected running time. In fact, for the
program LIST_SORT, the expected running time is proportional to n^2,
where n is the number of numbers to be sorted. A much more efficient
sorting program can be constructed if a slightly more complicated data
structure, the binary tree, is used. The resulting program, TREE_SORT,
has an expected running time proportional to $n \log_2 n$ instead of n^2.

It is quite difficult to write nonrecursive programs to process trees,
so we will think of trees as recursive structures right from the start.
Using this approach, a **binary tree** of integers is either empty or is an
integer, followed by two binary trees of integers, called the *left subtree*
and *right subtree*.

8.3.1 Sorting with Trees

To sort numbers with a tree, we will construct a special kind of ordered
binary tree with the property that the number at the "top" or "root"
node of the tree is greater than all the numbers in its left subtree and less
than or equal to all the numbers in its right subtree. This partitioning of
the tree into a left subtree containing smaller numbers and a right subtree
containing larger numbers is exactly analogous to the partitioning of a
list into smaller and larger sublists that makes quicksort an efficient algorithm. This property will hold not only for the most accessible node at
the "top" of the tree (paradoxically called the "root" of the tree), but
for all nodes of the tree. To illustrate this kind of tree, suppose a file of
integers contains the numbers 265, 113, 467, 264, 907, and 265 in the
order given. To build an ordered binary tree containing these numbers,
first start with an empty tree. Then read in the first number, 265, and
place it in a node at the root of the tree, as shown in Figure 8-9.

When the next number is read, it is compared with the first. If it is
less than the first number, it is placed as a node in the left subtree; if it is

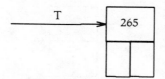

Figure 8-9 The root of a tree.

greater than or equal to the first number, it is placed in the right subtree. In our example, 113 < 265, so a node containing 113 is created and the left subtree pointer of the node containing 265 is set to point to it, as shown in Figure 8-10.

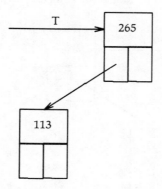

Figure 8-10 Adding the number 113 to the tree.

The next number is 467, and it is placed in the right subtree of 265 because it is larger than 265. The result is shown in Figure 8-11.

The next number is 264, so it is placed in the left subtree of 265. It is then compared with 113, the occupant of the top of the left subtree. Since 264 ≥ 113, it is placed in the right subtree of the one with 113 at the top to obtain the tree shown in Figure 8-12.

The next number 907 is larger than 265, so it is compared with 467 and put in the right subtree of the node containing 467, as shown in Figure 8-13.

The final number 265 is equal to the number in the root node. An insertion position is therefore sought in the right subtree of the root. Since 265 < 467, it is put to the left of 467, as shown in Figure 8-14. Notice that the two nodes containing the number 265 are not even adjacent, nor is the node containing the number 264 adjacent to either node with key 265. This doesn't matter. When the tree is printed, they will come out in the right order.

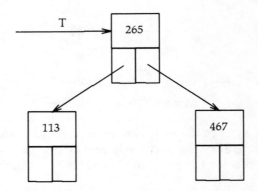

Figure 8-11 Adding the number 467 to the tree.

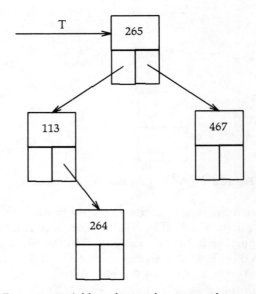

Figure 8-12 Adding the number 264 to the tree.

8.3.2 Type Declarations for Trees

The declaration for the node of a tree is similar to the declaration for the node of a linked list, except that the node must contain two pointers, one to the left subtree and one to the right subtree. As with lists, we could have TREE be a derived data type, which implies it must be a structure with one component, a pointer to the node of a tree. But just to be different, let's not put the tree operations in a module. Having made this decision, the extra syntax needed to select the pointer component using

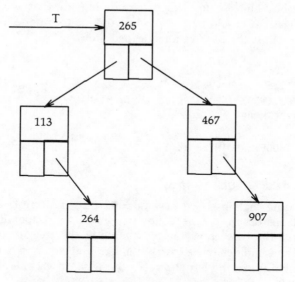

Figure 8-13 Adding the number 907 to the tree.

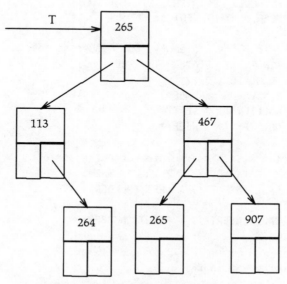

Figure 8-14 The final ordered binary tree.

the % symbol clutters up the program enough that we will simply declare things that would be trees to be pointers to a node, the root node of the tree. Thus, the declarations needed are

```
TYPE NODE
   INTEGER :: VALUE
   TYPE (NODE), POINTER :: LEFT, RIGHT
END TYPE NODE

TYPE (NODE), POINTER :: T
```

8.3.3 The INSERT Subroutine

The subroutine that inserts a new number into the tree is a straightforward implementation of the following informal recipe: if the tree is empty, make the new entry the only node of the tree; if the tree is not empty and the number to be inserted is less than the number at the root, insert the number in the left subtree; otherwise, insert the number in the right subtree.

```
RECURSIVE SUBROUTINE INSERT (T, NUMBER)

   IMPLICIT NONE
   TYPE (NODE), POINTER, INTENT (INOUT) :: T   ! Really a tree.
   INTEGER, INTENT (IN) :: NUMBER

   ! If (sub)tree is empty, put number at root
   IF (.NOT. ASSOCIATED (T)) THEN
      ALLOCATE (T)
      T % VALUE = NUMBER
      NULLIFY (T % LEFT)
      NULLIFY (T % RIGHT)

   ! otherwise, insert into correct subtree
   ELSE IF (NUMBER < T % VALUE) THEN
      CALL INSERT (T % LEFT, NUMBER)
   ELSE
      CALL INSERT (T % RIGHT, NUMBER)
   END IF

END SUBROUTINE INSERT
```

8.3.4 Printing the Tree in Order

The recipe for printing the nodes of the tree follows from the way the tree has been built. It is simply to print in order the values in the left subtree of the root, print the value at the root node, then print in order the values in the right subtree. This subroutine is shown in the following complete program that sorts a file of integers by reading them all in, constructing an ordered binary tree, and then printing out the values in the tree in infix order.

```
PROGRAM TREE_SORT
! Sorts a file of integers by building a
! tree, sorted in infix order.
! This sort has expected behavior n log n,
! but worst case (input is sorted) n ** 2.

   TYPE NODE
      INTEGER :: VALUE
      TYPE (NODE), POINTER :: LEFT, RIGHT
   END TYPE NODE

   IMPLICIT NONE
   TYPE (NODE), POINTER :: T  ! A tree
   INTEGER :: NUMBER, IOS

   NULLIFY (T)  ! Start with empty tree
   DO
      READ (*, *, IOSTAT = IOS) NUMBER
      IF (IOS < 0) EXIT
      CALL INSERT (T, NUMBER) ! Put next number in tree
   END DO
   PRINT_TREE (T)  ! Print nodes of tree in infix order

CONTAINS

   RECURSIVE SUBROUTINE INSERT (T, NUMBER)

      IMPLICIT NONE
      TYPE (NODE), POINTER, INTENT (INOUT) :: T  ! A tree
      INTEGER, INTENT (IN) :: NUMBER
```

```
            ! If (sub)tree is empty, put number at root
            IF (.NOT. ASSOCIATED (T)) THEN
               ALLOCATE (T)
               T % VALUE = NUMBER
               NULLIFY (T % LEFT)
               NULLIFY (T % RIGHT)
            ! Otherwise, insert into correct subtree
            ELSE IF (NUMBER < T % VALUE) THEN
               CALL INSERT (T % LEFT, NUMBER)
            ELSE
               CALL INSERT (T % RIGHT, NUMBER)
            END IF

        END SUBROUTINE INSERT

        RECURSIVE SUBROUTINE PRINT_TREE (T)
        ! Print tree in infix order

           IMPLICIT NONE
           TYPE (NODE), POINTER, INTENT (IN) :: T  ! A tree

           IF (ASSOCIATED (T)) THEN
              CALL PRINT_TREE (T % LEFT)
              PRINT *, T % VALUE
              CALL PRINT_TREE (T % RIGHT)
           END IF

        END SUBROUTINE PRINT_TREE

     END PROGRAM TREE_SORT
```

8.3.5 Exercise

1.   Experiment with the program TREE_SORT, sorting different quantities of randomly generated integers to determine an approximate formula for the complexity of the program. It should be proportional to $n \log_2 n$.

8.4 Case Study: Finding the Median

A common problem is to find the median of a set of numbers. One example is to find the score at the fiftieth percentile in a set of test scores. One way to compute the median is to sort the test scores and pick out the one half way through the list. However, the best sorting algorithms involve execution time that is proportional to $n \log n$, where n is the number of scores. We will illustrate a method whose execution time, on the average, is proportional to n.

One of the interesting features of this solution is that it actually does a more general computation: finding the kth number in order from a list of n numbers. This is one example of the strange phenomenon that it is sometimes easier to solve a more general problem than the one posed, particularly if the solution involves recursion.

Here is the way the algorithm works. Arbitrarily pick one number from the list. Split the list into three lists, one containing those numbers less than the number picked, a second containing the numbers equal to the number picked, and a third list containing the numbers larger than the one picked. Count the numbers, respectively s, e, and l, in each of the three lists. If the kth number is to be found and there are k or more numbers in the list of smaller numbers, then the kth number must be in that list, so the problem reduces to that of finding the kth number in the list of smaller numbers. Otherwise, if $k \leq s + e$, the sum of the sizes of the smaller and equal lists together, the number sought is equal to each number in the list of equal numbers. If neither of these cases is true, then the number sought is the $(k - s - e)$th number in the list of larger numbers.

To see how this works, suppose we are to find the fifth number (the median) of the following nine numbers: 43, 28, 56, 72, 43, 34, 62, 62, and 97. Suppose the first number, 43, is picked to form the partition into smaller, equal, and larger numbers. Then the list of smaller numbers is 28, 34; the list of equal numbers is 43, 43; and the list of larger numbers is 56, 72, 62, 62, 97. Since there are four numbers in the combined smaller and equal lists, the fifth number of the original list is the first number of the list of larger numbers. The process is applied again, let's say with 56 as the picked number. Then the list of smaller numbers is empty; the list of equal numbers is 56; and the list of larger numbers is 72, 62, 62, 97. In this case the number we are looking for is 56.

This process is described recursively, so it makes sense to write a recursive procedure to do the calculation. A very important decision involves the manner in which the lists are to be represented. It is certainly possible to put the numbers in arrays, but the sizes of the lists are all different and it turns out that it is necessary to insert and delete numbers from the list only at one end, so a linked list is an excellent choice.

A linked list for which insertions and deletions are made only at one end is called a **stack**. Stacks arise in many sorts of applications, so it is not a bad idea to have a module of routines to manipulate stacks. We shall construct some of the procedures handy to have for manipulating stacks of integers. The structure of the module and the data types used look much like our previous list module. Also, since they are just like the previous versions, we can include in the module immediately the function NEW that returns an empty stack and the logical function EMPTY that tests to see if a stack is empty.

```
MODULE STACK_OF_INTEGERS

    PRIVATE :: NODE

    TYPE NODE
       INTEGER :: VALUE
       TYPE (STACK) :: REST_OF_STACK
    END TYPE NODE

    TYPE STACK
       PRIVATE
       TYPE (NODE), POINTER :: TOP
    END TYPE STACK

CONTAINS

    FUNCTION NEW () RESULT (NEW_RESULT)

       IMPLICIT NONE
       TYPE (STACK) :: NEW_RESULT
       NULLIFY (NEW_RESULT % TOP)

    END FUNCTION NEW

    FUNCTION EMPTY (S) RESULT (EMPTY_RESULT)

       IMPLICIT NONE
       TYPE (STACK), INTENT (IN) :: S
       LOGICAL :: EMPTY_RESULT

       EMPTY_RESULT = .NOT. ASSOCIATED (S % TOP)

    END FUNCTION EMPTY

       . . .

    END MODULE STACK_OF_INTEGERS
```

Insertion of a new integer into a stack is always done at the top of the stack and so is simpler than the INSERT procedure for a general linked list. The operation is said to **push** the integer onto the stack.

```
SUBROUTINE PUSH (S, NUMBER)

    IMPLICIT NONE
    TYPE (STACK), INTENT (INOUT) :: S
    INTEGER, INTENT (IN) :: NUMBER
    TYPE (NODE), POINTER :: TMP_PTR

    ALLOCATE (TMP_PTR)
    TMP_PTR % VALUE = NUMBER
    TMP_PTR % REST_OF_STACK % TOP => S % TOP
    S % TOP => TMP_PTR

END SUBROUTINE PUSH
```

The other natural operation is to **pop** a number from the stack and return the value popped. It will be assumed that the stack always is checked to be sure it is not empty before the pop operation is executed.

```
SUBROUTINE POP (S, NUMBER)

    IMPLICIT NONE
    TYPE (STACK), INTENT (INOUT) :: S
    INTEGER, INTENT (OUT) :: NUMBER
    TYPE (NODE), POINTER :: TMP_PTR

    TMP_PTR => S % TOP
    NUMBER = TMP_PTR % VALUE
    S % TOP => TMP_PTR % REST_OF_STACK % TOP
    DEALLOCATE (TMP_PTR)

END SUBROUTINE POP
```

Now we can concentrate on the job of writing the procedure that finds the *k*th number in a given list. It will be assumed that the list will be in the form of a variable of type STACK. If this is not the case, it is pretty easy to convert an array of integers, for example, into a stack of integers by pushing them one by one onto an initially empty stack. As described above, the procedure SELECT picks an arbitrary number from the list to use as the test element. In our case we pick the number at the head of the stack, since that one is most accessible. Then SELECT forms three lists containing (a) the numbers less than the one picked, (b) the numbers equal to the one picked, and (c) the numbers greater than the one picked. Actually there is no reason to construct the list of equal numbers, but only to record how many there are. We also need to record the size of the other two lists. Then the procedure is called recursively using the appropriate sublist.

```
RECURSIVE SUBROUTINE SELECT (S, K, NUMBER, ERROR)

    USE STACK_OF_INTEGERS

    IMPLICIT NONE
    TYPE (STACK), INTENT (INOUT) :: S
    INTEGER, INTENT (IN) :: K
    INTEGER, INTENT (OUT) :: NUMBER
    LOGICAL, INTENT (OUT) :: ERROR
    TYPE (STACK) :: SMALLER, LARGER
    INTEGER :: NUMBER_SMALLER, NUMBER_EQUAL, NUMBER_LARGER

    IF (EMPTY (S)) THEN
        ERROR = .TRUE.

    ELSE
        CALL POP (S, NUMBER)
        IF (EMPTY (S)) THEN
            ERROR = (K /= 1)

        ELSE
            CALL SPLIT (S, NUMBER, SMALLER, NUMBER_SMALLER, &
                        NUMBER_EQUAL, LARGER, NUMBER_LARGER)

            IF (K <= NUMBER_SMALLER) THEN
                CALL SELECT (SMALLER, K, NUMBER, ERROR)
            ELSE IF (K <= NUMBER_SMALLER + NUMBER_EQUAL) THEN
                ! K is the correct value
                ERROR = .FALSE.
```

```
            ELSE
               CALL SELECT (LARGER, &
                  K - NUMBER_SMALLER - NUMBER_EQUAL, NUMBER, ERROR)
            END IF
         END IF
      END IF

END SUBROUTINE SELECT
```

The only remaining task is to write a subroutine that splits the list into the three parts.

```
SUBROUTINE SPLIT (S, PICKED, SMALLER, NUMBER_SMALLER,  &
                  NUMBER_EQUAL, LARGER, NUMBER_LARGER)

   USE STACK_OF_INTEGERS

   IMPLICIT NONE
   TYPE (STACK), INTENT (INOUT) :: S
   INTEGER, INTENT (IN) :: PICKED
   TYPE (STACK), INTENT (OUT) :: SMALLER, LARGER
   INTEGER, INTENT (OUT) :: &
         NUMBER_SMALLER, NUMBER_EQUAL, NUMBER_LARGER
   INTEGER :: NUMBER

   SMALLER = NEW ()
   LARGER = NEW ()
   NUMBER_SMALLER = 0
   NUMBER_EQUAL = 1
   NUMBER_LARGER = 0

   DO
      IF (EMPTY (S)) EXIT
      CALL POP (S, NUMBER)
      IF (NUMBER < PICKED) THEN
         CALL PUSH (SMALLER, NUMBER)
         NUMBER_SMALLER = NUMBER_SMALLER + 1
```

```
        ELSE IF (NUMBER > PICKED) THEN
          CALL PUSH (LARGER, NUMBER)
          NUMBER_LARGER = NUMBER_LARGER + 1
        ELSE
          NUMBER_EQUAL = NUMBER_EQUAL + 1
        END IF
      END DO

  END SUBROUTINE SPLIT
```

8.4.1 Modifications for Large Nodes

If instead of being just a single number, each item from which the kth item is to be selected consists of a huge structure type with a numeric key field, one must be very careful not to move nodes around; otherwise the time of moving nodes might be larger than the efficiently small amount of time spent comparing nodes in the recursive selection algorithm above. The principal culprit is that every time a number is pushed or popped from a stack, it is copied into a separate variable that is not part of a node. If whole structures were to be copied in the same way in PUSH and POP, much time would be lost.

The solution is to write new subroutines PUSH_NODE and POP_NODE that push a node (and not a value) onto the top of a stack and pop a node (not a value) off the top of a stack. The subroutine SPLIT can now pop a node from the input stack and push it onto the appropriate sublist merely by reassigning pointers without copying the entire value structure in the node. The modified subroutines PUSH_NODE, POP_NODE, and SPLIT are given below. Modifying the rest of the program is left as an exercise.

```
    SUBROUTINE SPLIT (S, PICKED, SMALLER, NUMBER_SMALLER,  &
                      NUMBER_EQUAL, LARGER, NUMBER_LARGER)

      USE STACK_OF_INTEGERS

      IMPLICIT NONE
      TYPE (STACK), INTENT (INOUT) :: S
      INTEGER, INTENT (IN) :: PICKED
      TYPE (STACK), INTENT (OUT) :: SMALLER, LARGER
      INTEGER, INTENT (OUT) :: &
          NUMBER_SMALLER, NUMBER_EQUAL, NUMBER_LARGER
      TYPE (NODE), POINTER :: TMP_PTR
```

```
      SMALLER = NEW ()
      LARGER = NEW ()
      NUMBER_SMALLER = 0
      NUMBER_EQUAL = 1
      NUMBER_LARGER = 0

   DO
      IF (EMPTY (S)) EXIT
      CALL POP_NODE (S, TMP_PTR)
      IF (TMP_PTR % KEY < PICKED) THEN
          CALL PUSH_NODE (SMALLER, TMP_PTR)
          NUMBER_SMALLER = NUMBER_SMALLER + 1
      ELSE IF (TMP_PTR % KEY > PICKED) THEN
          CALL PUSH_NODE (LARGER, TMP_PTR)
          NUMBER_LARGER = NUMBER_LARGER + 1
      ELSE
          DEALLOCATE (TMP_PTR)
          NUMBER_EQUAL = NUMBER_EQUAL + 1
      END IF
   END DO

END SUBROUTINE SPLIT

SUBROUTINE PUSH_NODE (S, NODE_PTR)

   IMPLICIT NONE
   TYPE (STACK), INTENT (INOUT) :: S
   TYPE (NODE), POINTER, INTENT (IN) :: NODE_PTR

   NODE_PTR % REST_OF_STACK % TOP => S % TOP
   S % TOP => NODE_PTR

END SUBROUTINE PUSH_NODE

SUBROUTINE POP_NODE (S, NODE_PTR)

   IMPLICIT NONE
   TYPE (STACK), INTENT (INOUT) :: S
   TYPE (NODE), POINTER, INTENT (OUT) :: NODE_PTR
```

```
        NODE_PTR => S % TOP
        S % TOP => NODE_PTR % REST_OF_STACK % TOP

    END SUBROUTINE POP_NODE
```

8.4.2 Exercises

1. Experiment with the program SELECT, finding the median of different quantities of randomly generated integers to determine an approximate formula for the complexity of the program. The execution time should be proportional to n.

2. Complete the modification of the procedures in the module STACK_OF_INTEGERS to be efficient when dealing with stacks of large structures, as was done for the subroutines PUSH_NODE, POP_NODE, and SPLIT.

3. Another way to handle the problem of manipulating stacks of objects that are not single values, such as integers, but perhaps are large structures or arrays, is to replace the value field in each node with a pointer to the object that is to be placed in the stack. That is, instead of manipulating stacks of objects, manipulate stacks of pointers to the objects. Modify the procedures in the module STACK_OF_INTEGERS to process stacks of large structures or arrays of values by this scheme.

8.5 Arrays of Pointers

In Fortran, it is not possible to have an array of pointers. However, the same effect can be achieved with an array of structures, each of which has a single component that is a pointer variable.

8.5.1 A Poor Sorting Algorithm

We begin with a very simple, but very inefficient, subroutine that sorts an array of real numbers. This should never be used to sort more than a few dozen numbers, but it is pretty easy to remember and write in a hurry, if necessary. Anyway, the point of this discussion is not to get a good sorting algorithm, but show how pointers can be used.

```
    SUBROUTINE BAD_SORT (NUMBERS)
    ! Uses an inefficient sorting algorithm
    ! Moves type REAL data when swapping
```

```
IMPLICIT NONE
REAL, DIMENSION (:), INTENT (INOUT) :: NUMBERS
INTEGER :: I, J
REAL :: N

DO I = 1, SIZE (NUMBERS) - 1
   DO J = I + 1, SIZE (NUMBERS)
      IF (NUMBERS (I) > NUMBERS (J)) THEN
         N = NUMBERS (I)
         NUMBERS (I) = NUMBERS (J)
         NUMBERS (J) = N
      END IF
   END DO
END DO

END SUBROUTINE BAD_SORT
```

Let's also suppose that instead of sorting an array of real numbers, we must sort an array of large data structures, one component of which is a key that determines the order of the data in the sorted list. An example might be structures, one for each person, maintained by the U.S. Internal Revenue Service. It might be desirable to sort the structures based on social security number, for example. Thus, we may have structures of type PERSON_TYPE with one component being SSN, the social security number that identifies each taxpayer.

```
TYPE PERSON_TYPE

   INTEGER :: SSN
   . . . ! A lot of other stuff

END TYPE PERSON_TYPE
```

The subroutine BAD_SORT would have to be modified to the following.

```
SUBROUTINE BAD_SORT (RECORDS)
! Uses inefficient sorting algorithm
! Moves whole records when swapping

   IMPLICIT NONE
   TYPE (PERSON_TYPE), DIMENSION (:), INTENT (INOUT) :: RECORDS
   TYPE (PERSON_TYPE) :: R
   INTEGER :: I, J
```

```
    DO I = 1, SIZE (RECORDS) - 1
        DO J = I + 1, SIZE (RECORDS)
            IF (RECORDS (I) % SSN > RECORDS (J) % SSN) THEN
                R = RECORDS (I)
                RECORDS (I) = RECORDS (J)
                RECORDS (J) = R
            END IF
        END DO
    END DO

END SUBROUTINE BAD_SORT
```

Now we not only have a subroutine that uses an inefficient sorting algorithm, but it wastes a lot of time moving large amounts of data around every time it finds two records out of order and swaps them.

A way around this last difficulty is to create an array of pointers to the structures and instead of moving the structures, just swap the pointers. The argument to the following function is not an array of objects of type PERSON_TYPE, but an array of structures containing just one component, which is a pointer to an object of type PERSON_TYPE.

```
TYPE PERSON_PTR_TYPE
    TYPE (PERSON_TYPE), POINTER :: PTR
END TYPE PERSON_PTR_TYPE

TYPE (PERSON_PTR_TYPE), DIMENSION (:), ALLOCATABLE :: POINTERS
```

It is necessary to declare the array of structures of type PERSON_TYPE to have the TARGET attribute.

```
TYPE (PERSON_TYPE), DIMENSION (NUMBER_OF_PERSONS), TARGET :: RECORDS
```

First, we can set things up so that the first pointer in the array POINTERS points to the first record, the second pointer points to the second record, and so on.

```
ALLOCATE (POINTERS (SIZE (RECORDS)))
DO I = 1, SIZE (RECORDS)
    POINTERS (I) % PTR  => RECORDS (I)
END DO
```

Now we can write a subroutine that will do the sorting in the sense that it will change the array of pointers so that the first pointer points to the record with the smallest key, the second pointer points to the record with the second smallest key, and so on. The main argument to this sorting routine is the array of pointers, not the array of objects to be sorted.

```
SUBROUTINE BAD_SORT (POINTERS)
! Still uses inefficient algortithm
! but now moves only pointers when swapping

   IMPLICIT NONE
   TYPE (PERSON_PTR_TYPE), DIMENSION (:), INTENT (INOUT) ::  &
        POINTERS
   TYPE (PERSON_PTR_TYPE) :: P
   INTEGER :: I, J

   DO I = 1, SIZE (POINTERS) - 1
      DO J = I + 1, SIZE (POINTERS)
         IF (POINTERS (I) % PTR % SSN >  &
             POINTERS (J) % PTR % SSN) THEN
            P = POINTERS (I)
            POINTERS (I) = POINTERS (J)
            POINTERS (J) = P
         END IF
      END DO
   END DO

   END SUBROUTINE BAD_SORT
```

As can be seen, the subroutine is pretty much the same, except that the array argument is a different type and one more indirect reference is needed to access the value of an SSN: namely, POINTERS (I) % PTR % SSN is used in place of NUMBER (I). Notice that ordinary assignment is used for the variable P and the elements of the array POINTERS because they are structures and not pointers, even though their only component is a pointer.

8.5.2 A Good Sorting Algorithm for Records

Next we combine an efficient algorithm with the pointer techniques of the previous section that replace the time-consuming action of copying large records with the much faster operation of changing pointers to these records. We use the better quick sort algorithm written in Sections 4.3 and 4.4, modified below to use the array names of this chapter. Also, since we have been discussing "bad" sorting algorithms and have a subroutine BAD_SORT, we modify it to an internal subroutine

BAD_SUBLIST_SORT to do the sorting for very small lists, where it actually is faster than quick sort.

```
SUBROUTINE QUICK_SORT (NUMBERS)

   IMPLICIT NONE
   REAL, DIMENSION (:), INTENT (INOUT) :: NUMBERS
   CALL QUICK_SORT_1 (1, SIZE (NUMBERS))

CONTAINS

   RECURSIVE SUBROUTINE QUICK_SORT_1 (LEFT_END, RIGHT_END)

      IMPLICIT NONE
      INTEGER, INTENT (IN) :: LEFT_END, RIGHT_END
      INTEGER :: I, J
      REAL :: CHOSEN, T

      IF (RIGHT_END < LEFT_END + 6) THEN
         ! Use interchange sort for small lists
         CALL BAD_SUBLIST_SORT (LEFT_END, RIGHT_END)
      ELSE
         ! Use partition  or "quick" sort
         CHOSEN = NUMBERS ((LEFT_END + RIGHT_END) / 2)
         I = LEFT_END - 1; J = RIGHT_END + 1

         DO
            ! Scan list from left end
            ! until element >= chosen is found
            DO
               I = I + 1; IF (NUMBERS (I) >= CHOSEN) EXIT
            END DO
            ! Scan list from right end
            ! until element <= chosen is found
            DO
               J = J - 1; IF (NUMBERS (J) <= CHOSEN) EXIT
            END DO
            IF (I < J) THEN
               ! Swap two out of place elements
               T = NUMBERS (I)
               NUMBERS (I) = NUMBERS (J)
               NUMBERS (J) = T
```

```
            ELSE IF (I = J) THEN
                I = I + 1; EXIT
            ELSE
                EXIT
            END IF
        END DO

        IF (LEFT_END < J) CALL QUICK_SORT_1 (LEFT_END, J)
        IF (I < RIGHT_END) CALL QUICK_SORT_1 (I, RIGHT_END)
    END IF

END SUBROUTINE QUICK_SORT_1

SUBROUTINE BAD_SUBLIST_SORT (LEFT_END, RIGHT_END)

    IMPLICIT NONE
    INTEGER, INTENT (IN) :: LEFT_END, RIGHT_END
    INTEGER :: I, J
    REAL :: T

    DO I = LEFT_END, RIGHT_END - 1
        DO J = I + 1, RIGHT_END
            IF (NUMBERS (I) > NUMBERS (J)) THEN
                T = NUMBERS (I)
                NUMBERS (I) = NUMBERS (J)
                NUMBERS (J) = T
            END IF
        END DO
    END DO

    END SUBROUTINE BAD_SUBLIST_SORT

END SUBROUTINE QUICK_SORT
```

The modifications that need to be made are the same as those for converting the bad sorting algorithm on the same data type to a pointer algorithm on records. Basically, we always move objects of PERSON_PTR_TYPE, which is a structure with one component. That component is a pointer to the record of type PERSON_TYPE that we want to avoid moving. When we need to reference a key value for comparison, we do it indirectly from the array of pointers. In effect, the current Ith social security number in the list is referenced by POINTERS (I)

% PTR % SSN. The following subroutines and declarations show the modifications.

```
TYPE PERSON_TYPE

   INTEGER :: SSN
   . . . ! A lot of other stuff

END TYPE PERSON_TYPE

TYPE PERSON_PTR_TYPE
   TYPE (PERSON_TYPE), POINTER :: PTR
END PERSON_PTR_TYPE

   . . .

TYPE (PERSON_TYPE), DIMENSION (NUMBER_OF_PERSONS),  &
                    TARGET :: RECORDS
TYPE (PERSON_PTR_TYPE), DIMENSION (:), ALLOCATABLE :: POINTERS
   . . .

ALLOCATE (POINTERS (SIZE (RECORDS))
DO I = 1, SIZE (RECORDS)
   POINTERS (I) % PTR => RECORDS (I)
END DO
CALL QUICK_SORT (POINTERS)
   . . .

SUBROUTINE QUICK_SORT (POINTERS)

   IMPLICIT NONE
   TYPE (PERSON_PTR_TYPE), DIMENSION (:),  &
                          INTENT (INOUT) :: POINTERS
   CALL QUICK_SORT_1 (1, SIZE (POINTERS))

   CONTAINS

   RECURSIVE SUBROUTINE QUICK_SORT_1 (LEFT_END, RIGHT_END)

      IMPLICIT NONE
      INTEGER, INTENT (IN) :: LEFT_END, RIGHT_END
      INTEGER :: I, J
      TYPE (PERSON_PTR_TYPE) :: CHOSEN, T
```

```
IF (RIGHT_END < LEFT_END + 6) THEN
   ! Use interchange sort for small lists
   CALL BAD_SUBLIST_SORT (LEFT_END, RIGHT_END)
ELSE
   ! Use partition ("quick") sort
   CHOSEN = POINTERS ((LEFT_END + RIGHT_END) / 2)
   I = LEFT_END - 1; J = RIGHT_END + 1

   DO
      ! Scan list from left end
      ! until element >= chosen is found
      DO
         I = I + 1
         IF (POINTERS (I) % PTR % SSN >=  &
               CHOSEN % PTR % SSN) EXIT
      END DO
      ! Scan list from right end
      ! until element <= chosen is found
      DO
         J = J - 1
         IF (POINTERS (J) % PTR % SSN <=  &
               CHOSEN % PTR % SSN) EXIT
      END DO
      IF (I < J) THEN
         ! Swap two out of place elements
         T = POINTERS (I); POINTERS (I) = POINTERS (J);
         POINTERS (J) = T
      ELSE IF (I = J) THEN
         I = I + 1; EXIT
      ELSE
         EXIT
      END IF
   END DO

   IF (LEFT_END < J) CALL QUICK_SORT_1 (LEFT_END, J)
   IF (I < RIGHT_END) CALL QUICK_SORT_1 (I, RIGHT_END)
END IF

END SUBROUTINE QUICK_SORT_1
```

```
        SUBROUTINE BAD_SUBLIST_SORT (LEFT_END, RIGHT_END)

    IMPLICIT NONE
    INTEGER, INTENT (IN) :: LEFT_END, RIGHT_END
    INTEGER :: I, J
    REAL :: T

    DO I = LEFT_END, RIGHT_END - 1
       DO J = I + 1, RIGHT_END
          IF (POINTERS (I) % PTR % SSN >  &
              POINTERS (J) % PTR % SSN) THEN
              T = POINTERS (I); POINTERS (I) = POINTERS (J)
              POINTERS (J) = T
          END IF
       END DO
    END DO

    END SUBROUTINE BAD_SUBLIST_SORT

END SUBROUTINE QUICK_SORT
```

9

Input and Output

The facilities needed to do simple input and output tasks were described in Chapter 1, and many examples of these statements were discussed throughout the other chapters. Sometimes it is necessary to use the more sophisticated input/output features of Fortran. This chapter describes in some detail these features, including direct access input/output, nonadvancing input/output, the use of internal files, file connection statements, the INQUIRE statement, file positioning statements, and formatting.

The input/output statements are

READ
PRINT
WRITE
OPEN
CLOSE
INQUIRE
BACKSPACE
ENDFILE
REWIND

The OPEN and CLOSE statements deal with the connection between an input/output unit and a file; the INQUIRE statement provides the means to find out things about a file or unit; the READ, WRITE, and PRINT statements are the ones that do the actual data transfer; and the BACK-SPACE, ENDFILE, and REWIND statements affect the position of the file.

Since this chapter is needed only for the more sophisticated kinds of input and output, it is organized a little bit differently from other chapters. The first part contains a discussion of some fundamental ideas needed for a thorough understanding of how Fortran input/output works. The next part of the chapter contains a description and examples of the special kinds of data transfer input/output statements. Then there is a description of the OPEN, CLOSE, INQUIRE, BACKSPACE, REWIND, and ENDFILE statements. The final part contains a more detailed description of formatting than that provided in Chapter 1.

Input and output operations deal with collections of data called *files*. The data are organized into *records*, which may correspond to a line on a computer terminal, a line on a printout, or a part of a disk file. The descriptions of records and files in this chapter are to be considered abstractions and do not necessarily represent the way data is stored physically on any particular device. For example, a Fortran program may produce a file of answers. This file might be printed, and the only remaining physical representation of the file would be the ink on the paper. Or it might be written onto magnetic tape and remain there for a few years, eventually to be erased when the tape is used to store other information.

Before discussing further the general properties of files, we will discuss the properties of records.

9.1 Records

There are two kinds of records, data records and end-of-file records. A **data record** is a sequence of values. Thus, a data record may be represented schematically as a collection of small boxes, each containing a value, as shown in Figure 9-1.

The values in a data record may be represented in one of two ways: formatted or unformatted. If the values are characters readable by a person, each character is one value and the data is **formatted**. For example, a record may contain the four character values "6" "," "1" and "1" that are intended to represent the two numbers, 6 and 11. In this case, the record might be represented schematically as Figure 9-2.

Unformatted data consists of values represented just as they are stored in computer memory. For example, if integers are stored using an

Figure 9-1 Schematic representation of the values in a record.

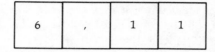

Figure 9-2 A record with four character values.

eight-bit binary representation, an unformatted record consisting of two integer values, 6 and 11 might look like Figure 9-3.

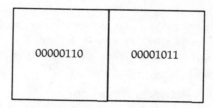

Figure 9-3 An unformatted record with two integer values.

9.1.1 Formatted Records

A **formatted record** is one that contains only formatted data. A formatted record may be created by a person typing at a terminal or by a Fortran program that converts values stored internally into character strings that form readable representations of those values. When formatted data is read into the computer, the characters must be converted to the computer's internal representation of values, which is often a binary representation. Even character values may be converted from one character representation in the record to another internal representation. The length of a formatted record is the number of characters in it; the length may be zero.

9.1.2 Unformatted Records

An **unformatted record** is one that contains only unformatted data. Unformatted records usually are created by running a Fortran program, although, with the knowledge of how to form the bit patterns correctly, they could be created by other means. Unformatted data often requires less space on an external device. Also, it is usually faster to read and write unformatted data because no conversion is required. However, it is not as suitable for reading by humans, and usually it is not suitable for transferring data from one computer to another because the internal representation of values is machine dependent. The length of an unformatted data record depends on the number of values in it, but is measured in some processor-dependent units; it may be zero. The length of an unformatted record that will be produced by a particular output list may be determined by the INQUIRE statement (9.6).

9.1.3 End-of-File Records

The other kind of record is the **end-of-file record**, which, at least conceptually, has no values and has no length. There can be at most one end-of-file record in a file and it must be the last record of a file. It is used to mark the end of a file.

An end-of-file record may be written explicitly by the programmer using the ENDFILE statement. An end-of-file record also is written implicitly when the last data transfer statement involving the file was an output statement and

1. a BACKSPACE statement is executed,

2. a REWIND statement is executed, or

3. the program is terminated without an error condition.

9.1.4 Printing of Formatted Records

Sometimes output records are sent to a device that interprets the first character of the record as a control character. This is usually the case with line printers. If a formatted record is printed on such a device, the first character of the record is not printed but instead is used to control vertical spacing. The remaining characters of the record, if any, are printed in one line beginning at the left margin.

The first character of such a record must be of default character type and determines vertical spacing, as shown in Table 9-1.

If there are no characters in the record, a blank line is printed.

Sometimes it may be difficult to determine if the first character of each record is going to be interpreted as a carriage control character. On some systems it is done on terminals and on some it is not. The first character in a record is almost always interpreted in this way by line printers and probably rarely so interpreted prior to storing on a disk or

Table 9-1 Carriage control characters.

Character	Vertical Spacing Before Printing
Blank	One line (single spacing)
0	Two lines (double spacing)
1	To first line of next page (begin new page)
+	No advance (overprint on top of old line)

magnetic tape. The only way to know is to read the manual for the system you are using or to experiment.

9.2 Files

A **file** is a collection of records. A file may be represented schematically with each box representing a record, as shown in Figure 9-4.

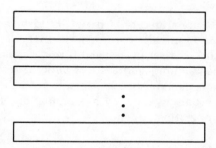

Figure 9-4 Schematic representation of records in a file.

The records of a file must be either all formatted or all unformatted, except that they may contain an endfile record as the last record. A file may have a name, but the length of the names and the characters that may be used in the names depend on the system being used. The set of names that are allowed often is determined by the operating system as well as the Fortran compiler.

A distinction is made between files that are located on an external device, such as a disk, and files in memory accessible to the program. The two kinds of files are

1. External files

2. Internal files

The use of the files is illustrated schematically in Figure 9-5.

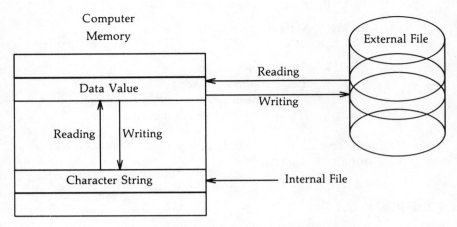

Figure 9-5 Internal and external files.

9.2.1 External Files

External files usually are stored on a peripheral device, such as a tape, a disk, or a computer terminal. For each external file, there is a set of allowed access methods, a set of allowed forms (formatted or unformatted), a set of allowed actions, and a set of allowed record lengths. How these characteristics are established is dependent on the computer system you are using, but usually is done by a combination of requests by users of the files and the operating system.

9.2.2 Internal Files

Internal files are stored in memory as values of character variables. The character values may be created using all the usual means of assigning character values or they may be created with an output statement using the variable as an internal file. If the variable is a scalar, the file has just one record; if the variable is an array, the file has one record for each element of the array. Only formatted sequential access is permitted on internal files.

9.2.3 Existence of Files

Certain files are known to the processor and are available to an executing program; these files are said to **exist** at that time. For example, a file may not exist because it is not anywhere on the disks accessible to a system. A file may not exist to a particular program because the user of the program is not authorized to access the file. For example, Fortran programs usually are not permitted to access special system files, such as the operating system or the compiler, in order to protect them from user modification. The INQUIRE statement may be used to determine whether or not a file exists.

In addition to files that are made available to programs by the processor for input, output, and other special purposes, programs may create files needed during and after program execution. When the program creates files, they are said to exist, even if no data has been written into the file. A file no longer exists after it has been deleted. Any of the input/output statements may refer to files that exist for the program at that point during execution. Some of the input/output statements (INQUIRE, OPEN, CLOSE, WRITE, PRINT, REWIND, and ENDFILE) may refer to files that do not exist. For example, a WRITE statement may create a file that does not exist and put data into that file. An internal file always exists.

9.2.4 File Access Methods

There are two kinds of access methods for external files:

1. Sequential access

2. Direct access

Sequential access to the records in the file begins with the first record of the file and proceeds sequentially to the second record, and then to the next record, record by record. The records are accessed in the order that they appear in the file. It is not possible to begin at some particular record within the file without reading from the current record down to that record in sequential order.

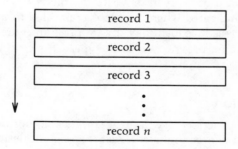

Figure 9-6 Sequential access.

When a file is being accessed sequentially, the records are read and written sequentially. For example, if the records are written in any arbitrary order using direct access and then read using sequential access, the records are read beginning with record number one of the file, regardless of when it was written.

When a file is accessed directly, the records are selected by record number. Using this identification, the records may be read or written in any order. For example, it is possible to write record number 47 first, then write record number 13. In a new file, this produces a file represented by Figure 9-7. Either record may be written without first accessing the other.

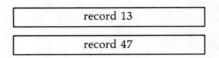

Figure 9-7 A file written using direct access.

The following rules apply when accessing a file directly:

1. If a file is to be accessed directly, all of the records must be the same length.

2. It is not possible to delete a record using direct access.

3. List-directed input/output and nonadvancing input/output are prohibited.

4. An internal file must be accessed sequentially.

Each file has a set of permissible access methods, which usually means that it may be accessed either sequentially or directly. However, it is possible that a file may be accessed by either method. The actual file access method used to read or write the file is *not* a property of the file itself, but is indicated when the file is connected to a unit. The same file may be accessed sequentially by a program, then later accessed directly by the same program, if both types of access are permitted for the file.

9.2.5 File Position

Each file being processed by a program has a **position**. During the course of program execution, records are read or written, causing the position of the file to change. Also, there are Fortran statements that cause the position of a file to change; an example is the BACKSPACE statement.

The **initial point** is the point just before the first record. The **terminal point** is the point just after the last record. If the file is empty, the initial point and the terminal point are the same.

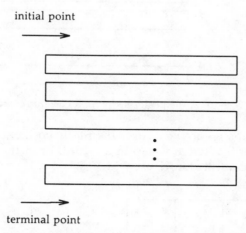

Figure 9-8 Initial and terminal points of a file.

A file may be positioned between records. In the example pictured in Figure 9-9, the file is positioned between records 2 and 3. In this case, record 2 is the preceding record and record 3 is the next record. Of course, if a file is positioned at its initial point, there is no preceding record, and there is no next record if it is positioned at its terminal point.

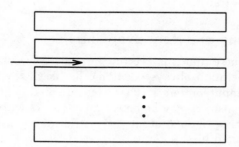

Figure 9-9 A file positioned between records.

There may be a current record during execution of an input/output statement or after completion of a nonadvancing input/output statement as shown in Figure 9-10, where record 2 is the current record.

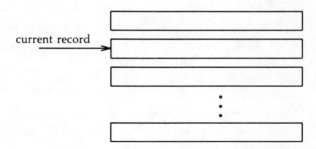

Figure 9-10 A file positioned with a current record.

When there is a current record, the file is positioned at the initial point of the record, between values in a record, or at the terminal point of the record as illustrated in Figure 9-11.

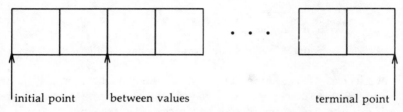

Figure 9-11 Positions within a record of a file.

An internal file is always positioned at the beginning of a record just prior to data transfer.

9.2.6 Advancing and Nonadvancing I/O

Advancing input/output is record oriented. Completion of an input/output operation always positions the file at the end of a record. Nonadvancing input/output is character oriented. After reading and writing, the file position may be between characters within a record.

Nonadvancing input/output is restricted to use with external sequential formatted files.

9.2.7 Units and File Connection

Input/output statements refer to a particular file by specifying its unit. For example, the READ and WRITE statements do not refer to a file directly, but refer to a unit number, which must be connected to a file.

The unit number for an external file is a nonnegative integer. The name of an internal file also is called a unit; it is a character variable.

Rules and restrictions for units:

1.   The * specifies a processor determined unit number. It is the same unit number that the processor would use if a READ or PRINT statement appeared without the unit number. The unit specified by an asterisk may be used only for formatted sequential access.

2.   File positioning, file connection, and inquiry must use external units.

3.   A unit number identifies one and only one unit in a Fortran program. That is, a unit number is global to an entire program; a particular file may be connected to unit 9 in one procedure and referred to through unit 9 in another procedure.

Only certain unit numbers may be used on a particular computing system. The unit numbers that may be used are said to **exist**. Some unit numbers on some processors are always used for data input (for example, unit 5), others are always used for output (for example, unit 6). Input/output statements must refer to units that exist, except for those that close a file or inquire about a unit. The INQUIRE statement may be used to determine whether or not a unit exists.

To transfer data to or from an external file, the file must be connected to a unit. Once the connection is made, most input/output statements use the unit number instead of using the name of the file directly. An internal file always is connected to the unit that is the name of the character variable. There are two ways to establish connection between a unit and an external file:

1.   Execution of an OPEN statement in the executing program

2.   Preconnection by the operating system

Only one file may be connected to a unit at any given time. If the unit is disconnected after its first use on a file, it may be reconnected later to another file or it may be reconnected later to the same file. A file that is not connected to a unit may not be used in any statement except the OPEN, CLOSE, or INQUIRE statements. Some units may be preconnected to files for each Fortran program by the operating system, without any action necessary by the program. For example, on most systems, units 5 and 6 are always preconnected to the default input and default output files, respectively. Preconnection of units also may be done by the operating system when requested by the user in the operating system command language. In either of these cases, the user program does not require an OPEN statement to connect the file; it is preconnected.

9.3 Data Transfer Statements

The **data transfer statements** are the READ, WRITE, and PRINT statements. In previous chapters we have seen examples of various kinds of data transfer statements. The general forms for the data transfer statements are as follows. Optional parts of a statement appear in square brackets.

> READ (*io-control-spec-list*) [*input-item-list*]
> READ *format* [, *input-item-list*]
> WRITE (*io-control-spec-list*) [*output-item-list*]
> PRINT *format* [, *output-item-list*]

9.3.1 The Format Specifier

The format specifier (*format* in the syntax for the PRINT statement and the short form of the READ statement) may be a character expression or the label of a FORMAT statement indicating **explicit formatting**, an asterisk (*) indicating list-directed or default formatting, or an integer variable that is assigned the label of a FORMAT statement. Using a FORMAT statement is considered obsolete.

9.3.2 The Control Information List

The input/output control specification list must contain a unit specifier of the form

> [UNIT] = *io-unit*

and may contain at most one each of the following optional items:

> [FMT =] *format*
> [NML =] *namelist-group-name*
> REC = *scalar-int-expr*
> IOSTAT = *scalar-int-variable*
> ERR = *label*
> END = *label*
> ADVANCE = *scalar-default-char-expr*
> SIZE = *scalar-int-variable*
> EOR = *label*

The input/output unit must be a nonnegative integer indicating an external unit connected to a file, an asterisk indicating a processor-dependent external unit, or an internal unit. If the keyword UNIT does appear with the unit specifier, then the unit specifier must be the first item in the list. In this case, the keyword FMT or NML may be omitted from the format or namelist specifier and this item must be second in the list. It is not permitted (and does not make sense) to have both a format and a namelist specifier.

The allowed forms of a format are the same within a control information list as they are in the PRINT statement and the short form of the READ statement.

There are lots of additional rules about which combinations of these items may occur; some of these rules will be covered in the discussion of various types of data transfer statements in the following sections.

9.3.3 The Input/Output List

The input/output list consists basically of variables in a READ statement and expressions in a WRITE or PRINT statement. In addition, in any of the statements, the input/output list may contain an input/output implied DO list.

9.3.4 External Formatted Advancing Sequential Access I/O

The title of this section is a mouthful, but this is the kind of input/output that has been illustrated throughout the book. For formatted input and output, the file consists of characters. These characters are converted into representations suitable for storing in computer memory during input and converted from an internal representation to characters on output. When a file is accessed sequentially, records are processed in the order in which they appear in the file. Advancing input/output means that the file is positioned after the end of the last record read or written when the input/output is finished.

The general form for input/output statements is given later in this chapter, but templates that may be used to construct explicitly formatted sequential access data statements are

```
READ ( [ UNIT = ] unit-number &
    , [ FMT = ] format &
    [ , IOSTAT = scalar-int-variable ] &
    [ , ERR = label ] &
    [ , END = label ] &
    [ , ADVANCE = scalar-default-char-expr ] &
    ) [ io-list ]
```

```
WRITE ( [ UNIT = ] unit-number &
        , [ FMT = ] format &
        [ , IOSTAT = scalar-int-variable ] &
        [ , ERR = label ] &
        [ , ADVANCE = scalar-default-char-expr ] &
        ) [ io-list ]
```

and

```
PRINT format [ , io-list ]
```

The symbols FMT= may be omitted only if UNIT= is omitted. The *format* may be the label of a FORMAT statement, a character expression whose value is a format specification, or an asterisk indicating list-directed default formatting. For advancing input/output, the expression in the ADVANCE specifier must evaluate to YES, if it is present; nonadvancing input/output is discussed in Section 9.3.5. The ADVANCE specifier must not be present if the format is an asterisk designating list-directed formatting.

Examples of formatted reading are

```
READ (5, FMT_100, ERR = 99, END = 100) A, B, (C (I), I = 1, 40)
READ (9, FMT = "(2F20.5)", IOSTAT = IEND) X, Y
READ (UNIT = 5, FMT = "(5E20.0)", ADVANCE = "YES")   &
     (Y (I), I = 1, KK)
READ *, X, Y
```

Examples of formatted writing are

```
WRITE (9, FMT_103, IOSTAT = IS, ERR = 99) A, B, C, S
WRITE (UNIT = 7, FMT = *, ERR = 9) X
WRITE (*, "(F10.5)") X
PRINT "(A, E14.6)", " Y = ", Y
```

When an advancing sequential access input/output statement is executed, reading or writing of data begins with the next character in the file. If a previous input/output statement was a nonadvancing statement, the next character transferred may be in the middle of a record, even if the statement being executed is an advancing statement. The difference between the two is that an advancing input/output statement always leaves the file positioned at the end of the record.

The IOSTAT specifier may be used to check for end of file or an error condition. The ERR specifier may be used to cause a branch to a labeled statement if there is an error condition and the END specifier may be used to cause a branch to a labeled statement if the end of the file is encountered.

> *Style Note:* Avoid the use of ERR= and END= options whenever possible because they use the obsolete feature of statement labels. In most cases, use of the IOSTAT option followed by a test of the IOSTAT result is the preferred substitute.

9.3.5 Nonadvancing Data Transfer

Like advancing input/output, the file is read or written beginning with the next character; however, nonadvancing input/output leaves the file positioned after the last character read or written, rather than skipping to the end of the record. Nonadvancing input/output is sometimes called *partial record* or *stream* input/output. It may be used only with explicitly formatted external files connected for sequential access.

Templates that may be used to construct nonadvancing input/output statements are

```
READ ( [ UNIT = ] unit-number &
     , [ FMT = ] format &
     , ADVANCE = scalar-default-char-expr &
     [ , SIZE = scalar-int-variable ] &
     [ , EOR = label ] &
     [ , IOSTAT = scalar-int-variable ] &
     [ , ERR = label ] &
     [ , END = label ] &
     ) [ io-list ]
```

and

```
WRITE ( [ UNIT = ] unit-number &
      , [ FMT = ] format &
      , ADVANCE = scalar-default-char-expr &
      [ , IOSTAT = scalar-int-variable ] &
      [ , ERR = label ] &
      ) [ io-list ]
```

The scalar character expression in the ADVANCE= specifier must evaluate to NO for nonadvancing input/output. The symbols FMT= may be omitted only if UNIT= is omitted. The format may be the label of a FORMAT statement or a character expression whose value is a format specification; it must not be an asterisk designating list-directed formatting.

The SIZE= variable is assigned the number of characters read on input. The EOR branch is taken if an end of record is encountered during input.

The IOSTAT specifier may be used to check for an end of file, end of record, or error condition. The ERR specifier may be used to cause a branch if there is an error condition, and the END specifier may be used to cause a branch if the end of the file is encountered on input.

One of the important uses of nonadvancing input/output occurs when the size of the records is not known and it is necessary to read the input one character at a time. To illustrate this, the following program counts the number of characters in a file. IOSTAT values for end-of-record and end-of-file are required to be negative, but are otherwise processor dependent. The values –2 and –1 are typical, but the manual for you system should be consulted.

```
PROGRAM CHAR_COUNT
    IMPLICIT NONE
    INTEGER, PARAMETER :: END_OF_RECORD = -2
    INTEGER, PARAMETER :: END_OF_FILE = -1
    CHARACTER (LEN = 1) :: C
    INTEGER :: COUNT, IOS

    COUNT = 0
    DO
        READ (*, "(A)", ADVANCE = "NO", IOSTAT = IOS) C
        IF (IOS == END_OF_RECORD) THEN
            CYCLE
        ELSE IF (IOS == END_OF_FILE) THEN
            EXIT
        ELSE
            COUNT = COUNT + 1
        END IF
    END DO

    PRINT *, "The number of characters in the file is ", COUNT
END PROGRAM CHAR_COUNT
```

Another obvious use is to print part of a line at one place in a program and finish the line later. If things are implemented properly, it also should be possible to use nonadvancing input/output to supply a prompt to a terminal and have the user type in data on the same line. This is not absolutely guaranteed, because many systems consider input from a terminal and output to the terminal to involve two different files. Here is a simple example:

```
PROGRAM TEST_SIGN
   IMPLICIT NONE
   INTEGER :: NUMBER
   WRITE (*, *, ADVANCE = "NO"), "Type in any integer: "
   READ *, NUMBER
   WRITE (*, *, ADVANCE = "NO"), "The number", NUMBER, "is "
   IF (NUMBER > 0) THEN
      PRINT *, "positive."
   ELSE IF (NUMBER == 0) THEN
      PRINT *, "zero."
   ELSE
      PRINT *, "negative."
   END IF
END PROGRAM TEST_SIGN

RUN TEST_SIGN

Type in any number: 36
The number 36 is positive.
```

9.3.6 Data Transfer on Internal Files

Transferring data from machine representation to characters or from characters back to machine representation is done between two variables in an executing program. A formatted sequential access input or output statement is used. The format is used to interpret the characters. The internal file and the internal unit are the same character variable.

Templates that may be used to construct data transfer statements on an internal file are

READ ([UNIT =] *char-variable* &
    , [FMT =] *format* &
    [, IOSTAT = *scalar-int-variable*] &
    [, ERR = *label*] &
    [, END = *label*] &
) [*io-list*]

and

WRITE ([UNIT =] *char-variable* &
    , [FMT =] *format* &
    [, IOSTAT = *scalar-int-variable*] &
    [, ERR = *label* &
) [*io-list*]

The optional symbols FMT= may be omitted only if UNIT= is omitted.

Examples of data transfer statements on internal files are

```
READ (CHAR_124, FMT_100, IOSTAT = IO_ERR) MARY, X, J, NAME
WRITE (UNIT = CHAR_VAR, FMT = *) X
```

Some rules and restrictions for using internal files are

1.   The unit must be a character variable whose scope includes the data transfer statement.

2.   Each record of an internal file is a scalar character variable.

3.   If the file is an array or an array section, each element of the array or section is a scalar character variable and thus a record. The order of the records is the order of the array elements (for arrays of rank two and greater, the first subscript varies most rapidly). The length, which must be the same for each record, is the length of one array element.

4.   If the character variable is an array or part of an array that has the allocatable attribute, the variable must be allocated before its use as a unit identifier.

5.   If the number of characters written is less than the length of the record, the remaining characters are set to blank. If the number of characters is greater than the length of the record, the remaining characters are truncated.

6.   The records in an internal file are defined when the record is written. An internal file also may be defined by a character assignment statement, or some other means.

7.   To read a record in an internal file, it must have been defined.

8.   An internal file is always positioned at the beginning before a data transfer occurs.

9.   Only formatted sequential access is permitted on internal files. Namelist formatting is prohibited.

10.   File connection, positioning, and inquiry must not be used with internal files.

11.   The use of the IOSTAT, ERR, and END specifiers is the same as for external files.

As a simple example of the use of internal files, the following WRITE statement converts the value of the integer variable N into the character string S of length 10:

```
WRITE (S, "(I10)") N
```

If N = 999, the string S would be "*bbbbbbb*999", where "*b*" represents a blank character. To make the conversion behave a little differently, we can force the first character of S to be a sign (9.8.18) and make the rest of the characters digits, using as many leading zeros as necessary (9.8.5).

```
WRITE (S, "(SP, I10.9)") N
```

Now if N = 999, the string S will have the value "+000000999".

Another use of internal input/output is to read data from a file directly into a character string, examine it to make sure it has the proper form for the data that is supposed to be read, then read it with formatting conversion from the internal character string variable to the variables needed to hold the data. To keep the example simple, suppose that some input data record is supposed to contain 10 integer values, but they have been entered into the file as 10 integers separated by colons. List-directed input requires that the numbers be separated by blanks or commas. One option is to read in the data, examine the characters one at a time, and build the integers; but list-directed input will do everything except find the colon separators. So another possibility is to read in the record, change the colons to commas, and use an internal list-directed READ statement to convert the character string into 10 integer values.

```
CHARACTER (LEN = 100) INTERNAL_RECORD
INTEGER, DIMENSION (10) :: NUMBERS
   . . .
READ (*, "(A)") INTERNAL_RECORD
DO
    COLON_POSITION = INDEX (INTERNAL_RECORD, ":")
    IF (COLON_POSITION == 0) EXIT
    INTERNAL_RECORD (COLON_POSITION : COLON_POSITION) = ","
END DO
READ (INTERNAL_RECORD, FMT = *) NUMBERS
```

Of course, in a real program, some error checking should be done to make sure that the internal record has the correct format after the colons are converted to commas.

9.3.7 Unformatted Input/Output

For unformatted input and output, the file consists of values stored using the same representation used in program memory. This means that no conversion is required during input and output. Unformatted input/output may be done using both sequential and direct access.

Templates that may be used to construct unformatted access data statements are

```
READ ( [ UNIT = ] unit-number &
       [ , REC = record-number ] &
       [ , IOSTAT = scalar-int-variable ] &
       [ , ERR = label ] &
       [ , END = label ] &
     ) [ io-list ]
```

and

```
WRITE ( [ UNIT = ] unit-number &
        [ , REC = record-number ] &
        [ , IOSTAT = scalar-int-variable ] &
        [ , ERR = label ] &
      ) [ io-list ]
```

Examples of unformatted access reading are

```
READ (5, ERR = 99, END = 100) A, B, (C (I), I = 1, 40)
READ (UNIT = 9, REC = 14, IOSTAT = IEND) X, Y
READ (5) Y
```

Examples of unformatted access writing are

```
WRITE (9, IOSTAT = IS, ERR = 99) A, B, C, S
WRITE (ERR = 99, UNIT = 7) X
WRITE (9, REC = NEXT_RECORD_NUMBER) X
```

If the access is sequential, the file is positioned at the beginning of the next record prior to data transfer and positioned at the end of the record when the input/output is finished, because nonadvancing unformatted input/output is not permitted.

The IOSTAT, ERR, and END specifiers may be used in the same ways they are used for formatted input/output.

Unformatted access is very useful when creating a file of data that must be saved from one execution of a program and used for a later execution of the program. Suppose, for example that a program deals with the inventory of a large number of automobile parts. The data for each part (in our simple example) consists of the part number and the quantity in stock.

```
TYPE PART
    INTEGER :: ID_NUMBER, QTY_IN_STOCK
END TYPE PART

TYPE (PART), DIMENSION (10000) :: PART_LIST
INTEGER :: NUMBER_OF_PARTS
```

Suppose the integer variable NUMBER_OF_PARTS records the number of different parts that are stored in the array PART_LIST. At the end of the program, the number of parts and the entire part list can be saved in the file named PART_FILE with the following statements:

```
OPEN (UNIT = 9, FILE = "PART_FILE", POSITION = "REWIND",  &
      FORM = "UNFORMATTED", ACTION = "WRITE")
WRITE (9), NUMBER_OF_PARTS, PART_LIST (1:NUMBER_OF_PARTS)
```

At the beginning of the next execution of the program, the inventory can be read back into memory with the statements:

```
OPEN (UNIT = 9, FILE = "PART_FILE", POSITION = "REWIND",  &
      FORM = "UNFORMATTED", ACTION = "READ", STATUS = "OLD")
READ (9), NUMBER_OF_PARTS, PART_LIST (1:NUMBER_OF_PARTS)
```

9.3.8 Direct Access Data Transfer

When a file is accessed directly, the record to be processed is given by reference to the record number. The file may be formatted or unformatted.

Templates that may be used to construct direct access data statements are

```
READ ( [ UNIT = ] unit-number &
       [ , [ FMT = ] format ] &
       , REC = record-number &
       [ , IOSTAT = scalar-int-variable ] &
       [ , ERR = label ] &
       ) [ io-list ]
```

and

```
WRITE ( [ UNIT = ] unit-number ] &
        [ , [ FMT = ] format ] &
        , REC = record-number &
        [ , IOSTAT = scalar-int-variable ] &
        [ , ERR = label ] &
      ) [ io-list ]
```

FMT= may be omitted only if UNIT= is omitted. The *format* must not
be an asterisk.

Examples of direct access input/output statements are

```
READ (7, FMT_X, REC = 32, ERR = 99) A
READ (UNIT = 10, REC = 34, IOSTAT = IO_STATUS, ERR = 99) A, B, D
WRITE (8, "(2F15.5)", REC = N + 2) X, Y
```

The IOSTAT and ERR specifiers are used just as they are with
sequential access. The END specifier is not used with direct access.

To illustrate the use of direct access files, let us consider the simple
automobile parts example used in Section 9.3.7 to illustrate unformatted
input/output. In this example, suppose that the parts list is so large that
it is not feasible to read the entire list into memory. Instead, each time
information about a part is needed, just the information about that one
part is read from an external file. To do this in a reasonable amount of
time, the file must be stored on a device such as a disk, where each part
is accessible as readily as any other. Analogous but more realistic examples might involve the bank accounts for all customers of a bank or tax
information on all tax payers in one country. This time a structure is
not needed, because the only information in the file is the quantity on
hand. The part identification number is used as the record number of
the record in the file used to store the information for the part having
that number. Also, the array is not needed because the program deals
with only one part at a time.

Suppose we just need a program that looks up the quantity in stock
for a given part number. This program queries the user for the part
number, looks up the quantity on hand by reading one record from a
file, and prints out that quantity.

```
PROGRAM PART_INFO
   IMPLICIT NONE
   INTEGER :: PART_NUMBER, QTY_IN_STOCK

   PRINT *, "Enter part number"
   READ *, PART_NUMBER
```

```
OPEN (UNIT = 9, FILE = "PART_LIST", ACCESS = "DIRECT",  &
      FORM = "UNFORMATTED", ACTION = "READ", STATUS = "OLD")
READ (UNIT = 9, REC = PART_NUMBER) QTY_IN_STOCK
PRINT *, "The quantity in stock is ", QTY_IN_STOCK
END PROGRAM PART_INFO
```

Of course, the program could be a little more sophisticated by using a loop to repeat the process of asking for a part number and providing the quantity in stock. Also, there must be other programs that create and maintain the file that holds the database of information about the parts. A more complex organization for the file may be necessary if the range of legal part numbers greatly exceeds the actual number of different parts for which information is saved.

9.4 The OPEN Statement

The OPEN statement establishes a connection between a unit and an external file and determines the connection properties. After this is done, the file can be used for data transfers (reading and writing) using the unit number. It is not necessary to execute an OPEN statement for files that are preconnected to a unit.

The OPEN statement may appear anywhere in a program and, once executed, the connection of the unit to the file is valid in the main program or any subprogram for the remainder of that execution, unless a CLOSE statement affecting the connection is executed.

If a file is connected to one unit, it may not be connected to a different unit at the same time.

9.4.1 Changing the Connection Properties

Execution of an OPEN statement may change the properties of a connection that is already established. The properties that may be changed are those indicated by BLANK=, DELIM=, PAD=, ERR=, and IOSTAT=. If new values for DELIM, PAD, and BLANK are specified, these will be used in subsequent data transfer statements; otherwise, the old ones will be used. However, the parameters in ERR and IOSTAT from a previous connection are used only until another OPEN statement is encountered; after that they have no effect. If no ERR or IOSTAT appear in the new OPEN statement, no ERR or IOSTAT action can result from subsequent input/output.

9.4.2 Syntax Rule for the OPEN Statement

The form of the OPEN statement is

OPEN (*connect-spec-list*)

where the permissible connection specifications are

[UNIT =] *external-file-unit*
IOSTAT = *scalar-int-variable*
ERR = *label*
FILE = *file-name-expr*
STATUS = *scalar-char-expr*
ACCESS = *scalar-char-expr*
FORM = *scalar-char-expr*
RECL = *scalar-int-expr*
BLANK = *scalar-char-expr*
POSITION = *scalar-char-expr*
ACTION = *scalar-char-expr*
DELIM = *scalar-char-expr*
PAD = *scalar-char-expr*

Examples are

```
OPEN (STATUS = "SCRATCH", UNIT = 9)
OPEN (8, FILE = "PLOT_DATA", ERR = 99, ACCESS = "DIRECT")
```

Some rules and restrictions for the OPEN statement are

1. An external unit number is required. If the keyword UNIT is omitted, the external unit must be the first item in the list.

2. A specifier may appear at most once in any OPEN statement.

3. The FILE= specifier must appear if the STATUS= is OLD, NEW, or REPLACE; the FILE= specifier must not appear if the STATUS is SCRATCH.

4. The character expression established for many of the specifiers must contain permitted values in a list of alternative values as described below. For example, OLD, NEW, UNKNOWN, REPLACE, and SCRATCH are permitted for the STATUS= specifier; any other combination of letters is not permitted. Trailing blanks in any specifier are ignored.

9.4.3 The Connection Specifiers

IOSTAT=	The IOSTAT specifier must be an integer variable. It is given a value that is a positive integer if there is an error condition, a negative integer if there is an end-of-file or end-of-record condition, and zero if none of these conditions is true. The values returned for end of file and end of record are processor dependent.
ERR=	The program branches to the label in the ERR= specifier if an error occurs.
FILE=	The FILE= specifier indicates the name of the file to be connected. If the name is omitted, the connection could be made to a processor-determined file.
STATUS=	The value of the STATUS= specifier must be OLD, NEW, UNKNOWN, REPLACE, or SCRATCH. OLD refers to a file that must exist. NEW refers to a file that must not exist. UNKNOWN refers to a processor-dependent status. If the status is REPLACE and the file does not exist, it is created and given a status of OLD. If the status is REPLACE and the file does exist, it is deleted, a new file is created with the same name, and its status is changed to OLD. SCRATCH refers to a scratch file that exists only until termination of execution of the program or until a CLOSE is executed on that unit. Scratch files must be unnamed.
ACCESS=	The value of the ACCESS= specifier must be DIRECT or SEQUENTIAL. DIRECT refers to direct access. SEQUENTIAL refers to sequential access. The method must be an allowed access method for the file. If the file is new, the allowed access methods given to the file must include the one indicated.
FORM=	The value of the FORM= specifier must be FORMATTED or UNFORMATTED. FORMATTED indicates that all records will be formatted. UNFORMATTED indicates that all records will be unformatted. If the file is

connected for direct access, the default is
UNFORMATTED. If the file is connected for
sequential access, the default is FORMATTED.
If the file is new, the allowed forms given to the
file must include the one indicated.

RECL=

The RECL= specifier has a positive value that
specifies the length of each record if the access
method is DIRECT or the maximum length of a
record if the access method is SEQUENTIAL. If
the file is connected for formatted input/output,
the length is the number of characters. If the
file is connected for unformatted input/output,
the length is measured in processor-dependent
units. The length may, for example, be the
number of computer words. If the file exists,
the length of the record specified must be an
allowed record length. If the file does not exist,
the file is created with the specified length as an
allowed length.

BLANK=

The BLANK= specifier has a value that is
NULL or ZERO and may be specified only for
files connected for FORMATTED input/output.
If there is no blank specifier, the default is
NULL. If NULL is specified, all blanks in
numeric fields are ignored; a field of all blanks
would evaluate to zero. If ZERO is specified, all
blanks except leading blanks are interpreted as
zero.

POSITION=

The value of the POSITION= specifier must be
ASIS, REWIND, or APPEND. ASIS leaves the
file position unchanged for a connected file and
unspecified for a file that is not connected.
REWIND positions the file at its initial point.
APPEND positions the file at the terminal point
or just ahead of an endfile record, if there is
one. The file must be connected for sequential
access. If the file is new, it is positioned at its
initial point. The default value is ASIS, permitting an OPEN statement to change other connection properties of a file that is already connected
without changing its position.

ACTION= The value of the ACTION= specifier must be READ, WRITE, or READWRITE. READ indicates that WRITE, PRINT, and ENDFILE are prohibited. WRITE indicates that READ statements are prohibited. READWRITE indicates that any input/output statement is permitted. The default is READWRITE.

DELIM= The value of the DELIM= specifier must be APOSTROPHE, QUOTE, or NONE. APOSTROPHE and QUOTE indicate that the delimiting character for character constants written in list-directed or namelist formatting is the apostrophe or quotation mark, respectively. In this case, an occurrence of the designated character within a character constant will be doubled. NONE indicates that character constants will not be delimited. The default is NONE. The specifier is permitted only for a file connected for formatted input/output; it is ignored for formatted input.

PAD= The PAD= specifier has a value YES or NO. YES means that blank padding is used when the input list requires more data than the record contains. NO means that the input list must contain the data that the input list and formatting require. The default is YES.

9.5 The CLOSE Statement

Execution of a CLOSE statement terminates the connection of a file to a unit. Any connections not closed explicitly by a CLOSE statement are closed by the operating system when the program terminates. The form of the CLOSE statement is

    CLOSE (close-spec-list)

The items in the close specification list may be selected from

    [UNIT =] external-file-unit
    IOSTAT = scalar-int-variable
    ERR = label
    STATUS = scalar-char-expr

Examples are

```
CLOSE (ERR = 99, UNIT = 9)
CLOSE (8, IOSTAT = IR, STATUS = "KEEP")
```

Some rules for the CLOSE statement are

1.   An external unit number is required. If the keyword UNIT is omitted, the external unit must be the first item in the list.

2.   A CLOSE statement may refer to a unit that is not connected or does not exist, but it has no effect. This is not considered an error.

3.   The STATUS= specifier must have a value that is KEEP or DELETE. If it is KEEP, the file continues to exist after closing the file. If it has the value of DELETE, the file will not exist after closing the file. The default value is KEEP, except that the default for SCRATCH files is DELETE.

4.   The rules for the ERR= and IOSTAT= parameters are the same as for the OPEN statement.

5.   A specifier must not appear more than once in a CLOSE statement.

6.   Connections that have been closed may be reopened at a later point in an executing program. The new connection may be to the same or to a different file.

9.6 The INQUIRE Statement

The INQUIRE statement provides the capability of determining information about a file's existence, connection, access method, or other properties during execution of a program. For each property inquired about, a scalar variable is supplied; that variable is given a value that answers the inquiry. The variable may be tested and optional execution paths selected in a program based on the answer returned. The inquiry specifiers are indicated by keywords in the INQUIRE statement. A file inquiry may be made by unit number, by the file name, or by an output list that might be used in an unformatted direct access output statement.

The form of an inquiry by unit number or file name is

INQUIRE (*inquire-spec-list*)

An **inquiry by unit** must include the following in the inquire specification list:

[UNIT =] *external-file-unit*

If the keyword UNIT is omitted, it must be the first item in the list.

An **inquiry by name** must include the following in the inquire specification list:

FILE = *file-name*

The expression for the file name may refer to a file that is not connected or does not exist. The value for the name must be acceptable to the processor. You may not inquire both by unit and by name with the same INQUIRE statement.

In addition, the inquire specification list may contain the following items. The type of the item following the keyword is indicated; each item following the keyword and equals sign must be a scalar variable, except for the label following the ERR= specifier. Each character variable must be default kind, except the one following NAME=.

    IOSTAT = *integer*
    ERR = *label*
    EXIST = *logical*
    OPENED = *logical*
    NUMBER = *integer*
    NAMED = *logical*
    NAME = *character*
    ACCESS = *character*
    SEQUENTIAL = *character*
    DIRECT = *character*
    FORM = *character*
    FORMATTED = *character*
    UNFORMATTED = *character*
    RECL = *integer*
    NEXTREC = *integer*
    BLANK = *character*
    POSITION = *character*
    ACTION = *character*
    READ = *character*
    WRITE = *character*
    READWRITE = *character*
    DELIM = *character*
    PAD = *character*

The form of an INQUIRE statement used to determine the length of an output item list is

INQUIRE (IOLENGTH = *scalar-int-variable*) *output-item-list*

Examples of the INQUIRE statement are

```
INQUIRE (9, EXIST = EX)
INQUIRE (FILE = "T123", OPENED = OP, ACCESS = AC)
INQUIRE (IOLENGTH = IOLEN)  X, Y, CAT
```

9.6.1 The IOLENGTH Inquiry

The length value returned in the scalar integer variable will be an acceptable value that can be used later as the value of the RECL= specifier in an OPEN statement to connect a file whose records will hold the data indicated by the output list of the INQUIRE statement.

9.6.2 Specifiers for Inquiry by Unit or File Name

This section describes the syntax and effect of the inquiry specifiers that may appear in the unit and file forms of the INQUIRE statement. The values returned in the inquiry specification list are those current at that point in the execution of the program.

As with the other input/output statements in this chapter, there is a status parameter and an error condition parameter. If an error condition occurs, all the inquiry parameters are undefined except the status parameter. The IOSTAT and ERR inquiry specifiers indicate error condition information about the inquiry statement execution itself.

EXIST=	If the inquiry is by unit, the logical variable indicates whether or not the unit exists. If the inquiry is by file, the logical variable indicates whether or not the file exists.
OPENED=	If the inquiry is by unit, the logical variable indicates whether or not the unit is connected to some file. If the inquiry is by file, the logical variable indicates whether or not the file is connected to some unit.
NUMBER=	The value returned is the number of the unit connected to the file. If there is no unit connected to the file, the value is –1.
NAMED=	The scalar logical value is true if and only if the file has a name.
NAME=	The value is the name of the file if the file has a name; otherwise the designated variable becomes undefined. The processor may return a name

different from the one specified in the FILE= by the program, since a user identifier or some other processor requirement for file names may be added. The name returned will be acceptable for use in a subsequent OPEN statement. The case (upper or lower) used is determined by the processor.

ACCESS=
The value returned is SEQUENTIAL if the file is connected for sequential access, DIRECT if the file is connected for direct access, or UNDEFINED if the file is not connected.

SEQUENTIAL=
The value returned is YES if sequential access is an allowed method, NO if sequential access is not an allowed method, or UNKNOWN if the processor does not know if sequential access is allowed.

DIRECT=
The value returned is YES if direct access is an allowed method, NO if direct access is not an allowed method, or UNKNOWN if the processor does not know if direct access is allowed.

FORM=
The value returned is FORMATTED if the file is connected for formatted input/output, UNFORMATTED if the file is connected for unformatted input/output, or UNDEFINED if the file is not connected.

FORMATTED=
The value returned is YES if formatted input/output is permitted for the file, NO if formatted input/output is not permitted for the file, or UNKNOWN if the processor cannot determine if formatted input/output is permitted for the file.

UNFORMATTED=
The value returned is YES if unformatted input/output is permitted for the file, NO if unformatted input/output is not permitted for the file, or UNKNOWN if the processor cannot determine if unformatted input/output is permitted for the file.

RECL=
The integer value returned is the maximum record length of the file. For a formatted file, the length is in characters. For an unformatted

file, the length is in processor-dependent units. If the file does not exist, the specified variable becomes undefined.

NEXTREC=

The integer value returned is one more than the last record number read or written in a file connected for direct access. If no records have been processed, the value is 1. The specified variable becomes undefined if the file is not connected for direct access or if the file position is indeterminate because of a previous error condition.

BLANK=

The value returned is NULL if null blank control is in effect, ZERO if zero blank control is in effect, or UNDEFINED if the file is not connected for formatted input/output or if the file is not connected at all.

POSITION=

The value returned is REWIND if the file is connected with its position at the initial point, APPEND if the file is connected with its position at the end point, ASIS if the file is connected without any position change, or UNDEFINED if the file is not connected, is connected for direct access, or if any repositioning has occurred since the file was connected.

ACTION=

The value returned is READ if the file is connected limiting the access to input, WRITE if the file is connected limiting the access to output, READWRITE if the file is connected for input and output, or UNDEFINED if the file is not connected.

READ=

The value returned is YES if READ is one of the allowed actions for the file, NO if READ is not one of the allowed actions for the file, or UNKNOWN if the processor is unable to determine if READ is one of the allowed actions for the file.

WRITE=

The value returned is YES if WRITE is one of the allowed actions for the file, NO if WRITE is not one of the allowed actions for the file, or UNKNOWN if the processor is unable to determine if WRITE is one of the allowed actions for the file.

READWRITE=

The value returned is YES if READWRITE is one of the allowed actions for the file, NO if READWRITE is not one of the allowed actions for the file, or UNKNOWN if the processor is unable to determine if READWRITE is one of the allowed actions for the file.

DELIM=

The value returned indicates the way character strings in list-directed and namelist formatted output will be delimited. It is APOSTROPHE if an apostrophe is used as the delimiter, QUOTE if the quotation mark is used as the delimiter, NONE if there is no delimiting character, or UNDEFINED if the file is not connected or the file is not connected for formatted input/output.

PAD=

Two valid values may be returned. It is NO if the file was connected with the PAD = parameter set to NO. Otherwise, it is YES.

9.6.3 Table of Values Assigned by INQUIRE

Table 9-2 indicates the values assigned to the various variables by the execution of an INQUIRE statement.

9.7 File Positioning Statements

Execution of a data transfer usually changes the position of a file. In addition, there are three statements whose main purpose is to change the position of a file. Changing the position backwards by one record is called **backspacing**. Changing the position to the beginning of the file is called **rewinding**. The ENDFILE statement writes an endfile record and positions the file after the endfile record.

The syntax of the file positioning statements is

BACKSPACE *external-file-unit*
BACKSPACE (*position-spec-list*)
REWIND *external-file-unit*
REWIND (*position-spec-list*)
ENDFILE *external-file-unit*
ENDFILE (*position-spec-list*)

A position specification may by any of the following:

Table 9-2 Values assigned by the INQUIRE statement.

Specifier	INQUIRE by File		INQUIRE by Unit	
	Unconnected	Connected	Connected	Unconnected
EXIST =	.TRUE. if file exists, .FALSE. otherwise		.TRUE. if unit exists, .FALSE. otherwise	
OPENED =	.FALSE.		.TRUE.	.FALSE.
NUMBER =	−1		unit no.	−1
NAMED =	.TRUE.		.TRUE. if file named, .FALSE. otherwise	.FALSE.
NAME =	filename (may not be same as FILE= value)		filename if named, else undefined	undefined
ACCESS =	UNDEFINED	SEQUENTIAL or DIRECT		UNDEFINED
SEQUENTIAL =	YES, NO, or UNKNOWN			UNKNOWN
DIRECT =	YES, NO, or UNKNOWN			UNKNOWN
FORM =	UNDEFINED	FORMATTED or UNFORMATTED		UNDEFINED
FORMATTED =	YES, NO, or UNKNOWN			UNKNOWN
UNFORMATTED =	YES, NO, or UNKNOWN			UNKNOWN
RECL =	undefined	if direct access, record length; else maximum record length		undefined
NEXTREC =	undefined	if direct access, next record #; else undefined		undefined
BLANK =	UNDEFINED	NULL, ZERO, or UNDEFINED		UNDEFINED
DELIM =	UNDEFINED	APOSTROPHE, QUOTE, NONE, or UNDEFINED		UNDEFINED
PAD =	YES	YES or NO		YES
POSITION =	UNDEFINED	REWIND, APPEND, ASIS, or UNDEFINED		UNDEFINED
ACTION =	UNDEFINED	READ, WRITE, or READ/WRITE		UNDEFINED
IOLENGTH =	RECL= value for *output-item-list*			

```
[ UNIT = ] external-file-unit
IOSTAT = scalar-int-variable
ERR = label
```

Examples of file positioning statements are

```
BACKSPACE 9
BACKSPACE (ERR = 99, UNIT = 8, IOSTAT = STATUS)
REWIND (ERR = 102, UNIT = 10)
ENDFILE (10, IOSTAT = IERR)
ENDFILE (11)
```

As with the other input/output statements, if the keyword UNIT is omitted, that specifier must be first in the list. There must be an external unit specifier.

Rules and restrictions for file positioning statements:

1. The BACKSPACE, REWIND, and ENDFILE statements may be used only to position external files.

2. The external file unit number is required.

3. The files must be connected for sequential access.

4. If the keyword UNIT is not used, the external file unit number must be the first parameter in the list.

5. The branch target label used in the ERR parameter must be in the same scoping unit as the positioning statement.

9.7.1 The BACKSPACE Statement

Execution of a BACKSPACE statement causes the file to be positioned before the current record if there is a current record, or before the preceding record if there is no current record. If there is no current record and no preceding record, the position of the file is not changed. If the preceding record is an endfile record, the file becomes positioned before the endfile record. If a BACKSPACE statement causes the implicit writing of an endfile record and if there is a preceding record, the file becomes positioned before the record that precedes the endfile record.

If the file is already at its initial point, a BACKSPACE statement does not affect it. If the file is connected, but does not exist, backspacing is prohibited. Also, backspacing over records written using list-directed or namelist formatting is prohibited.

9.7.2 The REWIND Statement

A REWIND statement positions the file at its initial point. Rewinding has no effect on the position of a file already at its initial point. If a file does not exist but it is connected, rewinding the file is permitted but has no effect.

9.7.3 The ENDFILE Statement

The ENDFILE writes an endfile record and positions the file after the endfile record written. Writing records past the endfile record is prohibited. After executing an ENDFILE statement, it is necessary to execute a BACKSPACE or a REWIND to position the file ahead of the endfile record before reading or writing the file. If the file is connected but does not exist, writing an endfile record creates the file.

9.8 Formatting

Data usually is stored in memory as the values of variables in some binary form. For example, the integer 6 may be stored as 0000000000000110, where the 1s and 0s represent bits. On the other hand, formatted data records in a file consist of characters. Thus, when data is read from a formatted record, it must be converted from characters to the internal representation and when data is written to a formatted record, it must be converted from the internal representation into a string of characters. A **format specification** provides the information needed to determine how these conversions are to be performed. The format specification is basically a list of **edit descriptors**, one for each data value in the input/output list of the data transfer statement.

A format specification is written either as a character string or in a FORMAT statement. The FORMAT statement is described in Chapter 10. The character expression, when evaluated, must be a valid format specification including the parentheses. Using these methods is called **explicit formatting**.

There are two other cases where formatting of a different sort applies. These are list-directed and namelist formatting. Formatting (that is, conversion) occurs without specifically providing the editing information usually contained in a format specification. In these cases, the editing or formatting is implicit. List-directed editing, also called default formatting, is explained in Section 9.8.21; namelist formatting is discussed briefly in Chapter 10.

Some rules and restrictions pertaining to format specifications are

1. Any information may appear following the last right parenthesis in the format; this has no effect.

2. If the expression is a character array, the format is derived in array element order.

3. If the expression is an array element, the format must be entirely contained within that element.

9.8.1 Format Specifications

The items that make up a format specification are **edit descriptors**, which may be **data edit descriptors**, **control edit descriptors**, or **character string edit descriptors**. Each data list item must have a corresponding data edit descriptor; other descriptors control spacing, tabulation, etc. The use of character string edit descriptors is considered obsolete and so are discussed in Chapter 10.

Each format item has one of the following forms:

[r] *data-edit-desc*
control-edit-desc
char-string-edit-desc
[r] (*format-item-list*)

where r is an integer literal constant called a **repeat factor**; it must be a positive integer.

Examples:

```
READ (*, "(5E10.1, I10)") MAX_VALUES, K
PRINT "(A, 2I5)", "The two values are: ", N (1), N (2)
```

The data edit descriptors have the following forms:

I w [. m]
B w [. m]
O w [. m]
Z w [. m]
F w . d
E w . d [E e]
EN w . d [E e]
ES w . d [E e]
G w . d [E e]
L w
A [w]
D w . d

w and e must be positive integer literal constants and d and m must be nonnegative integer literal constants.

The value of m, d, and e may be restricted further by the value of w. I, B, O, Z, F, E, EN, ES, G, L, A, and D indicate the manner of editing.

In each case, w designates the width of the field in the file, that is, the number of characters transferred to or from the file. Also, as explained below in the description of each edit descriptor, m is the number of digits in the number field, d is the number of digits after the decimal point, and e is the number of digits in the exponent.

The control edit descriptors have the forms:

T n
TL n
TR n
n X
[r] /
:
S
SS
SP
k P
BN
BZ

where k is a signed integer literal constant and n is a positive integer literal constant.

In kP, k is called the **scale factor**.

T, TL, TR, X, slash, colon, S, SP, SS, P, BN, and BZ indicate the manner of editing.

9.8.2 Formatted Data Transfer

When formatted data transfer is taking place, the next item in the input/output list is matched up with the next data edit descriptor to determine the form of conversion between the internal representation of the data and the string of characters in the formatted record. Before this matching process occurs, the input/output list is considered to be expanded by writing out each element in an array and each component in a structure, and expanding any implied DOs. Analogously, the repeated edit descriptors are considered to be expanded and the whole specification is considered to be repeated as often as necessary to accommodate the entire list, as explained below regarding the use of parentheses. Let's take an example:

```
PRINT "(I5, 2(I3, TR1, I4), I5)", I, (N (I), I = 1, 4), I
```

The expanded input/output list would be

```
I, N (1), N (2), N (3), N (4), I
```

and the expanded list of data edit descriptors would be:

```
I5, I3, I4, I3, I4, I5
```

As the formatting proceeds, each input/output list item is read or written with a conversion as specified by its corresponding data edit descriptor. The control edit descriptors affect the editing process at the point they occur in the list of edit descriptors.

An empty format specification such as ( ) is restricted to input/output statements without a list of items. The effect on input is that one record is skipped in the input file. The effect on output is that no characters are written to the record. Note that complex data type items require two data edit descriptors of the same type.

Control edit descriptors do not require a corresponding data item in the list. When the data items are completely processed, any control edit descriptors occurring next in the expanded list of edit descriptors are processed and then the formatting terminates.

9.8.3 Parentheses in a Format Specification

The action indicated by parentheses in a format specification depends on the nesting level.

The rules are the following:

1. When the rightmost parenthesis is encountered and there are no more data items, format control terminates.

2. When the rightmost parenthesis is encountered and there are more data items, format control continues beginning at the rightmost left parenthesis in the specification. This may be at the beginning of the format if there are no nested parentheses. A slash edit descriptor is considered to occur after processing the right parenthesis and before processing the left parenthesis.

3. If there is a repeat factor encountered when reverting to the left parenthesis, the repeat before the parenthesis is reused.

4. Scale factors, sign control, and blank interpretation are not affected. They remain in effect for the duration of the format processing.

9.8.4 Numeric Editing

There are seven edit descriptors that cover numeric editing: I, F, E, EN, ES, D, and G. The following rules apply to all of them.

On input:

1. Leading blanks are not significant.

2. Within a field, the way blanks are interpreted is dependent on defaults for preconnected or internal files, the BLANK= specifier, and any BN or BZ blank control edit descriptors in effect. The default is to treat blanks as zero; the BLANK= specifier may establish a different default for a file, and the BN and BZ edit descriptors may override that default during the execution of part or all of one input/output statement.

3. Plus signs may be omitted in the input data.

4. In numeric fields that have a decimal point such as F, E, EN, ES, D, or G, the decimal point in the input field overrides placement of the decimal point by the edit descriptor.

On output:

1. A positive or zero internal value may have a plus sign, depending on the sign edit descriptors used.

2. The number is right justified in the field. Leading blanks may be inserted.

3. If the number or the exponent is too large for the field width specified in the edit descriptor, the output field is filled with asterisks. The processor must not produce asterisks when elimination of optional characters, such as the optional plus sign indicated by the SP edit descriptor, will make the output small enough to fit into the output field.

9.8.5 Integer Editing

The integer edit descriptors are

$I w[.m]$
$B w[.m]$
$O w[.m]$
$Z w[.m]$
$G w$

w is the field width; m is the least number of digits to be output. m has no affect on an input field. If m is omitted, its default value is 1.

The value of m must not exceed the value of w. Leading zeros pad an integer field to the value of m. The field on output consists of an optional sign and the magnitude of the integer number without leading zeros, except in the case of padding to the value of m. Blanks are output if the magnitude is zero and $m = 0$. I editing produces a decimal integer using the digits 0–9; B editing produces a binary integer using the digits 0 and 1; O editing produces an octal integer using the digits 0–7; and Z editing produces a hexadecimal integer using the digits 0–7 and A–F. G editing usually produces the same output as I editing for integers.

   Input. The character string in the file must be an optionally signed integer constant using only the digits permitted by the edit descriptor.

   Output. The field consists of leading blanks, followed by an optional sign, followed by the unsigned value of the integer. At least one digit must be output unless m is 0 and the output value is 0.

   Example:

```
READ (5, "(I5, B8)") I, J
```

If the input field is

   *bbb*2401110101

I is read using the integer I5 edit descriptor. J is read with a B8 edit descriptor, where the digits allowed are 0 and 1. The resulting values of I and J are 24 and 117, respectively.

9.8.6 Real Editing

The forms of the edit descriptors for real values are

   $Fw.d$
   $Ew.d[Ee]$
   $ENw.d[Ee]$
   $ESw.d[Ee]$
   $Dw.d$
   $Gw.d[Ee]$

9.8.7 The F Edit Descriptor

F editing converts to or from a string of w digits with d places after the decimal point. d must not be greater than w. The number may be signed.

   Input. If the input field contains a decimal point, the value of d has no effect. If there is no decimal point, a decimal point is inserted in front of the rightmost d digits. There may be more digits in the number than the processor can use. On input, the number may contain an E or D indicating an exponent value. If there is a scale factor kP in effect (9.8.19) and there is no exponent field in the input, the number in the input is multiplied by 10^{-k} before it is assigned to the variable in the input list.

Output. The number is an optionally signed floating-point number with a decimal point, rounded to d digits after the decimal point. If the number is less than one, the processor may place a zero in front of the decimal point. At least one zero must be output if no other digits would appear. If the number does not fit into the output field, the entire field is filled with asterisks.

Example:

```
READ (5, "(F10.2, F10.3)") X, Y
```

If the input field is

```
bbbb6.42181234567890
```

the values assigned to X and Y are 6.4218 and 1234567.89, respectively. The value of d is ignored for X because the input field contains a decimal point.

9.8.8 The E and D Edit Descriptors

For E and D editing, the field representing the floating-point number contains w characters, including an exponent. d and e must not be greater than the length, w. The number of digits after the decimal is changed if a scale factor is indicated.

Input. The form is the same as for F editing, where either E or D may indicate an exponent.

Output. The form of the output field for a scale factor of zero is

$$[\ \pm\ ]\ [0]\ .\ x_1 x_2 \cdots x_d\ exp$$

Example: if Y $= -212.12$ and Z $= 26592.12$,

```
WRITE (6, "(2E15.3)") Y, Z
```

produces the output record

```
bbbbb-0.212E+03bbbbbbb0.266E+05
```

Note that the first blank in the record may be used as carriage control and not printed.

9.8.9 The EN Edit Descriptor

EN is the engineering edit descriptor.

Input. The form is the same as for F editing.

Output. The output of the number is in the form of engineering notation, where the exponent is divisible by three and the absolute value of the mantissa is greater than or equal to 1 and less than 1000, except when the output value is 0.

Example:

```
WRITE (6, "(EN12.3)") B
```

The form of the output field is

$[\ \pm\ ]\ yyy.x_1x_2 \cdots x_d\,exp$

Examples of output using the EN descriptor are found in Table 9-3.

Table 9-3 Examples of output using the EN edit descriptor.

Internal value	Output field using SS, EN12.3
6.421	6.421E+00
−.5	−500.000E−03
.0217	21.70E−03
4721.3	4.721E+03

9.8.10 The ES Edit Descriptor

ES is the scientific edit descriptor.

Input. The form is the same as for F editing.

Output. The output of the number is in the form of scientific notation; the absolute value of the mantissa is greater than or equal to 1 and less than 10, except when the output value is 0.[1]

Example:

```
WRITE (6, "(ES12.3)") B
```

---

1. The effect of the ES edit descriptor could be achieved in Fortran 77 with the use of the 1P edit descriptor. However, the 1P edit descriptor affects all following real edit descriptors, often with results not intended or expected by the programmer.

The form of the output field is

$$[\pm] \; y.x_1x_2 \cdots x_d \, exp$$

Examples of output using the ES descriptor are found in Table 9-4.

Table 9-4 Examples of output using the ES edit descriptor.

Internal value	Output field using SS, ES12.3
6.421	6.421E+00
−.5	−5.000E−01
.0217	2.170E−02
4721.3	4.721E+03

9.8.11 Complex Editing

Editing of complex numbers requires two real edit descriptors, one for the real part and one for the imaginary part. Different edit descriptors may be used, including integer edit descriptors. Data read for a complex quantity, even if read using an integer edit descriptor, is converted to type real and, by the rules of conversion for assignment to complex, the kinds of both parts of a complex quantity are made the same. Other controls and characters may be inserted between the specification for the real and imaginary parts.

Example:

```
COMPLEX CM (2)
READ (5, "(4E7.2)") (CM (I), I = 1, 2)
WRITE (6, "(2 (F7.2, A, F7.2, A))") &
      (REAL (CM (I)), " + ", AIMAG (CM (I)), " I ", I = 1, 2)
```

If the input record is

bb55511bbb2146bbbb100bbbb621

the values assigned to CM (1) and CM (2) are $555.11 + 21.46i$ and $1 + 6.21i$, respectively, and the output record is

b555.11b+bbb21.46bIbbbb1.00b+bbbb6.21bIb

9.8.12 The G Edit Descriptor

The G edit descriptor may be used to edit real and complex values.

Input. The rules for F editing are followed.

Output. Either E or F editing is used, depending on the magnitude of the number. The scale factor affects only those numbers that are formatted using E editing.

Example: if X = 87.532,

```
PRINT "(G10.1)", X
```

produces the output:

*bbbbbb*87.6

One blank may be used for carriage control, if the record is printed.

9.8.13 Logical Editing

The edit descriptors used for logical editing are

Lw
Gw

w is the field width.

Generalized logical editing, Gw, follows the rules for Lw editing.

Input. The input field for a logical value consists of any number of blanks, followed by an optional period, followed by T or F, followed by anything. Valid input fields for true include T, TRUE, .TRUE., .T, and THURSDAY_AFTERNOON, although the last is poor practice.

Output. The output field consists of $w - 1$ leading blanks, followed by T or F.

Example:

```
WRITE (6, "(2L7") L1, L2
```

If L1 and L2 are true and false, respectively, the output record will be

*bbbbbb*T*bbbbb*F

9.8.14 Character Data Editing

The edit descriptors for character editing are

A[w]

G[w]

w is the field width measured in characters. If w is omitted, the length of the data object being read in or written out is used as the field width.

Input. Let *len* be the length of the data object being read. If w is greater than *len*, the rightmost *len* characters in the input field are read. If w is less than *len*, the input is padded with "blanks" on the right. If the character datum is not the default kind, the character used for "blank padding" is processor dependent.

Output. If w is greater than *len*, blanks are added on the left. If w is less than *len*, the leftmost w characters will appear in the output field. Unlike numeric fields, asterisks are not written if the data does not fit in the specified field width.

Example:

```
CHARACTER (LEN = *), PARAMETER :: &
      SLOGAN = "SAVE THE RIVER"
WRITE (*, "(A)") SLOGAN
```

produces the output record:

SAVE*b*THE*b*RIVER

9.8.15 Position Editing

Position edit descriptors control relative tabbing left or right in the record before the next list item is processed. The edit descriptors for tabbing are

Tn	tab to position n
TLn	tab left n positions
TRn	tab right n positions
nX	tab right n positions

n must be a positive integer constant.

The Tn edit descriptor positions the record just before character n, so that if a character is put into or taken from the record, it will be the nth character in the record. TRn and nX move right n characters. TLn moves left n characters.

If, because of execution of a nonadvancing input/output statement, the file is positioned within a record at the beginning of an input/output statement, the value of n in a Tn edit descriptor refers to the nth character from the initial position, and left tabbing may not position that record any farther left than its initial position.

Input. The T descriptor may position either forward or backward. A position to the left of the current position allows input to be processed twice. The X descriptor always moves forward and skips characters.

Output. The positioning does not transmit characters and does not by itself cause the record to be shorter or longer. Positions that are skipped are blank filled, unless filled later in the processing. A character may be replaced by subsequent descriptors, but the positioning descriptors do not carry out the replacement.

Example: if X = 12.66 and Y = –8654.123,

```
PRINT "(F9.2, 6X, F9.3)", X, Y
```

produces the record:

*bbbb*12.66*bbbbbb*–8654.123

```
PRINT "(F9.2, T7, F9.3)", X, Y
```

produces the record:

*bbbb*12–8654.123

9.8.16 Slash (/) Editing

The current record is ended when a slash is encountered in a format specification. The slash edit descriptor consists of the single slash character (/).

Input. If the file is connected for sequential access, the file is positioned at the beginning of the next record. The effect is to skip the remainder of the current record. For direct access, the record number is increased by one. A record may be skipped entirely on input.

Output. If the file is connected for sequential access, the file is positioned at the beginning of a new record. For direct access, the record number is increased by one, and this record becomes the current record. An empty record is blank filled.

Example:

```
PRINT "(F5.1, /, 2F6.1)", A, B, C
```

produces two records:

*bb*1.1
*bbb*2.2*bbb*3.3

9.8.17 Colon Editing

The colon edit descriptor consists of the single colon character (:).

If the list of items in the formatted READ or WRITE statement is exhausted, a colon stops format processing at that point. It has no effect if there is more data.

Example:

```
FMT_SPEC = "(3F5.2, :, ""STOP"")"
WRITE (5, FMT_SPEC) A, B, C
```

produces

bb1.1bb2.2bb3.3

The characters STOP are not printed because the output list is exhausted when the colon edit descriptor is processed.

Example:

```
FMT_SPEC = "(3 (F5.2, :, "",""))"
WRITE (5, FMT_SPEC) A, B, C
```

produces

bb1.1,bb2.2,bb3.3

Because of the colon edit descriptor, a comma is not written after the third number.

9.8.18 Sign Editing

Sign editing applies to numeric fields only; it controls the printing of the plus sign. It only applies to output. The sign edit descriptors are

S	optional plus is processor dependent
SP	optional plus must be printed
SS	optional plus must not be printed

The S edit descriptor indicates that the printing of optional plus signs is up to the processor. SP indicates that optional plus signs must be printed. SS indicates that optional plus signs must not be printed. The occurrence of these descriptors applies until another one (S, SP, SS) is encountered in the format specification.

Example:

```
WRITE (6, "(SP, 2F10.2)") (X (K), K = 1, 2)
```

produces the record:

bbbbb+1.46*bbb*+234.12

9.8.19 Scale Factors

The kP edit descriptor indicates scaling, where the scale factor k is a signed integer literal constant.

The scale factor is zero at the beginning of a formatted input/output statement. When a kP descriptor occurs, all succeeding numeric fields processed with an I, F, E, EN, ES, D, or G edit descriptor are scaled by k, until another scale factor occurs.

Input. The external number equals the internal number multiplied by a scale factor 10^k. The scale factor has no effect if the input field has an exponent.

Output. I and F descriptors are not affected by a scale factor on output. For E and D descriptors, the nonexponent part of the number appearing in the output is multiplied by 10^k and the exponent is reduced by k. The G edit descriptor is not affected by the scale factor if the number will print correctly with an F edit descriptor. Otherwise the G descriptor is the same as the E descriptor. EN and ES editing is not affected by a scale factor on output.

Consider the following example:

```
READ (*, "(3P, F5.0)") X
WRITE (*, "(E20.5)") X
WRITE (*, "(3P, E20.5)") X
```

When this program is run with the following input:

```
10.23
```

the resulting output is

```
0.10230E-01
102.300E-04
```

Note that when the value 10.23 is read, it is converted to the internal value 0.01023 by multiplying by 10^{-3}, but the value printed is the same value as the internal value—only its format is different.

9.8.20 Blanks in Numeric Fields

Blanks other than leading blanks may be interpreted as zero or blanks as determined by the blank edit descriptors:

BN   ignore blanks in numeric input fields

BZ   treat blanks in numeric input fields as zeros

The interpretation is for input fields only; output fields are not affected. See the interpretation of blanks specifier in the BLANK= keyword in the OPEN statement. If NULL, the blanks are ignored and treated as if they were not in the input field. If, however, a BZ is encountered in the format specification, the blanks are interpreted as zeros in succeeding numeric fields. A BN or BZ edit descriptor overrides the BLANK= specifier for the duration of the current READ statement.

Example:

```
READ (5, "(I5, BZ, I5)") N1, N2
```

If the input record is

ᵬ9ᵬ9ᵬ9ᵬ9ᵬ9

the values assigned to N1 and N2 are 99 and 90909, respectively.

9.8.21 List-Directed Formatting

List-directed formatting, also called default formatting, is one of the implicit formatting conventions in Fortran, selected by using an asterisk (*) in place of an explicit format specification in a READ, WRITE, or PRINT statement. List-directed editing occurs based on the type of each list item.

Example:

```
READ (5, *) A, B, C
```

Some rules and restrictions relating to list-directed formatting are

1.   The record consists of values and value separators.

2.   If there are no list items, an input record is skipped or an output record that is empty is written.

Values. The values allowed are

null	a null value as in ,, (no value between separators)
c	a literal or nondelimited character constant
r*c	r repetitions of the constant c
r*	r repetitions of the null value

Embedded blanks are not allowed except in a character constant.
Separators. The separators allowed are

,	a comma, optionally preceded or followed by contiguous blanks
/	a slash, optionally preceded or followed by contiguous blanks
	a blank between two nonblank values

Input values generally are accepted as list-directed input if they are accepted in explicit formatting with an edit descriptor. There are some exceptions. They are

1. The type must agree with the next item in the list.

2. Blank editing is not allowed and blanks are never zeros.

3. Embedded blanks are not allowed, except within a character constant.

4. Complex items in the list include the parentheses for a complex constant. Blanks may occur before or after the comma. An example is

    (1.2, 5.666)

5. Logical items must not use value separators as the optional characters following the T or F.

6. When a character constant is continued beyond the current record, the end of record must not be between any quotes or apostrophes that are doubled because they are the same character as the character constant delimiter. Value separators may be representable characters in the constant.

7. In certain cases, the delimiters are not required for character constants on input. The constant then ends with the first blank, comma, slash, or end of record. In this case, delimiters (' and ") need only appear once to be accepted as representable characters in the constant.

8. If *len* is the length of the next input list item, and if

$len \leq w$	the leftmost *len* characters of the constant are used
$len > w$	the w characters of the constant are used and the field is blank filled on the right

A null value is encountered if

1.   There is no value between separators.

2.   The record begins with a value separator.

3.   The $r*$ form is used.

Rules and Restrictions:

1.   An end of record does not signify a null value.

2.   The null value does not change the next list item.

3.   In complex number input, the entire constant may be null, but not one of the parts.

4.   If a slash terminates input, the rest of the list items are treated as though a null value had been read. This applies to remaining items in a DO.

Example:

```
REAL X (2)
READ (5, *) I, X
```

If the input record is

```
b6,,2.418
```

the result is that $I = 6$, $X (1)$ is unchanged, and $X (2) = 2.418$.

List-directed output uses the same conventions that are used for list-directed input. There are a few exceptions that are noted below for each of the intrinsic types. Blanks and commas are used as separators except for certain character constants that may contain a separator as part of the constant. The processor begins new records as needed, at any point in the list of output items. A new record does not begin in the middle of a number, except that complex numbers may be separated between the real and the imaginary parts. Very long character constants are the exception; they may be split across record boundaries. Slashes and null values are never output. Each new record begins with a blank for carriage control, except for delimited character constants. The processor has the option of using the repeat factor, r * c.

Integer. The effect is as though an Iw edit descriptor were used.

Real. The effect is as though an F or an E edit descriptor were used. The output result depends on the magnitude of the number, and the processor has some selection in this case.

Complex. The real and imaginary parts are enclosed in parentheses and separated by a comma (with optional blanks surrounding the comma). If the length of the complex number is longer than a record, the processor may separate the real and imaginary parts on two records.

Logical. List-directed output prints T or F depending on the value of the logical data object.

Character. Character constants are output based on the value of the delimiter, DELIM=, in the OPEN statement for that unit. If there is no delimiter, or the value is NONE:

1.   Constants are not delimited.

2.   Constants are not surrounded by value separators.

3.   Only one quote or apostrophe is output for each quote and apostrophe embedded in the character constant.

4.   A blank is inserted in new records for carriage control.

If the delimiter is QUOTE or APOSTROPHE:

1.   Constants are delimited.

2.   Constants are surrounded by value separators.

3.   Embedded delimiters are doubled in the output.

4.   Optional kind parameters and underscores are allowed if applicable.

5.   No blanks are inserted in the record for carriage control.

10

Obsolete Features

Because Fortran is one of the oldest commonly used high-level languages, there are many features that should be considered obsolete in the sense that they should not be used in constructing new programs. However, lots of programs that have used these features are still being compiled and run. As a Fortran programmer, you may be asked to modify or convert a program containing these features and should know something about what they do. This chapter contains a brief description of these features with some guidelines for converting the features to more modern ones. To obtain more detailed information about these features, you should consult the standard itself or a more complete reference work such as *The Fortran 90 Handbook* by Adams, Brainerd, Martin, Smith, and Wagener, McGraw-Hill, 1990.

10.1 Control of Flow

10.1.1 Labels

A Fortran statement may be preceded by a **label**, which is a string of digits. The label is used to refer to the statement from other places within the same program unit. Any digits that occur at the beginning of a statement must constitute a label because no statement can begin with a digit. Leading zeros are insignificant in a label, so that the labels 11, 011, and 0011 are all considered to be the same label, but 01, 10, and 100 are all different labels. One of the digits in a label must be nonzero.

10.1.2 The Arithmetic IF Statement

An example of an arithmetic IF statement is

```
IF (X - Y) 100, 200, 300
```

Any expression may occur within the parentheses. The expression is evaluated. If it is negative, control is transferred to the first label (100); if it is zero, control is transferred to the second label (200); if it is positive, control is transferred to the third label (300). The IF construct or IF statement should be used to replace the arithmetic IF statement.

10.1.3 Old Forms of the DO Loop and the CONTINUE Statement

The DO statement may have a label following the keyword DO, in which case, the loop ends with a statement having that label, rather than with an END DO statement. The END DO statement is new in Fortran 90, but prior to that, careful programmers used the CONTINUE statement to end DO loops. The CONTINUE statement has no effect and may be used anywhere, but usually was used to mark the end of a DO loop. DO loops may end with any statement, however, and more than one DO loop may terminate with the same statement, as in

```
DO 10 I = 1, 100
   DO 10 J = 1, 100
10    A (I, J) = I + J
```

This example is straightforward, but when a program contains branches to the terminating statement, either from within the inner loop or from within the outer loop, it is very difficult to tell what is going on.

All such forms of the DO loop can be rewritten using the DO construct, the EXIT statement, and the CYCLE statement.

10.1.4 Real DO Variables

DO variables that are type real may be used, but this is considered poor practice by some people. Because of the possibility of roundoff error with real values, DO blocks with real DO variables do not always execute the expected number of times. Such loops can be replaced by those using integer DO variables. For example,

```
DO R = 0.1, 0.9, 0.1
   . . .
END DO
```

can be rewritten as

```
DO I = 1, 9
   R = 0.1 * I
   . . .
END DO
```

10.1.5 The Alternate Return

It is possible to use a label preceded with an asterisk (*) as an actual argument in a subroutine call, such as

```
CALL SUBR_ALT (X, Y, *100, *200, *300)
```

If in the called subroutine, a statement such as

```
RETURN 2
```

is executed, where an integer expression follows the keyword RETURN, that expression is evaluated getting an integer value, say n, and, back in the calling program, a branch is made to the nth label in the list of labels that are arguments. In our example, a branch is made to the statement with label 200 because $n = 2$.

A better scheme is to use an integer variable to return a value to the calling program and let the calling program test the value and perform the necessary operations. For example,

```
CALL SUBR_ALT (X, Y, RETURN_CODE)
SELECT CASE (RETURN_CODE)
    . . .
```

10.1.6 The GO TO Statement

The GO TO statement causes a simple transfer of control to the statement with the label following the keyword GO TO. For example,

```
GO TO 87122
```

causes a branch to the statement with label 87122. This labeled statement must be in the same main program or procedure as the GO TO statement. There are a few cases for which the GO TO statement can be effective, but almost all of the time, an IF construct, DO construct, EXIT statement, CYCLE statement, or SELECT CASE construct should be used instead.

10.1.7 The Computed GO TO Statement

The computed GO TO involves an integer expression and a list of labels. The expression is evaluated, giving a value n. Then a branch is made to the nth label in the list. For example,

```
GO TO I (100, 200, 300)
```

causes a branch to the statement labeled 100, 200, or 300, depending on whether the value of I is 1, 2, or 3, respectively. Other control constructs can always be used. For example,

```
SELECT CASE (I)
   CASE (1)
      . . .
   CASE (2)
      . . .
   CASE (3)
      . . .
END SELECT
```

10.1.8 The ASSIGN and Assigned GO TO Statements

The statement

```
ASSIGN 200 TO I
```

allows an assigned GO TO statement to use the value of I as a label. The simple form of the assigned GO TO looks just like the ordinary GO TO except that a variable is used in place of the label.

```
GO TO I
```

A list of labels in parentheses is permitted after the variable, in which case the value of one of those labels must be the label currently assigned to the variable.

```
GO TO I (100, 200, 300)
```

10.1.9 The DO WHILE Statement

Although the DO WHILE version of the DO construct was added in Fortran 90, it is already obsolete because it provides only the special case of exiting a loop at the top, whereas the EXIT statement allows an exit from any point in the loop. A consistent use of the EXIT statement makes the exit condition explicit and all loops with exit will look similar. The statement

```
DO WHILE (.NOT. CONVERGED)
```

can be replaced by

```
DO
    IF (CONVERGED) EXIT
```

or even

```
DO; IF (CONVERGED) EXIT
```

if you like the looks of this better. Moreover, these forms explicitly reference the condition of exit rather than its negation.

10.1.10 The RETURN Statement

The RETURN statement causes execution of a procedure to terminate with control given back to the calling program. With the use of modern control constructs, a procedure should always stop by coming to the end of the procedure.

10.1.11 The STOP Statement

The STOP statement causes execution of a program to stop. With the use of modern control constructs, a program should always stop by coming to the end of the program.

10.1.12 The PAUSE Statement

The PAUSE statement used to be used to suspend execution of a program so that the console lights could be examined and the "run" button pushed again to resume execution of the program. It is now often implemented as a WRITE statement to the user followed by a READ statement to wait until the user responds, so it has very little functionality not provided by other features.

10.2 Data

10.2.1 The IMPLICIT Statement

The IMPLICIT statement may be used to indicate that each undeclared variable has a type based on its first letter. For example

```
IMPLICIT REAL (A-Z)
```

indicates that all undeclared variables are to be of type real, and

```
IMPLICIT INTEGER (A-K, M-Z), LOGICAL (L)
```

indicates that all undeclared variables beginning with the letter L are to be of type logical and all other undeclared variables are to be of type integer.

If there is no IMPLICIT NONE statement in a program unit, all undeclared variables have a type determined as if the program unit contained the following IMPLICIT statement:

```
IMPLICIT REAL (A-H, O-Z), INTEGER (I-N)
```

___

That is, all variables beginning with the letters I, J, K, L, M, or N are of type integer and all others are of type real. An IMPLICIT statement can be used to override some of the default typing so that, for example, if a program contained only the following single IMPLICIT statement

```
IMPLICIT COMPLEX (C)
```

all undeclared variables beginning with the letters I–N would be of type integer, those beginning with the letter C would be of type complex, and all others would be of type real.

10.2.2 Type Declaration Statements

There are many different forms that may be used in declaration statements. In particular, there is a statement form for almost every data attribute. For example, X can be declared a real array with the DIMENSION statement, as well as with the REAL statement.

```
REAL X
DIMENSION X (20, 30)
```

Character strings can be declared in myriad ways, particularly if they are arrays or have a specified kind parameter. Here are a few of the equivalent ways to declare the variable to be a 4 × 5 array of character strings, each of length 20.

```
CHARACTER NAME (4, 5) * 20
CHARACTER NAME (4, 5) * (20)
CHARACTER :: NAME (4, 5) * (20)
CHARACTER * 20 NAME (4, 5)
CHARACTER * (20) NAME (4, 5)
CHARACTER * (20) :: NAME (4, 5)
CHARACTER (LEN = 20) :: NAME (4, 5)
CHARACTER (LEN = 20), DIMENSION (4, 5) :: NAME
CHARACTER, DIMENSION (4, 5) :: NAME * 20
CHARACTER, DIMENSION (4, 5) :: NAME * (20)
```

If, in addition, the variable NAME is to have KIND type parameter KANJI (assumed to be an integer parameter), there are the following options:

```
CHARACTER (KIND = KANJI) :: NAME (4, 5) * 20
CHARACTER (KIND = KANJI) :: NAME (4, 5) * (20)
CHARACTER (20, KANJI) :: NAME (4, 5)
CHARACTER (20, KIND = KANJI) :: NAME (4, 5)
CHARACTER (LEN = 20, KIND = KANJI), DIMENSION (4, 5) :: NAME
CHARACTER (KIND = KANJI, LEN = 20), DIMENSION (4, 5) :: NAME
```

The meaning of all of these different forms should be apparent to the knowledgeable reader of other programs, but when new programs are written or old ones revised, one style of declarations should be used consistently, as is done in this book.

10.2.3 The DATA Statement

The **DATA statement** provides a way to give variables initial values. The syntax is a bit unusual, but the following examples should allow you to understand how to interpret a DATA statement. The DATA statement is not needed as variables may be initialized in a type statement, as described in 1.3.1, or with an assignment statement.

```
CHARACTER (LEN = 10)  NAME
INTEGER, DIMENSION (0:9) :: MILES
REAL, DIMENSION (100, 100) :: SKEW
TYPE PERSON
    INTEGER :: AGE
    CHARACTER (LEN = 20) :: NAME
END TYPE PERSON
TYPE (PERSON) MY_NAME, YOUR_NAME
DATA NAME / 'JOHN DOE' /, MILES / 10 * 0 /
DATA ((SKEW (K, J), J = 1, K), K = 1, 100) / 5050 * 0.0 /
DATA ((SKEW (K, J), J = K + 1, 100), K = 1, 99) / 4950 * 1.0 /
DATA MY_NAME / PERSON (21, 'JOHN SMITH') /
DATA YOUR_NAME % AGE, YOUR_NAME % NAME / 35, 'FRED BROWN' /
```

The character variable NAME is initialized with the value JOHN DOE with padding on the right because the length of the constant is less than the length of the variable. All ten elements of the integer array MILES are initialized to zero. The two-dimensional array SKEW is initialized so that the lower triangle of SKEW is zero and the strict upper triangle is one. The structures MY_NAME and YOUR_NAME are declared using the derived type PERSON. MY_NAME is initialized by a structure constructor. YOUR_NAME is initialized by supplying a separate value for each component.

Note that a DATA statement may contain implied DO loops similar to those that may occur in array constructors.

A DATA statement is one of the few places that binary, octal, and hexadecimal constants may occur, so if you want to initialize an integer using a constant of one of these types, the DATA statement is the only choice.

```
INTEGER :: N
DATA N / Z"FFFF" /   ! Initializes N to hexadecimal FFFF
```

10.2.4 The DOUBLE PRECISION Data Type

One of the kinds of reals corresponds to what is called **DOUBLE PRECISION**. Variables of this type also can be declared using the DOUBLE PRECISION type statement. Constants of this type are written with an exponent letter "D" instead of "E", as in the example 5.67D–22.

10.2.5 Hollerith Data

Prior to Fortran 77, it was possible to assign characters to variables of other data types with a constant that begins with a character count and the letter "H", as in the string

```
4HWALT
```

This was removed from Fortran 77, but the H edit descriptor, which looks just like the Hollerith constant, was kept. All uses of Hollerith data and H edit descriptors can be replaced with the use of the character data type. Most programmers gleefully abandoned the H edit descriptor with its error-prone character counting and used the character constant descriptor introduced in Fortran IV and standardized in Fortran 77.

10.2.6 Common Blocks

Common blocks provide a mechanism for creating values that can be shared between program units. How values get shared using common blocks depends on the arrangement of variables in the common blocks. Although the names of the common blocks themselves are global, none of the variables within the blocks are global; values are shared between two variables simply by the fact that they occupy corresponding positions within the same common block. Suppose the following COMMON statements occur within two subroutines named S1 and S2.

```
SUBROUTINE S1
  COMMON / CMN / A, B (2)
  . . .

SUBROUTINE S2
  COMMON / CMN / C, X
  COMPLEX C
  . . .
```

Because C is complex, it corresponds to two real values, so A in S1 shares values with the real part of C in S2. Similarly B (1) in S1 corresponds to the complex part of C in S2, and B (2) in S1 corresponds to X in S2. Many programmers who use common blocks try to ensure that COMMON statements declaring the same common blocks in two different program units are identical; this avoids complicated sharing mechanisms and errors that are difficult to detect.

All uses of common blocks can be replaced by modules.

10.2.7 The EQUIVALENCE Statement

The EQUIVALENCE statement establishes a value-sharing scheme within a program unit in much the same way the common blocks do in different program units. For example,

```
COMPLEX Z
REAL X (2), Y (2)
EQUIVALENCE (X, Z), (Y (1), X (2))
```

cause X and the real part of Z to share storage and cause X (2), Y (1), and the imaginary part of Z to share storage.

The introduction of modules, dynamic storage allocation, pointers, structures, and the intrinsic TRANSFER function makes the use of EQUIVALENCE unnecessary.

10.2.8 Block Data Program Unit

A **block data program unit** provides a mechanism to initialize data in common blocks. It may contain only type declarations and IMPLICIT, PARAMETER, COMMON, DIMENSION, EQUIVALENCE, DATA, and SAVE statements. The use of modules makes the use of block data program units unnecessary.

10.3 Input/Output

10.3.1 Namelist Input/Output

Namelist input/output accomplishes two different things. It provides a mechanism for naming the objects that may occur in an input/output list (as you might expect), but only in namelist input/output statements. It also provides a mechanism whereby the input data may contain values for only a portion of the variables in the input list. Here are two very simple examples.

```
REAL A (3)
CHARACTER (LEN = 3) CHAR
COMPLEX X
LOGICAL LL
NAMELIST / TOKEN / I, A, CHAR, X, LL
READ (*, NML = TOKEN)
```

If the input record is

```
&TOKEN A(1:2) = 2*1.0  LL = T  CHAR = NOP  X = (2.4,0.0)
```

results of the READ are

I	unchanged
A (1)	1.0
A (2)	1.0
A (3)	unchanged
CHAR	NOP
X	(2.4, 0.0)
LL	T

To illustrate namelist output:

```
NAMELIST / TURN / I, X
WRITE (*, NML = TURN)
```

produces the output record:

```
&TURN  I = 20  X = 2.468
```

Although namelist input/output has been around for a long time in the form of vendor extensions, it was added to standard Fortran only recently. It can be useful in some circumstances, but it is an extremely poorly designed feature and there are many restrictions on its use with other features of Fortran, so it is best not to use it unless absolutely necessary.

10.3.2 The FORMAT Statement

Perhaps the most common use of a label is with a FORMAT statement. This provides an alternative (and formerly the only) way to have one format be used by several input/output statements. In the statements

```
PRINT 15, X, " and " N
15 FORMAT (F5.1, A, I4)
```

the format specification is placed in a FORMAT statement. The digits 15 in the PRINT and FORMAT statements form a statement label. They identify the FORMAT statement so that the PRINT statement can refer to it.

As illustrated by the example above, the FORMAT statement consists of the keyword FORMAT followed by a format specification. FORMAT statements are not executable statements. Thus, they do not have to appear immediately following the PRINT statements that reference them. However, this is a reasonable place for FORMAT statements that are used only once. If several PRINT statements use the same FORMAT statement, many programmers put the FORMAT statement at the end of the program. The same effect is achieved in Fortran 90 by assigning the format specification to a character variable.

10.3.3 Character String Edit Descriptors

The character string edit descriptors are

> ' characters '
> " characters "
> nH characters

The apostrophe and quote edit descriptors have the form of character constants and cause those constants to be placed in the output. The Hollerith descriptor nH . . . may be used to print the n characters following the H. These edit descriptors must not be used on input.

To print one of the delimiting characters in the output field, use two consecutive apostrophes or quotes. The field width is basically the length of the character constant, but doubled quotes or apostrophes are counted as single characters.

Example:

```
      WRITE (6, 110) TEMP
  110 FORMAT (15H TEMPERATURE = , F13.6)
```

produces the record:

    *b*TEMPERATURE*b*=*bbbb*32.120001

So also do the statements

```
      WRITE (6, 120) TEMP
  120 FORMAT (' TEMPERATURE = ', F13.6)
```

which avoids counting characters in the Hollerith constant. The following equivalent ways to produce the record were available in Fortran 77:

```
      WRITE (6, '('' TEMPERATURE = '', F13.6)') TEMP

      CHRFMT = '('' TEMPERATURE = '', F13.6)')
      WRITE (6, CHRFMT) TEMP

      WRITE (6, '(A, F13.6)') ' TEMPERATURE = ', TEMP
```

If a character string edit descriptor occurs in a format specification that is a literal constant delimited by apostrophes, two apostrophes must be written to represent each apostrophe in the format specification. If a format specification is, in turn, a character constant delimited by apostrophes, there must be two apostrophes for each delimiter and each apostrophe within the constant must be represented by four apostrophes. See the example below. The use of quote marks for delimiters is similar. One way to avoid problems is to use delimiters different from the characters within the format specification, if possible. However, the best way to avoid the problem is to put the character expression in the input/output list instead of the format specification as shown in the second example.

Example:

```
      PRINT '(''I can''''t hear you'')'

      PRINT "(A)", "I can't hear you"
```

10.4 Miscellaneous

10.4.1 Fixed Source Form

There is a second format that may be used to write Fortran programs. With **fixed source form**, positions 1–5 can be used only for labels; position 6, if it contains any character except a blank or zero, indicates that the line is a continuation of the previous line; and the main part of the statement must fall in positions 7–72. Positions 73 to the end of the record are ignored. A "C" or "*" in position one indicates that the entire line is a comment. The exclamation point (!) may be used to indicate comments, just as it does in the free source form used in this book. The semicolon (;) may be used to separate statements. Blank characters are insignificant in fixed source form, which is a major difference. Many older Fortran programs are written in fixed source form, which was once the only acceptable form and the only standard form until the adoption of Fortran 90.

Each program unit must use one form or the other; they cannot be mixed. There must be some way for the programmer to indicate whether a program unit is written in fixed form or written in free form, but that mechanism varies from one system to another. Check the manual for the system you are using to see how this is done.

10.4.2 Intrinsic Functions

Intrinsic functions that can be used with only one data type have been superceded by generic versions. For example, the function CABS finds the absolute value of a complex number, but the function ABS can be used to find the absolute value of a number of any numeric data type. It is always best to use the generic version.

10.4.3 The Statement Function

It is possible to define and use a function in a program, subroutine, or function by giving a one-line definition of a **statement function**. An example is

```
PROGRAM FUNCTION_EXAMPLE

   F (X) = X ** 2 - 1
   . . .
   Y = F (A + 2 * B)
   . . .

END PROGRAM FUNCTION_EXAMPLE
```

If more than one line is needed to define the function, a statement function cannot be used. All uses of statement functions can be replaced by internal functions.

10.4.4 Assumed-Size Arrays

An **assumed-size array** is a dummy argument for which the upper bound in the last dimension is declared to be an asterisk (*). This indicates that the extent of the array in that dimension, and hence its size, is not known. It is up to the programmer to make sure that elements of the assumed-size dummy argument match up correctly with the corresponding actual argument.

All uses of assumed-size arrays can be replaced by uses of assumed-shape arrays, in which all bounds are assumed from the actual argument by declaring the bounds to be a colon (:).

10.4.5 INCLUDE Line

An **include line** contains the keyword INCLUDE and a character literal constant. The meaning of the constant is not specified, but probably is a file name on most systems. The include line is replaced by included text, such as the contents of a specified file.

Although the include line might be useful in some simple cases, the use of modules is recommended instead.

10.4.6 The ENTRY Statement

The **ENTRY statement** allows one program unit to define more than one procedure. This may be useful when two procedures share some computations but still are different. A classic example is the computation of the trigonometric functions sine and cosine. Cosines of certain angles are computed as sines of related angles, and vice versa. In the following simple example, $g(x) = f(x)$ and $h(x) = f(|x|)$:

```
FUNCTION H (X)
    XX = ABS (X)
    GO TO 10
ENTRY G (X)
    XX = X
10 H = F (XX)
END FUNCTION H
```

10.4.7 Vendor Extensions

In many respects, any features in the Fortran system provided by a vendor that are not in the standard should be treated as obsolete, however new they may be. Every Fortran compiler is required to have a mechanism that will flag all nonstandard syntax. This feature always should be enabled during development and debugging.

Vendor extensions never should be used for the programmers' convenience or to achieve a small gain in efficiency. Use of such extensions will prevent the program from being run on different systems, perhaps even those provided later by the same vendor.

There are some circumstances in which it is necessary to use vendor extensions to standard Fortran in a program. One is to construct programs that are not possible to write in standard Fortran. Examples might be some real-time processing applications or a program that must manipulate special registers of a computer. The other use of nonstandard features is to achieve major improvements in efficiency on sections of code that use very large amounts of computing resources. Examples of this are provided by vendor extensions to access special vector-processing hardware. Fortran now has array processing facilities that should eliminate most of these uses. However, the next generation of machines may have special facilities for asynchronous parallel processing, and it might be necessary to introduce special language facilities to utilize these facilities most effectively.

If it is really necessary to use vendor extensions, do it only in those parts of the program that require them, and document their use thoroughly.

Syntax Rules

This appendix contains two parts. The first part is an extraction of all syntax rules and constraints in the order in which they occur in the Fortran standard. The second part is a cross reference with an entry for each terminal symbol and each nonterminal symbol in the syntax rules.

A.1 Notation Used in the Syntax Rules

Syntax rules are used to help describe the form that Fortran lexical tokens, statements, and constructs may take. These syntax rules are expressed in a variation of Backus-Naur form (BNF) in which

1. Characters from the Fortran character set are to be written as shown, except where otherwise noted.

2. Lowercase italicized letters and words (often hyphenated and abbreviated) represent general syntactic classes for which specific syntactic entities must be substituted in actual statements.

    Some common abbreviations used in syntactic terms are

    stmt   for   statement   *attr*   for   attribute

expr	for	expression	*decl*	for	declaration
spec	for	specifier	*def*	for	definition
int	for	integer	*desc*	for	descriptor
arg	for	argument	*op*	for	operator

3.   The syntactic metasymbols used are

is   introduces a syntactic class definition
or   introduces a syntactic class alternative
[ ]   encloses an optional item
[ ] ... encloses an optionally repeated item
         which may occur zero or more times
■   continues a syntax rule

4.   Each syntax rule is given a unique identifying number of the form R*snn*, where *s* is a one- or two-digit section number of the Fortran standard and *nn* is a two-digit sequence number within that section. The syntax rules are distributed as appropriate throughout the text, and are referenced by number as needed. Some rules in Sections 2 and 3 of the Fortran standard are more fully described in later sections; in such cases, the section number *s* is the number of the later section where the rule is repeated.

5.   The syntax rules are not a complete and accurate syntax description of Fortran, and cannot be used to generate automatically a Fortran parser; where a syntax rule is incomplete, it is accompanied by the corresponding constraints.

6.   A **constraint** is a restriction on the syntax rule that is capable of being checked by a compiler. Standard-conforming Fortran compilers must have the capability of detecting all deviations from the rules and the constraints given in this appendix.

An example of the use of syntax rules is

int-literal-constant   **is**   *digit* [*digit*] ...

The following forms are examples of forms for an integer literal constant allowed by the above rule:

digit
digit digit
digit digit digit digit
digit digit digit digit digit digit digit digit

When specific entities are substituted for *digit*, actual integer literal constants might be

4
67
1999
10243852

A.1.1 Assumed Syntax Rules

To minimize the number of additional syntax rules and convey appropriate constraint information, the following rules are assumed. The letters "*xyz*" stand for any legal syntactic class phrase.

xyz-list	**is**	*xyz* [, *xyz*] ...
xyz-name	**is**	*name*
scalar-xyz	**is**	*xyz*

Contraint: *scalar-xyz* must be scalar.

A.1.2 Syntax Conventions and Characteristics

1.   Any syntactic class name ending in "*-stmt*" follows the source form statement rules: it must be delimited by end-of-line or semicolon and may be labeled unless it forms part of another statement (such as an IF or WHERE statement). Conversely, everything considered to be a source form statement is given a "*-stmt*" ending in the syntax rules.

2.   The rules on statement ordering are described rigorously in the definition of *program-unit* (R202-R216). Expression hierarchy is described rigorously in the definition of *expr* (R723).

3.   The suffix "*-spec*" is used consistently for specifiers, such as keyword type parameters, keyword actual arguments, and input/output statement specifiers. It also is used for type declaration attribute specifications (for example, "*array-spec*" in R512), and in a few other cases.

4.   When reference is made to a type parameter, including the surrounding parentheses, the term "selector" is used. See, for example, "*length-selector*" (R507) and "*kind-selector*" (R505).

5.   The term "*subscript*" (for example, R615, R616, and R617) is used consistently in array definitions.

A.2 Syntax Rules and Constraints

Each of the following sections contains the syntax rules and constraints from one section of the Fortran standard.

A.2.1 Introduction

A.2.2 Fortran Terms and Concepts

R201	*executable-program*	**is**	*program-unit*
			[*program-unit*] ...
R202	*program-unit*	**is**	*main-program*
		or	*external-subprogram*
		or	*module*
		or	*block-data*
R1101	*main-program*	**is**	[*program-stmt*]
			[*specification-part*]
			[*execution-part*]
			[*internal-subprogram-part*]
			end-program-stmt
R203	*external-subprogram*	**is**	*function-subprogram*
		or	*subroutine-subprogram*
R1218	*function-subprogram*	**is**	*function-stmt*
			[*specification-part*]
			[*execution-part*]
			[*internal-subprogram-part*]
			end-function-stmt
R1222	*subroutine-subprogram*	**is**	*subroutine-stmt*
			[*specification-part*]
			[*execution-part*]
			[*internal-subprogram-part*]
			end-subroutine-stmt
R1104	*module*	**is**	*module-stmt*
			[*specification-part*]
			[*module-subprogram-part*]
			end-module-stmt
R1110	*block-data*	**is**	*block-data-stmt*
			[*specification-part*]
			end-block-data-stmt
R204	*specification-part*	**is**	[*use-stmt*] ...
			[*implicit-part*]
			[*declaration-construct*] ...
R205	*implicit-part*	**is**	[*implicit-part-stmt*] ...
			implicit-stmt
R206	*implicit-part-stmt*	**is**	*implicit-stmt*
		or	*parameter-stmt*
		or	*format-stmt*
		or	*entry-stmt*
R207	*declaration-construct*	**is**	*derived-type-def*
		or	*interface-block*
		or	*type-declaration-stmt*
		or	*specification-stmt*
		or	*parameter-stmt*
		or	*format-stmt*

		or	*entry-stmt*
		or	*stmt-function-stmt*
R208	*execution-part*	is	*executable-construct*
			[*execution-part-construct*] ...
R209	*execution-part-construct*	is	*executable-construct*
		or	*format-stmt*
		or	*data-stmt*
		or	*entry-stmt*
R210	*internal-subprogram-part*	is	*contains-stmt*
			internal-subprogram
			[*internal-subprogram*] ...
R211	*internal-subprogram*	is	*function-subprogram*
		or	*subroutine-subprogram*
R212	*module-subprogram-part*	is	*contains-stmt*
			module-subprogram
			[*module-subprogram*] ...
R213	*module-subprogram*	is	*function-subprogram*
		or	*subroutine-subprogram*
R214	*specification-stmt*	is	*access-stmt*
		or	*allocatable-stmt*
		or	*common-stmt*
		or	*data-stmt*
		or	*dimension-stmt*
		or	*equivalence-stmt*
		or	*external-stmt*
		or	*intent-stmt*
		or	*intrinsic-stmt*
		or	*namelist-stmt*
		or	*optional-stmt*
		or	*pointer-stmt*
		or	*save-stmt*
		or	*target-stmt*
R215	*executable-construct*	is	*action-stmt*
		or	*case-construct*
		or	*do-construct*
		or	*if-construct*
		or	*where-construct*
R216	*action-stmt*	is	*allocate-stmt*
		or	*assignment-stmt*
		or	*backspace-stmt*
		or	*call-stmt*
		or	*close-stmt*
		or	*computed-goto-stmt*
		or	*continue-stmt*
		or	*cycle-stmt*
		or	*deallocate-stmt*
		or	*endfile-stmt*
		or	*end-function-stmt*
		or	*end-program-stmt*
		or	*end-subroutine-stmt*
		or	*exit-stmt*
		or	*goto-stmt*
		or	*if-stmt*
		or	*inquire-stmt*
		or	*nullify-stmt*
		or	*open-stmt*
		or	*pointer-assignment-stmt*

		or	*print-stmt*
		or	*read-stmt*
		or	*return-stmt*
		or	*rewind-stmt*
		or	*stop-stmt*
		or	*where-stmt*
		or	*write-stmt*
		or	*arithmetic-if-stmt*
		or	*assign-stmt*
		or	*assigned-goto-stmt*
		or	*pause-stmt*

Constraint: An *execution-part-construct* must not contain an *end-function-stmt*, an *end-program-stmt*, or an *end-subroutine-stmt*.

A.2.3 Characters, Lexical Tokens, and Source Form

R301	*character*	is	*alphanumeric-character*
		or	*special-character*
R302	*alphanumeric-character*	is	*letter*
		or	*digit*
		or	*underscore*
R303	*underscore*	is	_
R304	*name*	is	*letter* [*alphanumeric-character*] ...

Constraint: The maximum length of a *name* is 31 characters.

R305	*constant*	is	*literal-constant*
		or	*named-constant*
R306	*literal-constant*	is	*int-literal-constant*
		or	*real-literal-constant*
		or	*complex-literal-constant*
		or	*logical-literal-constant*
		or	*char-literal-constant*
		or	*boz-literal-constant*
R307	*named-constant*	is	*name*
R308	*int-constant*	is	*constant*

Constraint: *int-constant* must be of type integer.

R309	*char-constant*	is	*constant*

Constraint: *char-constant* must be of type character.

R310	*intrinsic-operator*	is	*power-op*
		or	*mult-op*
		or	*add-op*
		or	*concat-op*
		or	*rel-op*
		or	*not-op*
		or	*and-op*
		or	*or-op*
		or	*equiv-op*
R708	*power-op*	is	**
R709	*mult-op*	is	*
		or	/
R710	*add-op*	is	+
		or	–
R712	*concat-op*	is	//
R714	*rel-op*	is	.EQ.
		or	.NE.
		or	.LT.

		or	.LE.
		or	.GT.
		or	.GE.
		or	= =
		or	/ =
		or	<
		or	< =
		or	>
		or	> =
R719	*not-op*	is	.NOT.
R720	*and-op*	is	.AND.
R721	*or-op*	is	.OR.
R722	*equiv-op*	is	.EQV.
		or	.NEQV.
R311	*defined-operator*	is	*defined-unary-op*
		or	*defined-binary-op*
		or	*generic-intrinsic-op*
R704	*defined-unary-op*	is	. *letter* [*letter*] ... .
R724	*defined-binary-op*	is	. *letter* [*letter*] ... .
R312	*generic-intrinsic-op*	is	*intrinsic-operator*

Constraint: A *defined-unary-op* and a *defined-binary-op* must not contain more than 31 letters and must not be the same as any *intrinsic-operator* or *logical-literal-constant*.

R313	*label*	is	*digit* [*digit* [*digit* [*digit* [*digit*]]]]

Constraint: At least one digit in a *label* must be nonzero.

A.2.4 Intrinsic and Derived Data Types

R401	*signed-digit-string*	is	[*sign*] *digit-string*
R402	*digit-string*	is	*digit* [*digit*] ...
R403	*signed-int-literal-constant*	is	[*sign*] *int-literal-constant*
R404	*int-literal-constant*	is	*digit-string* [_ *kind-param*]
R405	*kind-param*	is	*digit-string*
		or	*scalar-int-constant-name*
R406	*sign*	is	+
		or	–

Constraint: The value of *kind-param* must be nonnegative.

Constraint: The value of *kind-param* must specify a representation method that exists on the processor.

R407	*boz-literal-constant*	is	*binary-constant*
		or	*octal-constant*
		or	*hex-constant*

Constraint: A *boz-literal-constant* may appear only in a DATA statement.

R408	*binary-constant*	is	B ' *digit* [*digit*] ... '
		or	B " *digit* [*digit*] ... "

Constraint: *digit* must have one of the values 0 or 1.

R409	*octal-constant*	is	O ' *digit* [*digit*] ... '
		or	O " *digit* [*digit*] ... "

Constraint: *digit* must have one of the values 0 through 7.

R410	*hex-constant*	is	Z ' *hex-digit* [*hex-digit*] ... '
		or	Z " *hex-digit* [*hex-digit*] ... "
R411	*hex-digit*	is	digit
		or	A
		or	B

		or	C
		or	D
		or	E
		or	F

R412 *signed-real-literal-constant* **is** [*sign*] *real-literal-constant*

R413 *real-literal-constant* **is** *significand* [*exponent-letter exponent*] [_ *kind-param*]
 or *digit-string exponent-letter exponent* [_ *kind-param*]

R414 *significand* **is** *digit-string* . [*digit-string*]
 or . *digit-string*

R415 *exponent-letter* **is** E
 or D

R416 *exponent* **is** *signed-digit-string*

Constraint: If both *kind-param* and *exponent-letter* are present, *exponent-letter* must be E.

Constraint: The value of *kind-param* must specify an approximation method that exists on the processor.

R417 *complex-literal-constant* **is** (*real-part* , *imag-part*)

R418 *real-part* **is** *signed-int-literal-constant*
 or *signed-real-literal-constant*

R419 *imag-part* **is** *signed-int-literal-constant*
 or *signed-real-literal-constant*

R420 *char-literal-constant* **is** [*kind-param* _] ' [*rep-char*] ... '
 or [*kind-param* _] " [*rep-char*] ... "

Constraint: The value of *kind-param* must specify a representation method that exists on the processor.

R421 *logical-literal-constant* **is** .TRUE. [_ *kind-param*]
 or .FALSE. [_ *kind-param*]

Constraint: The value of *kind-param* must specify a representation method that exists on the processor.

R422 *derived-type-def* **is** *derived-type-stmt*
 [*private-sequence-stmt*] ...
 component-def-stmt
 [*component-def-stmt*] ...
 end-type-stmt

R423 *private-sequence-stmt* **is** PRIVATE
 or SEQUENCE

R424 *derived-type-stmt* **is** TYPE [, *access-spec* ::] *type-name*

Constraint: The same *private-sequence-stmt* must not appear more than once in a given *derived-type-def*.

Constraint: If SEQUENCE is present, all derived types specified in component definitions must be sequence types.

Constraint: An *access-spec* (5.1.2.2) or a PRIVATE statement within the definition is permitted only if the type definition is within the specification part of a module.

Constraint: If a component of a derived type is of a type declared to be private, either all components of the derived type must be private or the derived type must be private.

Constraint: A derived type *type-name* must not be the same as the name of any intrinsic type nor the same as any other accessible derived *type-name*.

R425 *end-type-stmt* **is** END TYPE [*type-name*]

Constraint: If END TYPE is followed by a *type-name*, the *type-name* must be the same as that in the corresponding *derived-type-stmt*.

R426 *component-def-stmt* **is** *type-spec* [[, *component-attr-spec-list*] ::] ■
 ■ *component-decl-list*

R427 *component-attr-spec* **is** POINTER
 or DIMENSION (*component-array-spec*)

Constraint: No *component-attr-spec* may appear more than once in a given *component-def-stmt*.

Constraint: If the POINTER attribute is not specified for a component, a *type-spec* in the *component-def-stmt* must specify an intrinsic type or a previously defined derived type.

Constraint: If the POINTER attribute is specified for a component, a *type-spec* in the *component-def-stmt* must specify an intrinsic type or any accessible derived type including the type being defined.

R428   *component-array-spec*   **is**   *explicit-shape-spec-list*
                                                        or   *deferred-shape-spec-list*

R429   *component-decl*   **is**   *component-name* [(*component-array-spec*)] ■
                                      ■ [* *char-length*]

Constraint: If the POINTER attribute is not specified, each *component-array-spec* must be an *explicit-shape-spec-list*.

Constraint: If the POINTER attribute is specified, each *component-array-spec* must be a *deferred-shape-spec-list*.

Constraint: The * *char-length* option is permitted only if the type specified is character.

Constraint: A *char-length* in a *component-decl* must be an integer constant expression.

Constraint: Each bound in the *explicit-shape-spec* (R428) must be an integer constant expression.

R430   *structure-constructor*   **is**   *type-name* (*expr-list*)
R431   *array-constructor*   **is**   (/ *ac-value-list* /)
R432   *ac-value*   **is**   *expr*
                    or   *ac-implied-do*
R433   *ac-implied-do*   **is**   (*ac-value-list* , *ac-implied-do-control*)
R434   *ac-implied-do-control*   **is**   *ac-do-variable* = *scalar-int-expr* , ■
                                      ■ *scalar-int-expr* [, *scalar-int-expr*]
R435   *ac-do-variable*   **is**   *scalar-int-variable*
Constraint: *ac-do-variable* must be a named variable.
Constraint: Each *ac-value* in the sequence must have the same type and type parameters.

A.2.5 Data Object Declarations and Specifications

R501   *type-declaration-stmt*   **is**   *type-spec* [[, *attr-spec*] ... ::] *entity-decl-list*
R502   *type-spec*   **is**   INTEGER [*kind-selector*]
                    or   REAL [*kind-selector*]
                    or   DOUBLE PRECISION
                    or   COMPLEX [*kind-selector*]
                    or   CHARACTER [*char-selector*]
                    or   LOGICAL [*kind-selector*]
                    or   TYPE (*type-name*)
R503   *attr-spec*   **is**   PARAMETER
                    or   *access-spec*
                    or   ALLOCATABLE
                    or   DIMENSION (*array-spec*)
                    or   EXTERNAL
                    or   INTENT (*intent-spec*)
                    or   INTRINSIC
                    or   OPTIONAL
                    or   POINTER
                    or   SAVE
                    or   TARGET
R504   *entity-decl*   **is**   *object-name* [(*array-spec*)] ■
                                    ■ [* *char-length*] [= *initialization-expr*]
                    or   *function-name* [(*array-spec*)] [* *char-length*]

R505   *kind-selector*   **is**   ([KIND =] *scalar-int-initialization-expr*)

Constraint: The same *attr-spec* must not appear more than once in a given *type-declaration-stmt*.

Constraint: The *function-name* must be the name of an external function, an intrinsic function, a function dummy procedure, or a statement function.

Constraint: The = *initialization-expr* must appear if the statement contains a PARAMETER attribute (5.1.2.1).

Constraint: If = *initialization-expr* appears, a double colon separator must appear before the *entity-decl-list*.

Constraint: The = *initialization-expr* must not appear if *object-name* is a dummy argument, a function result, an object in a named common block unless the type declaration is in a block data program unit, an object in blank common, an allocatable object, a pointer, an external name, an intrinsic name, or an automatic object.

Constraint: The * *char-length* option is permitted only if the type specified is character.

Constraint: The ALLOCATABLE attribute may be used only when declaring an array that is not a dummy argument or a function result.

Constraint: An array declared with a POINTER or an ALLOCATABLE attribute must be specified with an *array-spec* that is a *deferred-shape-spec-list* (5.1.2.4.3).

Constraint: The *array-spec* for a *function-name* that does not have the pointer attribute must be an *explicit-shape-spec-list*.

Constraint: The *array-spec* for a *function-name* that does have the pointer attribute must be a *deferred-shape-spec-list*.

Constraint: An object must not have both the TARGET attribute and the PARAMETER attribute.

Constraint: If the POINTER attribute is specified, the INTENT, EXTERNAL, and INTRINSIC attributes must not be specified.

Constraint: If the TARGET attribute is specified, The EXTERNAL and INTRINSIC attributes must not be specified.

Constraint: The PARAMETER attribute must not be specified for dummy arguments, pointers, functions, or objects in a common block.

Constraint: The INTENT and OPTIONAL attributes may be specified only for dummy arguments.

Constraint: An entity must not have the PUBLIC attribute if its type has the PRIVATE attribute.

Constraint: The SAVE attribute must not be specified for an object that is in a common block, a dummy argument, a procedure, a function result, or an automatic data object.

Constraint: An entity must not have the EXTERNAL attribute if it has the INTRINSIC attribute.

Constraint: An entity in a *type-declaration-stmt* must not have the EXTERNAL or INTRINSIC attribute specified unless it is a function.

Constraint: An array must not have both the ALLOCATABLE attribute and the POINTER attribute.

Constraint: An entity must not be given explicitly any attribute more than once in a scoping unit.

Constraint: The value specified in a *kind-selector* must be nonnegative.

R506   *char-selector*   **is**   *length-selector*
                                     or   ([LEN=] *type-param-value* , ■
                                               ■ [KIND=] *scalar-int-initialization-expr*)
                                     or   (KIND= *scalar-int-initialization-expr* ■
                                               ■ [, LEN= *type-param-value*])

R507   *length-selector*   **is**   ([LEN =] *type-param-value*)
                                     or   * *char-length* [,]

R508   *char-length*   **is**   (*type-param-value*)

			or *scalar-int-literal-constant*

Constraint: The optional comma in a *length-selector* is permitted only if no double colon separator appears in the *type-declaration-stmt*.

R509	*type-param-value*	**is**	*specification-expr*
		or	*
R510	*access-spec*	**is**	PUBLIC
		or	PRIVATE

Constraint: An *access-spec* attribute may appear only in the *specification-part* of a module.

R511	*intent-spec*	**is**	IN
		or	OUT
		or	INOUT

Constraint: The INTENT attribute may appear only in the *specification-part* of a subprogram or interface body (12.3.2.1).

Constraint: The INTENT attribute must not be specified for a dummy argument that is a dummy procedure or a dummy pointer.

R512	*array-spec*	**is**	*explicit-shape-spec-list*
		or	*assumed-shape-spec-list*
		or	*deferred-shape-spec-list*
		or	*assumed-size-spec*

Constraint: The maximum rank is seven.

R513	*explicit-shape-spec*	**is**	[*lower-bound* :] *upper-bound*
R514	*lower-bound*	**is**	*scalar-int-expr*
R515	*upper-bound*	**is**	*scalar-int-expr*

Constraint: An explicit-shape array whose bounds depend on the values of nonconstant expressions must be a dummy argument, a function result, or an automatic array of a procedure.

Constraint: The bounds in an explicit-shape array declaration must be specification expressions (7.1.6.2).

R516	*assumed-shape-spec*	**is**	[*lower-bound*] :
R517	*deferred-shape-spec*	**is**	:
R518	*assumed-size-spec*	**is**	[*explicit-shape-spec-list* ,] [*lower-bound* :] *

Constraint: The function name of an array-valued function must not be declared as an assumed-size array.

R519	*intent-stmt*	**is**	INTENT (*intent-spec*) [::] *dummy-arg-name-list*

Constraint: An *intent-stmt* may appear only in the *specification-part* of a subprogram or an interface body (12.3.2.1).

Constraint: *dummy-arg-name* must not be the name of a dummy procedure or a dummy pointer.

R520	*optional-stmt*	**is**	OPTIONAL [::] *dummy-arg-name-list*

Constraint: An *optional-stmt* may occur only in the scoping unit of a subprogram or an interface block.

R521	*access-stmt*	**is**	*access-spec* [[::] *access-id-list*]
R522	*access-id*	**is**	*use-name*
		or	*generic-spec*

Constraint: An *access-stmt* may appear only in the scoping unit of a module. Only one accessibility statement with an omitted *access-id-list* is permitted in the scoping unit of a module.

Constraint: Each *access-id* must be the name of a named variable, nonintrinsic procedure, derived type, named constant, or namelist group.

Constraint: A *access-id* in a PUBLIC statement must not be the name of a module procedure that has a dummy argument or function result of a type that has PRIVATE accessibility, and such a procedure must not be given PUBLIC accessibility by default.

R523	*save-stmt*	**is**	SAVE [[::] *saved-entity-list*]

R524   *saved-entity*   **is**   *object-name*
                                          or   / *common-block-name* /

Constraint: An *object-name* must not be a dummy argument name, a procedure name, a function result name, an automatic data object name, a namelist group name, or the name of an entity in a common block.

Constraint: If a SAVE statement with an omitted saved entity list occurs in a scoping unit, no other explicit occurrence of the SAVE attribute or SAVE statement is permitted in the same scoping unit.

R525   *dimension-stmt*   **is**   DIMENSION [::] *array-name* (*array-spec*) ■
                                          ■ [, *array-name* (*array-spec*)] ...

R526   *allocatable-stmt*   **is**   ALLOCATABLE [::] *array-name* ■
                                          ■ [(*deferred-shape-spec-list*)] ■
                                          ■ [, *array-name* [(*deferred-shape-spec-list*)]] ...

Constraint: The *array-name* must not be a dummy argument or function result.

Constraint: If the DIMENSION attribute for an *array-name* is specified elsewhere in the scoping unit, the *array-spec* must be a *deferred-shape-spec-list*.

R527   *pointer-stmt*   **is**   POINTER [::] *object-name* ■
                                          ■ [(*deferred-shape-spec-list*)] ■
                                          ■ [, *object-name* [(*deferred-shape-spec-list*)]] ...

Constraint: The INTENT attribute must not be specified for an *object-name*.

Constraint: If the DIMENSION attribute for an *object-name* is specified elsewhere in the scoping unit, the *array-spec* must be a *deferred-shape-spec-list*.

Constraint: The PARAMETER attribute must not be specified for *object-name*.

R528   *target-stmt*   **is**   TARGET [::] *object-name* [(*array-spec*)] ■
                                          ■ [, *object-name* [(*array-spec*)]] ...

Constraint: The PARAMETER attribute must not be specified for an *object-name*.

R529   *data-stmt*   **is**   DATA *data-stmt-set* [[,] *data-stmt-set*] ...

R530   *data-stmt-set*   **is**   *data-stmt-object-list* / *data-stmt-value-list* /

R531   *data-stmt-object*   **is**   *variable*
                                          or   *data-implied-do*

R532   *data-stmt-value*   **is**   [*data-stmt-repeat* *] *data-stmt-constant*

R533   *data-stmt-constant*   **is**   *scalar-constant*
                                          or   *signed-int-literal-constant*
                                          or   *signed-real-literal-constant*
                                          or   *structure-constructor*
                                          or   *boz-literal-constant*

R534   *data-stmt-repeat*   **is**   *scalar-int-constant*

R535   *data-implied-do*   **is**   (*data-i-do-object-list* , *data-i-do-variable* = ■
                                          ■ *scalar-int-expr* , *scalar-int-expr* [, *scalar-int-expr*])

R536   *data-i-do-object*   **is**   *array-element*
                                          or   *data-implied-do*

Constraint: *array-element* must not be a subobject with a constant parent.

R537   *data-i-do-variable*   **is**   *scalar-int-variable*

Constraint: *data-i-do-variable* must be a named variable.

Constraint: The DATA statement repeat factor must be positive or zero. If the DATA statement repeat factor is a named constant, it must have been declared previously in the scoping unit or made accessible by use association or host association.

Constraint: If a *data-stmt-constant* is a *structure-constructor*, each component must be a constant expression.

Constraint: A variable whose name or designator is included in a *data-stmt-object-list* or a *data-i-do-object-list* must not be: a dummy argument, made accessible by use association or host association, in a named common block unless the DATA statement is in a block data program unit, in a blank common block, a function name, a function result name, an automatic object, a pointer, or an allocatable array.

Constraint: A subscript in an array element *data-i-do-object* must be an expression whose primaries are either constants or DO variables of the containing *data-implied-do*s.

Constraint: A *scalar-int-expr* of a *data-implied-do* must involve as primaries only constants or DO variables of the containing *data-implied-do*s.

R538	*parameter-stmt*	**is**	PARAMETER (*named-constant-def-list*)
R539	*named-constant-def*	**is**	*named-constant* = *initialization-expr*
R540	*implicit-stmt*	**is**	IMPLICIT *implicit-spec-list*
		or	IMPLICIT NONE
R541	*implicit-spec*	**is**	*type-spec* (*letter-spec-list*)
R542	*letter-spec*	**is**	*letter* [– *letter*]

Constraint: If IMPLICIT NONE is specified in a scoping unit, it must precede any PARAMETER statements that appear in the scoping unit and there must be no other IMPLICIT statements in the scoping unit.

Constraint: If the minus and second letter appear, the second letter must follow the first letter alphabetically.

R543	*namelist-stmt*	**is**	NAMELIST / *namelist-group-name* / ■
			■ *namelist-group-object-list* ■
			■ [[,] / *namelist-group-name* / ■
			■ *namelist-group-object-list*] ...
R544	*namelist-group-object*	**is**	*variable-name*

Constraint: A *namelist-group-object* must not be an array dummy argument with nonconstant bounds, a variable with assumed parameters, an automatic object, a pointer, a structure containing a pointer, an allocatable array, or a subobject of any of the preceding objects.

Constraint: If a *namelist-group-name* has the PUBLIC attribute, no item in the *namelist-group-object-list* may have the PRIVATE attribute.

R545	*equivalence-stmt*	**is**	EQUIVALENCE *equivalence-set-list*
R546	*equivalence-set*	**is**	(*equivalence-object* , *equivalence-object-list*)
R547	*equivalence-object*	**is**	*variable-name*
		or	*array-element*
		or	*substring*

Constraint: An *equivalence-object* must not be a dummy argument, a pointer, an allocatable array, a nonsequence structure, a sequence structure containing a pointer, an automatic object, a function name, an entry name, a result name, or a subobject of any of the preceding objects.

Constraint: Each subscript or substring range expression in an *equivalence-object* must be an integer initialization expression (7.1.6.1).

Constraint: If an *equivalence-object* is of type default integer, default real, double precision real, default complex, default logical, or numeric sequence type, all of the objects in the equivalence set must be of these types.

Constraint: If an *equivalence-object* is of type default character or character sequence type, all of the objects in the equivalence set must be of these types.

Constraint: If an *equivalence-object* is of a derived type that is not a numeric sequence or character sequence type, all of the objects in the equivalence set must be of the same type.

Constraint: If an *equivalence-object* is of an intrinsic type other than default integer type, default real type, double precision real type, default complex type, default logical type, or default character type, all of the objects in the equivalence set must be of the same type with the same kind type parameter values.

R548	*common-stmt*	**is**	COMMON [/ [*common-block-name*] /] ■
			■ *common-block-object-list* ■
			■ [[,] / [*common-block-name*] / ■
			■ *common-block-object-list*] ...

R549   *common-block-object*   **is**   *variable-name* [(*explicit-shape-spec-list*)]

Constraint: Only one appearance of a given *variable-name* is permitted in all *common-block-object-list*s within a scoping unit.

Constraint: A *common-block-object* must not be a dummy argument, an allocatable array, an automatic object, a function name, an entry name, or a result name.

Constraint: Each bound in the *explicit-shape-spec* must be an integer initialization expression.

Constraint: If a *common-block-object* is of a derived type, it must be a sequence type (4.4.1).

Constraint: If a *variable-name* appears with an *explicit-shape-spec-list*, it must not have the POINTER attribute.

A.2.6 Use of Data Objects

R601   *variable*   **is**   *scalar-variable-name*
                                     or   *array-variable-name*
                                     or   *subobject*

Constraint: *array-variable-name* must be the name of a *variable* that is an array.

Constraint: *subobject* must not be a subobject designator (for example, a substring) whose parent is a constant.

R602   *subobject*   **is**   *array-element*
                                     or   *array-section*
                                     or   *structure-component*
                                     or   *substring*

R603   *logical-variable*   **is**   *variable*

Constraint: *logical-variable* must be of type logical.

R604   *default-logical-variable*   **is**   *variable*

Constraint: *default-logical-variable* must be of type default logical.

R605   *char-variable*   **is**   *variable*

Constraint: *char-variable* must be of type character.

R606   *default-char-variable*   **is**   *variable*

Constraint: *default-char-variable* must be of type default character.

R607   *int-variable*   **is**   *variable*

Constraint: *int-variable* must be of type integer.

R608   *default-int-variable*   **is**   *variable*

Constraint: *default-int-variable* must be of type default integer.

R609   *substring*   **is**   *parent-string* (*substring-range*)

R610   *parent-string*   **is**   *scalar-variable-name*
                                     or   *array-element*
                                     or   *scalar-structure-component*
                                     or   *scalar-constant*

R611   *substring-range*   **is**   [*scalar-int-expr*] : [*scalar-int-expr*]

Constraint: *parent-string* must be of type character.

R612   *structure-component*   **is**   *parent-structure* % *component-name*

R613   *parent-structure*   **is**   *scalar-variable-name*
                                     or   *array-variable-name*
                                     or   *array-element*
                                     or   *array-section*
                                     or   *structure-component*
                                     or   *named-constant*

Constraint: If *parent-structure* is an array, the component must not be an array and must not have the pointer attribute.

Constraint: *parent-structure* must be of derived type.

Constraint: *component-name* must be a component from the derived-type definition of the type of *parent-structure*.

R614 *array-element*   is *parent-array* (*subscript-list*)

Constraint: The number of subscripts must equal the rank of the array.

R615 *array-section*   is *parent-array* (*section-subscript-list*) [(*substring-range*)]

Constraint: If *substring-range* is present, *parent-array* must be of type character.

Constraint: At least one *section-subscript* must be a *subscript-triplet* or *vector-subscript*.

Constraint: The number of *section-subscript*s must equal the rank of the array.

R616 *parent-array*   is *array-name*
                               or *structure-component*

Constraint: A *structure-component* may appear only if the component specified is an array.

R617 *subscript*   is *scalar-int-expr*

R618 *section-subscript*   is *subscript*
                               or *subscript-triplet*
                               or *vector-subscript*

R619 *subscript-triplet*   is [*subscript*] : [*subscript*] [: *stride*]

R620 *stride*   is *scalar-int-expr*

R621 *vector-subscript*   is *int-expr*

Constraint: A *vector-subscript* must be an integer array expression of rank one.

Constraint: The second *subscript* must not be omitted from a *subscript-triplet* in the last dimension of an assumed-size array.

R622 *allocate-stmt*   is ALLOCATE (*allocation-list* ■
                                   ■ [, STAT = *stat-variable*])

R623 *stat-variable*   is *scalar-int-variable*

Constraint: The *stat-variable* must not be allocated within the ALLOCATE statement in which it appears.

R624 *allocation*   is *allocate-object* [(*explicit-shape-spec-list*)]

R625 *allocate-object*   is *variable-name*
                               or *structure-component*

Constraint: Each *allocate-object* must be a pointer or an allocatable array.

Constraint: A bound in an *allocation explicit-shape-spec* must not be an expression involving as a primary an array inquiry function (13.10.15) whose argument is any other object in the same ALLOCATE statement.

Constraint: The number of *explicit-shape-spec*s in an *allocation explicit-shape-spec-list* must be the same as the rank of the pointer or allocatable array.

R626 *nullify-stmt*   is NULLIFY (*pointer-object-list*)

R627 *pointer-object*   is *variable-name*
                               or *structure-component*

Constraint: Each *pointer-object* must have the POINTER attribute.

R628 *deallocate-stmt*   is DEALLOCATE (*allocate-object-list* ■
                                   ■ [, STAT = *stat-variable*])

Constraint: Each *allocate-object* must be a pointer or an allocatable array.

Constraint: The *stat-variable* must not be deallocated within the same DEALLOCATE statement.

A.2.7 Expressions and Assignment

R701 *primary*   is *constant*
                               or *constant-subobject*
                               or *variable*
                               or *array-constructor*
                               or *structure-constructor*

		or	*function-reference*
		or	(*expr*)
R702	*constant-subobject*	is	*subobject*

Constraint: *subobject* must be a subobject designator whose parent is a constant.

Constraint: A *variable* that is a *primary* must not be an assumed-size array.

R703	*level-1-expr*	is	[*defined-unary-op*] *primary*
R704	*defined-unary-op*	is	. *letter* [*letter*] ... .

Constraint: A *defined-unary-op* must not contain more than 31 letters and must not be the same as any *intrinsic-operator* or *logical-literal-constant*.

R705	*mult-operand*	is	*level-1-expr* [*power-op mult-operand*]
R706	*add-operand*	is	[*add-operand mult-op*] *mult-operand*
R707	*level-2-expr*	is	[[*level-2-expr*] *add-op*] *add-operand*
R708	*power-op*	is	**
R709	*mult-op*	is	*
		or	/
R710	*add-op*	is	+
		or	−
R711	*level-3-expr*	is	[*level-3-expr concat-op*] *level-2-expr*
R712	*concat-op*	is	//
R713	*level-4-expr*	is	[*level-3-expr rel-op*] *level-3-expr*
R714	*rel-op*	is	.EQ.
		or	.NE.
		or	.LT.
		or	.LE.
		or	.GT.
		or	.GE.
		or	==
		or	/=
		or	<
		or	<=
		or	>
		or	>=
R715	*and-operand*	is	[*not-op*] *level-4-expr*
R716	*or-operand*	is	[*or-operand and-op*] *and-operand*
R717	*equiv-operand*	is	[*equiv-operand or-op*] *or-operand*
R718	*level-5-expr*	is	[*level-5-expr equiv-op*] *equiv-operand*
R719	*not-op*	is	.NOT.
R720	*and-op*	is	.AND.
R721	*or-op*	is	.OR.
R722	*equiv-op*	is	.EQV.
		or	.NEQV.
R723	*expr*	is	[*expr defined-binary-op*] *level-5-expr*
R724	*defined-binary-op*	is	. *letter* [*letter*] ... .

Constraint: A *defined-binary-op* must not contain more than 31 letters and must not be the same as any *intrinsic-operator* or *logical-literal-constant*.

R725	*logical-expr*	is	*expr*

Constraint: *logical-expr* must be type logical.

R726	*char-expr*	is	*expr*

Constraint: *char-expr* must be type character.

R727	*default-char-expr*	is	*expr*

Constraint: *default-char-expr* must be of type default character.

R728	*int-expr*	is	*expr*

Constraint: *int-expr* must be type integer.

R729	*numeric-expr*	is	*expr*

Constraint: *numeric-expr* must be of type integer, real or complex.

R730	*initialization-expr*	**is**	*expr*
R731	*char-initialization-expr*	**is**	*char-expr*
R732	*int-initialization-expr*	**is**	*int-expr*
R733	*logical-initialization-expr*	**is**	*logical-expr*
R734	*specification-expr*	**is**	*scalar-int-expr*

Constraint: The *scalar-int-expr* must be a restricted expression.

R735 *assignment-stmt* **is** *variable = expr*

Constraint: A *variable* in an *assignment-stmt* must not be an assumed-size array.

R736 *pointer-assignment-stmt* **is** *pointer-object = > target*

R737	*target*	**is**	*variable*
		or	*function-reference*

Constraint: The *pointer-object* must have the POINTER attribute. The target object must have one of the attributes TARGET or POINTER or it must be a subobject of an object with one of these attributes.

Constraint: The *target* must be of the same type, type parameters, and rank as the pointer.

Constraint: The *target* must not be an array section with a vector subscript.

Constraint: The *function-reference* must deliver a pointer result.

R738 *where-stmt* **is** WHERE (*mask-expr*) *assignment-stmt*

R739 *where-construct* **is** *where-construct-stmt*
        [*assignment-stmt*] ...
        [*elsewhere-stmt*
          [*assignment-stmt*] ...]
        end-where-stmt

R740	*where-construct-stmt*	**is**	WHERE (*mask-expr*)
R741	*mask-expr*	**is**	*logical-expr*
R742	*elsewhere-stmt*	**is**	ELSEWHERE
R743	*end-where-stmt*	**is**	END WHERE

Constraint: In each *assignment-stmt*, the *mask-expr* and the variable being defined must be arrays of the same shape.

A.2.8 Execution Control

R801 *block* **is** [*execution-part-construct*] ...

R802 *if-construct* **is** *if-then-stmt*
        block
        [*else-if-stmt*
          block] ...
        [*else-stmt*
          block]
        end-if-stmt

R803	*if-then-stmt*	**is**	[*if-construct-name* :] IF (*scalar-logical-expr*) THEN
R804	*else-if-stmt*	**is**	ELSE IF (*scalar-logical-expr*) THEN [*if-construct-name*]
R805	*else-stmt*	**is**	ELSE [*if-construct-name*]
R806	*end-if-stmt*	**is**	END IF [*if-construct-name*]

Constraint: If the *if-then-stmt* of an *if-construct* is identified by an *if-construct-name*, the corresponding *end-if-stmt* must specify the same *if-construct-name*. If the *if-then-stmt* of an *if-construct* is not identified by an *if-construct-name*, the corresponding *end-if-stmt* must not specify an *if-construct-name*. If an *else-if-stmt* or *else-stmt* is identified by an *if-construct-name*, the corresponding *if-then-stmt* must specify the same *if-construct-name*.

R807 *if-stmt* **is** IF (*scalar-logical-expr*) *action-stmt*

Constraint: The *action-stmt* in the *if-stmt* must not be an *if-stmt, end-program-stmt, end-function-stmt,* or *end-subroutine-stmt.*

R808 *case-construct* **is** *select-case-stmt*
        [*case-stmt*
           block] ...
        end-select-stmt

R809 *select-case-stmt* **is** [*case-construct-name* :] SELECT CASE (*case-expr*)

R810 *case-stmt* **is** CASE *case-selector* [*case-construct-name*]

R811 *end-select-stmt* **is** END SELECT [*case-construct-name*]

Constraint: If the *select-case-stmt* of a *case-construct* is identified by a *case-construct-name,* the corresponding *end-select-stmt* must specify the same *case-construct-name.* If the *select-case-stmt* of a *case-construct* is not identified by a *case-construct-name,* the corresponding *end-select-stmt* must not specify a *case-construct-name.* If a *case-stmt* is identified by a *case-construct-name,* the corresponding *select-case-stmt* must specify the same *case-construct-name.*

R812 *case-expr* **is** *scalar-int-expr*
       or *scalar-char-expr*
       or *scalar-logical-expr*

R813 *case-selector* **is** (*case-value-range-list*)
       or DEFAULT

Constraint: No more than one of the selectors of one of the CASE statements may be DEFAULT.

R814 *case-value-range* **is** *case-value*
       or *case-value* :
       or : *case-value*
       or *case-value* : *case-value*

R815 *case-value* **is** *scalar-int-initialization-expr*
       or *scalar-char-initialization-expr*
       or *scalar-logical-initialization-expr*

Constraint: For a given *case-construct,* each *case-value* must be of the same type as *case-expr.* For character type, length differences are allowed, but the kind type parameters must be the same.

Constraint: A *case-value-range* using a colon must not be used if *case-expr* is of type logical.

Constraint: For a given *case-construct,* the *case-value-ranges* must not overlap; that is, there must be no possible value of the *case-expr* that matches more than one *case-value-range.*

R816 *do-construct* **is** *block-do-construct*
       or *nonblock-do-construct*

R817 *block-do-construct* **is** *do-stmt*
          do-block
          end-do

R818 *do-stmt* **is** *label-do-stmt*
       or *nonlabel-do-stmt*

R819 *label-do-stmt* **is** [*do-construct-name* :] DO *label* [*loop-control*]

R820 *nonlabel-do-stmt* **is** [*do-construct-name* :] DO [*loop-control*]

R821 *loop-control* **is** [,] *do-variable* = *scalar-numeric-expr* , ■
         ■ *scalar-numeric-expr* [, *scalar-numeric-expr*]
       or [,] WHILE (*scalar-logical-expr*)

R822 *do-variable* **is** *scalar-variable*

Constraint: The *do-variable* must be a scalar integer, default real, or double precision real named variable.

Constraint: Each *scalar-numeric-expr* in *loop-control* must be of type integer, default real, or double precision real

R823 *do-block* **is** *block*

R824	*end-do*	**is**	*end-do-stmt*
		or	*continue-stmt*
R825	*end-do-stmt*	**is**	END DO [*do-construct-name*]

Constraint: If the *do-stmt* of a *block-do-construct* is identified by a *do-construct-name*, the corresponding *end-do* must be an *end-do-stmt* specifying the same *do-construct-name*. If the *do-stmt* of a *block-do-construct* does not so specify a *do-construct-name*, the corresponding *end-do* must not specify a *do-construct-name*.

Constraint: If the *do-stmt* is a *nonlabel-do-stmt*, the corresponding *end-do* must be an *end-do-stmt*.

Constraint: If the *do-stmt* is a *label-do-stmt*, the corresponding *end-do* must be identified with the same *label*.

R826	*nonblock-do-construct*	**is**	*action-term-do-construct*
		or	*outer-shared-do-construct*
R827	*action-term-do-construct*	**is**	*label-do-stmt*
			do-body
			do-term-action-stmt
R828	*do-body*	**is**	[*execution-part-construct*] ...
R829	*do-term-action-stmt*	**is**	*action-stmt*

Constraint: A *do-term-action-stmt* must not be a *continue-stmt*, a *goto-stmt*, a *return-stmt*, a *stop-stmt*, an *exit-stmt*, a *cycle-stmt*, an *end-function-stmt*, an *end-subroutine-stmt*, an *end-program-stmt*, an *arithmetic-if-stmt*, or an *assigned-goto-stmt*.

Constraint: The *do-term-action-stmt* must be identified with a label and the corresponding *label-do-stmt* must refer to the same label.

R830	*outer-shared-do-construct*	**is**	*label-do-stmt*
			do-body
			shared-term-do-construct
R831	*shared-term-do-construct*	**is**	*outer-shared-do-construct*
		or	*inner-shared-do-construct*
R832	*inner-shared-do-construct*	**is**	*label-do-stmt*
			do-body
			do-term-shared-stmt
R833	*do-term-shared-stmt*	**is**	*action-stmt*

Constraint: A *do-term-shared-stmt* must not be a *goto-stmt*, a *return-stmt*, a *stop-stmt*, an *exit-stmt*, a *cycle-stmt*, an *end-function-stmt*, an *end-subroutine-stmt*, an *end-program-stmt*, an *arithmetic-if-stmt*, or an *assigned-goto-stmt*.

Constraint: The *do-term-shared-stmt* must be identified with a label and all of the *label-do-stmts* of the *shared-term-do-construct* must refer to the same label.

R834	*cycle-stmt*	**is**	CYCLE [*do-construct-name*]

Constraint: If a *cycle-stmt* refers to a *do-construct-name*, it must be within the range of that *do-construct*; otherwise, it must be within the range of at least one *do-construct*

R835	*exit-stmt*	**is**	EXIT [*do-construct-name*]

Constraint: If an *exit-stmt* refers to a *do-construct-name*, it must be within the range of that *do-construct*; otherwise, it must be within the range of at least one *do-construct*.

R836	*goto-stmt*	**is**	GO TO *label*

Constraint: The *label* must be the statement label of a branch target statement that appears in the same scoping unit as the *goto-stmt*.

R837	*computed-goto-stmt*	**is**	GO TO (*label-list*) [,] *scalar-int-expr*

Constraint: Each *label* in *label-list* must be the statement label of a branch target statement that appears in the same scoping unit as the *computed-goto-stmt*.

R838	*assign-stmt*	**is**	ASSIGN *label* TO *scalar-int-variable*

Constraint: The *label* must be the statement label of a branch target statement or *format-stmt* that appears in the same scoping unit as the *assign-stmt*.

Constraint: *scalar-int-variable* must be of type default integer.

R839   *assigned-goto-stmt*   **is**   GO TO *scalar-int-variable* [[,] (*label-list*)]

Constraint: Each *label* in *label-list* must be the statement label of a branch target statement that appears in the same scoping unit as the *assigned-goto-stmt*.

Constraint: *scalar-int-variable* must be of type default integer.

R840   *arithmetic-if-stmt*   **is**   IF (*scalar-numeric-expr*) *label* , *label* , *label*

Constraint: Each *label* must be the label of a branch target statement that appears in the same scoping unit as the *arithmetic-if-stmt*.

Constraint: The *scalar-numeric-expr* must not be of type complex.

R841   *continue-stmt*   **is**   CONTINUE

R842   *stop-stmt*   **is**   STOP [*stop-code*]

R843   *stop-code*   **is**   *scalar-char-constant*
                                             or   *digit* [*digit* [*digit* [*digit* [*digit*]]]]

Constraint: *scalar-char-constant* must be of type default character.

R844   *pause-stmt*   **is**   PAUSE [*stop-code*]

A.2.9 Input/Output Statements

R901   *io-unit*   **is**   *external-file-unit*
                                             or   *
                                             or   *internal-file-unit*

R902   *external-file-unit*   **is**   *scalar-int-expr*

R903   *internal-file-unit*   **is**   *default-char-variable*

Constraint: The *char-variable* must not be an array section with a vector subscript.

R904   *open-stmt*   **is**   OPEN (*connect-spec-list*)

R905   *connect-spec*   **is**   [UNIT=] *external-file-unit*
                                             or   IOSTAT= *scalar-default-int-variable*
                                             or   ERR= *label*
                                             or   FILE= *file-name-expr*
                                             or   STATUS= *scalar-default-char-expr*
                                             or   ACCESS= *scalar-default-char-expr*
                                             or   FORM= *scalar-default-char-expr*
                                             or   RECL= *scalar-int-expr*
                                             or   BLANK= *scalar-default-char-expr*
                                             or   POSITION= *scalar-default-char-expr*
                                             or   ACTION= *scalar-default-char-expr*
                                             or   DELIM= *scalar-default-char-expr*
                                             or   PAD= *scalar-default-char-expr*

R906   *file-name-expr*   **is**   *scalar-default-char-expr*

Constraint: If the optional characters UNIT= are omitted from the unit specifier, the unit specifier must be the first item in the *connect-spec-list*.

Constraint: Each specifier must not appear more than once in a given *open-stmt*; an *external-file-unit* must be specified.

Constraint: The *label* used in the ERR= specifier must be the statement label of a branch target statement that appears in the same scoping unit as the OPEN statement.

R907   *close-stmt*   **is**   CLOSE (*close-spec-list*)

R908   *close-spec*   **is**   [UNIT=] *external-file-unit*
                                             or   IOSTAT= *scalar-default-int-variable*
                                             or   ERR= *label*
                                             or   STATUS= *scalar-default-char-expr*

Constraint: If the optional characters UNIT= are omitted from the unit specifier, the unit specifier must be the first item in the *close-spec-list*.

Constraint: Each specifier must not appear more than once in a given *close-stmt*; an *external-file-unit* must be specified.

Constraint: The *label* used in the ERR= specifier must be the statement label of a branch target statement that appears in the same scoping unit as the CLOSE statement.

R909	*read-stmt*	**is**	READ (*io-control-spec-list*) [*input-item-list*]
		or	READ *format* [, *input-item-list*]
R910	*write-stmt*	**is**	WRITE (*io-control-spec-list*) [*output-item-list*]
R911	*print-stmt*	**is**	PRINT *format* [, *output-item-list*]
R912	*io-control-spec*	**is**	[UNIT=] *io-unit*
		or	[FMT=] *format*
		or	[NML=] *namelist-group-name*
		or	REC= *scalar-int-expr*
		or	IOSTAT= *scalar-default-int-variable*
		or	ERR= *label*
		or	END= *label*
		or	ADVANCE= *scalar-default-char-expr*
		or	SIZE= *scalar-default-int-variable*
		or	EOR= *label*

Constraint: An *io-control-spec-list* must contain exactly one *io-unit* and may contain at most one of each of the other specifiers.

Constraint: An END=, EOR=, or SIZE= specifier must not appear in a *write-stmt*.

Constraint: The *label* in the ERR=, EOR=, or END= specifier must be the statement label of a branch target statement that appears in the same scoping unit as the data transfer statement.

Constraint: A *namelist-group-name* must not be present if an *input-item-list* or an *output-item-list* is present in the data transfer statement.

Constraint: An *io-control-spec-list* must not contain both a *format* and a *namelist-group-name*.

Constraint: If the optional characters UNIT= are omitted from the unit specifier, the unit specifier must be the first item in the control information list.

Constraint: If the optional characters FMT= are omitted from the format specifier, the format specifier must be the second item in the control information list and the first item must be the unit specifier without the optional characters UNIT=.

Constraint: If the optional characters NML= are omitted from the namelist specifier, the namelist specifier must be the second item in the control information list and the first item must be the unit specifier without the optional characters UNIT=.

Constraint: If the unit specifier specifies an internal file, the *io-control-spec-list* must not contain a REC= specifier or a *namelist-group-name*.

Constraint: If the REC= specifier is present, an END= specifier must not appear, a *namelist-group-name* must not appear, and the *format*, if any, must not be an asterisk specifying list-directed input/output.

Constraint: An ADVANCE= specifier may be present only in a formatted sequential input/output statement with explicit format specification (10.1) whose control information list does not contain an internal file unit specifier.

Constraint: If an EOR= specifier is present, and ADVANCE= specifier also must appear.

R913	*format*	**is**	*default-char-expr*
		or	*label*
		or	*
		or	*scalar-default-int-variable*

Constraint: The *label* must be the label of a FORMAT statement that appears in the same
scoping unit as the statement containing the format specifier.

R914   *input-item*   is   *variable*
                                    or   *io-implied-do*

R915   *output-item*   is   *expr*
                                    or   *io-implied-do*

R916   *io-implied-do*   is   (*io-implied-do-object-list* , *io-implied-do-control*)

R917   *io-implied-do-object*   is   *input-item*
                                    or   *output-item*

R918   *io-implied-do-control*   is   *do-variable* = *scalar-numeric-expr* , ■
                                          ■ *scalar-numeric-expr* [, *scalar-numeric-expr*]

Constraint: A *variable* that is an *input-item* must not be an assumed-size array.

Constraint: The *do-variable* must be a scalar of type integer, default real, or double precision real.

Constraint: Each *scalar-numeric-expr* in an *io-implied-do-control* must be of type integer,
default real, or double precision real.

Constraint: In an *input-item-list*, an *io-implied-do-object* must be an *input-item*. In an
output-item-list, an *io-implied-do-object* must be an *output-item*.

R919   *backspace-stmt*   is   BACKSPACE *external-file-unit*
                                    or   BACKSPACE (*position-spec-list*)

R920   *endfile-stmt*   is   ENDFILE *external-file-unit*
                                    or   ENDFILE (*position-spec-list*)

R921   *rewind-stmt*   is   REWIND *external-file-unit*
                                    or   REWIND (*position-spec-list*)

R922   *position-spec*   is   [UNIT =] *external-file-unit*
                                    or   IOSTAT = *scalar-default-int-variable*
                                    or   ERR = *label*

Constraint: The *label* in the ERR= specifier must be the statement label of a branch target statement that appears in the same scoping unit as the file positioning
statement.

Constraint: If the optional characters UNIT= are omitted from the unit specifier, the unit
specifier must be the first item in the *position-spec-list*.

Constraint: A *position-spec-list* must contain exactly one *external-file-unit* and may contain at most one of each of the other specifiers.

R923   *inquire-stmt*   is   INQUIRE (*inquire-spec-list*)
                                    or   INQUIRE (IOLENGTH = *scalar-default-int-variable*) ■
                                          ■ *output-item-list*

R924   *inquire-spec*   is   [UNIT =] *external-file-unit*
                                    or   FILE = *file-name-expr*
                                    or   IOSTAT = *scalar-default-int-variable*
                                    or   ERR = *label*
                                    or   EXIST = *scalar-default-logical-variable*
                                    or   OPENED = *scalar-default-logical-variable*
                                    or   NUMBER = *scalar-default-int-variable*
                                    or   NAMED = *scalar-default-logical-variable*
                                    or   NAME = *scalar-default-char-variable*
                                    or   ACCESS = *scalar-default-char-variable*
                                    or   SEQUENTIAL = *scalar-default-char-variable*
                                    or   DIRECT = *scalar-default-char-variable*
                                    or   FORM = *scalar-default-char-variable*
                                    or   FORMATTED = *scalar-default-char-variable*
                                    or   UNFORMATTED = *scalar-default-char-variable*
                                    or   RECL = *scalar-default-int-variable*
                                    or   NEXTREC = *scalar-default-int-variable*
                                    or   BLANK = *scalar-default-char-variable*
                                    or   POSITION = *scalar-default-char-variable*

> or ACTION = *scalar-default-char-variable*
> or READ = *scalar-default-char-variable*
> or WRITE = *scalar-default-char-variable*
> or READWRITE = *scalar-default-char-variable*
> or DELIM = *scalar-default-char-variable*
> or PAD = *scalar-default-char-variable*

Constraint: An *inquire-spec-list* must contain one FILE= specifier or one UNIT= specifier, but not both, and at most one of each of the other specifiers.

Constraint: In the inquire by unit form of the INQUIRE statement, if the optional characters UNIT= are omitted from the unit specifier, the unit specifier must be the first item in the *inquire-spec-list*.

A.2.10 Input/Output Editing

R1001 *format-stmt*   is   FORMAT *format-specification*
R1002 *format-specification* is   ([*format-item-list*])

Constraint: The *format-stmt* must be labeled.
Constraint: The comma used to separate *format-item*s in a *format-item-list* may be omitted as follows:

1. Between a P edit descriptor and an immediately following F, E, EN, D, or G edit descriptor (10.6.5)

2. Before a slash edit descriptor when the optional repeat specification is not present (10.6.2)

3. After a slash edit descriptor

4. Before or after a colon edit descriptor (10.6.3)

R1003 *format-item*   is   [*r*] *data-edit-desc*
                           or   *control-edit-desc*
                           or   *char-string-edit-desc*
                           or   [*r*] (*format-item-list*)
R1004 *r*   is   *int-literal-constant*

Constraint: *r* must be positive.
Constraint: *r* must not have a kind parameter specified for it.

R1005 *data-edit-desc*   is   I *w* [. *m*]
                           or   B *w* [. *m*]
                           or   O *w* [. *m*]
                           or   Z *w* [. *m*]
                           or   F *w* . *d*
                           or   E *w* . *d* [E *e*]
                           or   EN *w* . *d* [E *e*]
                           or   ES *w* . *d* [E *e*]
                           or   G *w* . *d* [E *e*]
                           or   L *w*
                           or   A [*w*]
                           or   D *w* . *d*
R1006 *w*   is   *int-literal-constant*
R1007 *m*   is   *int-literal-constant*
R1008 *d*   is   *int-literal-constant*
R1009 *e*   is   *int-literal-constant*

Constraint: *w* and *e* must be positive and *d* and *m* must be zero or positive.
Constraint: *w*, *m*, *d*, and *e* must not have kind parameters specified for them.

R1010 *control-edit-desc* is   *position-edit-desc*
                            or   [*r*] /

or :
or *sign-edit-desc*
or *k* P
or *blank-interp-edit-desc*

R1011 *k*   is *signed-int-literal-constant*
Constraint: *k* must not have a kind parameter specified for it.

R1012 *position-edit-desc*   is T *n*
                                        or TL *n*
                                        or TR *n*
                                        or *n* X

R1013 *n*   is *int-literal-constant*
Constraint: *n* must be positive.
Constraint: *n* must not have a kind parameter specified for it.

R1014 *sign-edit-desc*   is S
                                        or SP
                                        or SS

R1015 *blank-interp-edit-desc*   is BN
                                        or BZ

R1016 *char-string-edit-desc*   is *char-literal-constant*
                                        or *c* H *rep-char* [*rep-char*] ...

R1017 *c*   is *int-literal-constant*
Constraint: *c* must be positive.
Constraint: *c* must not have a kind parameter specified for it.
Constraint: The *rep-char* in the *c*H form must be of default character type.
Constraint: The *char-literal-constant* must not have a kind parameter specified for it.

A.2.11 Program Units

R1101 *main-program*   is [*program-stmt*]
                                   [*specification-part*]
                                   [*execution-part*]
                                   [*internal-subprogram-part*]
                                   end-program-stmt

R1102 *program-stmt*   is PROGRAM *program-name*
R1103 *end-program-stmt*   is END [PROGRAM [*program-name*]]
Constraint: In a *main-program*, the *execution-part* must not contain a RETURN statement or an ENTRY statement.
Constraint: The *program-name* may be included in the *end-program-stmt* only if the optional *program-stmt* is used and, if included, must be identical to the *program-name* specified in the *program-stmt*.
Constraint: An automatic object must not appear in the *specification-part* (R204) of a main program.

R1104 *module*   is *module-stmt*
                                   [*specification-part*]
                                   [*module-subprogram-part*]
                                   end-module-stmt

R1105 *module-stmt*   is MODULE *module-name*
R1106 *end-module-stmt*   is END [MODULE [*module-name*]]
Constraint: If the *module-name* is specified in the *end-module-stmt*, it must be identical to the *module-name* specified in the *module-stmt*.
Constraint: A module *specification-part* must not contain a *stmt-function-stmt* or a *format-stmt*.
Constraint: An automatic object must not appear in the *specification-part* (R204) of a module.

R1107	*use-stmt*	**is**	USE *module-name* [, *rename-list*]
		or	USE *module-name* , ONLY : [*only-list*]
R1108	*rename*	**is**	*local-name* = > *use-name*
R1109	*only*	**is**	*access-id*
		or	[*local-name* = >] *use-name*

Constraint: Each *access-id* must be a public entity in the module.

Constraint: Each *use-name* must be the name of a public entity in the module.

R1110	*block-data*	**is**	*block-data-stmt*
			[*specification-part*]
			end-block-data-stmt
R1111	*block-data-stmt*	**is**	BLOCK DATA [*block-data-name*]
R1112	*end-block-data-stmt*	**is**	END [BLOCK DATA [*block-data-name*]]

Constraint: The *block-data-name* may be included in the *end-block-data-stmt* only if it was provided in the *block-data-stmt* and, if included, must be identical to the *block-data-name* in the *block-data-stmt*.

Constraint: A *block-data specification-part* may contain only USE statements, type declaration statements, IMPLICIT statements, PARAMETER statements, derived-type definitions, and the following specification statements: COMMON, DATA, DIMENSION, EQUIVALENCE, INTRINSIC, POINTER, SAVE, and TARGET.

Constraint: A type declaration statement in a *block-data specification-part* must not contain the ALLOCATABLE, EXTERNAL, INTENT, OPTIONAL, PRIVATE, or PUBLIC attribute specifiers.

A.2.12 Procedures

R1201	*interface-block*	**is**	*interface-stmt*
			[*interface-body*] ...
			[*module-procedure-stmt*] ...
			end-interface-stmt
R1202	*interface-stmt*	**is**	INTERFACE [*generic-spec*]
R1203	*end-interface-stmt*	**is**	END INTERFACE
R1204	*interface-body*	**is**	*function-stmt*
			[*specification-part*]
			end-function-stmt
		or	*subroutine-stmt*
			[*specification-part*]
			end-subroutine-stmt
R1205	*module-procedure-stmt*	**is**	MODULE PROCEDURE *procedure-name-list*
R1206	*generic-spec*	**is**	*generic-name*
		or	OPERATOR (*defined-operator*)
		or	ASSIGNMENT (=)

Constraint: An *interface-body* must not contain an *entry-stmt, data-stmt, format-stmt,* or *stmt-function-stmt.*

Constraint: The MODULE PROCEDURE specification is allowed only if the *interface-block* has a *generic-spec.*

Constraint: An *interface-block* must not appear in a BLOCK DATA program unit.

Constraint: An *interface-block* in a subprogram must not contain an *interface-body* for a procedure defined by that subprogram.

R1207	*external-stmt*	**is**	EXTERNAL *external-name-list*
R1208	*intrinsic-stmt*	**is**	INTRINSIC *intrinsic-procedure-name-list*
R1209	*function-reference*	**is**	*function-name* ([*actual-arg-spec-list*])

Constraint: The *actual-arg-spec-list* for a function reference must not contain an *alt-return-spec.*

R1210	*call-stmt*	**is**	CALL *subroutine-name* [([*actual-arg-spec-list*])]
R1211	*actual-arg-spec*	**is**	[*keyword* =] *actual-arg*
R1212	*keyword*	**is**	*dummy-arg-name*
R1213	*actual-arg*	**is**	*expr*
		or	*variable*
		or	*procedure-name*
		or	*alt-return-spec*
R1214	*alt-return-spec*	**is**	* *label*

Constraint: The *keyword* = must not appear if the interface of the procedure is implicit in the scoping unit.

Constraint: The *keyword* = may be omitted from an *actual-arg-spec* only if the *keyword* = has been omitted from each preceding *actual-arg-spec* in the argument list.

Constraint: Each *keyword* must be the name of a dummy argument in the explicit interface of the procedure.

Constraint: A *procedure-name actual-arg* must not be the name of an internal procedure and must not be the generic name of a procedure (12.3.2.1, 13.1). If it is the name of an intrinsic function, it must be a specific name for the function (13.12).

Constraint: The *label* used in the *alt-return-spec* must be the statement label of a branch target statement that appears in the same scoping unit as the *call-stmt*.

R1215	*function-subprogram*	**is**	*function-stmt*
			[*specification-part*]
			[*execution-part*]
			[*internal-subprogram-part*]
			end-function-stmt
R1216	*function-stmt*	**is**	[*prefix*] FUNCTION *function-name* ■
		■	([*dummy-arg-name-list*]) [RESULT (*result-name*)]

Constraint: The *result-name* must not appear in any specification statement in the scoping unit of the function subprogram.

R1217	*prefix*	**is**	*type-spec* [RECURSIVE]
		or	RECURSIVE [*type-spec*]
R1218	*end-function-stmt*	**is**	END [FUNCTION [*function-name*]]

Constraint: If RESULT is specified, *result-name* must not be the same as *function-name*.

Constraint: FUNCTION must be present on the *end-function-stmt* of an internal or module function.

Constraint: An internal function must not contain an ENTRY statement.

Constraint: An internal function must not contain an *internal-subprogram-part*.

Constraint: If a *function-name* is present on the *end-function-stmt*, it must be identical to the *function-name* specified in the *function-stmt*.

R1219	*subroutine-subprogram*	**is**	*subroutine-stmt*
			[*specification-part*]
			[*execution-part*]
			[*internal-subprogram-part*]
			end-subroutine-stmt
R1220	*subroutine-stmt*	**is**	[RECURSIVE] SUBROUTINE *subroutine-name* ■
		■	[([*dummy-arg-list*])]
R1221	*dummy-arg*	**is**	*dummy-arg-name*
		or	*
R1222	*end-subroutine-stmt*	**is**	END [SUBROUTINE [*subroutine-name*]]

Constraint: SUBROUTINE must be present on the *end-subroutine-stmt* of an internal or module subroutine.

Constraint: An internal subroutine must not contain an ENTRY statement.

Constraint: An internal subroutine must not contain an *internal-subprogram-part*.

Constraint: If a *subroutine-name* is present on the *end-subroutine-stmt*, it must be identical to the *subroutine-name* specified in the *subroutine-stmt*.

R1223 *entry-stmt* **is** ENTRY *entry-name* [([*dummy-arg-list*]) ■
■ [RESULT (*result-name*)]]

Constraint: An *entry-stmt* may appear only in an *external-subprogram* or *module-subprogram*. An *entry-stmt* must not appear within an *executable-construct*.

Constraint: RESULT may be present only if the *entry-stmt* is contained in a function subprogram.

Constraint: Within the subprogram containing the *entry-stmt*, the *entry-name* must not appear as a dummy argument in the FUNCTION or SUBROUTINE statement or in another ENTRY statement and it must not appear in an EXTERNAL statement.

Constraint: A *dummy-arg* may be an alternate return indicator only if the ENTRY statement is contained in a subroutine subprogram.

Constraint: If RESULT is specified, *result-name* must not be the same as *entry-name*.

R1224 *return-stmt* **is** RETURN [*scalar-int-expr*]

Constraint: The *return-stmt* must be contained in the scoping unit of a function or subroutine subprogram.

Constraint: The *scalar-int-expr* is allowed only in the scoping unit of a subroutine subprogram.

R1225 *contains-stmt* **is** CONTAINS
R1226 *stmt-function-stmt* **is** *function-name* ([*dummy-arg-name-list*]) = *scalar-expr*

Constraint: The *scalar-expr* may be composed only of constants (literal and named), references to scalar variables and array elements, references to functions and function dummy procedures, and intrinsic operators. If a reference to another statement function appears in *scalar-expr*, its definition must have been provided earlier in the scoping unit.

Constraint: Named constants in *scalar-expr* must have been declared earlier in the scoping unit. If array elements appear in *scalar-expr*, the parent array must have been declared as an array earlier in the scoping unit. If a scalar variable, array element, function reference, or dummy function reference is typed by the implicit typing rules, its appearance in any subsequent type declaration statement must confirm this implied type and the values of any implied type parameters.

Constraint: The *function-name* and each *dummy-arg-name* must be specified, explicitly or implicitly, to be scalar data objects.

Constraint: A given *dummy-arg-name* may appear only once in any *dummy-arg-name-list*.

Constraint: Each scalar variable reference in *scalar-expr* may be either a reference to a dummy argument of the statement function or a reference to a variable within the same scoping unit as the statement function statement.

A.2.13 Intrinsic Procedures

A.2.14 Scope, Association, and Definition

A.3 Cross References

The following is a cross reference of all syntactic symbols used in the BNF, giving the rule in which they are defined and all rules in which they are referenced.

The symbols are sorted alphabetically within three categories: nonterminal symbols that are defined, nonterminal symbols that are not defined, and terminal symbols. Note that except for those ending with -*name*, the only undefined nonterminal symbols are *letter*, *digit*, *special-character*, and *rep-char*. Symbols ending with -*name* are defined by the rule:

    xyz-name   is *name*

Before processing the cross references, all occurrences of -*list* and *scalar-* in the symbol names were removed.

Symbol	Defined in	Referenced in			
ac-do-variable	R435	R434			
ac-implied-do	R433	R432			
ac-implied-do-control	R434	R433			
ac-value	R432	R431	R433		
access-id	R522	R521	R1109		
access-spec	R510	R424	R503	R521	
access-stmt	R521	R214			
action-stmt	R216	R215	R807	R829	R833
action-term-do-construct	R827	R826			
actual-arg	R1213	R1211			
actual-arg-spec	R1211	R1209	R1210		
add-op	R710	R310	R707		
add-operand	R706	R706	R707		
allocatable-stmt	R526	R214			
allocate-object	R625	R624	R628		
allocate-stmt	R622	R216			
allocation	R624	R622			
alphanumeric-character	R302	R301	R304		
alt-return-spec	R1214	R1213			
and-op	R720	R310	R716		
and-operand	R715	R716			
arithmetic-if-stmt	R840	R216			
array-constructor	R431	R701			
array-element	R614	R536	R547	R602	R610	R613
array-section	R615	R602	R613		
array-spec	R512	R503	R504	R525	R528
assign-stmt	R838	R216			
assigned-goto-stmt	R839	R216			
assignment-stmt	R735	R216	R738	R739	
assumed-shape-spec	R516	R512			
assumed-size-spec	R518	R512			
attr-spec	R503	R501			
backspace-stmt	R919	R216			
binary-constant	R408	R407			
blank-interp-edit-desc	R1015	R1010			
block	R801	R802	R808	R823	
block-data	R1110	R202			
block-data-stmt	R1111	R1110			
block-do-construct	R817	R816			
boz-literal-constant	R407	R306	R533		
c	R1017	R1016			
call-stmt	R1210	R216			
case-construct	R808	R215			

Symbol	Defined in	Referenced in			
case-expr	R812	R809			
case-selector	R813	R810			
case-stmt	R810	R808			
case-value	R815	R814			
case-value-range	R814	R813			
char-constant	R309	R843			
char-expr	R726	R731	R812		
char-initialization-expr	R731	R815			
char-length	R508	R429	R504	R507	
char-literal-constant	R420	R306	R1016		
char-selector	R506	R502			
char-string-edit-desc	R1016	R1003			
char-variable	R605				
character	R301				
close-spec	R908	R907			
close-stmt	R907	R216			
common-block-object	R549	R548			
common-stmt	R548	R214			
complex-literal-constant	R417	R306			
component-array-spec	R428	R427	R429		
component-attr-spec	R427	R426			
component-decl	R429	R426			
component-def-stmt	R426	R422			
computed-goto-stmt	R837	R216			
concat-op	R712	R310	R711		
connect-spec	R905	R904			
constant	R305	R308	R309	R533	R610 R701
constant-subobject	R702	R701			
contains-stmt	R1225	R210	R212		
continue-stmt	R841	R216	R824		
control-edit-desc	R1010	R1003			
cycle-stmt	R834	R216			
d	R1008	R1005			
data-edit-desc	R1005	R1003			
data-i-do-object	R536	R535			
data-i-do-variable	R537	R535			
data-implied-do	R535	R531	R536		
data-stmt	R529	R209	R214		
data-stmt-constant	R533	R532			
data-stmt-object	R531	R530			
data-stmt-repeat	R534	R532			
data-stmt-set	R530	R529			
data-stmt-value	R532	R530			
deallocate-stmt	R628	R216			
declaration-construct	R207	R204			
default-char-expr	R727	R905	R906	R908	R912 R913
default-char-variable	R606	R903	R924		
default-int-variable	R608	R905	R908	R912	R913 R922
		R923	R924		
default-logical-variable	R604	R924			
deferred-shape-spec	R517	R428	R512	R526	R527
defined-binary-op	R724	R311	R723		
defined-operator	R311	R1206			
defined-unary-op	R704	R311	R703		
derived-type-def	R422	R207			
derived-type-stmt	R424	R422			

Symbol	Defined in	Referenced in				
digit-string	R402	R401	R404	R405	R413	R414
dimension-stmt	R525	R214				
do-block	R823	R817				
do-body	R828	R827	R830	R832		
do-construct	R816	R215				
do-stmt	R818	R817				
do-term-action-stmt	R829	R827				
do-term-shared-stmt	R833	R832				
do-variable	R822	R821	R918			
dummy-arg	R1221	R1220	R1223			
e	R1009	R1005				
else-if-stmt	R804	R802				
else-stmt	R805	R802				
elsewhere-stmt	R742	R739				
end-block-data-stmt	R1112	R1110				
end-do	R824	R817				
end-do-stmt	R825	R824				
end-function-stmt	R1218	R216	R1204	R1215		
end-if-stmt	R806	R802				
end-interface-stmt	R1203	R1201				
end-module-stmt	R1106	R1104				
end-program-stmt	R1103	R216	R1101			
end-select-stmt	R811	R808				
end-subroutine-stmt	R1222	R216	R1204	R1219		
end-type-stmt	R425	R422				
end-where-stmt	R743	R739				
endfile-stmt	R920	R216				
entity-decl	R504	R501				
entry-stmt	R1223	R206	R207	R209		
equiv-op	R722	R310	R718			
equiv-operand	R717	R717	R718			
equivalence-object	R547	R546				
equivalence-set	R546	R545				
equivalence-stmt	R545	R214				
executable-construct	R215	R208	R209			
executable-program	R201					
execution-part	R208	R1101	R1215	R1219		
execution-part-construct	R209	R208	R801	R828		
exit-stmt	R835	R216				
explicit-shape-spec	R513	R428	R512	R518	R549	R624
exponent	R416	R413				
exponent-letter	R415	R413				
expr	R723	R430	R432	R701	R723	R725
		R726	R727	R728	R729	R730
		R735	R915	R1213	R1226	
external-file-unit	R902	R901	R905	R908	R919	R920
		R921	R922	R924		
external-stmt	R1207	R214				
external-subprogram	R203	R202				
file-name-expr	R906	R905	R924			
format	R913	R909	R911	R912		
format-item	R1003	R1002	R1003			
format-specification	R1002	R1001				
format-stmt	R1001	R206	R207	R209		
function-reference	R1209	R701	R737			
function-stmt	R1216	R1204	R1215			

Symbol	Defined in	Referenced in			
function-subprogram	R1215	R203	R211	R213	
generic-intrinsic-op	R312	R311			
generic-spec	R1206	R522	R1202		
goto-stmt	R836	R216			
hex-constant	R410	R407			
hex-digit	R411	R410			
if-construct	R802	R215			
if-stmt	R807	R216			
if-then-stmt	R803	R802			
imag-part	R419	R417			
implicit-part	R205	R204			
implicit-part-stmt	R206	R205			
implicit-spec	R541	R540			
implicit-stmt	R540	R205	R206		
initialization-expr	R730	R504	R539		
inner-shared-do-construct	R832	R831			
input-item	R914	R909	R917		
inquire-spec	R924	R923			
inquire-stmt	R923	R216			
int-constant	R308	R534			
int-expr	R728	R434	R514	R515	R535	R611
		R617	R620	R621	R732	R734
		R812	R837	R902	R905	R912
		R1224			
int-initialization-expr	R732	R505	R506	R815	
int-literal-constant	R404	R306	R403	R508	R1004	R1006
		R1007	R1008	R1009	R1013	R1017
int-variable	R607	R435	R537	R623	R838	R839
intent-spec	R511	R503	R519		
intent-stmt	R519	R214			
interface-block	R1201	R207			
interface-body	R1204	R1201			
interface-stmt	R1202	R1201			
internal-file-unit	R903	R901			
internal-subprogram	R211	R210			
internal-subprogram-part	R210	R1101	R1215	R1219	
intrinsic-operator	R310	R312			
intrinsic-stmt	R1208	R214			
io-control-spec	R912	R909	R910		
io-implied-do	R916	R914	R915		
io-implied-do-control	R918	R916			
io-implied-do-object	R917	R916			
io-unit	R901	R912			
k	R1011	R1010			
keyword	R1212	R1211			
kind-param	R405	R404	R413	R420	R421
kind-selector	R505	R502			
label	R313	R819	R836	R837	R838	R839
		R840	R905	R908	R912	R913
		R922	R924	R1214		
label-do-stmt	R819	R818	R827	R830	R832
length-selector	R507	R506			
letter-spec	R542	R541			
level-1-expr	R703	R705			
level-2-expr	R707	R707	R711		
level-3-expr	R711	R711	R713		

Symbol	Defined in	Referenced in			
r	R1004	R1003	R1010		
read-stmt	R909	R216			
real-literal-constant	R413	R306	R412		
real-part	R418	R417			
rel-op	R714	R310	R713		
rename	R1108	R1107			
return-stmt	R1224	R216			
rewind-stmt	R921	R216			
save-stmt	R523	R214			
saved-entity	R524	R523			
section-subscript	R618	R615			
select-case-stmt	R809	R808			
shared-term-do-construct	R831	R830			
sign	R406	R401	R403	R412	
sign-edit-desc	R1014	R1010			
signed-digit-string	R401	R416			
signed-int-literal-constant	R403	R418	R419	R533	R1011
signed-real-literal-constant	R412	R418	R419	R533	
significand	R414	R413			
specification-expr	R734	R509			
specification-part	R204	R1101	R1104	R1110	R1204	R1215
		R1219			
specification-stmt	R214	R207			
stat-variable	R623	R622	R628		
stmt-function-stmt	R1226	R207			
stop-code	R843	R842	R844		
stop-stmt	R842	R216			
stride	R620	R619			
structure-component	R612	R602	R610	R613	R616	R625
		R627			
structure-constructor	R430	R533	R701		
subobject	R602	R601	R702		
subroutine-stmt	R1220	R1204	R1219		
subroutine-subprogram	R1219	R203	R211	R213	
subscript	R617	R614	R618	R619	
subscript-triplet	R619	R618			
substring	R609	R547	R602		
substring-range	R611	R609	R615		
target	R737	R736			
target-stmt	R528	R214			
type-declaration-stmt	R501	R207			
type-param-value	R509	R506	R507	R508	
type-spec	R502	R426	R501	R541	R1217
underscore	R303	R302			
upper-bound	R515	R513			
use-stmt	R1107	R204			
variable	R601	R531	R603	R604	R605	R606
		R607	R608	R701	R735	R737
		R822	R914	R1213		
vector-subscript	R621	R618			
w	R1006	R1005			
where-construct	R739	R215			
where-construct-stmt	R740	R739			
where-stmt	R738	R216			
write-stmt	R910	R216			

Symbol	Defined in	Referenced in
`*`		R809 R813 R821 R837 R839 R840 R904 R907 R909 R910 R916 R919 R920 R921 R923 R1002 R1003 R1206 R1209 R1210 R1216 R1220 R1223 R1226 R429 R504 R507 R509 R518 R532 R709 R901 R913 R1214
`**`		R1221
`+`		R708
`,`		R406 R710 R417 R424 R426 R433 R434 R501 R506 R507 R518 R525 R526 R527 R528 R529 R535 R543 R546 R548 R622 R628 R821 R837 R839 R840 R909
`-`		R911 R916 R918 R1107
`.`		R406 R542 R710
`.AND.`		R414 R704 R724 R1005
`.EQ.`		R720
`.EQV.`		R714
`.FALSE.`		R722
`.GE.`		R421
`.GT.`		R714
`.LE.`		R714
`.LT.`		R714
`.NE.`		R714
`.NEQV.`		R714
`.NOT.`		R722
`.OR.`		R719
`.TRUE.`		R721
`/`		R421 R524 R530 R543 R548 R709 R1010
`/)`		R431
`//`		R712
`/=`		R714
`:`		R513 R516 R517 R518 R611 R619 R803 R809 R814 R819 R820 R1010 R1107
`::`		R424 R426 R501 R519 R520 R521 R523 R525 R526 R527 R528
`<`		R714
`<=`		R714
`=`		R434 R504 R505 R507 R535 R539 R622 R628 R735 R821 R918 R922 R923 R924 R1206 R1211 R1226
`==`		R714
`=>`		R736 R1108 R1109
`>`		R714
`>=`		R714
A		R411 R1005
ACCESS		R924
ACCESS=		R905
ACTION		R924

Symbol	Defined in	Referenced in			
ACTION=		R905			
ADVANCE=		R912			
ALLOCATABLE		R503	R526		
ALLOCATE		R622			
ASSIGN		R838			
ASSIGNMENT		R1206			
B		R408	R411	R1005	
BACKSPACE		R919			
BLANK		R924			
BLANK=		R905			
BLOCK		R1111	R1112		
BN		R1015			
BZ		R1015			
C		R411			
CALL		R1210			
CASE		R809	R810		
CHARACTER		R502			
CLOSE		R907			
COMMON		R548			
COMPLEX		R502			
CONTAINS		R1225			
CONTINUE		R841			
CYCLE		R834			
D		R411	R415	R1005	
DATA		R529	R1111	R1112	
DEALLOCATE		R628			
DEFAULT		R813			
DELIM		R924			
DELIM=		R905			
DIMENSION		R427	R503	R525	
DIRECT		R924			
DO		R819	R820	R825	
DOUBLE		R502			
E		R411	R415	R1005	
ELSE		R804	R805		
ELSEWHERE		R742			
EN		R1005			
END		R425	R743	R806	R811	R825
		R1103	R1106	R1112	R1203	R1218
		R1222			
END=		R912			
ENDFILE		R920			
ENTRY		R1223			
EOR=		R912			
EQUIVALENCE		R545			
ERR		R922	R924		
ERR=		R905	R908	R912	
ES		R1005			
EXIST		R924			
EXIT		R835			
EXTERNAL		R503	R1207		
F		R411	R1005		
FILE		R924			
FILE=		R905			
FMT=		R912			
FORM		R924			

B

Intrinsic Procedures

There are four classes of intrinsic procedures: inquiry functions, elemental functions, transformational functions, and subroutines.

B.1 Intrinsic Functions

An **intrinsic function** is an inquiry function, an elemental function, or a transformational function. An **inquiry function** is one whose result depends on the properties of its principal argument other than the value of this argument; in fact, the argument value may be undefined. An **elemental function** is one that is specified for scalar arguments but may be applied to array arguments, as described in Section B.2. All other intrinsic functions are **transformational functions**; they almost all have one or more array-valued arguments or an array-valued result.

Generic names of intrinsic functions are listed in B.10. In most cases, generic functions accept arguments of more than one type and the type of the result is the same as the type of the arguments. **Specific names** of intrinsic functions with corresponding generic names are listed in Section B.12.

If an intrinsic function is used as an actual argument to a procedure, its specific name must be used and it may be referenced in the procedure only with scalar arguments. If an intrinsic function does not have a specific name, it must not be used as an actual argument.

B.2 Elemental Intrinsic Procedures

B.2.1 Elemental Intrinsic Function Arguments and Results

If a generic name or a specific name is used to reference an elemental intrinsic function, the shape of the result is the same as the shape of the argument with the greatest rank. If the arguments are all scalar, the result is scalar. For those elemental intrinsic functions that have more than one argument, all arguments must be conformable (i.e., have the same shape). In the array-valued case, the values of the elements, if any, of the result are the same as would have been obtained if the scalar-valued function had been applied separately, in any order, to corresponding elements of each argument. Arguments called KIND must always be specified as scalar integer initialization expressions.

B.2.2 Elemental Intrinsic Subroutine Arguments

If a generic name is used to reference an elemental intrinsic subroutine, either all actual arguments must be scalar or all INTENT (OUT) arguments must be arrays of the same shape, and the remaining arguments must be conformable with them. In the case that the INTENT (OUT) arguments are arrays, the values of the elements, if any, of the results are the same as would be obtained if the subroutine with scalar arguments were applied separately, in any order, to corresponding elements of each argument.

B.3 Positional Arguments or Argument Keywords

All intrinsic procedures may be invoked with either positional arguments or argument keywords. The descriptions in Sections B.10 and B.11 give the keyword names and positional sequence. A keyword is required for an argument only if a preceding optional argument is omitted.

B.4 Argument Presence Inquiry Function

The inquiry function PRESENT permits an inquiry to be made about the presence of an actual argument associated with a dummy argument that has the OPTIONAL attribute.

B.5 Numeric, Mathematical, Character, and Bit Procedures

B.5.1 Numeric Functions

The elemental functions INT, REAL, DBLE, and CMPLX perform type conversions. The elemental functions AIMAG, CONJG, AINT, ANINT, NINT, ABS, MOD, SIGN, DIM, DPROD, MODULO, FLOOR, CEIL-ING, MAX, and MIN perform simple numeric operations.

B.5.2 Mathematical Functions

The elemental functions SQRT, EXP, LOG, LOG10, SIN, COS, TAN, ASIN, ACOS, ATAN, ATAN2, SINH, COSH, and TANH evaluate elementary mathematical functions.

B.5.3 Character Functions

The elemental functions ICHAR, CHAR, LGE, LGT, LLE, LLT, IACHAR, ACHAR, INDEX, VERIFY, ADJUSTL, ADJUSTR, SCAN, and LEN_TRIM perform character operations. The transformational function REPEAT returns repeated concatenations of a character string argument. The transformational function TRIM returns the argument with trailing blanks removed.

B.5.4 Character Inquiry Function

The inquiry function LEN returns the length of a character entity. The value of the argument to this function need not be defined. It is not necessary for a processor to evaluate the argument of this function if the value of the function can be determined otherwise.

B.5.5 Kind Functions

The inquiry function KIND returns the kind type parameter value of an integer, real, complex, logical, or character entity. The transformational function SELECTED_REAL_KIND returns the real kind type parameter value that has at least the decimal precision and exponent range specified by its arguments. The transformational function SELECTED_INT_KIND returns the integer kind type parameter value that has at least the decimal exponent range specified by its argument.

B.5.6 Logical Function

The elemental function LOGICAL converts between objects of type logical with different kind type parameter values.

B.5.7 Bit Manipulation and Inquiry Procedures

The bit manipulation procedures consist of a set of ten functions and one subroutine. Logical operations on bits are provided by the functions IOR, IAND, NOT, and IEOR; shift operations are provided by the functions ISHFT and ISHFTC; bit subfields may be referenced by the function IBITS and by the subroutine MVBITS; single-bit processing is provided by the functions BTEST, IBSET, and IBCLR.

For the purposes of these procedures, a bit is defined to be a binary digit w located at position k of a nonnegative integer scalar object based on a model nonnegative integer defined by

$$ j = \sum_{k=0}^{s-1} w_k \times 2^k $$

and for which w_k may have the value 0 or 1. An example of a model number compatible with the examples used in Section B.7.1 would have $s = 32$, thereby defining a 32-bit integer.

An inquiry function BIT_SIZE is available to determine the parameter s of the model. The value of the argument of this function need not be defined. It is not necessary for a processor to evaluate the argument of this function if the value of the function can be determined otherwise.

Effectively, this model defines an integer object to consist of s bits in sequence numbered from right to left from 0 to $s - 1$. This model is valid only in the context of the use of such an object as the argument or result of one of the bit manipulation procedures. In all other contexts, the model defined for an integer in B.7.1 applies. In particular, whereas the models are identical for $w_{s-1} = 0$, they do not correspond for $w_{s-1} = 1$ and the interpretation of bits in such objects is processor dependent.

B.6 Transfer Function

The function TRANSFER specifies that the physical representation of the first argument is to be treated as if it were one of the type and type parameters of the second argument with no conversion.

B.7 Numeric Manipulation and Inquiry Functions

The numeric manipulation and inquiry functions are described in terms of a model for the representation and behavior of numbers on a processor. The model has parameters which are determined so as to make the model best fit the machine on which the executable program is executed.

B.7.1 Models for Integer and Real Data

The model set for integer i is defined by

$$ i = s \times \sum_{k=1}^{q} w_k \times r^{k-1} $$

where r is an integer exceeding one, q is a positive integer, each w_k is a nonnegative integer less than r, and s is $+1$ or -1. The model set for real x is defined by

$$ x = \begin{cases} 0 & or \\ s \times b^e \times \sum_{k=1}^{p} f_k \times b^{-k}, \end{cases} $$

where b and p are integers exceeding one; each f_k is a nonnegative integer less than b, except f_1 which is also nonzero; s is $+1$ or -1; and e is an integer that lies between some integer maximum e_{max} and some integer minimum e_{min} inclusively. For $x = 0$, its exponent e and digits f_k are defined to be zero. The integer parameters r and q determine the set of model integers, and the integer parameters b, p, e_{min}, and e_{max} determine the set of model floating point numbers. The parameters of the integer and real models are available for each integer and real data type implemented by the processor. The parameters characterize the set of available numbers in the definition of the model. The numeric manipulation and inquiry functions provide values related to the parameters and other constants related to them. Examples of these functions in this section use the models:

$$i = s \times \sum_{k=1}^{31} w_k \times 2^{k-1}$$

and

$$x = 0 \ \ or \ \ s \times 2^e \times \left[\tfrac{1}{2} + \sum_{k=2}^{24} f_k \times 2^{-k} \right], \quad -126 \le e \le 127$$

B.7.2 Numeric Inquiry Functions

The inquiry functions RADIX, DIGITS, MINEXPONENT, MAX-EXPONENT, PRECISION, RANGE, HUGE, TINY, and EPSILON return scalar values related to the parameters of the model associated with the type and type parameters of the arguments. The value of the arguments to these functions need not be defined, pointer arguments may be disassociated, and array arguments need not be allocated.

B.7.3 Floating Point Manipulation Functions

The elemental functions EXPONENT, SCALE, NEAREST, FRACTION, SET_EXPONENT, SPACING, and RRSPACING return values related to the components of the model values (B.7.1) associated with the actual values of the arguments.

B.8 Array Intrinsic Functions

The array intrinsic functions perform the following operations on arrays: vector and matrix multiplication, numeric or logical computation that reduces the rank, array structure inquiry, array construction, array manipulation, and geometric location.

B.8.1 The Shape of Array Arguments

The transformational array intrinsic functions operate on each array argument as a whole. The shape of the corresponding actual argument must therefore be defined; that is, the actual argument must be an array section, an assumed-shape array, an explicit-shape array, a pointer that is associated with a target, an allocatable array that has been allocated, or an array-valued expression. It must not be an assumed-size array.

Some of the inquiry intrinsic functions accept array arguments for which the shape need not be defined. Assumed-size arrays may be used as arguments to these functions; they include the function LBOUND and certain references to SIZE and UBOUND.

B.8.2 Mask Arguments

Some array intrinsic functions have an optional MASK argument that is used by the function to select the elements of one or more arguments to be operated on by the function. Any element not selected by the mask need not be defined at the time the function is invoked.

The MASK affects only the value of the function, and does not affect the evaluation, prior to invoking the function, of arguments that are array expressions.

A MASK argument must be of type logical.

B.8.3 Vector and Matrix Multiplication Functions

The matrix multiplication function MATMUL operates on two matrices, or on one matrix and one vector, and returns the corresponding matrix-matrix, matrix-vector, or vector-matrix product. The arguments to MATMUL may be numeric (integer, real, or complex) or logical arrays. On logical matrices and vectors, MATMUL performs Boolean matrix multiplication.

The dot product function DOT_PRODUCT operates on two vectors and returns their scalar product. The vectors are of the same type (numeric or logical) as for MATMUL. For logical vectors, DOT_PRODUCT returns the Boolean scalar product.

B.8.4 Array Reduction Functions

The array reduction functions SUM, PRODUCT, MAXVAL, MINVAL, COUNT, ANY, and ALL perform numerical, logical, and counting operations on arrays. They may be applied to the whole array to give a scalar result or they may be applied over a given dimension to yield a result of rank reduced by one. By use of a logical mask that is conformable with the given array, the computation may be confined to any subset of the array (for example, the positive elements).

B.8.5 Array Inquiry Functions

The function ALLOCATED returns a value true if the array argument is currently allocated, and returns false otherwise. The functions SIZE, SHAPE, LBOUND, and UBOUND return, respectively, the size of the array, the shape, and the lower and upper bounds of the subscripts along each dimension. The size, shape, or bounds must be defined.

The values of the array arguments to these functions need not be defined.

B.8.6 Array Construction Functions

The functions MERGE, SPREAD, PACK, and UNPACK construct new arrays from the elements of existing arrays. MERGE combines two conformable arrays into one array by an element-wise choice based on a logical mask. SPREAD constructs an array from several copies of an actual argument (SPREAD does this by adding an extra dimension, as in forming a book from copies of one page). PACK and UNPACK respectively gather and scatter the elements of a one-dimensional array from and to positions in another array where the positions are specified by a logical mask.

B.8.7 Array Reshape Function

RESHAPE produces an array with the same elements and a different shape.

B.8.8 Array Manipulation Functions

The functions TRANSPOSE, EOSHIFT, and CSHIFT manipulate arrays. TRANSPOSE performs the matrix transpose operation on a two-dimensional array. The shift functions leave the shape of an array unaltered but shift the positions of the elements parallel to a specified dimension of the array. These shifts are either circular (CSHIFT), in which case elements shifted off one end reappear at the other end, or end-off (EOSHIFT), in which case specified boundary elements are shifted into the vacated positions.

B.8.9 Array Location Functions

The functions MAXLOC and MINLOC return the location (subscripts) of an element of an array that has maximum and minimum values, respectively. By use of an optional logical mask that is conformable with the given array, the reduction may be confined to any subset of the array.

B.8.10 Pointer Association Status Inquiry Functions

The function ASSOCIATED tests whether a pointer is currently associated with any target, with a particular target, or with the same target as another pointer.

B.9 Intrinsic Subroutines

Intrinsic subroutines are supplied by the processor and have the special definitions given in Section B.11. An intrinsic subroutine is referenced by a CALL statement that uses its name explicitly. The name of an intrinsic subroutine must not be used as an actual argument.

B.9.1 Date and Time Subroutines

The subroutines DATE_AND_TIME and SYSTEM_CLOCK return integer data from the date and real-time clock. The time returned is local, but there are facilities for finding out the difference between local time and Coordinated Universal Time.

B.9.2 Pseudorandom Numbers

The subroutine RANDOM returns a pseudorandom number or an array of pseudorandom numbers. The subroutine RANDOM_SEED initializes or restarts the pseudorandom number sequence.

B.9.3 Bit Copy Subroutine

The subroutine MVBITS copies a bit field from a specified position in one integer object to a specified position in another.

B.10 Generic Intrinsic Functions

For all of the intrinsic procedures, the arguments shown are the names that must be used for keywords when using the keyword form for actual arguments. For example, a reference to CMPLX may be written in the form CMPLX (REAL_PART, COMPLEX_PART, M) or in the form CMPLX (Y = COMPLEX_PART, KIND = M, X = REAL_PART).

Many of the argument keywords have names that are indicative of their usage. For example,

KIND	Describes the KIND of the result
STRING, STRING_A	An arbitrary character string
BACK	Indicates a string scan is to be from right to left (backward)
MASK	A mask that may be applied to the arguments
DIM	A selected dimension of an array argument

B.10.1 Argument Presence Inquiry Function

PRESENT (A)   Argument presence

B.10.2 Numeric Functions

ABS (A)   Absolute value
AIMAG (Z)   Imaginary part of a complex number
AINT (A, KIND)   Truncation to whole number
   Optional KIND
ANINT (A, KIND)   Nearest whole number
   Optional KIND
CEILING (A)   Least integer greater than or equal to number
CMPLX (X, Y, KIND)   Conversion to complex type
   Optional Y, KIND
CONJG (Z)   Conjugate of a complex number
DBLE (A)   Conversion to double precision real type
DIM (X, Y)   Positive difference
DPROD (X, Y)   Double precision real product
INT (A, KIND)   Conversion to integer type
   Optional KIND
FLOOR (A)   Greatest integer less than or equal to number
MAX (A1, A2, A3,...)   Maximum value
   Optional A3,...
MIN (A1, A2, A3,...)   Minimum value
   Optional A3,...
MOD (A, P)   Remainder function
MODULO (A, P)   Modulo function
NINT (A, KIND)   Nearest integer
   Optional KIND
REAL (A, KIND)   Conversion to real type
   Optional KIND
SIGN (A, B)   Transfer of sign

B.10.3 Mathematical Functions

ACOS (X)   Arccosine
ASIN (X)   Arcsine
ATAN (X)   Arctangent
ATAN2 (Y, X)   Arctangent
COS (X)   Cosine
COSH (X)   Hyperbolic cosine
EXP (X)   Exponential
LOG (X)   Natural logarithm
LOG10 (X)   Common logarithm (base 10)
SIN (X)   Sine
SINH (X)   Hyperbolic sine
SQRT (X)   Square root
TAN (X)   Tangent
TANH (X)   Hyperbolic tangent

B.10.4 Character Functions

ACHAR (I)	Character in given position in ASCII collating sequence
ADJUSTL (STRING)	Adjust left
ADJUSTR (STRING)	Adjust right
CHAR (I, KIND) Optional KIND	Character in given position in processor collating sequence
IACHAR (C)	Position of a character in ASCII collating sequence
ICHAR (C)	Position of a character in processor collating sequence
INDEX (STRING, SUBSTRING, BACK) Optional BACK	Starting position of a substring
LEN_TRIM (STRING)	Length without trailing blank characters
LGE (STRING_A, STRING_B)	Lexically greater than or equal
LGT (STRING_A, STRING_B)	Lexically greater than
LLE (STRING_A, STRING_B)	Lexically less than or equal
LLT (STRING_A, STRING_B)	Lexically less than
REPEAT (STRING, NCOPIES)	Repeated concatenation
SCAN (STRING, SET, BACK) Optional BACK	Scan a string for a character in a set
TRIM (STRING)	Remove trailing blank characters
VERIFY (STRING, SET, BACK) Optional BACK	Verify the set of characters in a string

B.10.5 Character Inquiry Function

LEN (STRING)	Length of a character entity

B.10.6 Kind Functions

KIND (X)	Kind type parameter value
SELECTED_INT_KIND (R)	Integer kind type parameter value, given range
SELECTED_REAL_KIND (P, R)	Real kind type parameter value, given precision and range

B.10.7 Logical Function

LOGICAL (L, KIND) Optional KIND	Convert between objects of type logical with different kind type parameters

B.10.8 Numeric Inquiry Functions

DIGITS (X)	Number of significant digits in the model
EPSILON (X)	Number that is almost negligible compared to one
HUGE (X)	Largest number in the model
MAXEXPONENT (X)	Maximum exponent in the model

MINEXPONENT (X)	Minimum exponent in the model
PRECISION (X)	Decimal precision
RADIX (X)	Base of the model
RANGE (X)	Decimal exponent range
TINY (X)	Smallest positive number in the model

B.10.9 Bit Inquiry Function

BIT_SIZE (I)	Number of bits in the model

B.10.10 Bit Manipulation Functions

BTEST (I, POS)	Bit testing
IAND (I, J)	Logical AND
IBCLR (I, POS)	Clear bit
IBITS (I, POS, LEN)	Bit extraction
IBSET (I, POS)	Set bit
IEOR (I, J)	Exclusive OR
IOR (I, J)	Inclusive OR
ISHFT (I, SHIFT)	Logical shift
ISHFTC (I, SHIFT, SIZE)	Circular shift
Optional SIZE	
NOT (I)	Logical complement

B.10.11 Transfer Function

TRANSFER (SOURCE, MOLD, SIZE)	Treat first argument as if
Optional SIZE	of type of second argument

B.10.12 Floating Point Manipulation Functions

EXPONENT (X)	Exponent part of a model number
FRACTION (X)	Fractional part of a number
NEAREST (X, S)	Nearest different processor number in given direction
RRSPACING (X)	Reciprocal of the relative spacing of model numbers near given number
SCALE (X, I)	Multiply a real by its base to an integer power
SET_EXPONENT (X, I)	Set exponent part of a number
SPACING (X)	Absolute spacing of model numbers near given number

B.10.13 Vector and Matrix Multiply Functions

DOT_PRODUCT (VECTOR_A, VECTOR_B)	Dot product of two rank-one arrays
MATMUL (MATRIX_A, MATRIX_B)	Matrix multiplication

B.10.14 Array Reduction Functions

ALL (MASK, DIM) Optional DIM	True if all values are true
ANY (MASK, DIM) Optional DIM	True if any value is true
COUNT (MASK, DIM) Optional DIM	Number of true elements in an array
MAXVAL (ARRAY, DIM, MASK) Optional DIM, MASK	Maximum value in an array
MINVAL (ARRAY, DIM, MASK) Optional DIM, MASK	Minimum value in an array
PRODUCT (ARRAY, DIM, MASK) Optional DIM, MASK	Product of array elements
SUM (ARRAY, DIM, MASK) Optional DIM, MASK	Sum of array elements

B.10.15 Array Inquiry Functions

ALLOCATED (ARRAY)	Array allocation status
LBOUND (ARRAY, DIM) Optional DIM	Lower dimension bounds of an array
SHAPE (SOURCE)	Shape of an array or scalar
SIZE (ARRAY, DIM) Optional DIM	Total number of elements in an array
UBOUND (ARRAY, DIM) Optional DIM	Upper dimension bounds of an array .

B.10.16 Array Construction Functions

MERGE (TSOURCE, FSOURCE, MASK)	Merge under mask

PACK (ARRAY, MASK, VECTOR)
    Optional VECTOR
	Pack an array into an array of rank one
	    under a mask

SPREAD (SOURCE, DIM, NCOPIES)	Replicates array by adding a dimension

UNPACK (VECTOR, MASK,
        FIELD)
	Unpack an array of rank one into an array
	    under a mask

B.10.17 Array Reshape Function

RESHAPE (SOURCE, SHAPE,
        PAD, ORDER)
    Optional PAD, ORDER
	Reshape an array

B.10.18 Array Manipulation Functions

CSHIFT (ARRAY, SHIFT, DIM)	Circular shift
EOSHIFT (ARRAY, SHIFT, BOUNDARY, DIM)	End-off shift
Optional BOUNDARY	
TRANSPOSE (MATRIX)	Transpose of an array of rank two

B.10.19 Array Location Functions

MAXLOC (ARRAY, MASK)	Location of a maximum value in an array
Optional MASK	
MINLOC (ARRAY, MASK)	Location of a minimum value in an array
Optional MASK	

B.10.20 Pointer Association Status Inquiry Function

ASSOCIATED (POINTER, TARGET)	Association status or comparison
Optional TARGET	

B.11 Intrinsic Subroutines

DATE_AND_TIME (ALL, COUNT, MSECOND, SECOND, MINUTE, HOUR, DAY, MONTH, YEAR, ZONE)	Obtain date and time
Optional ALL, COUNT, MSECOND, SECOND, MINUTE, HOUR, DAY, MONTH, YEAR, ZONE	
MVBITS (FROM, FROMPOS, LEN, TO, TOPOS)	Copies bits from one integer to another
RANDOM (HARVEST)	Returns pseudorandom number
RANDOM_SEED (SIZE, PUT, GET)	Initializes or restarts the
Optional SIZE, PUT, GET	pseudorandom number generator
SYSTEM_CLOCK (COUNT, COUNT_RATE, COUNT_MAX)	Obtain data from the system clock
Optional COUNT, COUNT_RATE, COUNT_MAX	

B.12 Specific Names for Intrinsic Functions

Specific Name	Generic Name	Argument Type
ABS (A)	ABS (A)	default real
ACOS (X)	ACOS (X)	default real
AIMAG (Z)	AIMAG (Z)	default complex
AINT (A)	AINT (A)	default real
ALOG (X)	LOG (X)	default real
ALOG10 (X)	LOG10 (X)	default real

• AMAX0 (A1,A2,A3,...) Optional A3,...	REAL (MAX (A1, A2,A3,...)) Optional A3,...	default integer
• AMAX1 (A1,A2,A3,...) Optional A3,...	MAX (A1, A2,A3,...) Optional A3,...	default real
• AMIN0 (A1,A2,A3,...) Optional A3,...	REAL (MIN (A1, A2,A3,...)) Optional A3,...	default integer
• AMIN1 (A1,A2,A3,...) Optional A3,...	MIN (A1, A2,A3,...) Optional A3,...	default real
AMOD (A,P)	MOD (A,P)	default real
ANINT (A)	ANINT (A)	default real
ASIN (X)	ASIN (X)	default real
ATAN (X)	ATAN (X)	default real
ATAN2 (Y,X)	ATAN2 (Y,X)	default real
CABS (A)	ABS (A)	default complex
CCOS (X)	COS (X)	default complex
CEXP (X)	EXP (X)	default complex
• CHAR (I)	CHAR (I)	default integer
CLOG (X)	LOG (X)	default complex
CONJG (Z)	CONJG (Z)	default complex
COS (X)	COS (X)	default real
COSH (X)	COSH (X)	default real
CSIN (X)	SIN (X)	default complex
CSQRT (X)	SQRT (X)	default complex
DABS (A)	ABS (A)	double precision real
DACOS (X)	ACOS (X)	double precision real
DASIN (X)	ASIN (X)	double precision real
DATAN (X)	ATAN (X)	double precision real
DATAN2 (Y,X)	ATAN2 (Y,X)	double precision real
DCOS (X)	COS (X)	double precision real
DCOSH (X)	COSH (X)	double precision real
DDIM (X,Y)	DIM (X,Y)	double precision real
DEXP (X)	EXP (X)	double precision real
DIM (X,Y)	DIM (X,Y)	default real
DINT (A)	AINT (A)	double precision real
DLOG (X)	LOG (X)	double precision real
DLOG10 (X)	LOG10 (X)	double precision real
• DMAX1 (A1,A2,A3,...) Optional A3,...	MAX (A1,A2,A3,...) Optional A3,...	double precision real
• DMIN1 (A1,A2,A3,...) Optional A3,...	MIN (A1,A2,A3,...) Optional A3,...	double precision real
DMOD (A,P)	MOD (A,P)	double precision real
DNINT (A)	ANINT (A)	double precision real
DPROD (X,Y)	DPROD (X,Y)	default real
DSIGN (A,B)	SIGN (A,B)	double precision real
DSIN (X)	SIN (X)	double precision real
DSINH (X)	SINH (X)	double precision real
DSQRT (X)	SQRT (X)	double precision real
DTAN (X)	TAN (X)	double precision real

DTANH (X)	TANH (X)	double precision real
EXP (X)	EXP (X)	default real
• FLOAT (A)	REAL (A)	default integer
IABS (A)	ABS (A)	default integer
• ICHAR (C)	ICHAR (C)	default character
IDIM (X,Y)	DIM (X,Y)	default integer
• IDINT (A)	INT (A)	double precision real
IDNINT (A)	NINT (A)	double precision real
• IFIX (A)	INT (A)	default real
INDEX (STRING, SUBSTRING)	INDEX (STRING, SUBSTRING)	default character
• INT (A)	INT (A)	default real
ISIGN (A,B)	SIGN (A,B)	default integer
LEN (STRING)	LEN (STRING)	default character
• LGE (STRING_A, STRING_B)	LGE (STRING_A, STRING_B)	default character
• LGT (STRING_A, STRING_B)	LGT (STRING_A, STRING_B)	default character
• LLE (STRING_A, STRING_B)	LLE (STRING_A, STRING_B)	default character
• LLT (STRING_A, STRING_B)	LLT (STRING_A, STRING_B)	default character
• MAX0 (A1,A2,A3,...) Optional A3,...	MAX (A1,A2,A3,...) Optional A3,...	default integer
• MAX1 (A1,A2,A3,...) Optional A3,...	INT (MAX (A1,A2,A3,...)) Optional A3,...	default real
• MIN0 (A1,A2,A3,...) Optional A3,...	MIN (A1,A2,A3,...) Optional A3,...	default integer
• MIN1 (A1,A2,A3,...) Optional A3,...	INT (MIN (A1,A2,A3,...)) Optional A3,...	default real
MOD (A,P)	MOD (A,P)	default integer
NINT (A)	NINT (A)	default real
• REAL (A)	REAL (A)	default integer
SIGN (A,B)	SIGN (A,B)	default real
SIN (X)	SIN (X)	default real
SINH (X)	SINH (X)	default real
• SNGL (A)	REAL (A)	double precision real
SQRT (X)	SQRT (X)	default real
TAN (X)	TAN (X)	default real
TANH (X)	TANH (X)	default real

• These specific intrinsic function names must not be used as an actual argument. However, they may be enclosed in a function subprogram of a different name and be passed that way.

Index